COMING
ALIVE

CHINA AFTER MAO

CHINA AFTER MAO

Roger Garside

McGraw-Hill Book Company

New York   St. Louis   San Francisco
Hamburg   Mexico

1 2 3 4 5 6 7 8 9 DODO 8 7 6 5 4 3 2 1

LIBRARY OF CONGRESS CATALOGING IN PUBLICATION DATA

Garside, Roger.
Coming alive:
Bibliography: p.
Includes index.
1.   China--Politics and government--1976-
I.   Title.
DS779.26.G37   951.05'7   80-21730
ISBN 0-07-022914-7

Book design by Roberta Rezk.

To my mother and father

Acknowledgments

HAVING WATCHED China at close quarters from 1976 to 1979, I wanted to tell the story of how life returned to a nation that had been half-dead. The events of those years were testimony to the resilience of the human spirit. They showed that a nation could rouse itself from an Orwellian nightmare, and they proved that for educated Chinese of all ages the values and institutions of liberal democracy were far from irrelevant.

An invitation to spend a year writing and teaching at the U.S. Naval Postgraduate School on the beautiful Monterey Peninsula in California was heaven-sent. Claude Buss acted as my intermediary with heaven and, equally important, with Patrick Parker, Chairman of the School's National Security Affairs Department. I am grateful to all three for bringing me to a place where writing was a pleasure instead of a struggle.

My debt to Claude Buss goes further. This eternally youthful Professor Emeritus of Asian History from Stanford University, now teaching at the Naval Postgraduate School, let me draw without stint on his lifetime's experience of China and of writing and teaching.

My students at the school gave me stimulus and companionship—none more than Lieutenant Commander Hank Carde, Major Ed Ross, and Captain Rich Curasi.

The China-watching community in Peking in the years 1976 to 1979 had something of the quality of a co-educational monastery. Undistracted by the pleasures and complexities of life in other capitals, this closed community devoted itself single-mindedly to the study of China, reading, thinking and speaking of little else, even on so-called "social" occasions. This monomania suited me and I valued the close companionship that it gave me with others of my calling. Above all I would mention the original members of my own Gang of Four, Gerd Ahrens, Don Keyser and Shige Yoshida, and their worthy successors, especially Christian Hauswedell and Chris Szymanski. With Shyam Saran I exchanged many an interpretation and not a little information.

Nigel Wade of the *Daily Telegraph* was my companion of many a sortie to Tiananmen Square and Democracy Wall. Together we went "hunting wild, after the wildest beauty in the world . . . I mean the truth untold." (Forgive me, Wilfred Owen.) John Fraser of the Toronto *Globe and Mail* gave a transfusion of humor and humanity to our rather thin-blooded community. Alain Jacob of *Le Monde* brought us not only the urbanity of Paris but the sober appraisal of a man who knew well the "other communism," that of Moscow.

Yanfu and Annemarie Ma did much to help me understand the events I observed in their country. Any failures of understanding are mine alone.

My wife, Evelyne, was a source of strength when I needed it most.

In Monterey, Marianne Schippereit was a resourceful and painstaking helper who relieved me of many a chore.

My editor at McGraw-Hill, Beverly Jane Loo, quickly won my respect for her professional judgment, and my copy editor, Herb Kirk, proved to be as sensitive a word surgeon as ever took a scalpel to my prose.

Many others helped me on my way with encouragement or practical help. I thank them too.

I am indebted to my colleagues at the Foreign and Commonwealth Office in London, for permitting me to accept the invitation to spend a year at the U.S. Naval Postgraduate School, Monterey. I should also emphasize that the views expressed in this book are my own and should not be taken as representing in any way the views of either of these two institutions. In writing this book I have had no access to official material and have had to rely entirely on the not inconsiderable resources available to me in Monterey.

I acknowledge permission to reprint copyrighted material from the following:

Faber & Faber, for lines from T.S. Eliot's *The Waste Land*;

Chatto & Windus, for lines from Wilfrid Owen's "Strange Meeting."

Contents

A Note about Chinese Spelling

IN THIS BOOK, I have used the *pinyin* system for transcribing Chinese names and other words into the Roman alphabet, with a few exceptions. For instance, the capital of China appears here as Peking rather than the *pinyin* Beijing; *Peking* has more associations for me and will be more familiar to most readers. I have also retained the traditional (Wade-Giles) transcription for names of Hong Kong publications (which themselves continue to use this form) and for names of people now dead—like Chiang Kai-shek, whom the world knows only in this form.

The *pinyin* system is simple to read except for two letters:

q is pronounced like the *ch* in chicken, and

x is pronounced like the *s* in simple.

R. G.

Principal Personalities

CHEN YUN (Ch'en Yun). In the 1950s First Deputy Prime Minister and senior economic specialist. Later eclipsed.

DENG TO (Teng T'o). Editor-in-chief of *People's Daily* until 1958; later, anti-Mao satirist. Purged in Cultural Revolution.

DENG XIAOPING (Teng Hsiao-p'ing). Senior Vice-Premier and successor chosen by Zhou Enlai. For many years General Secretary of the Party. A pragmatist.

HUA GUOFENG (Hua Kuo-feng). Appointed Acting Prime Minister in early 1976.

JIANG QING (Chiang Ch'ing). Mao's wife, who hoped to succeed him as Chairman of the CPC.

LIN BIAO (Lin Piao). Marshal, Minister of Defense, and designated successor to Mao until his death in 1971.

LIU SHAOQI (Liu Shao-ch'i). Number two in Party and Head of State before the Cultural Revolution.

MAO ZEDONG (Mao Tse-tung). Leader of the Communist Party from 1935 until his death in September 1976.

PENG DEHUAI (P'eng Te-huai). Minister of Defense in the 1950s and critic of the Great Leap Forward.

WANG DONGXING (Wang Tung-hsing). Security chief and manager of the Party apparatus. Mao's former bodyguard.

WANG HONGWEN (Wang Hung-wen). Senior Vice-Chairman of the Party in his early forties. Rose to power during the Cultural Revolution.

WEI JINGSHENG (Wei Ching-sheng). Activist in democracy movement; leading editor of *Exploration*, jailed 1979.

XÙ SHIYU (Hsü Shih-you). Commander of the Canton Military Region. Supporter of Deng Xiaoping.

YE JIANYING (Yeh Chien-ying). Minister of Defense, 1976.

ZHANG CHUNQIAO (Chang Ch'un-ch'iao,. Leftist Vice-Premier since Cultural Revolution.

ZHOU ENLAI (Chou En-lai). Premier of the People's Republic from its foundation in 1949 until his death on 8 January 1976.

PROLOGUE

China Watch: Sha Tau Kok to Tiananmen

I BEGAN my China-watching on the China–Hong Kong border peering through a pair of binoculars. I spent a week in the Sha Tau Kok observation post commanding a small detachment of Gurkha soldiers of the British garrison in Hong Kong. The observation post was set high on a hillside not far from where the railway crosses into China. A flimsy fence of wire netting ran through the valley below us to divide the British Empire from Red China. The coexistence was peaceful. To our right we looked out across Mirs Bay. White sands backed by green hills made a curving shoreline and the waters of the wide bay were sprinkled with small islands. When I woke in the morning in my imperial outpost the sun came up "outa China 'crost the Bay!," as it had for Kipling in another part of the same Empire sixty years before. I would watch its rays touch the islands and skip across the rippled waters before I turned to observe the small detachment of the People's Liberation Army in the valley below us. They spent their days patrolling the border, playing basketball, and watching us. The task was of somewhat less than strategic importance, but it awakened my curiosity in what went on in the country that stretched fifteen hundred miles beyond the hills in front of me. It made me start a journey of inquiry.

Eighteen years later, in April 1976, I stood on Tiananmen Square in Peking in the midst of a political demonstration that was radically changing the course of Chinese politics. I was making progress on my journey.

In the years between, I had spent two more years in Hong Kong, studying Mandarin Chinese, and had gone on from that to my first stay in Peking, from 1968 to 1970. In those years I had seen the storm of the Cultural Revolution arise and subside, and had then worked to detect from which direction the wind would blow next. There were times I regretted the peace of the Hong Kong hills and the simplicity of watching China through binoculars, but the fascination of trying to figure out what was really happening in China never palled.

At first, Chinese politics looked utterly different from those of an elective democracy such as the United States or Britain. Although on paper there were constitutions of party and state, in fact politics were conducted with little regard to them. There were no elections at regular intervals to set a reassuring rhythm for political life and, of course, there were no election campaigns to provide a formal setting for "debating the issues." Occasionally a People's Congress or a Party Congress would be held, but even then there was no debate because disagreements in the public eye were considered destructive of party unity. The congress presented the outcome of inner-party debates, not the debates themselves. There was no question of rules for an equitable sharing of television and radio air time or access to the press: in China the aim of all political rivals was to monopolize the media.

In Britain and the U.S., that otherwise dangerous moment when power is transferred had been made one of dignity and grace, thanks to finely honed ritual. The outgoing American president would attend the inauguration of his successor. A newly appointed British prime minister would drive to Buckingham Palace to kiss the hand of the monarch, and the outgoing premier would pause on the steps of No. 10 Downing Street to say a few words to the press, wishing his successor well and looking forward to spending more time with his grandchildren. In China, by contrast, Premier Zhou Enlai would give some of his last strength to summoning the regional military commanders to his bedside, to appeal to them to keep the country united after his death.[1]

In the political culture in which I had grown up, the relationship between issues and individuals was explicit and it was considered legitimate to focus on the views of the individual candidates. In China, the one-party system obliged rivals to couch their appeals in terms of the correct line for the revolution to follow.

I learned to read the press in China differently from the way I read it at home. Because all papers were under control of the Party and were given explicit guidance on the line to take on the major issues of the hour, the press was the voice of authority as it could never be in a democracy. Editorials in the major papers were an occasional, not a daily, occurrence; they were written on instruction from above and published only after clearance by one or more of the highest ruling group, the twenty-one-member Politburo of the Central Committee of the Communist Party. In the absence of an elected parliament or congress, the press took on enhanced importance as a political battleground. In consequence, Chinese and foreigners alike studied the press as an authoritative guide to the thinking of national leaders. A major editorial must be read with the same attention one would give to a speech by the president of the United States. Small changes in emphasis, the reformulation of a set phrase, the appearance of a new slogan or the quiet dropping of an old one occurred only by design and reflected a political development whose meaning one must search for. Textual exegesis became so much a part of my life that I saw myself as a latter-day monk studying "biblical" texts to construct a view of reality.

The absence of a tradition of constitutional government had a devastating effect, at times of political crisis, on the freedom and dignity of the individual. The lack of elections made political contests take on a life-or-death character.

In Britain an incoming government would blame the rate of inflation, the level of unemployment, or the sluggish growth of the economy on its predecessor, but a Chinese leader in disgrace was condemned as the source of all evil. In China, the struggle was presented as one between Marxist–Leninist good and capitalist evil, with nothing between. So one year Liu Shaoqi was a highly respected head of state and "the number one capitalist-roader" the next.

I found that economics and traditional political culture reinforced the effects of the Soviet-style state to make Chinese politics extremely ruthless. The size and poverty of China rendered the consequences of the "wrong" outcome in a political struggle far more grave than in an economically developed country. A way must be found to lead a billion people out of poverty. Order and unity must be maintained among a quarter of mankind. The transition from strict dictatorship to something more tolerant of diversity was made perilous not only by the accumulated bitterness of the recent past but by millennia of emperor-worship.

But a closer acquaintance with Chinese politics modified the impression of utter strangeness. If China did not debate issues in election campaigns or on television talk shows, it suffered no lack of political campaigns designed to influence official and public opinion. Out of consideration (sometimes genuine, sometimes feigned) for party unity, the campaigns would be conducted in code—through historical or literary allegory—in their early stages. But these were genuine struggles being waged in the public eye, for those who could read the code, and the Chinese were expert code-breakers after centuries of practice. (The use of allegory was not introduced to Chinese politics by the Communist Party.)

Mao never submitted himself to the judgment of the electorate, but when he was running a major campaign to recapture power, the Cultural Revolution, his propagandists distributed millions of lapel badges. They did not bear slogans like ALL THE WAY WITH LBJ or I'M READY FOR TEDDY, but they promoted his image all the same. One could not accuse Mao of neglecting the role of personality in politics.

While Mao's struggle with the hierarchy of the Communist Party led him to destroy the rhythm of politics the party and state constitutions set out, it is possible to exaggerate the degree to which the rhythm of our own political lives is regulated by elections. American foreign policy is liable to change if the rival superpower invades a nation in Western Asia, and the change may be not only sudden but also more profound than a change wrought by a presidential election. The center of British politics might rest for twenty years on common ground that was not truly disputed as Conservative and Labour politicians replaced each other in office, then shift suddenly to the right in the space of a year or two. China did not differ from the U.S. and Britain in having periods of political immobility followed by times of rapid change.

If in China the role ritual played in politics was different from the one it played at home, it was nonetheless important. There was a large element of ritual evident daily in the way the newspapers were edited. It was partly a matter of stylized language, partly the way the paper was made up. The size of photographs of Chinese and foreign leaders, for instance, was determined solely by political and protocol considerations, not by the intrinsic interest of the picture itself. On public occasions the leaders of the nation must appear in a certain order and stand in carefully predetermined array. The public was entitled to read political significance into a change of order or placing. The protŏcol for greeting foreign leaders was as carefully regulated as in any nonrevolutionary society. On 1 January there was always a New Year's editorial, and if it failed to appear one was entitled to wonder why. One of the functions of ritual is to diminish the hazards of improvization and make life seem more secure by making it more predictable. Ritual certainly worked this way in China, and indeed it was much needed.

Looking at recent developments in China in a historical context, parallels with European history emerge. Since the death of Mao there has developed in China a strong movement to condemn the cult that raised him to the level of a deity and was a modern extension of emperor-worship. There is a parallel here with the decline of the divine right of kings that occurred in Europe in the seventeenth and eighteenth centuries. Hand in hand with this movement goes a deliberate drive to spread a scientific attitude to political doctrine, asserting the right and indeed the duty of all people to "take practice as the sole criterion of truth." Theories must be judged by their results in application and the Marxist classics must not be regarded as unalterable, universally applicable truth, to be accepted as they stand for all time and every place, as some fundamentalist Christians' regard the Bible. Young Chinese writers have drawn a parallel between this period in China and the Age of Enlightenment in Europe.

The China of 1976 made me think of Sophocles' trilogy of tragedies about the ancient Greek city-state of Thebes. As a young man, Oedipus liberated the city from the thrall of the Sphinx, which was terrorizing it and exacting a tribute of human sacrifice. In gratitude, the people made Oedipus their king. By the time that the play *Oedipus The King* opens, Thebes is once again in a deep crisis. There is blight in the fields and among the cattle and even the women have become sterile. A sense of death is settling on the city. A priest calls on Oedipus to save Thebes a second time. King Oedipus swears to punish whoever has brought disaster upon the city by his sins. The blind prophet Teiresias tells the king the truth: You yourself are to blame.

The third play of the trilogy, *Antigone*, takes place after the death of Oedipus, when a struggle for the succession is going on. A son of Oedipus, Polynices, has fallen in battle outside the walls of the city, and Creon, who has occupied the throne, issues an order forbidding anyone to bury the body. Polynices' sister Antigone sets loyalty to her brother above obedience to the edict of the state. She goes secretly to throw a few handfuls of sand over the body of Polynices, to give him that symbolic burial without which his soul is condemned to wander homeless forever. She performs the rite and slips away, but guards set by the king to watch the corpse discover what has been done and uncover it again. Antigone returns for another attempt, but this time she is caught by the guards. Brought face to face with the king, she does not seek his mercy but asserts that she was bound by a law higher than that of men to do what she did.

In the pages that follow some may see a parallel between the actions of Antigone and those of the crowds who in April 1976 conducted what they called a people's funeral ceremony for the late Premier Zhou Enlai in defiance of an official edict. Like Antigone, they chose their fate knowing full well the consequences of their action. Like her, they stood firm when their resolution was put to the test.

1

Funeral, with Thunderclouds

LATE IN THE AFTERNOON of Sunday, 11 January 1976, a small blue-and-white bus drew out of the gates of the Peking Hospital and drove toward Tiananmen Square followed by a line of one hundred black limousines. Laden with wreaths and draped with yellow and black streamers, it circled the square and passed the Gate of Heavenly Peace. The light of this winter's day was fading but there was still a patch of glory in the west. The cortege headed down the Avenue of Eternal Peace toward the Western Hills and the setting sun. Silent crowds lined the sidewalk, many weeping. Zhou Enlai, their Premier, was making his last journey, to the Babaoshan Cemetery of Fallen Revolutionaries

After cremation at Babaoshan, his ashes would be brought back to the old Imperial City. There they would rest for three days in a majestic building where emperors had once honored the memory of their ancestors. People from all walks of life would come to pay their last respects, and then, on 15 January, a memorial ceremony would be held in his honor in the Great Hall of the People. Finally Zhou's ashes would be scattered in the rivers, lakes, and seas of China and on its land, in accordance with his wishes. The compatriots living on Taiwan would not be forgotten: one part of his ashes would be scattered in the Taiwan Straits. He had said no memorial should be built for him.

Zhou's personal name, Enlai, can be translated as "Grace Comes." He had brought grace to the hard world of revolutionary politics and T.S. Eliot's words seemed to fit his manner of leaving it: he would become "grace dissolved in place."

But the people who lined the route from Tiananmen Square to Babaoshan were not in a mood to appreciate the poetry of this last act. They were anxious as well as sorrowful. There had been no public announcement that it was Zhou's wish that his body be cremated, or indeed that he would be cremated that day. But, somehow, the news spread like wildfire, and a million people had come to line the nine-mile route to the cemetery. At home, many had made white chrysanthemums, an emblem of mourning, from white silk paper. They held small bunches of them now in their hands as they waited quietly for the cortege to come by.

But the people at one point along the route were in a state of agitation. They suspected that the cremation had been ordered by people in the Politburo who wanted to prevent proper commemoration of Zhou's role in China's history as a prelude to suppressing his policies. The crowd wanted his body preserved in a mausoleum, but now they saw it being hurried away. It had lain in state for only two days, and out of a nation of nine hundred million only ten thousand "representatives of the masses" had been allowed to pay their last respects.* No plans for a memorial hall had been announced.

As the procession approached that section of the crowd which was particularly agitated, the mourners rushed forward. They blocked the road and forced the motorcade to halt. Officials got out of their black limousines to persuade the crowd that cremation was Zhou's own choice, but to no avail. On the contrary, suspicion grew when the crowd saw that Zhou's cho-

---

* Nine months later Mao's body would lie in state, not in a hospital but in the Great Hall of the People, and in the course of seven days would receive the homage of three hundred thousand people.

sen successor, Deng Xiaoping, was not in the cortege. Only two Politburo members were accompanying the body: Wang Hongwen, a symbol of the forces opposed to Deng and to Zhou's pragmatic legacy, and Wang Dongxing, Mao's former bodyguard who had played an important role in the Cultural Revolution. Zhou's frail seventy-two-year-old widow had to leave her car to assure the crowd personally that cremation was Zhou's own wish. Only then did they reluctantly open a path to let the vehicles through.[1]*

Zhou's death had stunned China. It was not unexpected; he had been in the hospital for more than a year and people knew he was dying, but nothing could have fully prepared them for this loss. The announcement was made early on the morning of Friday, 9 January, and many Chinese were quite unable to work properly that day. In Peking, foreigners could see how the Chinese around them were affected. The local staff of embassies, the interpreters working with foreign correspondents, the students of foreign-language teachers, the colleagues of foreign translators, and the roommates of foreign students were numb with grief.

Tiananmen Square, a vast open space in the heart of Peking that will hold one million people, lies between the Gate of Heavenly Peace (*Tiananmen* in Chinese) and another gate to the south, where the walls of Peking used to run. In the middle of the square stands the Monument to the People's Heroes, a soaring monolith commemorating those who died "for the Revolution." It stands on a marble terrace that stands on a lower, broader terrace outside which are lines of evergreen hedges.

On the first Sunday after Zhou's death, tens of thousands of Peking people came to the monument on their day of rest to pay spontaneous tribute to Zhou. They thronged the square, which usually sees only a light scattering of visitors. They moved in toward the monument. Young people, wearing red or black armbands on their drab winter tunics and overcoats, took turns standing at the foot of the monument to read poems or speeches extolling Zhou's memory. Their eulogy ended, they would

* Superscript numbers refer to notes concerning sources of information and quotations, which begin on page 435.

stand to attention and raise their clenched right fist to shoulder level in the Communist salute. Groups laid wreaths and sang the "*Internationale,*" the anthem of Communists everywhere.

As they sang their anthem that day they gave back to the well-worn words the force they had had when they were first put together a hundred years before: "There is no savior, there is no god . . . we must win our own salvation." Sung in honor of Zhou Enlai, who stood for rational socialism, these words were no mere ritual: they expressed a deep conviction, and more than a hint of defiance of those who forced the people to worship Mao as a savior and a demigod.

Their anthem ended, they moved away, and took the mourning flowers of white silk paper from their buttonholes to tie them to the evergreens beside the monument until it seemed that these bushes were blooming in the cold of winter to honor Zhou.

On Monday morning the *People's Daily* published a striking photograph of Zhou—his face exposed, the rest of his body draped in the party flag, with weeping mourners filing past. People seemed to read the appearance of this photograph as a sign of official approval for the expression of grief. More and more black armbands appeared, and quite suddenly all over the city men and women were to be seen crying openly. Foreigners realized that the city was overwhelmed by a sorrow as great as, if not greater than, that felt in the West at the death of John F. Kennedy.

On Monday, Tuesday, and Wednesday, Chinese and foreigners went to the former Hall of the Ancestors in the Imperial City to pay their respects to Zhou's ashes. The setting was a physical reminder of Zhou's work as a force for unity and continuity in China and the world, and of his qualities of loyalty and unpompous dignity. To approach the hall one walked through courtyards surrounded by buildings with vermilion walls and yellow-tiled roofs of bold and sweeping outline. To pass from courtyard to courtyard, through archways draped in yellow and black, was to follow an architectural progression of strength and grace. Halls, terraces, and walls related to each other in unity of style and harmony of proportion. Aged pines, symbols of endurance and loyalty, guarded the path. A funeral march was played over and over again.

At last one came to the courtyard where the Hall of the Ancestors stood, fronted by terraces of white marble, their balustrades finely carved in that pure, hard stone. On those terraces stood rank upon rank of wreaths of brightly colored silk-paper flowers. One after another, groups of mourners mounted the stone steps past the terraces, carrying their own wreaths, to the hall itself. Each group stood in silence for a few seconds before the small wooden casket of carved red lacquer that contained his ashes. The party flag, red with a yellow hammer and sickle, was draped over one half of the casket. Behind, a photograph showed Zhou as he had been in 1949. A simple modern ceremony in a setting of Ming-dynasty beauty was the best possible farewell to Zhou.

On Wednesday the ashes were taken from the Imperial City to the Great Hall of the People, where the main memorial ceremony would be held the next day. As the long cortege of black limousines emerged from the Imperial City and drove across Tiananmen Square to the Great Hall, the grandstands of ocher concrete flanking the Gate of Heavenly Peace were filled with spectators. Along the short route to the hall, crowds ten deep pressed forward against cordons of soldiers. As the cars moved past, soldiers and policemen wept with the crowd and cries of grief swelled to a mass clamor. This procession was taking away from them the last remains of a man who had held the People's Republic together when forces unleashed by Mao were threatening to tear it limb from limb. Without him, could the center hold, or would things fall apart once more?

At the memorial ceremony in the Great Hall the next day, Deng Xiaoping read the eulogy to the assembly of five thousand officials and "representatives of the masses." This was reassuring. He was Zhou's choice to succeed him as Premier. But where was Chairman Mao Zedong? He was absent without explanation. There was no protocol reason why he should not be there; he had attended earlier ceremonies for other comrades, such as the late Foreign Minister, Chen Yi. Was health the reason? Mao had received ten foreign visitors in the past four

months; all of them had found him very much alive, and a few
weeks later he would receive ex-President Nixon for an hour
and forty minutes. He had been to visit Zhou in the hospital
several times as the end approached, and one official said privately that Mao had been with Zhou half an hour before his
death. Yet the press made no mention of this.[2] His absence from
the memorial ceremony and his failure to pay any public tribute
to Zhou created great unease. In the weeks that followed he was
largely withdrawn from public view but his unseen presence
loomed over the political life of the nation.

After the memorial ceremony something happened which
can only have increased the anxiety of those who suspected that
Zhou's enemies in the Politburo were maneuvering against his
political legacy. (To foreigners it might come as a surprise that
Zhou had had enemies in the Party, but Chinese knew only too
well how often he had been attacked by the ultra-left.) The
period of mourning was declared at an end. An order from the
Party Center prohibited any further popular expressions of
mourning. People took off the black armbands they had so recently put on. All over the country, in factories, schools, farms,
mines, army units, neighborhoods—wherever people worked or
 ved—plans had been made to hold simple memorial ceremonies to express the affection and respect that people felt for
Zhou. Now, by order of the Party Center, these ceremonies
were forbidden. Even foreigners who wanted to show their respect for him were cautioned against public displays. A group of
African visitors about to return home from Shanghai airport
told their Chinese official escorts that they would like to observe
a minute's silence in Zhou's honor. They were asked not to do so
"out of consideration for Chairman Mao's feelings."

The press treatment of Zhou's death increased popular anxiety. The papers duly reported the memorial ceremony and the
eulogy delivered by Deng. They gave space to the formal tributes from foreign governments and fraternal parties. But as-
tonishingly little was published by Chinese about Zhou's fifty-
seven years of work for his nation and the Marxist revolution.
There was no word from Mao; and the Party's most authoritative
publication, the *Red Flag* monthly, printed not a single word of

tribute. There were no personal reminiscences by any of the countless ordinary citizens whose lives and affections he had touched. The provincial press and radio, under tight control from Peking, where the ultra-left had its hands on the main levers of the mass media, made no contribution. Denied any other outlet for their feelings, the mass of ordinary citizens took their wreaths and their eulogies to the Heroes' Monument in Tiananmen Square. Officials estimated that two million people paid homage in this way, but the press passed over their action in silence, as it had passed over the crowd of one million, who, unbidden, had lined the route to Babaoshan a few days before. It was as if the people had intruded as uninvited guests at an official reception. The only thing to do was to ignore them. But their action was a warning tremor of an earthquake of protest that would shake China three months later.

The loss of the man who had been Premier of the People's Republic since its establishment left a void that needed to be filled quickly. Since, with Mao's approval, Deng Xiaoping had been in day-to-day charge of the government and Party for almost a year, it was expected at home and abroad that he would succeed Zhou. The editors of *Time* magazine put a photograph of Deng Xiaoping on their cover, with the caption "Chou's Successor: Teng Hsiao-ping." But days passed without any announcement. Instead of smoothly inheriting Zhou's mantle, Deng disappeared from public view after delivering the eulogy on 15 January. His disappearance was closely followed by that of the Minister of Defense, Ye Jianying, and the senior economic specialist, Li Xiannian, both trusted associates of Zhou Enlai.

Chinese China-watchers in Hong Kong shared the unease of their compatriots in China. On the day that Zhou's death was announced, the editors of the independent daily paper *Ming Pao* had forecast that Zhou's passing would lead inevitably to "intensification of the struggle between the radicals and the moderates."

The foreign journalists and diplomats, whose job it was to explain to their readers and their governments back home what was going on, were puzzled and perplexed. One of them quoted to me Winston Churchill's description of Russia in 1939: "a riddle wrapped in a mystery inside an enigma."

There were a number of sources of information available to China-watchers about the situation in China, but none of them offered instant enlightenment. There was the Chinese press, stiff with jargon but sometimes spiced with encoded references to power struggles not yet ripe for public disclosure. There were "travelers' tales" from Hong Kong: China was the last major country so cut off from the outside world that travelers emerging from it would be seized upon by journalists for any clue they could offer as to what was happening there. There were mountains of transcripts of radio broadcasts from almost every province of China which after hours of laborious study yielded enlightenment on the reaction—or lack of it—in province X to the latest word from the center. And there was the evidence of people's own eyes and ears: Chinese regulations prevented the Chinese people from talking candidly with foreigners about politics, but foreigners could still observe the behavior of ordinary Chinese to glean some sense of how politics were affecting them. To draw political conclusions from isolated small changes of dress or behavior would have been ridiculous, but pieced together they gave some feel for the mood of Peking.

The official press was the daily bread of China-watchers and it was to the press they turned first. As usual, on 1 January the three most authoritative mouthpieces of the Communist Party, the *People's Daily*, the *Liberation Army Daily* (edited by the military wing of the party), and *Red Flag* monthly (the main theoretical journal), had published a joint editorial at the New Year. This was a major political statement to the nation and was discussed in the political study groups the Chinese were obliged to attend at work or in their neighborhood. It had been published with two 1965 poems by Mao and quoted from them extensively. Indeed, two lines from one of the poems had been chosen as the title:

> Nothing is hard in this world
> If you dare to scale the heights.

"Look!," the editorial began, "'Orioles sing, swallows swirl . . . everywhere,' our Party is full of vigor, our people are in high spirits, our country is flourishing, and the dictatorship of the proletariat is stronger than ever." From this euphoric opening it moved on to prepare people for a coming battle. A little over a year earlier Mao had issued a call for stability and unity, but now the editorial warned "Chairman Mao has taught us: 'Never forget classes and class struggle.' Recently Chairman Mao has again taught us 'stability and unity do not mean writing off class struggle; class struggle is the key link and everything else hinges on it.' "

The editorial became more specific. It denounced, in very strong terms, criticisms that had recently been made of Mao's policies for education. The writers alleged that the attempt to change these policies was designed to promote the interests of the "bourgeoisie" against the "proletariat." The terms were vague but the charge was grave. Moreover, the editorial writers went on to hint that the attempt to change educational policy was only the visible tip of an iceberg that was threatening to ram and sink the whole raft of policies and political arrangements put together after the Cultural Revolution. They accused an unidentified leader of wanting an official re-evaluation of the Cultural Revolution, the great upheaval Mao had launched in 1966 in the hope of regaining control of the country and renewing the vitality of the Communist revolution. Since the Cultural Revolution was always referred to in the most glowing terms, re-evaluation could only mean admitting the damage done by that upheaval. The unnamed leader's move was denounced as "a concentrated reflection of the current struggle between the two classes, the two roads, and the two lines [capitalist against proletarian]." Stability and unity, it seemed, were leaving China after a very brief stay.

The two poems accompanying the editorial had been written by Mao in 1965, when he was preparing the Cultural Revolution, but were published now for the first time. They were both characteristic of Mao's mood at that time; the first expressed Mao's usual vaulting ambition, beginning "I have long aspired to reach for the clouds," and ended with his famous boundless confidence: "Nothing is hard in this world / If you dare to scale the heights."

The second poem showed Mao as a hero of superhuman

stature, daring to face the reality of a world in turmoil. Publication implied that Mao was leading China toward a new upheaval like the Cultural Revolution, when he had thrown millions of Red Guards into battle against the whole hierarchy of the Communist Party.

For me, it was hard to believe that anyone was seriously contemplating a rerun of that disaster, but the editorial writers had claimed that the fate of the revolution hung in the balance, and they were obviously writing under instructions from the leftists in the Politburo, who claimed Mao's authority.

Was it true that the rightists were launching an offensive on a broad front, or were the leftists who controlled the press exaggerating in order to pave the way for launching an offensive themselves?

Posters had appeared at Peking's two main universities accusing the Minister of Education and a leading university administrator of having made a concerted effort to change the Maoist educational policies then in force. Certainly no rightist reform of education would have been launched without the backing of someone of the rank of Deng Xiaoping. But had Deng gone beyond education to attempt to "reverse" other "verdicts," as the editorial implied? If he had, it might explain why stormclouds were gathering and he had disappeared from public view.

An article in *Red Flag* was far more explicit in linking the issues of the day with the struggles of the past. The writer of this article reviewed party history from 1949 to the present and claimed that the recent attempt to reform educational policy was but the latest manifestation of a rightist line against which Mao had fought repeatedly in that quarter of a century. Earlier manifestations he identified were the attempts made in the 1950s by Liu Shaoqi (then number two in the Party) to maintain a mixed capitalist–socialist economy, to build up democratic institutions and reduce class struggle after the economy had been socialized. The would-be reformers of 1976 were linked by this writer to the intellectuals who had demanded freedom of expression and the rule of law twenty years before. They were alleged to be birds of the same feather as those who in 1958–

1959 had opposed the Great Leap Forward and had later advocated policies that would have reversed Mao's policy of the collectivization of land, revived private farming by individual families, and expanded free markets and used profitability as a guide to investment. The rightists had opposed the Cultural Revolution when Mao launched it and were now trying to undermine the policies and leaders who had emerged from it. Again, Deng was not named as the leader of today's rightists, but it was general knowledge that he had opposed Mao on a number of the issues listed.

The *Red Flag* article ended with instructions on how to conduct the "present-day struggle" that were strangely at variance with the magnitude of the issues at stake. The unity of the "more than ninety-five percent of the cadres and masses" was to be maintained, even though it was highly doubtful that present policies enjoyed anything like such a high level of support. The "great debate on the educational front" was to be conducted under the "leadership" (i.e., control) of Party committees at all levels; no "fighting groups," such as had been the agents of chaos in the Cultural Revolution, were to be formed. These contradictions showed that the left was not yet strong enough to unleash an all-out assault on the right. The thunderclouds were gathering but the storm had not yet broken. Still, I recalled that at the outset of the Cultural Revolution itself, similar restriction had been imposed by Mao's opponents, only to be swept aside within weeks. That upheaval had also begun with a "debate" on one front and had then spilled over to engulf every part of life. If there really was an attempt underway to condemn the Cultural Revolution and its fruits, and the leftists were determined to resist this, then the full fury of a storm could swiftly break upon China.

Days without Deng became weeks without Deng. On 6 February, when he had been out of sight for more than three weeks, there was a new thunderclap: the *People's Daily* alleged that the Party was threatened now as it had been in the Cultural Revolution by "Party people in authority taking the capitalist road." The reappearance of this phrase, once used to denounce Liu Shaoqi and Deng Xiaoping, reinforced the impression that the left wanted to launch a new Cultural Revolution even if it was being restrained by its opponents for the time being. According to the *People's Daily*, those who were trying to lead China back down the road to capitalism were mostly the same people who had been exposed and criticized before. This pointed the finger not only at Deng but also at other officials who, like him, had been struck down and then restored to power.

But the writer did not stop even there. He went on to make an accusation that seemed aimed at Zhou Enlai himself. Twelve months before, in January 1975, Zhou had enunciated a set of long-range goals for China: the modernization of agriculture, industry, science and technology, and national defense by the year 2000. These goals—dubbed the Four Modernizations—had no socialist, let alone Communist, coloring. They appealed to patriots of every political viewpoint. Now the *People's Daily* writer alleged that there was "a complete set of revisionist programs and lines hidden behind the Four Modernizations." This attack was sure to incur the wrath of the many who had respected Zhou and the pragmatic rational approach to government he symbolized.

The appearance of this article had been carefully timed, as we foreigners would realize within forty-eight hours. On 7 February the newly arrived Ambassador of Venezuela was summoned to the presence of the "Acting Prime Minister." He assumed he would be received by Deng Xiaoping. To his surprise, he found himself confronted by a man who stood not five feet tall, as Deng did, but nearer six. Being new to China, he was unable to identify his interlocutor immediately, but it was certainly not Deng Xiaoping. A brief, matter-of-fact report of the meeting appeared in the *People's Daily* the next day saying that the Ambassador had been received by Acting Premier Hua Guofeng. Hua indicated that his name would be put before a plenum of the Party Central Committee and then the National People's Congress for confirmation. Since Mao was Chairman of the Party and Hua was now slated for the top post on the government side, Deng had obviously been passed over.

Hua had been promoted from fifth-ranking Vice-Premier

over the heads of older, more experienced men who were better known in China and abroad. Was this appointment the product of a consensus in the leadership and designed to bring on a younger man to bridge the gap to a generation of younger leaders? Any such thoughts were dispelled when, ten days later, the *People's Daily* alleged that "unrepentant capitalist-roaders in the Party" had "unscrupulously split the Central Committee." There could be no further doubt: we were in the midst of a major political crisis.

A day or two later, wall posters appeared at universities in Peking and Shanghai, and on the streets of some other cities of China, attacking Deng Xiaoping in violent terms. Some identified him by name, others by quoting well-known remarks he had made. At Peking University, which Deng's opponents made a focal point in the campaign against him, posters called him evil-minded and urged his dismissal: "Let us drag him off his horse, so we can kick him."

But if Deng was down, he was still not out. The official press did not identify him by name and, by the rules of Chinese politics, that showed the battle was still in the balance. Posters at Peking University said Deng was persisting in his policy line; that showed that his political strength was far from exhausted. When a Foreign Ministry official was asked whether he still held his four important posts of Vice-Premier, Vice-Chairman of the Party, Vice-Chairman of the Party's Military Commission, and Chief of Staff, he replied that he knew of no change. Military attachés were told that Deng continued as Chief of Staff. An article by a unit of the Peking garrison, published in the *People's Daily* on 21 February, showed that the army was in no hurry to join the students and party propaganda men in condemning Deng.

On 3 March, Deng's opponents deployed the full authority of the *People's Daily* to pose the question "What should be done now?" and answered it by saying that the "most important lesson of the Great Proletarian Cultural Revolution is the [need] to mobilize the masses." The paper revived a Cultural Revolution quotation from Mao: "We have seen through some of the rightists, but others have not yet been unmasked. Some are being trusted and trained as our successors. People like Khrushchev are now lurking beside us." This was an ominous indication—the clearest yet—that the left would not be content with Deng's head only. Referring to Deng (still not by name), the article said "As we did during the Cultural Revolution, we must give him a shove in the back once again and see how he behaves." To underline the need for a mass movement, the article described the position of the rightists within the leadership as extremely strong.

At this juncture, millions of copies of a leaflet entitled "Continuing and Developing the Cultural Revolution" were distributed. The posters at the universities in Peking and the articles in the press all continued to claim that fundamental issues were at stake. "That Party person in power taking the capitalist road . . . has clung to the revisionist line of Liu Shaoqi and Lin Biao and has to this day refused to mend his ways. . . . The political program of those persons fanning up the Right deviationist wind is to try to change the Party's basic line so as to attain their criminal aim of restoring capitalism." The leftist-controlled press was singing the old refrain of Cultural Revolution days: the true revolutionaries of the left are defending the sacred cause against the rightist enemy within the Party's ranks.

In *Red Flag*, a writer signing himself Chi Heng described the struggle now developing as "yet another major trial of strength . . . between the proletariat and the bourgeoisie." His main theme was that the capitalist-roaders were people who had joined the Party when it was still pursuing "bourgeois democratic" policies. (Chi Heng was referring to those who had joined the Party before 1949, when it was pursuing liberal economic policies focused on reducing rents and interest rates but not abolishing private businesses or redistributing large landholdings except where these had been abandoned by their owners.) These capitalist-roaders, he alleged, had accepted this minimum program of the "new-democratic revolution," but when the questions of socialist ownership and planning were put on the agenda of the leadership from 1953 on, they favored continued reliance on a free market and a mixed economy in industry, agriculture, and commerce. They had never been reconciled to their defeat and now they wanted to turn the clock back. "There are still a few who have been profoundly influenced by bourgeois ideology but have not accepted the Party's education and remolding."

As one who was himself deeply influenced by "bourgeois ideology," I was highly intrigued by this allegation.

The Deputy Director of the Political Department at Qinghua University, a stronghold of the left, wrote for the *People's Daily* an account of the politics of the "unrepentant capitalist-roader," saying that he minimized the importance of class struggle, gave excessive attention to increasing production, presented himself as the leader most anxious to promote the Four Modernizations, most concerned about stability and unity and the livelihood of the people, and most considerate of the intellectuals. The article purported to be an attack, but reading the substance of the charges one wondered whether the writer's intention was not precisely the opposite.

On 10 March, the *People's Daily* published an editorial on the subject of the campaign, and as always it had to be read as an authoritative reflection of the views of the Party leadership. It must have been approved by at least one member of the Politburo. This *People's Daily* editorial of 10 March complained that the unrepentant capitalist-roader had never been a true Marxist, and after returning to power had broken a promise not to "reverse the verdict" of the Cultural Revolution. A new quotation from Mao was produced: "Reversing verdicts is not welcomed by the people." But in contrast to much of the less authoritative propaganda at this time, it set its face against unleashing the masses in the style of the Cultural Revolution. It reiterated earlier injunctions that the campaign must be controlled by the party leadership at all levels and that there must be no disruption of production or defense. It also repeated the ban on forming "fighting groups" and carrying on intercity liaison—a ban that was being flouted by students who had gone from Peking to Shanghai to stir up the campaign there.[3]

Equally important, the editorial issued a reminder that it was the long-established policy of the Party to reform rather than purge those who had erred ("treat the illness to cure the patient").

As March wore on more signs emerged that a high-level

attempt at reconciling Deng and Mao was under way—and that this was being resisted by the extreme leftists who claimed to speak for the aging Mao.

On 21 March, the *People's Daily* published a second indication that Deng was being offered the chance to remain in the leadership in some senior capacity if he would renounce his challenge to the status quo. The offer was addressed to Deng as clearly as if his name had been printed:

> The historic policy of the Party is "to learn from past mistakes to avoid future ones, and treat the illness to cure the patient." At this time, will the capitalist-roader who is trying to reverse verdicts change his bourgeois stand under the renewed criticism of the people of the whole country and risk their help? . . . Will he have a genuine change of heart and sincerely repent? People are watching to see what his attitude is.

Since the official press had still not named him as the object of the attacks, it was theoretically open to Deng to give a general assurance to the left and be restored to public life with a minimum loss of face by the two sides. The offer of amnesty seemed to indicate that Mao had given a sign of readiness to accept an assurance from Deng at face value.

But even as the offer was being publicized, the left was printing a "recent" remark by Mao about Deng that was focused more precisely and personally on him than anything printed before: "This person," Mao was reported to have said, "does not grasp class struggle; he has never referred to this key link. Still his theme of 'white cat, black cat,' making no distinction between Marxism and Imperialism."[4] (The white cat and the black cat had featured in the most famous or notorious example of Deng's pragmatic thinking. Speaking about agricultural policy in 1962, he had said that the most urgent task was to increase production, and added "In this context, even individual farming will do. It does not matter whether the cat is black or white, so long as it catches mice.")

These contradictory signals suggested that more moderate elements were still able to exercise some influence over Mao and were contending with the left for control over the ultimate authority he constituted.

Was a peace settlement really possible? To a foreign eye, the surface of life in Peking was calm, in unnerving contrast to the high drama evoked by the press and the full-blast wall-poster campaign in the universities of Peking. Which was reality: the calm in the streets or the drama in the press and on the walls?

The press was still vague about what Deng had said and done in 1975, but the posters showed that he had indeed launched a wide-ranging challenge to the status quo. And Deng was not a man who would turn back once he had set his hand to the plow. For their part, Deng's left-wing rivals in the successor generation wanted confrontation even if Mao would accept reconciliation. They wanted to use Mao's authority, while he still lived, to strike down Deng and many other veteran pragmatists. That was why they had dramatized the confrontation, presenting Deng as the political descendant of all those who had opposed Mao in the past twenty-five years, associating him with the long line of rightist policies defeated time and again by Mao and his supporters. The public took them at their word. They saw no reason to doubt that a leadership contest was under way. Everything they had lived through made it seem only too likely that the left, led by Mao, was once again struggling against the right.

For the past eight years, the "masses" had not been in the thick of the fray. Ever since the Cultural Revolution, they had quietly gone on with their shopping, or pedaled slowly home from work, while political struggle had been waged among the elite. They had acted as the audience at a shadow play, watching scene after scene in which the living were attacked or defended only by reference to the dead. The shadows of Confucius, the dictatorial First Emperor of Qin, and the bandit chief Song Jiang had been struggling as symbols for the ideas of Zhou Enlai, Mao Zedong, and Deng Xiaoping. The audience had hissed or cheered as instructed. But when Zhou died, the backdrop had been torn aside and the audience could see that the struggle now was not shadow to shadow, but hand to hand. It was time for them to stand up and join the fight.

The rightist challenge to the status quo and the leftist counterattack had set in motion forces which had acquired such momentum that neither Deng nor Mao could now restrain them if they wanted to.

Would the masses fight for the left or the right? The left seemed to assume that they had only to invoke the authority of Mao and the people would follow them. It had worked before; surely it would work again. But would Mao's record over the years justify that degree of confidence? Was the pragmatism of the right so unattractive to the people? Were the people really striding into 1976 with "revolutionary vigor," or was their mood quite different from what the propagandists painted? Could the propaganda machine make people believe that two and two made five? On the answers to these questions would depend the outcome of the test of strength for which the contending forces were now arrayed.

2

Mao Zedong: From Party Leader to Lone Ranger

IN THE SPRING OF 1976 Mao had just turned eighty-two and was ailing but, after fifty years as a major force shaping the Communist Party of China and its revolution, his words carried enormous authority. Indeed, they were presented to the people by the leftists who controlled the press as the utterances of an infallible demigod. His thought was treated as dogma; his portrait was carried in processions or displayed in homes with a reverence, sincere or feigned, which can only be compared with that shown to objects of religious worship.

Deng was not accorded any such "honors," but he was a vigorous seventy-one and showed every sign of outlasting Mao. The death of Zhou Enlai had for the moment tilted the political balance in favor of the left, but Mao was an aging champion, defending his title against a fitter, younger challenger.

Mao's power to command an unceasing display of obedience and reverence was all too evident, but I had to ask myself how the mass of Chinese regarded him in the privacy of their minds. He was a legend, indeed a myth as much as a political strategist, but in their everyday lives people lived with the tangible results of his strategy.

If one looked back far enough, to the years before 1949, Mao's achievements and genuine prestige were beyond doubt.

He had been proved correct in his belief that China's revolution must be made by armed peasants, not industrial workers. He had acted on this belief since 1927 and had shown courage and common sense in sticking to this strategy in opposition to the party leadership and the leaders of international communism. He had displayed strength of character in the nightmare retreat of the Long March from Jiangxi in the South of China to Yanan in the Northwest in 1935, keeping the Communist cause alive in the face of terrible odds. After the Long March there had come a period of phenomenal growth of the Communist Party's power, for which he could claim much credit: from 1935 to 1945 he had led his colleagues in developing the highly successful political strategy that combined a patriotic appeal to resist the Japanese invasion with liberal social and economic reforms. It had aroused such enthusiastic support wherever the party penetrated in the North China countryside that in twelve years the volunteer Red Army grew from a battered band of a few thousand men who had narrowly escaped total destruction by the Nationalists to a force of one million. The policies espoused by Mao in those years had been welcomed by many liberal intellectuals as well as a mass of peasants. The peasants welcomed the Party, which gave them relief from excessively high rents and interest rates and promised them land. Intellectuals welcomed them because they were honest and not corrupt and had shown themselves to be less oppressive than the Nationalists. The phenomenal growth of the Red Army demonstrated that its leader Mao was in tune with millions of his fellow countrymen. Edgar Snow, the American journalist, gave this impression of meeting Mao in 1936: "You feel that whatever there is extraordinary in this man grows out of the uncanny degree to which he synthesizes and expresses the urgent demands of millions of Chinese, and especially the peasantry."[1]

John Service, the American diplomat who spent eleven weeks in Yanan in 1944 and had an excellent opportunity to observe Mao and his colleagues, wrote of them: "A rather unexpected, and yet strong impression that grows with acquaintance is their *realism* and *practicality*. . . . Firmly and universally held is the belief that the test of everything is whether it works—in China. . . . There is no mysticism in their make-up . . . and no rigid adherence to a hardened dogma."[2]

Despite their great expansion, the Communist forces were still outnumbered four to one by the Nationalists as the civil war resumed in 1946, and their equipment was inferior. Leading an army to victory despite such odds ensured that Mao came to power as a hero.

The more difficult question was how far he had sustained that support in the three decades since 1949. There was evidence to show that he had, as the editorial writers claimed in 1976, repeatedly struggled with his colleagues in the Party to secure adoption of policies which carried China farther and farther to the left. He had accelerated the transition from private to public ownership, from the free market to a planned economy, at a pace never dreamed of before the Party came to power. When, in 1976, Mao's propagandists reviewed this history of inner-party struggle and listed the causes for which Mao had fought, they blithely ignored the possibility that their readers might actually make an independent judgment of the policies and the results they had produced. So divorced from the people were they, so arrogant in the exercise of their supposed power, that they simply assumed the assent of their readers.

The colleagues who had opposed Mao were not always the same ones. The pattern of alliances shifted, but the basic trend was toward greater isolation of Mao Zedong from his senior colleagues. There was one characteristic common to all these struggles: the opposition to Mao always included men at the very highest level of the Party.

Even in the hour of Mao's triumph over the Nationalists, there were some among his colleagues who had deep misgivings about how he might behave as a leader in the future. Some of these misgivings were expressed in essays written by Wu Han, a historian, who in the next fifteen years was to take his place in the long line of Chinese scholars who have risked death by admonishing their emperor. Such scholars showed as much courage as Old Testament prophets who denounced misrule by the leaders of Israel, or the corruption of the society of their day, knowing they would bring down great wrath upon their heads. (The perception of the Chinese scholars was, of course, attributed to their study of history and statecraft rather than words spoken by God.) Sometimes they used literary allusion and historical allegory to protect themselves from retribution; Wu Han was a master of the oblique technique of "pointing at the mulberry to upbraid the ash."

Wu expressed the distaste and anxiety that he—and others more highly placed—felt over the emerging cult of Mao. To make the point, he wrote that after living in Nationalist-controlled areas during World War II, he was shocked to find, when he came to live under Communist rule, that people there were encouraged to shout "Boundless life to Chairman Mao!" just as the Nationalists shouted "Boundless life to Chiang Kai-shek!" and as once people had shouted "Boundless life!" to the emperor of the day.[3]

Wu Han went further. He wrote an essay about a monk who in the fourteenth century A.D. made a praiseworthy contribution to the overthrow of the Yuan dynasty and then withdrew from public life. "My admiration for such a person is boundless," Wu commented. "He is someone who did not engage in revolution just to attain high office, a great man indeed!"[4] Mao read the essay and summoned Wu Han for an evening chat. As Wu wrote afterward, Mao "persuaded" him that a person must recognize his class membership as a revolutionary and should stay on to serve the revolutionary state.

Was this a discreet first attempt by Mao's colleagues to get him to recognize that his talents were better suited to capturing power than using it, and that he would be best assured of a glorious place in history if he retired in this moment of triumph? Three years later some of them sent him a letter that urged him to "take a rest," and Zhu De, a highly respected party veteran, went so far as to suggest that Mao share his party post of Chairman with others in rotation. Nine years and two Mao-made disasters after Wu Han's essay on the modest monk, the Chairman would be forced by his colleagues to retire to the "second line." Until then he would reject all such suggestions and instead would mount a series of interventions in which he used his prestige in the Party at large to overwhelm senior colleagues who gave him unwelcome advice.

In the middle and late 1950s an opinion group formed in the top party circles that advocated a gradualist approach to restructuring the economy and adoption of some aspects of the Yugoslav form of socialism, which emphasized worker control, greater reliance on market forces, and a mixture of private and state ownership in agriculture. Liu Shaoqi favored this approach, and its most influential spokesman was the first Deputy Prime Minister, Chen Yun. Chen, a self-taught economist and one of the very few men in the party leadership who had ever belonged to a trade union and earned their living in a city, encouraged more academic economists to write articles on these themes and wrote some himself. But Mao wanted a rapid transition to socialism and accused his opponents of "tottering along like a woman with bound feet, always complaining that others are going too fast."

In 1953 Mao overruled those in the leadership who wanted more reliance on market forces than on centralized planning. He went on to defeat those who sought to maintain and even expand the role of capitalist enterprises. In 1955, to get his way on the most fundamental issue of Chinese political economy, the ownership of land, he simply swept aside the policy formulated by his colleagues in the Central Committee. The Central Committee's policy was to move very gradually from private ownership of land to some form of socialism. The policy's premise was that mechanization must precede collectivization and it was envisaged that mechanization would take at least 15 years. Mao launched a mass movement to collectivize land immediately.

In launching the movement he could rely on the trust and prestige he and the Party had acquired in the eyes of the peasants by resisting the Japanese invader and, later, distributing land more equally. He also benefited, let it be said, from the widespread recognition, instilled by earlier mass movements, that it was dangerous to oppose the will of the Party. As a result, he was able to carry through collectivization at extraordinary speed: China's hundred million households surrendered their land to the collectives in eighteen months. Violence, on the scale used by Stalin, had been unnecessary.

The leaders who were opposed to collectivization at this stage created one reverse tide of disbanding tens of thousands of cooperatives, which in their view had been formed without proper preparation, and that was all. However, the speed of the transformation could not disguise the fact that collectivization had not grown out of a spontaneous grass-roots movement, but was an initiative by Mao from the top down. As such, it was just the reverse of the kind of leadership he had practiced so successfully in earlier years. Also, the speedy transformation did not guarantee that the policy would increase production or would always be accepted by most of the peasants.

In the same year that Mao was leading collectivization, he was also using his authority to reinforce the control of party administrators over intellectual creation. The literary critic Hu Feng had presented a 300,000-word report to the Central Committee arguing that the continuing imposition on writers of control by cultural officials and the fetters of an official dogma would result in cultural sterility. The cultural hierarchy in the Party rejected Hu Feng's views and called for them to be criticized, but Mao went further and insisted that Hu Feng be denounced by name as a counter-revolutionary and made the target of a nationwide campaign directed at him personally. Indeed, from this campaign Mao developed the first post-1949 mass purge directed at opponents within the Party.[5] Some 150,000 were investigated.[6]

In those years of the 1950s an influential body in the leadership was trying to build up democratic institutions and achieve a shift from mass movements to the rule of law and constitutional government. This group within the Chinese leadership was in tune with Khrushchev, who was building up "socialist legality" in the Soviet Union and denouncing Stalin's cult of personality. Since China was still in close alliance with the Soviet Union, Mao's colleagues, led by Liu Shaoqi and Deng Xiaoping, were able to use the momentum developed by Khrushchev's leadership to dominate the Eighth Congress of the Chinese Communist Party and thereby commit their party to the same goals. At the congress they curbed Mao's personal power, played down class struggle, and emphasized the need for laws and constitutional government. Mao saw that this would hinder him from carrying forward his brand of revolution through mass movements. He talked more and more about class struggle, and it was not long before he again burst the bonds of party discipline and collective leadership with which his colleagues had tried to bind him.

In 1957, in face of opposition from senior colleagues, Mao

launched the Hundred Flowers campaign. For six weeks he encouraged intellectuals to criticize the Party, hoping to drive home the need for a less bureaucratic style of work. He had no intention of reforming China's institutions. Mao had greatly underestimated the scope of the criticisms and demands for reform that would be made. When the true views of the intellectuals became clear, some of his colleagues advocated a program that would accommodate the demands for reform. Mao resisted this.[7] Instead, he insisted on an antirightist campaign that purged 300,000 intellectuals. The repression of the Hundred Flowers alienated a generation of intellectuals and denied the nation the full contribution they could have made.

Mao and his supporters showed no regret, but I could not believe that this history did not weigh heavily against him in the silent judgment of many whose opinion counted in China in 1976.

In foreign as well as domestic affairs Mao succeeded in swinging the pendulum away from the relatively pragmatic policies of the Eighth Congress. After the Korean war had been turned into a stalemate peace, Premier Zhou Enlai had developed an international strategy that stressed China's role as a Third World country rather than a center of Communist revolution. In the spirit of the Bandung Conference of African and Asian nations held in 1955 and in line with Khrushchev's concept of peaceful coexistence, China had adopted a stance that aroused hopes of accommodation with the "imperialist" powers in place of confrontation.

This was not the kind of strategy to appeal to the adventurous, combative side of Mao's nature. Reports of discussions that Mao held with India's Prime Minister Jawaharlal Nehru and with Khrushchev showed his mind running along very different lines. Ordinary men like Nehru or Khrushchev might fear the destructive power of the atom bomb and see in the dangers of nuclear conflict a reason why detente between the West and the Communist bloc should be pursued urgently. But a hero of Mao's stature would not fall prey to anxiety on this score. At the time of Hiroshima, he had dismissed the atom bomb as a paper tiger,[8] and in 1954—even as his prime minister, Zhou Enlai, was developing his "diplomacy of smiles"—Mao showed that he was made of sterner stuff. He told Nehru that if an atomic war was fought and "if the worst came to the worst and half of mankind died, the other half would remain while imperialism would be razed to the ground and the whole world would become socialist."[9]

This statement was put on public record later by the Chinese government in an official communiqué. It lends credence to the allegation made by a hostile witness, Nikita Khrushchev, that one day, as he and Mao lay by Mao's swimming pool discussing problems of war and peace, the Chairman said to him "Comrade Khrushchev, what do you think? If we compare the military might of the capitalist world with that of the socialist world, you'll see that we obviously have the advantage over our enemies. . . . All you have to do is provoke the Americans into military action, and I'll give you as many divisions as you need to crush them—a hundred, two hundred, one thousand divisions."[10] Here was a man in the mold of Tamerlane, the Turkish warrior whose conquests had stretched from the Volga River to the Persian Gulf.

Small wonder that people in China were taught to love the bomb. I remember clearly the gorgeous colors of the mushroom cloud of an early Chinese atomic bomb, celebrated in a poster on a brick wall in Tianjin in 1969. The wall was crumbling, the poster was tattered, but the bomb was still brilliant.

Small wonder either that when United States Secretary of State John Foster Dulles responded to Zhou Enlai's olive branches by reinforcing anti-Communist hawks in Taiwan and South Korea, Mao swung Chinese policy away from the spirit of Bandung to a more aggressive posture. In Moscow in 1957 he tried to encourage a test of strength with "imperialism" by a speech in which he declared that "The East wind prevails over the West wind." But Khrushchev would have none of it, and the Sino-Soviet alliance became doubly irksome to Mao. Not only did Khrushchev's anti-Stalinist domestic reforms encourage Mao's pragmatic colleagues in the Chinese Party, but the Soviet strategy of peaceful coexistence was a stumbling block to the cause of world revolution.

In the first year of Communist rule, Hu Feng had written:

> Mao stands like an idol,
> Speaks to the whole world,
> Gives order to time.

In 1957, Mao was straining to realize his destiny as one who, with his combination of willpower, political skill, vaulting ambition and capacity to dream great dreams, would dictate to Time the order of events. If it meant breaking up the coalitions that bound together the different wings of the Communist Party of China and linked the Party to the nonparty intellectuals, so be it. If it meant destroying the alliance with the Soviet Union, so be it. Petty-minded "revisionists" like Khrushchev had chosen for themselves and their nations the ignoble role in history of abandoning the revolution. China under Mao was destined for greater things. The break with the Soviet revisionists was not too high a price to pay for renewing the momentum of progress toward the utopia Mao envisioned for China. It was this vision which distinguished him from a vulgar warrior like Tamerlane, intent on conquest merely for the sake of glory and the pleasures great power can buy. And it was a vision very different from the prospect of material abundance held out to the Soviet Union by Khrushchev; that Mao scorned as "goulash communism." He was after a spiritual as well as material revolution and envisaged far-reaching changes emerging from tumultuous upheavals that would send shivers down Khrushchev's spine. His mind's eye would not even be satisfied by the natural scale of things. First he magnified the acts of nature and then dreamed on a supernatural scale:

> The waves on Lake Tungt'ing boil up
>   like snow reaching to the heavens,
> The people of the Long Island sing earth-shaking songs.
> Inspired by all this I would dream a dream equally vast,
> And see the Land of the Hibiscus wholly illuminated
>   by the light of the dawn.[11]

His utopia was inspired partly by the Marxist classics, partly by Chinese philosophy, and partly by his own experience as a guerrilla leader, particularly in Yanan in the 1940s. He rejected the twentieth-century trend toward specialization. He wanted people to realize a contemporary version of the ideal of the Renaissance man. Soldiers should practice farming, farmers and industrial workers should master each other's skills and engage in some of each other's work. The humblest peasant should be encouraged to write poetry and paint. The gaps between city and countryside, between intellectual and manual labor should be narrowed. The communal ownership of property would eliminate exploitation and greed. There would be freedom as well as discipline.

So, in 1958, sweeping aside the strong reservations of senior colleagues, he again used his personal prestige to mobilize the Party and the masses. The aim this time was to make a Great Leap Forward in the space of a few years from poverty to abundance, and from socialism to communism. The peasants, reorganized into communes, were to industrialize their villages and live an even more collective life.

But Mao's goals were not static. He wanted men to live in a state of permanent revolution. As soon as one revolutionary task was achieved the leaders must set a new one. To create an emotional climate in which people would be prepared to engage in this enormously ambitious project, reason itself was swept aside, replaced by blind faith in the wisdom of the Party, and above all its leader Mao. The press increasingly cast a supernatural aura over Mao. For example, it reported one of the Uygurs, a traditionally Moslem people, as telling him in 1958: "In the past we Uygur people greeted each other with the words 'Huda [Allah] protect you.' Today we have changed this into 'The Party protect you, Chairman Mao protect you.'"

As with the early moves to collectivization, the Great Leap came not from the grass roots upward but from Mao downward. Those who lacked blind faith in Mao and the Party obeyed out of fear. They knew from the purges of the past decade—including the antirightist campaign, which was still fresh in memory—that the price of resistance to a mass movement was usually one's liberty or one's life.

To achieve the impossible goals of increased production and industrialization inspired by Mao, officials drove the people beyond the limits of the human body until in some places peasants were too exhausted to harvest the crops they had planted. The sweeping reorganization of rural life brought economic disruption on a large scale. Strong resistance developed to the highly collectivized pattern of life that was imposed. Instead of abundance there came hunger and even starvation. Instead of a new enthusiasm for communism came disillusion. Despite harsh penalties, acts of counter-revolution multiplied and peasants, defying party policy, broke up collectives to revert to private farming. They had rejected what had been offered to them in the name of communism. No one would offer it again in a hurry.

Mao's attempt to lead his people beyond the limits of humanity and to act on a superhuman scale had left China farther away from utopia than before he began. But Mao was far from contrite. In June 1959 he revisited his birthplace for the first time since he had plunged into the "tornado" of peasant uprisings in 1927. When he reviewed the struggles of the past he paid handsome tribute to the courage of those who had sacrificed themselves for the revolution but went on to use language which put the makers of the revolution on a par with God:

> Only because so many sacrificed themselves,
>   did our wills become strong,
> So that we dared command the sun and moon
>   to bring a new day.[12]

One of Mao's most powerful colleagues, Minister of Defense Peng Dehuai, who was revered by his fellow countrymen for his role as commander of the Chinese forces in the Korean war, had also been looking at conditions in the countryside. What he found after the autumn harvest of 1958 confirmed the fears he had voiced since Mao had first promoted the idea of a Great Leap. He wrote a poem reflecting the sufferings of the peasants:

> Grain scattered on the ground, potato leaves withered;
> Strong young people have left for steel-making,
> Only children and old women reaped the crops,
> How can they pass the coming year?
> Allow me to appeal for the people![13]

Other critical voices began to be heard in public. In the very month that Mao was writing his poem praising the achievements of the revolution, Wu Han, the historian who had warned of the dangers of the Mao cult in 1950, was writing for the *People's Daily* an essay that put Mao and the results of New China's first decade in quite another light. Wu Han described how an honest official of the Ming dynasty, Hai Rui, had scolded the Emperor Jiaqing. Those with eyes to see knew that the scolding was intended for Mao; he made Hai Rui say:

> At present the tax and labor burden of the people are severalfold above those of normal times . . . You have spent so much money on the superstitious arts, increasingly so with the days. Because of you the ordinary people have reached total poverty. [Such deprivation] has reached the extreme in these ten years. . . . In your early years you may have done a few good deeds. But now? . . . The country has been dissatisfied with you for a long time . . . so set upon cultivating the Way* you have become bewitched; so attached to dictatorial methods, you have become dogmatic and biased.[14]

Mao's immediate punishment for creating a manmade disaster on a scale unprecedented in the ten years of Communist rule in China was remarkably light. He lost the post of head of state and was forced to cede day-to-day control of domestic affairs to Liu Shaoqi, who succeeded him, and Deng Xiaoping, who exercised managerial control over the Party as its General Secretary. Mao retained the chairmanship of the Party and the freedom to develop the polemic with the Soviet Union. He was able to repulse the frontal attack made on his leadership of the Great Leap Forward by Peng Dehuai and secure Peng's dismissal and his replacement as Minister of Defense by a man of Mao's own choice. He was subject to no public criticism. Instead, lower-level officials and the weather were blamed for the disaster.

Looking back from 1976, however, it was clear that the long-term cost to Mao of the failure of the Great Leap was far greater than the outward damage he sustained. While he would remain titular head of the Party and a symbol for China until his death, he would never truly regain the leadership of the whole Party or the whole nation. Reconciliation with those he had alienated would have required him to abandon his vision of utopia, his conviction that only through turmoil and combat

---

* I.e., the dogma of Marxism–Leninism and Mao Zedong Thought.

could men reach that utopia, and his attempts to rearrange the affairs of the universe on a scale that called for more-than-mortal powers. It would have also required a modicum of humility, a readiness to sacrifice the Ram of Pride in place of his sons and daughters.

In the years immediately following the Great Leap Forward, particularly 1961 and 1962, the rightists Liu and Deng ran domestic policy with scant regard for Mao's views. Their motto was "Take reality as your starting point," and their version of reality contrasted strikingly with the utopian view of China propagated abroad by self-proclaimed friends of China.

A policy called The Three Freedoms and One Contract was implemented on a trial basis. This permitted the extension of plots of land for private use, the extension of private markets, an increase in the number of small enterprises with sole responsibility for their own profits or losses, and the fixing of output quotas based on individual households. The last point meant that an agricultural collective could divide up its land among its households provided they contracted to deliver a quota of produce. It was a thorough repudiation of Mao's two great collectivization drives, but Liu and Deng were acting in that tradition of flexibility which Mao had helped establish in earlier days. As John Service had written in 1944, "Once a specific measure or policy has been found unsuccessful or unsuited to conditions, and after discussion has produced what seems to be a better substitute, there is no hesitation in admitting failure by making a change. This *adaptability* and *willingness to change* has been apparent in every field—military strategy taxation, land policy, education, mass organization."[15]

Deng Xiaoping and Peng Zhen, Mayor of Peking and a very senior member of the Politburo, encouraged and protected writers and academics who were prepared to speak out against Mao and his policies.

One of Deng's confidants went to see Wu Han to encourage him to write more about the Ming-dynasty official Hai Rui.[16] The result was not only another essay but a full-length play, *Hai Rui Dismissed from Office*, a powerful appeal for returning to the people the land which had been "forcibly seized" by the "local tyrants." The play went through seven drafts and Wu Han consulted his friends at every stage, but the end result was not a muffled protest; it was a clarion call for reversing Mao's policy of collectivization, for the rehabilitation of Mao's most fearsome critic, Peng Dehuai, and for redress of the injustices perpetrated by the power-holders on the common people.

In one of the most telling scenes, a corrupt magistrate goes through the motions of trying a nobleman's son who has seized the land of a peasant family, abducted the mother and daughter, and set his servants to beat the grandfather. The magistrate pretends he can see no scars on the old man's body, orders him to be beaten for bringing false accusations, and turns a deaf ear to his final plea: "Your Honor! There *are* scars on my body. How can you say there are not! Please re-examine my wounds, Your Honor!" Seeing that those who are supposed to ensure justice are in fact corrupted by the local tyrants, the peasants complain that they have no place to air their grievances. Before they were independent farmers; now, after the seizure of their land, they are tenant farmers of the unscrupulous local power-holders and so, as they tell an honest official who arrives at the village in disguise, they dare not protest too strongly.

The outrage of Mao and his followers at the staging of this play in the heart of the capital in 1961, can be imagined. Wu Han's highly placed protectors were not strong enough to prevent the play being taken off after only a very brief run. Nor could they defend Wu Han when, four years later, Mao launched the Cultural Revolution by attacking it, and he died under persecution. With his knowledge of Chinese history and Chinese politics Wu Han would have known the risks he was running when he wrote the play, but he had espoused a cause much larger than himself and so had taken his place in a long tradition of intellectuals of high principle and great courage. His play did not die with him, as we shall see.

Wu Han was not a lone voice. It may not have been an accident that the play had opened in Peking in the same month that a forum of writers in Shanghai heard Zhou Yang, the second most senior party commissar for cultural affairs,* deplore

---

*Deputy Director of the Propaganda Department of the Communist Party of China since 1949.

the growing cult of worship of Mao Zedong.[17] On another occasion Zhou Yang made a remarkable attack on the dictatorship of the proletariat (i.e., the dictatorship of the Communist Party, which rules China "on behalf of the proletariat"), a criticism that echoed the complaint of the peasants in Wu Han's drama: "There was no place to air our grievances."

> The dictatorship of the proletariat is ravenous [Zhou Yang said], more fearsome than the dictatorship of the bourgeoisie. In a bourgeois society, one can run when one violates the law, but when society is so tightly organized, where can one run to? . . . There is no place to vent one's grief and no place to submit an appeal; one is afraid that things written down in one's diary might be found out. . . . In our society, there is indeed the phenomenon that men are not treated as men.[18]

The man who most consistently criticized Mao in public at this time was Deng Tuo, who had been editor-in-chief of the *People's Daily* until he let his reservations about the Great Leap Forward show in the editorial policy of the paper in the summer of 1958. Peng Zhen, Mayor of Peking, then made him the city's chief party commissar for press and culture and encouraged him to air his views in the city's press. Deng Tuo was a Chinese version of Alexander Pope, the eighteenth-century English poet who satirized the follies of the great of his day behind the thinnest of protective veils. Like Pope, Deng Tuo combined wit and learning. Some of his satirical essays were reprinted by the newspapers of other major cities of China and he acquired a nationwide following among the intelligentsia, while the Western world remained in total ignorance until he too was hounded to death in the Cultural Revolution.

In 1961 and 1962 Deng Tuo ridiculed a number of Mao's more striking follies and satirized his more pretentious and pompous utterances. One essay, "Great Empty Talk," ridiculed the grandiloquent and vague style of some of Mao's poetry and slogans, such as "The East wind prevails over the West wind." Deng Tuo pretended that there was a child-poet in his neighborhood who "in recent times, mostly in imitation of the style of great poets, composed a lot of 'empty talk.'" Recently the boy had written an "Ode on Wild Grass" that was nothing but empty talk and ran:

Heaven is our Father,
Earth is our Mother,
Sun is our Wetnurse,
The East Wind is our Benefactor,
The West Wind is our Enemy.
We are a tuft of grass,
Some like us,
Some hate us,
No matter—we don't care,
We keep on growing.[19]

Reading that in the midst of the chaos of 1966 restored one's faith in China. Remembering it in 1976, one knew that there would be no easy victory for the left in the new test of political strength.

Preparation to undermine Mao in a directly political manner may also have been undertaken. For instance, Peng Zhen, acting on instructions from "someone even higher," is said to have organized a working group, led by Deng Tuo, to meet secretly to examine and report on documents that would provide evidence that Mao had acted in violation of party discipline. The documents they examined had been issued in the name of the Central Committee in the years 1958 to 1961 after approval by Mao alone, without formal discussion with other Central Committee members. When Peng was driven from office in the Cultural Revolution, his enemies claimed that the purpose of the study had been to unearth sufficient evidence to force Mao to step out of his position of Chairman of the Party.[20]

Such efforts to undermine his position did not weaken Mao's will. His extraordinary rise from chieftan of a thousand ragtag guerrillas in 1927 to the leadership of a nation of five hundred million in 1949 had made him a hero in his own eyes as well as in those of others. When the Great Leap Forward caused many of those who had once accepted Mao's leadership to pass into opposition to him and to express their opposition publicly, his heroic self-image was not dimmed. A man was not a true hero unless he could stand alone, and even in Yanan, in the days when he was most closely in tune and in touch with his colleagues and his fellow countrymen, Mao had conveyed a quality of spiritual isolation. The American Agnes Smedley, who had gained his friendship then, wrote: "His spirit dwelt within itself, isolating him. . . . His humor was often sardonic and grim, as if it sprang from deep caverns of spiritual seclusion. I had the impression that there was a door to his being that had never been opened to anyone."[21]

The Great Leap had not only alienated many of Mao's fellow countrymen, it had also provoked the break with the Soviet Union. China now faced the hostility of Russia as well as of America. To some of his colleagues this put China in a difficult and dangerous position, but Mao saw this isolation as confirmation of the heroic role China was playing under his leadership. The faint-hearted might quake at having to face the tiger of U.S. "imperialism" at the front gate and the Soviet bear at the back, but not Mao. He wrote in 1962: "Only the hero dares pursue the tiger, / Still less does any brave fellow fear the bear."[22]

"He was as stubborn as a mule, and a steel rod of pride and determination ran through his nature. I had the impression that he would wait and watch for years, but eventually would have his way."[23] This was another of Agnes Smedley's judgments of Mao in 1936 and 1937 that was to be confirmed twenty-five years later. After the reverse of the Great Leap, Mao waited and watched awhile. Then, in 1962, Liu Shaoqi and Deng Xiaoping mounted an attempt to have their pragmatic ideas of reform adopted as national policy. In a speech to seven thousand senior party officials, Liu demanded among other things a return to individual farming, the closing of loss-making enterprises, the free marketing of surplus production by the peasants, the expansion of rural free markets and higher prices for agricultural products, the rehabilitation of people who had been wrongly denounced as rightists, and the reconsideration of the case of Peng Dehuai. In a later speech, Liu went on to make demands, obviously aimed at Mao, that party members, no matter how great their role in the Party, should lead from within and not from without or above. They should "submit to the majority."

Mao decided that this was the moment to strike back. He succeeded in blocking the reforms and gave a hint that he would one day pass from the defensive to the offensive. He did so in a way designed to put himself on the side of "the people" and against high-handed party officials. The style of rule practiced then by Liu and Deng emphasized discipline and prompt obedience by the masses and junior officials to the instructions received from above. Mao warned party officials that they could not suppress people's views forever: "People will always want to speak their minds. Do you think they won't dare touch your arses, you fearsome tigers? Shit, they will!"[24]

He would see to it that they did. In the Cultural Revolution, he would use popular resentment of the Party's authoritarian rule, and of the privileges granted to its officials, to fuel the fire of a revolt by the people against the Party. He would be "alone, with the masses," as he put it to André Malraux. The party leader of 1949 would have completed his transformation into the Lone Ranger of the Chinese Revolution.

3

Mao: The Making and Unmaking of a Demigod

MAO HAD TURNED SEVENTY-ONE on 26 December 1964. He was already suffering from Parkinson's disease and could count on only a few more years of fully active political life. His next campaign might be his last. Believing that the revolution was being stifled by bureaucracy and materialism, he was preparing a great movement to renew the vitality of the Chinese revolution and to mobilize his fellow countrymen to remake society by drastically decentralizing it. He had a genuine but totally imprecise notion of making China democratic. In this movement, the Cultural Revolution, he would commission the youth of China to act as the vanguard in a massive attempt to remold those in power at every level of the party; to destroy the hold on men's minds of traditional Chinese and foreign culture, ideas, habits, and customs; and to reorder political and state power so that party officials would no longer form a privileged hierarchy "oppressing the people." While youth rebelled, the army, controlled by Mao's disciple, Minister of Defense Marshal Lin Biao, would provide discreet support. Mao's word would once more shape events. Because he would be bypassing and indeed attacking virtually the whole party hierarchy and would be directly leading youth in the assault, his personal authority would be crucial.

In January 1965, Mao told Edgar Snow that there was need for more deification of the individual in China.[1] Was this just a political strategy to reinforce the personal authority of a leader who saw himself as being alone with the masses, or did it reflect a deeper conviction that his ability to grasp the truth was so great as to give him superhuman power to change the world? If he had not believed this, would he have had the nerve to act on the scale he did act on? Would he have written, later in 1965, as he climbed again to his old guerrilla base in the Jinggang mountains, "I have long aspired to reach the clouds"? If his faith in himself had not far exceeded that of other men he could not have led so many to suspend disbelief, to ignore the laws of human gravity and "reach for the clouds" with him.

Superhuman imagery came easily to him in the poem "Two Birds: A Dialogue," which he wrote in the autumn of 1965, on the eve of the Cultural Revolution. The two birds in the dialogue are a cowardly sparrow who will do anything for a quiet, comfortable life, and a heroic roc unafraid of war and turmoil. The roc is a fabulous bird of prey so huge and strong that it could carry off the largest of animals. Mao identifies with the mighty bird of prey: his opponents at home and abroad are like the timid sparrow. The poem begins

> The roc wings fanwise
> Soaring ninety thousand *li**
> And rousing a raging cyclone.
> The blue sky on his back, he looks down
> To survey man's world with its towns and cities.
>
> Gunfire licks the heavens,
> Shells pit the earth.[2]

Terrified by the battle, the sparrow wants to escape to the peace and comfort of a jeweled palace. Filled with contempt, the roc dismisses peace as an illusion and the prospect of material ease as "farting nonsense." Revolutionary turmoil is the reality to be embraced, and the poem ends with the roc proclaiming "Look you, the world is being turned upside down."

Whether or not he himself believed in the superhuman

* Chinese kilometers.

image he projected, Mao knew he was appealing to feelings and practices of worship for the supreme ruler that were deeply rooted in Chinese society, as he made clear to Edgar Snow. For three thousand years the Chinese had worshiped their emperor as the Son of Heaven, an intermediary between the world of men and the powers above. The emperor's word was law. To criticize him was to risk execution. Theology and the power of the state combined forces to ensure that he was treated with reverence. As Mao was very much aware, such practices die hard. In the early days of his rule, country people had kow-towed before him during the National Day parades just as they had once kowtowed to the emperor.

Mao's revolutionary ideas made his rule very different from that of the emperors, but his style frequently echoed the imperial past. It was not only that people were encouraged to shout "Boundless life to Chairman Mao!" as once they had shouted "Boundless life!" to the emperors. In his use of the Imperial City for public appearances and for residence, in making calligraphic inscriptions for publications and monuments, and in the way he issued instructions in his own name rather than in the name of the Central Committee he associated himself with the imperial tradition. Even when he went one day to labor on the construction of the Ming Tombs reservoir, he was not so much breaking with the feudal past as renewing an ancient ritual, for the emperors had plowed a symbolic furrow every year. In his poetry and his informal talks, he seemed time and again to place himself in line of succession to China's emperors. So, inevitably, he inherited some of the worship they had enjoyed.

A musical extravaganza, *The East Is Red*, produced in 1964, first on stage, then as a film, was a major effort to build his cult. Its presentation of Mao, like countless others in the years that followed, was carefully ambiguous, pitching him somewhere be-tween man and god. A massed choir of one thousand, dressed to represent all the peoples of the world, sang "Chairman Mao is the sun in our hearts" as a thirty-foot-high image of him ap-peared in the "sky" formed by the backdrop. In the opening scene one hundred beautiful women dressed in long traditional Chinese gowns performed a dance as sunflowers facing a rising sun, and at its climax prostrated themselves on their backs before it while the choir sang "the sunflower seeks the rays of the sun." In once sequence of the film version, the screen showed an expanse of ocean, as a choir sang the opening lines of the title song:

> From the Red East rises the sun,
> There appears in China a Mao Zedong.

At this moment a huge ball of fire surged up over the horizon. It was the sun, magnified out of all proportion by a telescopic lens.

Soon there would be demands from the young that "The East Is Red" be made the national anthem. It was played and sung millions of times, and in this and a hundred other ways Mao was associated with the sun, one of the first objects of worship by primitive man.

To launch the Red Guards into the Cultural Revolution, Mao reviewed a total of eleven million of them on eight occasions in the summer of 1966. The first time, he appeared among them on Tian An Men Square at dawn. (At what other time should the sun make its first appearance?) The New China News Agency reported that the young people were exalted and exclaimed "Chairman Mao is here! Chairman Mao has come among us!"[3]

He retired into the Imperial City and would re-emerge two hours later to review the million assembled that day. As the crowd waited for him to reappear, they sang "From the Red East rises the Sun. / There appears in China a Mao Zedong." When Mao finally appeared, a hundred thousand Red Guard throats opened to greet him in frenzied adulation. Their demigod stood silent and remote from them, silhouetted on the Gate of Heavenly Peace. They chanted his name and title over and over again "Mao Zhuxi! Mao Zhuxi! Mao Zhuxi! Mao Zhuxi!" The chanting was rhythmic, urgent, yearning, and its pounding became more urgent because the yearning could not be satisfied. Teenage girls became hysterical, their faces contorted; they wept uncontrollably and, half-fainting, had to be supported by those next to them.

In Hong Kong, I heard a broadcast of the rally by chance.

Walking into the living room of Chinese friends I found them listening in silent horror as a high-pitched voice whipped a crowd to a delirium of fury. I could understand nothing of it and did not know what they were listening to. The savage frenzy made me think of Hitler's Nuremberg rallies, and yet the language was not German. Was it a dramatic recreation by a Chinese-language radio station? My friends told me that I had heard Lin Biao exhorting Red Guards to "Beat down the capitalist-roaders in power, beat down the reactionary bourgeois authorities, sweep away all wicked devils and evil spirits. Do away with the Four Old Things: old thought, old culture, old customs, and old habits. The Thoughts of Mao Zedong must rule, and transform the spirit until the power of the spirit transforms matter."[4] Mao was at Lin Biao's elbow as he delivered his speech, glancing over his shoulder at the text and smiling approvingly.

He himself did not address the Red Guards then or at any other time. He did, however, receive a group of youngsters who pinned a Red Guard armband on his sleeve. He asked the girl who pinned it on what her name was. She told him it was Song Pingping, and admitted that Pingping meant "Refined and Gentle." Did this name imply, Mao asked, that she did not want to do battle? Of course she wanted to do battle! Inspired by the man she thought of as "my Chairman," she changed her name to Yaowu, meaning "Will to Battle."[5]

Mao's apostles of destruction and rebirth marched away from the square inspired to take their orders literally. In the next months they not only destroyed such manifestations of old culture as books and paintings but also physically beat down many of their human targets, crippling and killing in the name of the Thought for which the claim was made "Where Mao Zedong Thought shines, there people see the way to fight for their liberation."

The press exhorted them to discard the notions of freedom, equality, and universal love for mankind. Humanism was to be despised. Mao, the hero-leader, possessed some of the characteristics of Nietzsche's superman and was determined to breed "in the storm and stress of revolutionary struggle" a younger generation who would embody those characteristics: an immensely strong will, a readiness to inflict suffering for a noble cause, and the courage to operate without norms of good and evil.

The Great Teacher taught the young that there is no such thing as objective truth, before which all men are equal. All truths were held to have a class character, not excluding those of the natural sciences. Newspaper editorials adopted a violence of language they had never used before. The *People's Daily* warned the "bourgeoisie" that "we shall leave you to rot, destroy you."[6] Taking their cue from this, Red Guards despised pity as a weakness and wrote "Let the landlord and bourgeois class, old and young gentlemen be pushed into the corner and let them cry! Let them jump as if struck by thunder! Let them tremble with fear! . . . A boat sinks and above a thousand boats sail on."[7] In this spirit hundreds of thousands of people—old and young—were killed, maimed, and tortured.*

Every resource of language was deployed to cast a supernatural aura around Mao Zedong and his Thought. Mao's chief propagandist, Yao Wenyuan, likened his Thought to a "massive cudgel" swung by a Golden Monkey. The brilliant light of the Thought, Yao wrote, would "penetrate all the dark corners and show up all the monsters and goblins in their true colors."[8]

Mao's enemies were "freaks and monsters"; a series of talks he had once delivered on literature and the arts was a "magic mirror" to detect demons. Determined to make a revolution that would "touch men to their very souls" and create a "new man in the socialist era," Mao saw the ghosts from the past holding him back. The poison of feudal and bourgeois ideas was being transmitted in all forms of culture. He called the Ministry of Culture the Ministry of Ghosts because it allowed figures from history and legend to crowd the theatrical stage and the pages of books.

The language of demonology sounds quaint, folkloric, and even comic to people in societies where literacy and the scientific spirit have been widespread for centuries, but China in

---

* AFP reported from Peking on 3 February 1979 that unofficial but usually reliable sources estimated that 400,000 people were killed during the Cultural Revolution.

1966 was in her first generation of mass literacy and only just emerging from millennia in which superstitions about ghosts and evil spirits exercised a strong hold over many minds. The spirit of scientific skepticism was a tender young plant easily overwhelmed by a revival of superstition allied to the modern jargon of Marxism–Leninism.

Contrary to party tradition under which Mao had been known as Comrade Mao Zedong, he was now referred to as "the Great Teacher, Great Leader, Great Commander and Great Helmsman Chairman Mao" and "Teacher of the People's Revolutions of the World." He was hailed as "the source of all wisdom." "All our victories are victories of the Thoughts of Mao Zedong," proclaimed Lin Biao, unconsciously echoing the propaganda for Big Brother in George Orwell's 1984. His Thought was made sacred, "a compass and spiritual food" of which every word was held to be worth ten thousand of anyone else's. Its value and power were constantly described in terms such as these:

> The thought of Mao Zedong is the sun in our heart, is the root of our life, is the source of all our strength. Through this, man becomes unselfish, daring, intelligent, able to do everything; he is not conquered by any difficulty and can conquer every enemy. The thought of Mao Zedong transforms man's ideology, transforms the Fatherland . . . through this the oppressed people of the world will rise.*

Little children were taught to sing:

> Father is dear, mother is dear
> But Chairman Mao is dearest of all.

* Quoted in Robert Jay Lifton, *Revolutionary Immortality* (London: Weidenfeld & Nicholson, 1969), pp. 72–73. I first read this book in Peking in 1968 and greatly valued its insights into the Cultural Revolution. I reread it eleven years later, after completing the first draft of this chapter. What I had learned of the Cultural Revolution in the years between had reinforced and enlarged the interpretation I had gained from Lifton. So well had it stood the test of time, and so fundamental had it remained to my understanding of Mao that there was very little that I then found to change in my draft or to disagree with in Lifton's book. I lay less emphasis than Lifton on Mao's desire to ensure the immortality of his revolution not because I dispute this central thesis but because I have found few words of Mao that bear directly on this preoccupation.

It was not only teenagers who were reduced to a state of tearful delirium. A film of the Ninth National Congress of the Communist Party in 1969 showed grown men and women, some of them veterans of the Long March, working themselves into a frenzy of emotion as they waited for Mao to appear on the stage of the Great Hall of the People. They jigged up and down, waving the little red book, calling his name over and over until tears rolled down their cheeks. When finally he appeared, these men and women, with a lifetime of service to the revolution behind them, people who had once called him comrade, yelped and bayed like animals in a mass orgy of adulation.

In the rebellion that Mao inspired, millions of people, from members of the Central Committee to the humblest peasants, were persecuted and their families suffered because of guilt by association. Of all the groups in society none suffered more than the intelligentsia.

The rebellion met fierce resistance from power-holders and chaos ensued in all fields. The story of the disruption of the economy, destruction of culture, degeneration of private morality and public order, and the suspension of all education above the primary level emerged piecemeal and, so long as Mao lived, no comprehensive accounting could be made. In the course of a tour of inspection in August and September 1967, Mao said, "I think this is a civil war!"[9] Responsible Chinese estimated the death toll at four hundred thousand.[10]

The causes of the catastrophe were Mao's subjectively formulated goals and his vague, sweeping instructions—but he blamed the young people. In July 1968, as the extent of the catastrophe emerged, he called a group of Red Guard leaders to his house and wept bitterly as he denounced their failure to make sense of his strategy. It was then that millions of young people were banished in wave after wave from the cities to resettle in the countryside.

Three months later, on 1 October, there was a live television broadcast of the National Day parade. At ten in the morning a thousand-man military band struck up "The East Is Red" and Mao emerged onto the Gate of Heavenly Peace. Here was a rare chance to look at him before the film editors and photoretouchers could get to work. The camera dwelt on him long and often, giving plenty of time for the viewer to see what marks had been left by the two and a half years of daring, struggle, and frustration. He glowered into the morning rays of that other sun in the sky. It was at that moment that his likeness to Tamerlane occurred to me: "His looks do menace heaven and dare the gods," Christopher Marlowe had written in *Tamburlaine the Great*. I could detect no glimmer of remorse for all the chaos Mao Zedong had unleashed, nor any trace of a new humility. But there was no longer any radiance in his daring. On a stage backdrop golden rays might still flicker from his head, but in real life I saw a gnarled oak that had been struck by lightning. There was still strength, but it was now a bleak strength devoid of that genial optimism I had seen in photographs taken before the Cultural Revolution. A tree that has been struck by lightning retains its appearance of strength for a while, but puts out no new leaves; its roots wither and its branches and trunk begin to crack and decay. So it was with Mao.

In the dismal years that followed, it became apparent that the outward strength was no longer matched by an iron will within. His once-indomitable resolve had been undermined by failure at a crucial moment in the Cultural Revolution. On 5 February 1967 forces loyal to him had seized power in Shanghai and proclaimed the establishment of the Shanghai People's Commune. All China was supposed to follow suit and establish "proletarian organs of administration" modeled on the Paris Commune of 1871. This would mean a radical democratization and decentralization of government in China. Seventeen days later, by order of the Party Center, Shanghai abandoned both the name and the principles of the Commune. In their place came a most unrevolutionary—indeed, thoroughly bureaucratic—Revolutionary Committee on which nonelected representatives of the military, the career officials, and "the masses" were supposed to work together.

Whether Mao backed away because his nerve failed him as he stood on the brink and surveyed the prospect the communes would bring or because his colleagues forced him to is less important than the fact that he did back away. After this moment of truth, his nerve would never be the same again. He had led China's youth to drive the enemy from the hilltop, and then he had ordered a retreat.

He did not renounce his vision or his belief in the need for struggle, but his will to pursue the vision and engage in struggle weakened. Mao's "victory" in the Cultural Revolution was Pyrrhic. His gains from the huge upheaval and the massive purging of the party were very limited. He had certainly failed to renew the dynamic of the revolution and he had failed to rebuild society. He had prolonged his power to block the reforms Liu and Deng had put forward in 1962, and he was able to ensure that social and economic policies took more account of his ideas. But he had to tolerate the rebuilding of the old bureaucratic order, the rehabilitation of leading opponents, and the destruction of ardent supporters. Not a few of those who had been the most active in executing his strategies of the past were stripped away from him. One of these was Chen Boda, his political secretary for more than thirty years and one of his main agents in the Cultural Revolution. He watched in silence as Chen was denounced as China's Trotsky. Mao's abandonment of Chen to his fate was a sign that he felt obliged to dissociate himself from much of his own past, because Chen had always been regarded as Mao's ideological alter ego and spokesman.

With Mao in decline, two main rival groups struggled to inherit his power. Lin Biao, formally proclaimed as his successor, led the left. Zhou Enlai spoke for those who favored a more pragmatic approach, although he never associated himself with Liu and Deng's 1962 reform program. The fiasco of the Cultural Revolution had drastically reduced Mao's influence among the party elite but it had not eliminated it. Both sides recognized that they needed the residual authority he possessed, so they bid for his approval of their policies. Often his role seemed to be limited to pronouncing his approval of the winner in the battles between these two groups. The relationship Zhou had built up with Mao over forty years enabled him to win Mao's endorsement in crucial conflicts with Lin Biao on both domestic and foreign policy issues. Zhou's final victory over Lin came in 1971 when an alleged plot by Lin to launch a coup d'etat was uncovered and Lin was reported to have died fleeing the country.

Thereafter, Zhou still had to face opposition from the left, now led by Mao's wife Jiang Qing and the other members of what would one day be called the Gang of Four. Mao could be persuaded to restrain these people on occasion but they were adept at presenting themselves as heirs to the radical side of Mao's thinking and they knew how to play on the old man's fears that after his death the right would undo much of what he had fought so long and so hard to achieve and maintain. So he never abandoned them. The result was instability and a never-ending series of compromises, which did not make for good government. There were no more wild adventures, but there was stagnation, and stifling of initiative.

The influence of the left was less strong in foreign affairs than in the domestic field. Zhou secured the cooperation of Mao in formulating a new strategy designed to put an end to China's diplomatic isolation. China won recognition from many non-communist states and new political relationships of the greatest importance for the future were begun with the United States and Japan. Despite the fact that this new strategy was the very antithesis of what Mao had promised in the 1960s, he played his role of elder statesman with total conviction. The new diplomacy was attributed to him personally, although Zhou Enlai probably deserves much of the credit. The great of the world followed one another in a steady stream to pay their respects to Mao in his study and to hear his admonitions on the need to resist the expansion of Soviet power. Men whose political lives had been based on promoting values and institutions that Mao had fought against with all his strength spoke of him with deep reverence.

Zhou Enlai then began to make his own arrangements for the succession, not only to Mao but also to himself. He knew that he did not have long in which to complete his work, because in 1972, when he was already seventy-four years old, he was told he had cancer. He began to assert himself as he had never done before in his forty years' political partnership with Mao. He did so with the utmost discretion, always deferring outwardly to Mao even as he set a course that departed from the Great Helmsman's.

He took the first major step in 1973 when he achieved the

restoration to the Politburo of Deng Xiaoping. When Mao had struck down Deng in the Cultural Revolution, he had called him a counter-revolutionary bent on restoring capitalism, second only in iniquity to Liu Shaoqi (who had died in 1969). Now, four hundred thousand deaths later, Mao acquiesced in the restoration to office of his foremost living opponent.

Deng was not obliged to make any public renunciation of his former views, yet it was obvious that he would be the strongest contender to succeed Mao as well as Zhou. The question was whether Mao had resigned himself to Deng shaping China's future or lacked the power to resist, so long as Zhou was alive.

In January 1975 Zhou brought off his last great act of state, the holding of the Fourth National People's Congress. The sessions of the NPC, China's nearest equivalent to a parliament, had always been well-ordered affairs with little or no opportunity for debate: the policies and appointments to be approved by each NPC had usually been settled by struggle and negotiation before the session opened. According to the state constitution, the NPC should have met once a year, but divisions within party and state had been so deep that no meeting had been possible for eleven years, since 1964, before the start of the Cultural Revolution.

As Zhou prepared for the Fourth NPC, Mao's wife Jiang Qing and her allies who had risen to power in the Cultural Revolution tried to get Mao's approval for their promotion to the commanding heights of the state apparatus. (Thanks to the Cultural Revolution they already occupied many of the top party posts.) Zhou not only succeeded in blocking them from any promotion, he also ensured that the congress consolidated Deng's return to power. Equally important, he used the congress platform to proclaim as China's goal for the next twenty-five years the modernization of agriculture, industry, national defense, and science and technology (the Four Modernizations), a goal that was more nationalist than Communist. Unable to dominate the congress, Mao boycotted it, making clear that his absence was due to politics, not failing health, by receiving foreign visitors while it was in session.

After the congress closed, Zhou took the next step in implementing his strategy for the succession. He obtained Mao's acquiescence in the appointment of Deng Xiaoping to take day-to-day charge of party and state affairs. (Neither Zhou nor Mao was any longer fit enough to carry the workload.)

Deng was very far from being a carbon copy of Zhou Enlai, and his seven years out of office from 1966 to 1973 had probably accentuated the differences between them. These years gave Deng a perspective on society he could not have gained in office. He became a worker in the messhall of a school for party officials, serving rice and vegetables to other members of the school. For a while he became head of the school before he was transferred to a factory. He had time to develop his own ideas on how the country should be run while Zhou was seeking, in domestic affairs, to make administrative sense out of Mao's ideas and, in foreign affairs, to harness Mao's weight to the new diplomacy.

In 1975, Deng had the strength and Zhou the charisma. The personalities of the Premier and his chosen successor differed in many other ways. Deng was tough where Zhou was suave; he was a master of the pungent phrase, where Zhou dealt in nuances. Deng lived "on the dangerous edge of things," whereas the prudent Zhou preferred to operate from the position of number two or number three in the leadership, seemingly loath to go out in front. Deng saw value in confrontations from time to time, while Zhou was the master of accommodation. Mao once complained that in the years when Deng and Liu Shaoqi were running the country they had treated him "like their dead parent at a funeral," never consulting him on policy matters. By contrast, Zhou always deferred to Mao and catered to his pride, without losing his own dignity. It was entirely in character that Deng had been swept from power in the Cultural Revolution while Zhou had remained at Mao's side throughout to preserve what he could of sanity and order and to rebuild the house of China after the tempest had passed.

If the Chinese nation had been a family, Zhou, who was loved by the people, would have played the role of mother and Mao, who was at first respected and later feared, that of the father. Zhou would be an intermediary between a difficult father and his recalcitrant children. Deng could never be anything but an alternative father. Oversimplifying, one might say that in the terms of one ancient Chinese explanation of cosmic creation and destruction, Zhou embodied the *Yin* (female and passive) force while Mao was its complement, *Yang* (male and active). Deng had too much of the *Yang* in him to complement Mao. If he tried to accommodate Mao for very long, he would lose his political character and integrity. Before his 1973 rehabilitation he had privately offered Mao the general assurance that he would "never go against the verdict [of the Cultural Revolution],"[11] but the meaning of that was open to question. In public he had never apologized for his political record. When his opponents called him an unrepentant capitalist-roader, they may or may not have mistaken the name of the road, but there could be no doubt that, whatever road he was on, he was unrepentant about his choice.

The physical contrast between Zhou and Deng was also striking. Slight of build, Zhou bore himself with an unadorned dignity that owed something to his mandarin family background. His face was handsome and grew more so with old age, until cancer began to take its toll. After his death, songs would be written praising the eyebrows that seemed to float, cloudlike, across his forehead. Deng was stocky and barrel-chested. No one would ever write poetry about his eyebrows; his face was as intelligent as Zhou's but had all the toughness to be expected of a man who liked to face issues and opponents head-on. Zhou had a courtly grace of manner, whereas Deng liked to play the "country boy," as he described himself to one visitor. This may have been a style he had cultivated, because one of Deng's fellow Szechwanese has told me that Deng was born into one of the eight great landowning families of Szechwan. Deng put this country style to political effect, making use of the capacious spittoons in the official reception rooms to reinforce a point he was making to a visitor—about the menace of the Soviet polar bear, for instance. Such a mannerism would have been unthinkable from Zhou or from Mao.

At five feet, Deng was very short by the standards of his generation, but he showed no special concern for his dignity and was adept at overcoming the cold pomposity of the cavernous rooms in the Great Hall of the People, where official visitors are received in Peking. He was quite capable of setting rolling an encounter with a British statesman known for his love of yachting by perching on the edge of his chair, leaning forward into the wind, and grasping an imaginary tiller. "You have had some victories in the past; how about the future?" he asked, and the rapport was re-established after a gap of three years full of vicissitudes for both men. In 1975, he looked younger than his seventy-one years. Even in repose, his face was rugged and as resilient as a soccer ball.

With Zhou he shared a quality of intellect that made him a masterful and stimulating interlocutor on any aspect of politics. His talk was spiced with a sardonic and sometimes grim humor that resembled Mao's.

Deng's allies and supporters in the Politburo in 1975 included Marshal Zhu De, who had once shared command of the Red Army with Mao; Marshal Ye Jianying, the Minister of Defense; Li Xiannian, the senior economic and financial expert; Xü Shiyu, Commander of the Canton Military Region; and Wei Guoqing, First Secretary of Guangdong province, of which Canton is the capital. A fifth, Liu Bocheng, was too ill to attend meetings but nevertheless would give his blessing to Deng, who had been his political commissar when he had been the Field Commander of the Second Field Army in 1948 and 1949, rolling up Chiang Kai-shek's armies from central China to the far South.

All these men commanded great influence among the elites of party, state, and army. Li had been in central government since his appointment as minister of finance in 1954. Ye had been Chief of Staff of the People's Liberation Army during World War II. General Xü and Wei Guoqing, from South China, could offer Deng a regional base of support—a vital ingredient in any political campaign. In the shadows stood other men whose seniority and circles of influence came close to those of Li and Ye even though they were not now members of the Poliburo. One such was Chen Yun, the economic expert, who since the 1950s had advocated a measured pace of economic development and structural change and had been repeatedly overruled by Mao. He had been fifth in the party hierarchy in 1956, and in earlier years had acted as prime minister when Zhou Enlai traveled abroad. Deng's allies included some of the toughest and most experienced political leaders alive. They had joined the Communist Party of China at its birth or in its infancy, and they had been in the thick of its struggle for power from the early 1920s. They had made the Long March with Mao. They had made great contributions to the Communist victory in 1949, but they now had to watch Mao's propagandists rewrite the history of the revolution to exalt Mao's role far above what it had been in reality, while theirs was obliterated. They had played a major role in building policies of the New China after 1949, but time and again Mao had swept aside their pragmatic approach to economic and social development.*

In all of this they were representative of hundreds of thousands of other, less prominent leaders in the army, the central bureaucracy, and the provincial administrations. Deng would have strong support if he played his cards right. It would be pointless and counterproductive to pretend otherwise. However, with Mao still alive and many power-holders wedded to the status quo, any challenge by Deng would have to be clear enough to act as a banner but not so provocative as to scare the many officials whose survival instinct had prompted them to go along with the left in recent years.

Deng knew that this appointment by no means gave him unfettered control of either party or state. More than half of the twenty-five people in the highest decision-making body, the Politburo, owed their position to the Cultural Revolution and had therefore profited by the fall of men like Deng. The three hundred or so people in the Central Committee had been

* The Chinese Communists insist that they are not pragmatists in the sense used by the American philosopher John Dewey, but they acknowledge that some of the terms and concepts of Marxists and "bourgeois pragmatists" are so similar as to cause confusion. My use of the word *pragmatist* in this book does not imply that I dispute the distinction drawn by the Chinese.

elected or re-elected to it at a time when Deng's influence was far from strong. Many of them also were beneficiaries of the Cultural Revolution.

Chief among the defenders of the status quo were Jiang Qing, Wang Hongwen, Zhang Chunquiao, and Yao Wenyuan. All of them were closely associated with Shanghai and were referred to as the Shanghai Gang by those who disliked them in China and in overseas Chinese communities. The city of Shanghai had been conceived on a mud flat on the coast of East China in a union of traditional China and dynamic European capitalism. In a hundred years it had grown from nothing to a city of eleven million people. It was a child of opportunity, a response to the commercial, industrial, intellectual, artistic, and political possibilities offered by the encounter between China and nineteenth-century Europe, and later the United States and Japan. As a child of opportunity, it was no stranger to opportunism. Being of mixed parentage, Shanghai knew it must live by its wits to survive and was not too fussy about the means it used. By the 1930s it had become one of the most exciting and least scrupulous cities in the world. It was easy to find fault with Shanghai, for its sins were all too well advertised, but it was a magnet that drew to itself many of the most enterprising and dynamic people in China. It was the New York of the Middle Kingdom.

When the capitalist system was in vogue, Shanghai had worked the system to its great material advantage. When socialism arrived, and politics rather than business enterprise became the ladder leading upward, Shanghainese were not slow to start climbing that way.

Jiang Qing had been drawn to the city as a very young actress in the 1930s. If her talents were limited, she quickly learned how to make the most of them in Shanghai style. When the Japanese occupied the city she left, not for the Communists' base, Yanan, but for the Nationalists' wartime capital, Chongqing. Professionally, her stay there was not very successful, and she moved on to Yanan. Photographs of that time show her looking pretty and full of vitality. To Mao, who had spent years fighting and marching in the mountains, her charm was great.

Several of his senior colleagues disapproved of the match, but he characteristically overrode their objections and Jiang Qing became his wife in his third consummated marriage. The price Mao and Jiang Qing paid was an understanding that she would stay out of public life, which she did for twenty years.

In the first two decades of Communist rule, Jiang Qing spent much of her time ill in bed and spent long periods in the Soviet Union for treatment. In the 1960s she was authorized by Mao to launch a reform of the theater and opera. This brought her into conflict with the Mayor of Peking, among others, and the results of her efforts earned her little popularity.

During the Cultural Revolution she came for the first time onto center stage in politics and exercised much power in the name of Mao. She showed none of Mao's sweeping imagination or political genius. Instead, she earned herself a reputation as a vindictive and petty-minded person.

Wang Hongwen had risen from being a political activist at the factory level in Shanghai at the start of the Cultural Revolution to the high post of a Vice-Chairman of the Communist Party by 1973, before he was forty. One of Wang's responsibilities was overseeing the civilian militia, a lightly armed, poorly trained, spare-time force organized by local party committees. The leftists saw the militia as a counterforce to the regular People's Liberation Army (PLA); they hoped that militia units could be used to promote or defend their cause in any confrontation. Wang was handsome and his "helicopter" promotion from shop-floor rebel to Vice-Chairman of the Party had made him a hero for some young workers, who would cheer when his image appeared on the cinema screen in documentary films.

Vice-Premier Zhang Chunqiao was the most credible of the Four as a political leader. He had a certain *gravitas* the others lacked, and his gaunt, bespectacled face made him look every inch the severe ideologue. For most of his career he had been in literary propaganda work, more as commissar than writer.

Yao Wenyuan, the fourth member of the group, was the Politburo member with overall responsibility for party propaganda and the mass media. He had first made history when, at Mao's request, he fired the opening shot of the Cultural

Revolution—an article denouncing those responsible for Wu Han's veiled attack on Mao, *Hai Rui Dismissed from Office*. A persistent rumor had it that he was Mao's son-in-law, married to a daughter of Mao and Jiang Qing. His father, a writer of some note, had been labeled a rightist in 1957. The father's fall from grace in 1957 cast a shadow over the son's prospects. But the younger Yao excised from his own earlier work all support for the liberal values for which his father had been condemned and quickly gained a reputation as a literary hatchet man of the left. He "arrived" with the Cultural Revolution. Under his guidance, the media sank to their low point of credibility and information, and reached their peak of ideological shrillness.

All four had worked closely with Mao in the Cultural Revolution and owed their national prominence to it. After being appointed to the national leadership they retained positions in Shanghai, with the aim of using China's largest city as a regional power base.

While the Four constantly emphasized their loyalty to Mao and his teachings, it was difficult to take their protestations at face value. They were men and women of a wholly different generation, the oldest twenty years younger than Mao. He was a characteristic product of rural, inland Hunan province, which had not been deeply marked by foreign influence. They had been formed by China's most sophisticated, cosmopolitan city. Having led a guerrilla army for twenty years, Mao could command guns as well as words, while their combat experience was limited to wielding a pen. He had spent fifty years forging policies by which men were governed, first in revolutionary bases and then in all China, while their experience of either economic or social administration was negligible.

The personal lives of the Four did not conform to the image of dedicated, puritanical revolutionaries they presented to the world. Jiang Qing exposed her own double standards to her American biographer, Roxane Witke. She imposed on the Chinese public a Puritan, anticosmopolitan ethic. In private, she indulged her taste for silk sheets, Western-style dresses, and lotus blossoms floating on reflecting pools. She watched foreign films in her private cinema and summoned the athletic young

Minister of Sport in the middle of the night as the fancy took her.

In Shanghai, Wang Hongwen gained the reputation of being a playboy. The aim of the Four was that eventually Jiang Qing should succeed Mao as Chairman of the Party, Wang Hongwen become chairman of the Standing Committee of the National People's Congress, and Zhang Chunqiao Prime Minister. They had already tried to obtain some or all of these appointments at the Fourth National People's Congress and failed. Undeterred by failure, they commissioned articles in the press that praised the historical role of women in the government of China. The Empress Lü, who had become the real ruler of the land after the death of her husband, Emperor Gao Zu of the Han dynasty, was presented in a particularly favorable light.

It was part of the tragedy of Mao's last years that those who most vociferously claimed to be his loyal disciples were so far inferior to him, in character and intellect. In the Cultural Revolution they had acted as his agents, but in his declining years they appeared at times to manipulate him for their own advantage. Mao had no one else to turn to, but he was not deceived.

In early 1973, Mao had written to Jiang Qing, saying "It is better not to see each other. You haven't carried out many of the things I talked to you about over the years." This was one instruction of Mao's that she did not publicize.

When the leader of the Australian Labour Party, Gough Whitlam, asked Mao where he had discovered Wang Hongwen, Mao replied with an offhand *Bu zhidao* (I don't know).

A fifth member of the Politburo, Wang Dongxing, owed his advancement to his personal loyalty to Mao and had played an important if unpublicized role in the Cultural Revolution. A burly, red-nosed man with a leathery skin, Wang had once been Mao's bodyguard. He now exercised considerable authority over the security apparatus and in the running of the Party machine. In the absence of any General Secretary of the Party, his position as Director of its General Office gave him great power over current Party documents and over the secret archives. He was also political commissar (and effectively commander) of the army's 8341 Unit, which guarded the national leadership. Wang worked discreetly, largely out of the public eye.

Among the fourteen members of the Politburo who owed their membership of that body to the Cultural Revolution were the Mayor of Peking and the commanders of the Peking and Shenyang Military Regions, who between them controlled the regional armed forces of the whole of north and northeast China.

Not all those who owed their position in the Politburo to the Cultural Revolution would support the Shanghai Gang in their political ambitions or would stand on the same ground in an ideological dispute. One of the exceptions was Vice-Premier Hua Guofeng, the Minister of Public Security, who enjoyed the trust of Zhou Enlai and Deng Xiaoping and was one of those younger leaders whom they were bringing on as part of the successor generation. But a substantial number did have reason to fear what might happen to them in the long run if Deng succeeded Zhou as premier. The Shanghai Gang could play on this fear.

People who had played a militant role in the Cultural Revolution, including the Shanghai Gang, exercised ultimate control over the press, radio, television, films, theater, publishing, music, and the issuance of briefing documents to the whole party. The only flow of communication they could not fully control was what a man might whisper to his family or to trusted friends or neighbors—back-lane news, as it was called—and even this they could often tap into because their influence over the security forces was strong. These people and hundreds of thousands of more junior officials who had climbed to power over the falling bodies struck down at Mao's command in 1966 to 1968 believed that their best hope of retaining power was to maintain the principle of Mao's infallibility. If they surrendered that, they would risk being swept away in the torrents of bitterness and opposition created by his disastrous leadership of the Cultural Revolution. So they pruned away some of the more extreme forms of Maoist idolatry that had been encouraged during the Cultural Revolution, hoping thereby to strengthen the cult.

In an attempt to gain popular acceptance for the dictatorial methods with which they muzzled popular dissatisfaction, the left used its control of the media to heap praise on Qin Shi Huang, an iron-willed ruler of the third century B.C. who had long been a symbol of dictatorship. They praised the dictatorial aspects of his rule as well as his unification of China, with which he has traditionally been credited. The parallel with Mao was clear. In a moment of daring, a Chinese confided in me "For two thousand years we Chinese have considered Qin Shi Huang to be bad, now He says we should admire him. We won't."

It was of a piece with the deification of Mao that the social and economic policies inspired by his ideas were presented as if they were immutable wisdom coming from a source that was more than human. It was not permitted to discuss them as the product of a man or men who were rational but fallible. To propose examining their results was an act of impiety equivalent to submitting the work of a priest to a cost-benefit analysis. To question them, let alone criticize them, was treated as blasphemy.

It was in this atmosphere that Deng set to work to spell out the reforms needed if China was to move toward the modernization goals set by the National People's Congress. He and his allies could not afford to delay if they were to take advantage of the momentum created by the congress and the protection afforded by Zhou Enlai while he lived. So in the spring of 1975, Deng launched that challenge to the political status quo which was to bring down on his head the fury of the left.

4

Deng's Challenge

FROM THE SPRING OF 1975, Deng began to take
the bull by the horns. In the course of the year, appointments
were made to the top positions in seven provinces; each was a
Deng supporter. In his meetings with foreign visitors, he exuded
self-confidence and brusqueness in place of the uncharacteristic
diffidence he had shown the year before. He encouraged a reconsideration of recruitment methods for higher education. He
convened a series of national conferences and high-level meetings to deal with pressing problems in such fields as iron and
steel, agriculture, defense industries, the coal industry, and the
armed forces and in the autumn he guided the drafting of three
policy documents.

In these documents the pulse of the urge to reform could be
felt through the covering of restrained language, but in his
speeches to the conferences and in his remarks on less formal
occasions Deng lowered the mask of caution and spoke with
candor. He made it quite clear that he thought the country was
in a mess, and that it was suffering from too much empty politics, too much emphasis on "class struggle" and too much dictatorship: "People are obliged to talk about class struggle every

month and every day and the class struggle cannot be relaxed even for an hour."*

"In many places there is political study after work as a daily rule," Deng said. "People who have babies are not allowed to go home to look after them. . . . This really is social oppression. . . . There is too much dictatorship and it should be relaxed a bit in the future."

Excessive emphasis on politics was damaging the economy, Deng believed. He and his followers wanted to "liberate the productive forces"—do what was necessary to encourage people to produce more. Rewards and punishments had been virtually abolished in industry: productivity bonuses had been eliminated and salary differentials reduced; enterprises had no power to shed surplus or incompetent labor. *Profit* was a dirty word. Overmanning was so prevalent that in some enterprises 30 to 40 percent of the workers never engaged in production but spent all their time on sports, propaganda, or "cultural" activities. The level of output per worker was low. One state enterprise in four was operating at a loss.

Deng's opponents were quick to attack him for emphasizing production, but he retorted: "No more criticism of the theory of productive forces; if it goes on, production will not rise! . . . You are criticizing putting profits in command, aren't you? It doesn't matter if we put profits in command a bit. Otherwise, what can the state depend on? . . . Nobody dares talk about production. Maintenance of equipment is bad, our technology is backward."

He quoted Lenin's view that the only way to judge whether political education had been effective was to see if production had increased. Politics divorced from economics were hollow. He reminded people that Mao had once said "In the last analysis, the impact upon the people . . . of any Chinese political party depends on whether and how much it helps to develop

* This and other quotations that follow are excerpts from speeches which Deng made in 1975. They were published for the first time in 1976, as part of the campaign to criticize him. Some then appeared on wall posters at the two main universities in Peking; others were published or read on the radio. Although they were made public by Deng's opponents, I see no reason to doubt their authenticity.

their productive forces," a Thought none of Mao's propagandists had quoted in recent years. Deng believed that one reason for the bad performance of the economy was that leftist ideologues had pushed aside and cowed people with technical competence, but lacked the expertise to do anything with the power they had acquired. Deng expressed his attitude toward the ideologues in blunt terms: "They sit on the lavatory, but they don't manage a shit!" (Chinese often use metaphors involving bodily functions to great effect. If President Truman had been Chinese he would not have said "If you can't stand the heat, get out of the kitchen!" but would have changed the location to the bathroom.)

Deng was scathing about the state of the arts, for which Jiang Qing had special responsibility. He regretted the suppression of traditional operas, which had been a truly popular art form (workingmen knew the stories, even the arias, by heart): "The old operas were performed for many years, yet this did not stop the revolution." He had no liking for the eight model revolutionary operas and ballets Jiang Qing had put in their place. "Cultural life is monotonous," he said; "how can eight shows satisfy an audience of eight hundred million people?" The press talked of a Hundred Flowers being in bloom but Deng remarked that the model operas were an example of one flower blossoming. That flower was obviously Jiang Qing.

Declining to go to one of Jiang Qing's productions, he commented "I would raise both hands to vote for her drama reform, but I wouldn't care to watch the show. With the model operas today, you just see a bunch of people running to and fro on the stage. No trace of art. No sense in bragging about them. Foreigners clap them, but only out of courtesy, not because they appreciate the show."

The Vienna Symphony Orchestra was more to Deng's taste. After a performance by this orchestra in Peking, he said "This is what I call food for the spirit. Revolution must have art in it. Only artistically talented people can really appreciate the substance of revolution. The model operas nowadays are no more than a gong-and-drum show. Go to a theatre and you find yourself on a battlefield."

Maoist propaganda had cast a mystic aura over the rural

production brigade at Dazhai, which had been set up as a model to be copied by the whole nation. Deng said Dazhai was only a unit that had done well in production and achieving high grain yields. It was "an example of production by hard, honest work." Visiting Dazhai had become an excuse for an outing in a country where people were not normally allowed to take holidays. "Nowadays scores of thousands of people are rushing to Dazhai. Are they coming to look at the scenery and climb the mountain or are they truly acquiring Dazhai's experience?"

When I visited Dazhai in 1976 I watched a column of more than a thousand visitors trudging along the mountainside past the fields. There were two guides, who walked at the head of the column; neither had a megaphone. The visitors displayed no interest in the fields they passed, and their faces were bored and blank. Their pilgrimage to this holy place of Chinese agriculture was nothing more than an uninformative country walk.

Deng castigated the armed forces, saying "In the past orders were obeyed as soon as they were issued. There was no need to repeat them. Nowadays, not only individuals but whole units disobey orders!" (This was no exaggeration; travelers to Hong Kong told how an entire division in East China had refused to move to another part of the country.) "Some military people have become arrogant," he went on. "Some army units have tense relations with each other. The relations of the army with the government and people are also rather tense. In the past, there was good unity, but that tradition has been lost." He recalled that "in the past when military comrades were sitting on a bus they would give up their seats to old people and to women with babies. Now some of them don't do that." The political power of the armed forces had grown too great: "They have become a power behind the throne. This has developed into regional factionalism." He found it necessary to remind the military that their first task was to learn to fight. He put an un-Maoist emphasis on weapons as opposed to the human factor. He summed up the problems of the forces in five words: "Thick-skinned, disunited, arrogant, soft, and lazy."

Deng clearly thought that things had gone topsy-turvy in China and that people had lost sight of what they were supposed to be doing. Just as the army had forgotten that its main task was to fight, so students had forgotten that their main task was to study: "Nowadays in schools we suddenly see the following situation. Students need not study—the Chairman said students are masters of their schools. . . . I demand that, in education at school, learning shall be made the main issue. . . . The level of college education at present is even lower than that of the secondary technical schools in the past. College students are far from being real college students. It is a real mess. The revolution in education has resulted in a lower quality of students and created a crisis."

It had become an article of faith that no one was ready for a university education unless he or she had worked in a factory or on a farm for a few years. Deng thought the country could not afford to make a rigid rule of this: "We should select good middle-school students to go directly to university." The low level of education was "hobbling the hind legs of the Four Modernizations."

The left had derided the idea of trailing along behind foreign countries in scientific research and proclaimed confidence in the limitless ability of the workers and peasants to storm the highest peaks of science. Deng sought to pour cold water on this attitude. As he looked at the educational scene, he saw "no trace of foreign languages, no mathematics, no physics, no chemistry. What high peaks are we climbing? We are not even climbing peaks of middle height. The peaks we surmount are low ones."

Schoolteachers had always proved an easy target when mass movements to uncover "bourgeois rightists" were under way. In the antirightist campaign of 1957, a hundred thousand had been purged. In the Cultural Revolution, virtually every school principal had lost his job and many had been tortured. Deng made the obvious comment no other leader had dared to make: "If teachers are despised and beaten, how can you arouse their enthusiasm?"

Commenting on the amount of time college students had spent on politics since the Cultural Revolution, he said: "Hou Baolin [China's favorite stand-up comedian who had been silenced by the left] once very aptly remarked that primary school pupils carry one pen, high school boys carry two, college students carry three, and illiterates carry four. Most college students now carry nothing but a brush for writing wall posters. They can't do anything else."

Deng spoke for the intelligentsia Mao had so distrusted. He was particularly dismayed by the low morale of China's scientists, because he saw science and technology as the key to modernization. He had people dig out statistics on the use or lack of use of research facilities and libraries by scientists and technicians, and quoted their reports:

> In the Research Institute for Non-Ferrous Metals, there are 800 technicians; in the last half year there have been 700 visitors to the library all told; that is an average of four visits a day.
>
> Out of 150,000 scientific and technical cadres in the Academy of Sciences, no one dares go into the research laboratories. They are all afraid of being disparaged as "white" specialists. The young are frightened and the old are frightened.
>
> Research personnel no longer read books nowadays. . . . Before the working day has ended, they go home and make their meals. If things go on like this, how can we reach "advanced world standards"?

Since the Cultural Revolution, the principles of open-door scientific research, in which large numbers of people were supposed to be involved, and of combining physical and intellectual labor, had been applied in such a way that highly qualified scientists from the giant Academy of Sciences were sent to labor in the field to conduct primitive experiments.

Research teams were dispersed and whole research institutes closed down. Deng thought this was crazy: "The Academy of Sciences is an academy of sciences and not an academy of production or of education. It is not an academy of cabbage cultivation; it is not an academy of beans. It is an academy which deals with the sciences and specifically with the natural sciences."

The low morale of scientists in China was remarked upon by some visiting scientists from abroad. One group of visitors estimated that the productivity of Chinese scientists was one fifth that of their colleagues in the West.

Deng was not wholly opposed to all the reforms introduced

after the Cultural Revolution, but he was opposed to the uncritical, unscientific attitudes with which they were regarded. The policies of recruiting university students from among the workers, peasants, and soldiers without centrally administered examinations, of training barefoot doctors, of sending city youth to the countryside after leaving school, of involving them in scientific experiments, of mixing academic study and physical labor were not simply treated as a set of social reforms to be judged on their merits; they were referred to as "the newborn things" and invested with magic properties by Mao's propagandists, because they flowed from his thinking. One result was that exaggerated expectations of the healing power of barefoot doctors were encouraged, and for ten years no full-length course in Western medicine was given in China—with the result that no one was graduated as a fully qualified doctor.

Deng's opponents claimed to be shocked when he said "Barefoot doctors cannot reach heaven at a single bound" and regarded their training as a step-by-step process: "The barefoot doctors have only just begun; their knowledge is slight. They can only treat a few common sicknesses. After some years, they will put on straw shoes; that is, their knowledge will have grown. A few years more, and they will wear cloth shoes." Deng walked out of a film that showed a barefoot doctor going well beyond his training and dismissed the film as ultraleftist.

Deng was unimpressed by those young officials who had been given extremely rapid promotion in recent years. He referred to their promotion as "helicopter" and "rocket" promotions: "As for the cadres [officials] who have risen by helicopter or rocket, they aren't good enough. They can go down again, while retaining their ranks. In the army there are company commanders who at a stroke have been promoted to the rank of army commander. It would be unacceptable even for them to become deputy commanders of battalions."

If Wang Hongwen, who had risen on a rocket from his textile factory in Shanghai, was not twisting in his seat by the time he had heard that, there was more for his discomfort: "Some people tend to criticize others in order to achieve fame, stamping on others' shoulders to move up to key positions. They only half understand others, but when they sniff out something they latch onto it and criticize it for a long time. This is because they have a lust for fame."

Deng called for the restoration to power of many more of the veteran officials who had been struck down by the Cultural Revolution and had not yet been "liberated." He encouraged those who were restored to power in these words: "You must go ahead boldly. As long as people say you are restoring capitalism, you have done your work well. . . . Be afraid of nothing. Don't be afraid of opposition or of being struck down. We have already been struck down once; why should we be afraid of being struck down a second time?"

The titles of the three policy documents drafted under Deng's guidance in 1975 were: "Outline Report on the Work of the Academy of Sciences"; "On the Accelerated Development of Industry"; and "On the General Program for All Work of the Party and the Country."[1] The paper on the Academy of Sciences was really a policy for the whole field of science. It called for a restoration of balance in the relations between politics and professionalism, production and scientific experimentation, and technically qualified people and the masses. It sought to restore respect for professional competence, research, work on basic theory, laboratory experiments, the contribution of individuals, the study of foreign experience, international scientific exchange, and debate and discussion of different scholastic viewpoints.

In most Third World countries—indeed, almost anywhere else—the principles set out in this paper would have seemed banal. In China they risked condemnation as heresy. To take one point alone, the exchange of scientific knowledge with foreigners, this would surely include foreign scientists coming to China to collaborate with Chinese scientists, to teach Chinese students or conduct exchanges in depth, and all this had been taboo for a decade.

The paper on industry opened with a blunt statement on the conditions prevailing in the sector. "Stealing, corruption, speculation, and conspiracy involving government officials as well as the employees of enterprises" were listed as major problems. "A small number of enterprises have serious capitalist tendencies. They are sabotaging the National Plan and engaging in illegal free production and free exchange." In other words, there was in existence a parallel economy, working on free-enterprise principles without regard to socialist planning.

The industry paper gave no examples, but the exploits of Wang Weichun illustrate what was going on. Wang was the Deputy Secretary for Economic Affairs in Henan province. This put him in an excellent position to organize, condone, and cover up breaches of financial and economic discipline on a vast scale. He and his son and their subordinates embezzled, misappropriated, and squandered disaster relief funds, provincial and national taxes, and other funds to a total of two billion U.S. dollars. Most of this was devoted to projects unauthorized by the planning authorities, many of them undertaken with the aim of making life more comfortable for officials, for instance by providing them with luxurious guest houses, more cars, and better offices at the expense of the ordinary people. This still left huge sums to be spent on food and drink at parties, held perhaps in the guest houses, and on gifts that would oil the wheels of their operations. In what seems to have been a decade under Wang's financial control, Henan province spent three billion dollars on a thousand unauthorized projects. In 1975, Wang concurrently held the post of relief work director in a prefecture hit by natural disaster. He encouraged subordinates in the county to ask the state for over two hundred million kilos of extra grain, all of which was diverted for nonrelief uses. Elsewhere in the province, in Gong county, officials, taking their cue from Wang, withheld from the state twenty million dollars in tax revenues and profits of state-run enterprises. Of this sum, most was spent on the illegal building of luxurious guest houses and office buildings and on the purchase of forty-three cars. A million dollars was spent on banquets and gifts. Wang recognized the merits of this financial administration by designating the county as an advanced model unit to be emulated throughout the province. Not all the other counties in Henan equalled Gong county's performance, but Xiangcheng county seems to have come close. Years after the county was hit by a flood, victims of that disaster were still living in straw huts whereas officials had found the means to hand out 110,000 cartons of cigarettes, 99,000 kilos of liquor and wine, 98,000 kilos of pork, and 280,000 kilos of grain as gifts or for parties.[2]

That the people of Henan were not alone in suffering from officials who abused their power on such a scale is shown by reports in the Chinese press of similar operations in other provinces. For example, in Heilongjiang there was a woman, Wang Shouxin, who used her position as manager of a fuel company to organize embezzlement that amounted to $320,000 over six years. She lavished furs, television sets, record players, tape recorders, electric fans, and eiderdown quilts on others—to buy their protection and cooperation—and on herself. Two hundred people from ninety units allegedly accepted these presents.[3] In Qinghai province, managers of a provincially owned farm machinery company used their positions to engage in a wide variety of black-market operations over a long period of time.[4]

A feature of these cases is that complaints were lodged against the officials detailing their malpractices long before any action was taken against them; the charges were simply ignored for years. The Qinghai operators kept their employees quiet by sharing some of the profits with them in the form of food.

"On the Accelerated Development of Industry" was highly critical of enterprise management in other ways also: "Management is in chaos; work productivity is low; product quality is poor, maintenance is expensive, costs are high, and breakdowns are frequent." The paper identified three categories of bad management: There were enterprises where the leadership was characterized by varying degrees of softness, slackness, and disunity. "These leaderships are frightened, they do not dare stick to principles. The good things are not praised, the bad things are not criticized." And there were enterprises where people who were both politically ignorant and inexperienced in production held power. "These people . . . make the most noise, pointing their fingers and calling the shots, accusing people and singing a high-sounding tune, but never working out concrete problems."

Finally, there were enterprises where out-and-out bad people were in power: "These elements steal and corrupt, speculate and cheat."

This industrial paper went on to prescribe remedies that would come as no surprise to an executive in a capitalist enterprise (Lenin had urged Soviet managers to learn from capitalism). There should be a proper system of post responsibility (the responsibilities of every job should be clearly defined); there should be a hierarchy of authority and the right kind of discipline; each ministry and enterprise must be familiar with the standards in its field in industrially developed countries and must establish plans and procedures to catch up and surpass them.

The recommendations on foreign trade policy were a radical departure from the extremely restrictive interpretation of the principle of self-reliance that had been followed for years; exports must be increased to permit more imports of advanced foreign technology, "hence the share of industrial and mining products [in total exports] must be increased." To speed up the exploitation of China's great reserves of coal and oil, consideration should be given to long-term credits and long-term contracts. Complete plants might be imported "to be paid back by our production of oil and coal."

While the paper on science and industry called for important changes, the third paper, "On the General Program of All Work for the Party and the Country," was political dynamite. The title announced a document of broad scope but gave no hint of the challenge it presented. The text itself bore a thick cosmetic coating of the orthodoxy of the day. Full honor was paid to Chairman Mao, his directives, his teachings, and his revolutionary line. Deng's pragmatic ally of yesteryear, Liu Shaoqi, was referred to in the standard terms of opprobrium: a "double-dealing counter-revolutionary" who had established a "bourgeois headquarters," sabotaged the dictatorship of the proletariat, and opposed Mao Zedong Thought.

But under these cosmetics could be seen Deng's pragmatic manifesto. "On the General Program" was a clear signal that Deng was preparing an assault on the legion of left-wing dogmatists who had prospered because of the Cultural Revolution, including those later to be known as the Gang of Four.

In Chinese politics the targets of an attack are seldom, if ever, named in the first phase of the campaign. Instead, their

political character is described with sufficient precision as to let
people know whom the attacker has in mind. If the opening
phase of the assault is successful, the attack is pressed home; if
not, a halt or retreat can be ordered with a minimum loss of face.
If and when the targets are named, the battle is all over bar the
shouting. Traditionally the decision to name the target of a campaign has been taken by the Central Committee or its Politburo.
Another reason for using general descriptions rather than names
is that, usually, the targets are not only a few individuals at the
top but all those who think and act like them—scores of thousands or hundreds of thousands of people whose names are not
listed anywhere, who can only be identified by those who live
and work with them. Chinese mass movements are managed by
symbolism in which nationally known figures are symbols for a
whole breed of people.

After the opening orthodoxies, "On the General Program"
launched into a description of its targets: "sham-Marxist political
swindlers" who disguised themselves as true revolutionaries,
making use of revolutionary slogans but distorting their meaning and sowing ideological confusion. The essential characteristic of these "successors to Lin Biao" was a mania for creating
factions: "They are permanently entangled in the struggle between this and that faction, between the so-called rebellious
faction and conservative faction, between the so-called new and
old cadres." "They topple good Party cadres . . . usurp leadership in some places and units, and exercise the dictatorship of
the bourgeoisie there." The left looked on itself as the rebel
faction and its leaders, like Wang Hongwen, used such slogans
as "going against the tide" to encourage opposition to more
pragmatic party leadership.

"On the General Program" warned: "With respect to 'rebellion,' we must examine which class one is rebelling against,
which class one is representing, in the rebellion. With respect to
'going against the tide,' we must examine the nature of the tide
one is going against . . . as Chairman Mao teaches us, we must
'smell with our nose and distinguish the good from the bad.'"

To the writers of the document, the bad included those who,
like Lin Biao, used ultraleftist phrases such as "holding high" the

banner of Mao Zedong Thought, who described the Thought as the "summit" of Marxism–Leninism, and based their political strategy on the establishment of the "absolute authority" of a political "genius." This of course was precisely what Mao's propagandists had done ever since 1966 to develop his cult. On this most explosive of all political issues, the authors insisted calmly but unequivocally that "there are no born geniuses in the world. . . . We must remember well Chairman Mao's teaching: 'The ideology, plans and methods of any great person can only be a reflection of the objective world. His raw materials and semi-finished products can come only from the practice of the masses or his own scientific experimentation. His brain can only serve the function of a processing factory making the finished products.'" The author warned that one should not take one's partial experiences as the universal truth.

When Central Committee members read the document's reminder that "No person or organization is allowed to stand above the Party," how could they not remember the way Mao had overridden his colleagues to launch the land collectivization and the Great Leap Forward? When they read "All Party members and cadres—old and new—must . . . take unity as the life of the Party, say and do things that will promote unity, and don't say or do things that will harm unity," how could they not think of how Mao had split the Party in the Cultural Revolution? Indeed, the authors of the paper condemned the indiscriminate attacks made on officials and others in the Cultural Revolution using the transparent device of ascribing the damage to Lin Biao rather than Mao. But no one would be in doubt as to whom they had in mind when they wrote "his policy toward revolutionary comrades was that of fierce struggle and merciless attack."

When "On the General Program" condemned those who "separate politics from economics and revolution from production, talking only about politics and revolution but not about economics and production," readers did not have to search far for heads on which this cap fitted.

"Revolution means liberating the productive forces" was the central positive message of the document. In contrast to the preoccupation of the left with ideological purity, the document resurrected a quotation from Mao that had long since been lost sight of:

> Chairman Mao taught us a long time ago: "Do we want to win the support of the masses? Do we want them to devote their strength to the front? If so, we must be with them, arouse their enthusiasm and initiative, be concerned with their welfare, work earnestly and sincerely in their interests, and solve all their problems of production and everyday life—the problem of salt, rice, housing, clothing, childbirth, etc."

Such attention to the material needs of the masses was heresy to people like Zhang Chunqiao in 1975.

The authors asserted that the standard of living of the masses should be improved as production increased. This too flew in the face of the orthodoxy of the day; no general wage increase had been granted for more than ten years.

There should be a new objective in reporting: "We must seek truth from facts and stand against reporting the good but not the bad. We advocate telling the truth and not lies." In the China of 1975, when Yao Wenyuan prevented hard realities from being published and aired instead a host of fantasies, these words were not banal; they were a promise of profound change.

Persisting in putting forward explosive statements in calm, low-key language, "On the General Program" called for rectification in every area of life in China, spelling out each field of activity by name lest there be any misunderstanding. To a Chinese Communist, *rectification* means making changes in the leadership as well as in policies. To make clear the gravity of their task, the writers set down that the "sham-Marxist political swindlers" were class enemies. "The struggle between them and the working class, poor and middle peasants, revolutionary cadres and revolutionary intellectuals is a life-and-death struggle."

"On the General Program" was written on 7 October 1975, but Deng's opponents had not waited for that to start their efforts to counter his influence. In March, Yao Wenyuan had written an article claiming that empiricism was the main danger in the party, an assertion clearly aimed at pragmatists like Deng. Attacks on this theme were developed in the months that followed. In September, the left began to attack Deng in one of those campaigns shot through with allegory that add to the fascination of China but sometimes make it hard to present Chinese politics with the seriousness they deserve. This campaign focused on the career of a twelfth-century bandit named Song Jiang. Song was a leading member of a bandit gang whose exploits were described in a fourteenth-century novel, *The Water Margin*, that Mao, like millions of his fellow countrymen, enjoyed reading. It was hardly a coincidence that when Deng had been in charge of southwest China from 1950 to 1954, he had taken the nickname Song Jiang and had given his close colleagues names of other members of the gang. The problem with Song Jiang in the eyes of the left in 1975 was that he had betrayed the principles for which the bandits, surprising though it may seem, had claimed to be fighting. To give weight to the campaign, the left quoted notes Mao had made in the margin of his copy of the book when rereading it in the recent past.

Deng laughed off the campaign, saying "Much ado about nothing . . . nowadays some people hear the wind blowing and immediately assume that it is raining. When they just hear of something they believe it has already happened. Some people think there's a movement going on because Song Jiang's capitulationism is being criticized."

In November, the Minister of Education came under fire from the left because of the questioning of established policies in his field. The left alleged that the Minister was backed by "the biggest rightist in the Party." Referring to the skeptical comments being made by Deng and others on barefoot doctors, the sending of youth to the countryside, the recruitment of workers, peasants, and soldiers to universities and other "newborn things," Mao was reported to have said "Let there be a great debate, and let the attacks on the newborn things be rebutted." This could not be laughed off like the *Water Margin* campaign, but it was still played in a minor key. The scope of Deng's criticisms of the present state of affairs and his proposals for reform were not released to the public, only hinted at darkly. Only when Zhou was safely dead did the full-scale counterattack begin.

When Deng had launched his challenge, it was obvious that

Mao might fight back. His mind was still clear enough to recognize the nature of Deng's initiative, and he had never blinded himself to the likelihood that sooner or later men would seek to undo what he had accomplished. In 1974, he had written to Zhou Enlai:

Our mission, unfinished, may take a thousand years.
The struggle tires us, and our hair is gray.
You and I, old friend, can we just watch our efforts
    being wasted away?

While Zhou Enlai lived, his personal power and his forty-year partnership with Mao exercised a restraining influence on the Chairman. His death gave Deng's opponents a chance to work on Mao's fears of seeing his life's work swept away and perhaps created an illusion in Mao's mind that he was now free of the political forces with which he had compromised since the Cultural Revolution, the forces of pragmatism Zhou had come to represent.

But he had neither the physical nor the mental strength left for a major campaign. His frailty was obvious to visitors. He insisted on rising to greet them but had to be supported by a nurse. His clothes hung baggily on his once-powerful frame. Having greeted his visitors, he relapsed into his chair. His face bore witness to his decades of struggle with his fellow men and with disease. His hands trembled.

He was losing the power of speech. On occasion, when he was having trouble in forming a sound, one of his interpreters would half-rise from her chair to peer down his throat as if she could catch the meaning by sight. When there was doubt as to what he had said, the interpreters would write down what they believed to be his words and show them to him for confirmation. Their role was reminiscent of that of the priestess in ancient Greece who interpreted the oracle at Delphi.

In Chinese mythology there is a character named Wu Gang who in seeking immortality committed crimes for which he was condemned to chopping down a tree that, every time he felled it, would spring up again to its former height. In his attempt to lead China toward communism, Mao had repeatedly chopped down the spontaneous shoots of capitalism which kept springing up in town and countryside alike. The anti-Deng campaign was a desperate last attempt by the aging Wu Gang of the Chinese revolution.

As that campaign unfolded, in February and March 1976, I tried to assess the mood of those toward whom the barrage of criticism of Deng was being directed.

5

A Nation Half Alive

"THE PEOPLE of the whole country are striding with revolutionary vigor into another militant spring. . . . The dismal darkness of the old China has been banished and in its place is a luxuriant and vibrant scene where 'orioles sing, swallows swirl, streams purl everywhere, and the road mounts skyward.' Isn't this exactly a miniature of our socialist motherland?" So ran *Red Flag*'s commentary on the two poems from Mao's pen published for the first time in January 1976.

This was not exactly a miniature of the scene that had greeted me as I re-entered China one day that month after six years away. Having traveled by train from Hong Kong, I sat in the airport lounge at Canton and looked around at the several dozen Chinese with whom I was to fly to Peking. They were not an animated group. Most of them sat in silence, and the few who talked did so in a desultory fashion. Hardly anyone read a newspaper, magazine, or book. The main pastime, for the men, was smoking. Clothes were drab and rumpled. Faces wore a bored or vacant look. The contrast with the animated, stylishly dressed Chinese I had left on the streets of Hong Kong that morning was depressing.

The flight crew of the Trident aircraft that was to take us from Canton to Peking walked through the departure hall. They were smartly dressed and there was a spring in their step. As they passed me, my eyes met those of an air hostess. My glance must have betrayed something more than the professional interest of a political observer, for it struck a spark of adventure in hers. I thought I saw in her bearing and her eyes a sense of life, but life that was carefully contained, biding its time.

How much had changed in the six years I had been away? The Chinese my family and I had encountered on our way from the border to the airport were more welcoming and much less tense than they had been in 1968. There was a fine new railway station in Canton. But apart from that, very little seemed to have changed, physically or spiritually.

The silence and passivity were so much as I remembered them that it was as if I had stepped outside China for six days, not six years. Even where the buildings and equipment were new, old habits remained unchanged. Canton's new railway station had a whole array of glass swinging doors, but all except two were kept locked.

We flew to Peking in a newly purchased aircraft, but the cabin crew ignored the meal-heating facilities and served cold food, and orange juice from an aluminum kettle. When we landed at Peking airport, our baggage was brought to us by the same single, antiquated conveyor belt that had been there six years before, and we still had to thrust our way through a dense crowd of passengers to retrieve our suitcases from a jumble on the floor.

I noticed half a dozen large jet airliners belonging to China's civil airline parked at Peking airport. Colleagues told me they were kept there idle day after day. China had bought a large number of aircraft, expecting to use them on international routes. Traffic rights had been negotiated, but for some reason the aircraft remained grounded, their engines deteriorating, tens of millions of U.S. dollars of hard-won foreign exchange earning no return. Seeing this waste of potential, I thought again of the stewardess. How long would it be before she and her Boeing could take off on an international route?

Installed in Peking, I could detect very little of that revolutionary vigor of which *Red Flag* had spoken, and few figurative swallows were swirling or orioles singing. Instead, in the streets, in the parks, in restaurants, wherever I went, I found the same eerie absence of serious conversation or animated chatter as in Canton airport. Each morning I watched the dark rivers of bicyclists flowing to work down the broad avenue outside our home. They pedaled slowly, in silence, with expressionless faces. ". . . so many, I had not thought death had undone so many."*

The commuter tide is a gloomy sight in any city, but in Peking it was more so. Neither going to work in the morning nor returning home in the evening did people seem to have anything to hurry for. The ideal in Peking has long been an unhurried life, but the tone of the city now was torpid rather than leisurely.

Physically, too, Peking was as drab in 1976 as I had left it in 1970. The windows, doors, and eaves of houses and apartments were still left unpainted for years. In place of the variety of earlier decades, shopfronts were now painted in a narrow range of colors. As the years had passed more and more graceful temples and family courtyards had been turned into factories and scarred with makeshift workshops and iron chimneys. When a new building gave pleasure to the eye, it was a remarkable occasion. This was a result of design rather than low-cost materials.

With its huge surplus labor force, China could have made Peking bright with flowers, but beauty itself had been suspect as a bourgeois value ever since the Cultural Revolution. Meeting so many bleak scenes, my eyes became inert. More often than not, to search the passing scene for sights that would give pleasure was to waste energy and court disappointment. I had to exert an effort of will to keep looking around me.

There was a tidiness to the city that reminded me of an army barracks. Public health had no doubt greatly benefited from the constant sweeping, but it was not only litter that tidy-minded administrators had swept away. People had gone too: the people who provide all kinds of low-cost services and goods on the streets of other cities in developing countries of Asia; they clut-

* T. S. Eliot, *The Waste Land*.

ter the roadside, but they fill a hundred gaps in the economic structure, gaps that bureaucrats never have the time or will to fill. The cobblers and shoe-shine men, the key-makers and umbrella repairers, the vendors of toys, watch-straps, and hair-ribbons, the men who keep stalls where you can buy a bowl of steaming noodles any time of day or late into the night. All these earn their livings, provide service, and give vitality to the city. Before 1949, Peking had its markets just outside the walls where traders sold products from farms and workshops nearby or melons from central Asia. But in 1976, the city administrators would banish a young man to the countryside rather than let him set himself up in a small line of business.* The left-wing ideologues were happy: they were suppressing "spontaneous shoots of capitalism," but everyone else was worse off.

One of the biggest surprises of my first tour in China had been to discover that the morale of the workers was low. Naïvely, I had come with images in my mind of men pushing wheelbarrows at the run. I had seen it in a hundred photographs and documentary films, but I never saw it in real life. I had expected to find at work the same skill and energy I had seen in Chinese communities in Hong Kong and Southeast Asia. I observed nothing of the kind. The work ethic had been destroyed so far as the majority of people were still concerned.

The *Red Flag* commentary on Mao's poems gave the impression that things were very different in 1976: "'Nothing is hard in this world / If you dare to scale the heights.' Like music that is full of vigor, these two concluding lines impart to us inexhaustible strength." The workmen who came to unpack our heavy baggage seemed not to have read the poems, for their strength was exhausted after half a day's work. When their predecessors (or perhaps they themselves) had packed up our belongings in December 1969 they had worked for four and a half hours out of a theoretical eight-hour day. We wanted to see whether the performance had changed over the years; so now, six years later, we discreetly timed them again: they worked four and a half hours in the day.

* Exceptions included vendors of popsicles in summer and candied apples in winter.

In the weeks that followed, one saw and heard a great deal of evidence that the morale of the work force was not high. It was not hard to come up with a partial explanation. Productivity bonuses had been abolished, under the influence of leftist dogma, since the Cultural Revolution. Material incentives generally were in disfavor, and there had been no general wage increase since the early 1960s, despite regular claims of increased production.

But compared with conditions before 1949, there had been major social and economic improvements. Nationwide, there had been a revolution in the standard of public health and the availability of schooling. All around me I could see evidence to confirm the official claims: on the streets of Peking, young adults towered over their grandparents, and virtually all the children in Peking attended secondary as well as primary schools. Before 1949 there had been unhealthy slums in the city. These had all gone. Much new housing had been built and public transportation had improved. The nation as a whole has scored remarkable achievements in many branches of industry and in exploiting her oil and coal reserves.[1] Why was it that appreciation of these achievements did not compensate for lack of growth in money incomes?

One reason was that the most noticeable improvements in the conditions of life, for those who had been most deprived before the Communists came to power, had been effected long before, in the 1950s. The more equitable and secure supply of basic foods, the new security of employment and of housing, the increased access to education—changes that rightly impressed those who could compare the old and new Chinas—were now taken for granted by many, especially by the young who had never known anything else. People were looking for further improvements, and there had not been many in recent years.

The amount of food grain distributed per head was no higher in 1976 than it had been in 1957. Staple foods were all still rationed. So was cotton cloth, production of which had only risen from eight meters per head in 1957 to about ten in 1976.*

* In 1976, cotton was still the cloth used in the great majority of garments. Wool was expensive and rare; synthetic-fiber production was increasing but still not great.

It was also a fact that China's economic performance had
been very much inferior to that of capitalist economies in East
and Southeast Asia. The growth rates and improvements in the
standard of living of all economic classes in Japan, South Korea,
Thailand, Malaysia, Hong Kong, and Taiwan had far outstripped
those in China. Although no information on this was ever published by the Chinese press, some knowledge of the facts had
certainly filtered into the cities from Overseas Chinese relatives
or through Canton province, where such knowledge was so
widespread that the province was a seemingly inexhaustible
source of emigrants, both legal and illegal. The steady flow of
remittances from relatives overseas was tangible proof for many
people.

The state of the economy was only part of the explanation
for the malaise that so palpably gripped society. Less tangible
social, cultural, educational, and political factors had surely contributed to it. In these areas it was evident that life in China had
not simply stagnated since 1966 but had deteriorated.

If the Chinese were finding little pleasure in their work,
their leisure time offered them few compensations. Before the
Cultural Revolution, a tradition had grown up of Saturday-night
dances in places where people worked and lived. Most factories,
offices, universities, and neighborhoods that had places to hold
dances would do so—genteel affairs that gave much pleasure to
millions of working people in Peking and other cities. These
were part of proletarian culture but did not conform to the
leftist ideologues' conception of a proletarian revolutionary line
for culture, so they had ceased in the Cultural Revolution.

Festivals like the Lantern Festival and the Dragon Boat Festival, which had once brightened the lives of people of all classes,
had not been organized for years.

Many years before, people had enjoyed making kites and
flying them in the autumn winds. They made magnificent kites,
some of them graceful and elegant, some designed to fight other
kites, but in 1976 the only kites to be seen in the air were poor
improvised things of no beauty or strength.

The Bei Hai Park, a place where Peking residents had once
enjoyed walking with their families to escape from the confines of their limited living space, and to delight in the lake and

trees and picturesque buildings, had been closed without explanation.

All forms of culture had been turned into weapons of political struggle. As a result, grace, beauty, humor, tenderness, and sensuality had all been eliminated from novels, films, television, plays, ballet, opera, poetry, music, and sculpture. The great comedians, playwrights, singers, dancers, novelists, actors, and actresses of the 1950s and 1960s had been banished from public view. The whole production of the highly professional Chinese film industry from its creation in the 1930s to 1966 had been consigned to oblivion.

The bookstores had been purged of virtually the entire heritage of Chinese and foreign literature, philosophy, and history, including the works of authors like Mao Dun and Ba Jin, who had done so much before 1949 to awaken the reading public to the need for radical change.

Peking's National Fine Arts Gallery was closed. No exhibition of any contemporary painting that deserved to be called art was on show anywhere in China.

A climate of repression of the sex instinct had been created that went far beyond a normal concern for public decency. Not a single love lyric was sung or read in public; not even the most scientific mention of sex was permitted in print. Were the ideologues of the left trying to kill Eros, lest he act as a pole of attraction rivaling their dogma? If so, they were fulfilling a prophecy made by George Orwell in his novel *1984*, which describes how life would be in Britain under a totalitarian regime.

The effects on society were clearly visible. Hairdressers would no longer wave hair. Women dared not offend the Puritan ethic by wearing dresses or the traditional *qi pao* with a slit skirt. Cosmetics were taboo in public and only the most audacious young lovers would hold hands on the street. Unmarried girls who became pregnant risked punishment of Victorian severity. They could be banished to the countryside or a remote city or even sentenced to labor camp. Their child might be forcibly removed from them.[2]

With the exception of a few showplaces like the Forbidden

City, museums possessing traditional works of art were closed to the Chinese public.

Occasionally since 1973 foreign orchestras had toured China, but for ten years the Chinese musicians who came to their concerts had been forbidden to play the music the foreigners played. They were not allowed to perform or even practice foreign music of any school. No foreign music was broadcast on radio or television.

Before the Cultural Revolution, the art of the stand-up comedian had been practiced with great skill. Men like Hou Baolin were philosopher-clowns who satirized the absurdities of society with punning wit and sharp social observation. He and his professional colleagues had been silenced, and some of them persecuted, since 1966.

In *1984*, Orwell describes an invention called the memory hole, which is heavily used by the Ministry of Truth to suppress and tamper with the record of the past. Every office in the ministry is equipped with a memory hole that gives access to a system of tubes connected to an ever-burning furnace in the basement. Officials of the ministry push into the hole paper and film bearing statements or images from the past that do not fit the current orthodoxy. The offensive evidence of the past is carried down the tubes and condemned to oblivion by the flames of the furnace.

In the China of 1976, there was no ministry of truth and no system of memory holes, but vast tracts of the past had been obliterated. To symbolize this policy, the very walls of Peking had been razed to the ground. (I had watched them go stone by stone in 1969, to be used in building air raid shelters—a flimsy protection against the reality of modern war.) This work of obliteration had been performed in the name of Chairman Mao's revolutionary line for culture, but the evidence pointed not to any grass-roots movement by the proletariat but rather to a top-down movement initiated by Jiang Qing before the Cultural Revolution. It was then enormously expanded under the slogan "Destroy the Four Olds," propagated with Mao's approval in 1966. In fact the nihilism of the Red Guards had been deeply resented by the proletariat itself.

When members of the proletariat wanted culture or enter-
tainment in 1976 they were faced by a choice between one form
of sterility and another. All works of fiction manipulated
cardboard characters who were nothing more than political or
social stereotypes, lacking any depth or individuality. Instead of
illuminating the area of life which they took as their subject
matter, they erected a painted screen between life and the public. The images on that screen were nothing more than the
simplicities of propaganda. There was no longer any place for
freshness of feeling, originality of thought, or subtlety of spirit.
In the "revolutionary" ballets produced under Jiang Qing's direction, grace had been eliminated from the movements of the
female dancers. Heroines danced in a style that expressed a
limited range of emotions: anger, militant resolve, hatred,
triumph, and steely optimism. The "model" works performed in
theaters, cinemas, and opera houses did not deal with the life of
China in 1976 but were set in the past. Only a tiny number of
feature films were produced on contemporary themes, and the
plots of these were thoroughly predictable.

Painting had been reduced to the level of poster art, and a
generation of talented painters inherited from pre-Communist
China had disappeared without trace.

Before 1966, hundreds of journals and magazines for a wide
range of readers from specialists to laymen had been published
on a great range of subjects. The natural and social sciences,
history, economics, world affairs, and the arts were covered for
the informed reader, and the cinema was covered for the film
fan. In 1976, they had all either been suspended from publication or reduced to a travesty of their former selves.

Arousing or maintaining in children enthusiasm for study
was a problem when the chairman of the Communist Party
himself was reported to have said "The more you study, the
more foolish you become," and the Chairman's propagandists
made a hero of a young man because he handed in a blank
answer sheet in an examination. Why should young people
strive to develop their minds when the Chairman had referred
to intellectuals as the "stinking ninth" category of bad elements
in society and his closest followers had taken his words so liter-

ally that anyone who became an expert or mastered a skill was liable to be denounced as bourgeois on that evidence alone? It was little wonder that wall posters had appeared, asking "What's the use of studying?"[3]

I visited Peking University, Liaoning University, and Jinan Technical College and found them half empty. The academic content of their courses had been cut by half compared with before the Cultural Revolution. At Liaoning University, the main university for the industrial heartland of Northeast China, the library shelves were covered in dust from disuse, and the stacks were out of bounds to the students. In the English literature section I could find no work written after 1949.

The daily press and even the Party's theoretical monthly *Red Flag* had reduced the language of politics to a litany. Jargon and dogma filled the pages. Words were used without precision. Instead they were exploited as shields and projectiles for political warfare. (For example, any policy attributed to Mao was simply asserted to be the proletarian revolutionary line. No evidence was produced to show how the proletariat had formed this line.) To my eye, the Chinese language as used in the press had become more dead than Latin or Greek. Only in the one functioning Protestant church in Peking did I find the language alive in all its old richness.

It was not only in the press that whole areas of life were simply never discussed. *All* writers knew that forbidden zones had been established which they must not enter. Some of the central ideas of Marx himself could not be touched upon: it was out of the question for anyone to propose ways of making a reality of "the self-government of the producers" or to discuss Marx's prediction that under socialism the state would wither away. No one would dare to recall the list of goals for socialism Marx had set out in his interview with the Chicago *Tribune* in January 1879. (The list began with universal, equal, direct suffrage through secret ballot, for all citizens over twenty years of age, in all elections and all votes. It included the abolition of all laws which limit or suppress the free expression of opinion, of thought and research, or the rights of publication, assembly and association.) The very notion of "socialist legality"—

building a system of laws and legal institutions—was taboo. In short, all discussion of China's political structure was off limits.

I could not know then, but I learned later, that back in 1969 a young man named Huang Xiang in the city of Guiyang in southwest China had written a poem which described his reaction to this stifling of the mind and the spirit:

I SEE A WAR

I see a war, an invisible war.
This war is waged in everyone's facial expression.
It is waged by numerous high-pitched loudspeakers.
It is waged in every pair of fearful and unstable eyes.
This war goes on within the nervous system in every brain.
It bombards every man, bombards every part and every aspect of
    man's physiological and psychological being.
The war is waged with invisible weapons,
Invisible bayonets, artillery, and bombs.
This is the war of all the evils.

This is the invisible extension of physical war,
It is a war waged in the show windows of bookstores,
In every library,
In every song taught to schoolchildren,
In every elementary-school textbook,
In every household.
In numerous mass meetings.
In each stereotyped movement, line, and image of the actors on
    stage.

I see the bayonets and spies, patrolling and spying between the
    lines of my poems,
Searching about in the conscience of every person.
A stubborn, ignorant, violent, feudal force
    Overruns everything, controls everything.

In the forefront of the attack by this unique, unprecedented and
    unrepeatable cultural dictatorship,
I see a group of wild animals trampling the spiritual world of man.
Oil paintings and canvases are lying to the people.
Poetry is panting in fear.
Music is crying.

Oh, invisible war, evil war,
You are the extension and continuation of 2500 years of war
   waged by feudal dictatorship.
You are the concentration and expansion of the war of spiritual enslavement that has been going on for 2500 years.

Come on, bomb, demolish, kill, hack down!
But people's democracy never dies,
The people's freedom of the spirit never dies.
Truth, Beauty, and Goodness which live within the heart of man
   can never be uprooted, never be snatched away.[4]

The gap between the rhetoric of "orioles singing, swallows
swirling" or the Chinese people "striding with revolutionary
vigor into another militant spring" and the realities of daily life
mocked the ordinary citizen of China.

Newspapers habitually published glowing success stories that
contained gross exaggerations or pure fabrication, but they were
not allowed to publish anything that showed the dark side of
Chinese society.* Accidents in industry, accidents to planes and
trains or on the roads, natural disasters, fires, epidemics of disease, unemployment, strikes, crime, the administration of justice, and the punishment of crime were taboo subjects. There
was no investigative journalism: the abuses of power by corrupt
cadres went unreported except during those rare periods when
the leadership decided to have a clean-up campaign.

A few thousand leading victims of the Cultural Revolution
had been restored to office, but hundreds of thousands of less
senior officials, technicians, and intellectuals who had been
purged for the same reasons looked in vain for rehabilitation,
and the press never mentioned their cases. With Mao's own

---

* Talking to officials reinforced this impression because they dared not
entrust their private thoughts to foreigners. I began to understand the agony
of Orwell's fictional Winston Smith, who, faced with the collective amnesia of
Britain in 1984, asked himself whether he alone possessed a memory of the
past. In 1976 I had to turn to other foreigners, to Chinese outside China, or to
an embassy library, protected by diplomatic privilege, for confirmation that the
past had indeed been the way I remembered it. As in 1984, one would occasionally get confirmation of one's memory from a "prole" who let slip a thought,
a gesture or an image that should have been erased: a sigh of regret for a dance
hall long since closed or a house where chrysanthemums had bloomed.

propagandists in ultimate charge of all public means of communication, not the least mention was made of any of the damage caused to millions of lives by the Cultural Revolution and
the Great Leap Forward before it.

Reading the press, novels, or any other Chinese publication,
I was tempted to think that a lobotomy had been performed on
China to remove that portion of the brain which contained the
public memory. With all means of communication choked with
the clichés of an official dogma, the Chinese were no longer
speaking or writing to each other in public about the realities of
their own past or present.

The ordinary citizen who was largely cut off from the true
thoughts and feelings of his fellow Chinese and from the true
facts of their lives was infinitely more isolated from the world
outside. Those, like Zhou Enlai, who were opposed to
obscurantism had managed to keep open one major window on
the world: a widely distributed daily newspaper published under
the forbidding title *Reference News*, which gave remarkably
broad coverage to international affairs and was based entirely on
reports published by foreign newspapers and news agencies.
However, the reports were selected to reinforce the party line
in foreign affairs and certainly did not provide a balanced picture
of the domestic affairs of foreign countries. With the exception
of *Reference News*, almost all the other officially controlled windows on the world had been shuttered since the Cultural Revolution, as far as the general public was concerned.

No public cinema and no television station in China ever
showed a film made in the United States, the Soviet Union, Japan,
Western Europe, or the Third World. No bookstore in China
sold any book published abroad or a Chinese translation of any
foreign work except some Marxist–Leninist classics. (Chinese
versions of foreign technical works may however have been
distributed directly to schools and colleges.) No book that described any foreign work of art from any period of human existence or gave any account of contemporary life abroad was on
sale. The Chinese people were called upon daily to reject and
denounce capitalism and Soviet revisionism without being given
even the most rudimentary account of either system. The

Chinese press proclaimed the superiority of the socialist system but never described to Chinese workers how their oppressed brothers and sisters across the four seas were living. The products of foreign societies were excluded with equal rigor: no foreign consumer product was on sale, and no foreign work of art—either original or in reproduction—was on public display anywhere in the country.

Chinese were expressly forbidden from having unofficial contact with the few foreigners who lived in Peking and other cities. This regulation was easy to enforce because, with the exception of students and a tiny number of trusted long-term residents, all foreigners lived in walled compounds guarded by soldiers who checked the papers of the Chinese who entered. It would have been very difficult for foreigners to visit the home of a Chinese without attracting the attention of the neighbors.

The chances of a Chinese going abroad to study were one in three million—out of a population of nine hundred million, about three hundred individuals were studying abroad. No Chinese could hope to take a holiday abroad unless he could wangle a visit to an Overseas Chinese relative, and in 1976 that was exceedingly hard. Why should people be allowed to take a holiday abroad when they were not entitled to holidays in China except the ten public holidays spaced out through the year?*

While adults were cut off from the past and the outside world, children could be given toy swords in the ancient style and a range of mechanical toys that gave glimpses of life in the West. In toy stores, Boeinglike airliners were ready for takeoff and American-style, chrome-encrusted open cars carried white men and their blonde girlfriends. Parents might only have a transistor radio, but their children could play with make-believe television sets. These toys had even remained on sale through the xenophobia and ultrapuritanism of the Cultural Revolution. So had clothes for children of a brightness and gaiety unthinkable for adults. Most memorable of these had been gaudy little round caps with crescent peaks of the kind boys wore on En-

---

* Certain categories of people were entitled to holidays. These included married couples assigned to work in different cities and newly married couples.

glish seafronts before the First World War. So much else had
been swept away, but these symbols of another set of values had
survived; if China excused its toddlers from the Puritan ethic,
then perhaps many grownups were only subscribing to it because they were forced to. Other signs pointed in the same
direction. In 1976, people were once again displaying a discreet
concern for their personal appearance: young men grew mus-
taches and dared to wear leather jackets in place of the eternal
blue cotton; young women would let a half-inch of pretty blouse
show at the collar of their drab Mao jackets, and lightweight
bicycles in vivid colors were sought after to replace the sturdy
black machines that had been the only ones sold until then. It
was my impression that, excluded from decision-making in public life and denied rewards for enterprise and initiative at work,
people were devoting their attention to their private lives, concentrating on the pursuit of the small permitted pleasures like
their choice of cloth, or sausage, or a toy for a child. Many in
China were walking on tiptoe, biding their time, believing that a
day would come when they could expand their spirits and live.

The system of controls to which people were subject was
centered upon their place of work, their unit, as it was called.
The unit was responsible for many aspects of life beyond work
itself. In its most developed form—for example a large state-
owned factory—the unit would provide the worker's pension,
medical benefits, and housing (single-sex dormitories for single
people, apartments for families). Marriages had to be approved
by the leadership of a worker's unit. If a couple wanted to have a
baby, they could apply for one of the births allotted to their unit
for the year ahead under the unified family-planning system. If
they wanted to divorce, the leadership of the unit would examine their reasons and form a view on the question. If they
wanted to buy a bicycle or a sewing machine, they would first
apply to their "leadership" for a letter of authority for the purchase. The unit distributed the industrial coupons they needed
to buy many other consumer goods and ration coupons for their
food and cloth. If they wanted to go to cinema or theater they
applied for tickets distributed by the unit. If one of them needed
to travel on personal or official business, he or she requested a

letter of authority from the unit. Without it they could not buy a railway ticket, and no hotel would accept them.

The unit was responsible for their behavior and for ensuring that their political thinking conformed to the current party line. To provide for their political education, the unit held obligatory political study sessions twice weekly. If they conducted themselves in a manner which pleased their leadership, the unit would look after them in a manner of a miniature welfare state. If they stepped out of line, there were many instruments available with which to discipline them.

Their unit was surrounded by a wall, and access to it was controlled by a gatekeeper. To many people this was no doubt reassuring, but the more independent spirits resented it.

The core of the leadership of all units was composed of Communist Party officials. They were appointed, not elected, and those who worked under them had no say in their appointment and no power to dismiss them. Young people who had been freed by Mao during the Cultural Revolution to roam China, far from the control of parents or party, resented the discipline of the unit as much as an earlier generation had resented the control of the extended family.

A worker did not choose his unit any more than he chose his line of work. The state decided what work school-leavers and college graduates should do and where they should do it. Once they were assigned to a unit they stayed there unless reassigned elsewhere. The system was not managed efficiently; of the generation of engineers and technicians trained before the Cultural Revolution only one in four was involved in work for which he or she had been trained.[5] This system may have been a relief to people who disliked taking responsibility for their own lives, but the more active spirits must have found it dampening their initiative and increasing their feeling that the state was their master and not their servant.

The weakness of the individual face-to-face with the state was very evident in the administration of justice. The Procuracy, which was supposed to ensure that those who should be tried were duly tried and that the police and courts did not abuse their powers, had been destroyed in the Cultural Revolution. It was now much easier for local powerholders to bully those whom they governed. In country districts particularly, there existed unscrupulous officials who felt free to take the law into their own hands. Some of them behaved in ways that must have prompted peasants to ask themselves whether their new masters were better or worse than the landlords of Old China.

To advance their own careers, the worst among them would claim that units under their command had produced far more grain than they really had and then, to "substantiate" the claim, they would force the peasants to hand over to the state grain they needed for their own consumption. The peasants went hungry while the officials were promoted. Some of the unscrupulous officials formed their own informer networks and strong-arm squads to track down and beat up anyone rash enough to expose them.

Of course, it was not only at the grass-roots level that officials were appointed rather than elected. No official holding any office in China in 1976 had been elected in an open, contested election in which nonmembers of the Party could vote.

In the twenty-six years of the People's Republic, its citizens had only once had an opportunity to take part in elections for a people's congress. That was in 1954, the first year of the first constitution. They had voted for delegates to their local people's congresses.* Delegates to the National People's Congress were then elected indirectly at two removes.

Since 1966 the leadership had been in constant state of flux but the people had had no say in any of the changes. When one leader was attacked, the masses (as they were revealingly termed) were merely called on to echo accusations formulated by a tiny number of top party men meeting in secret. And the manner in which the changes had been presented to the people showed as little respect for their intelligence as for the constitutions of party and state.

The 1966 disappearance and disgrace of the head of state, Liu Shaoqi, had been forced by Mao without even a decision by the full Central Committee. The people had then been asked to

* The vote was by a show of hands. Secret ballot had been ruled out on the grounds that the high level of illiteracy then prevailing made it impractical.

believe that this man, who had been Mao's Number Two in the Party for twenty years, was and had always been a capitalist at heart. Liu died in 1969, but his death was kept secret and had still not been revealed in 1976. The people had no right to be informed of the fate of their former head of state.

The announcement in July 1972 that Lin Biao had died while trying to escape after plotting an attempt on Mao's life hardly increased the leadership's image of stability. Nor did the fall of another ten of the twenty-one members of the Politburo in the same period.

Lin Biao's death had been kept secret for ten months, a brief time compared to the long silence on Liu but long enough to heighten the sense of instability. As in the case of Liu Shaoqi, respect for the party leadership was diminished by some of the charges made against Lin. The public was told that this man Mao had chosen as his Minister of Defense, and later as his successor, had been a military incompetent and his opponent since the 1920s. Either the people were being lied to or Mao had been foolish. Then there was a 180-degree turnabout on another of the charges leveled at the erstwhile successor: denounced first as an ultraleftist (a charge amply supported by Lin's public speeches), he was then relabeled an ultrarightist who throughout the Cultural Revolution had allegedly been intent on restoring capitalism. The authority of the party could hardly survive many more such displays of instability, inconsistency, and implausibility.

When, one evening in April 1973, Deng Xiaoping made his first public appearance for seven years (at a banquet for Prince Sihanouk), the official account of the occasion treated it as if it were a normal, everyday occurrence, as if indeed he had never been away. No public explanation was given as to how the "No. 2 Capitalist-Roader" had regained respectability. Apparently not even the Central Committee had been asked to approve the decision. Many were no doubt pleased by the news, but they can hardly have failed to reflect that it made a mockery of all the hours and all the sheets of poster paper that they had devoted to denouncing Deng some years before. More seriously, it was an acknowledgment that the whole Cultural Revolution had been a traumatic journey down a cul-de-sac. Mao had led China down the cul-de-sac and now, seven years later, he was letting Zhou Enlai lead the nation out again. Among "the masses," relief at the trend of events must have been accompanied by further reflections on Mao's fallibility.

Although the cult of Mao was shorn of some of its more ridiculous excesses, it was still maintained at a very high level of intensity. His frailty prevented him from appearing again in public in person, but his protégés kept his image and Thought constantly before the eyes of the people. No article on politics was complete if it did not wear the "hat and boots" of quotations from Mao: it must start and end with some of the Chairman's Thought. No action, indeed no thought, could be justified unless it were shown to be in accordance with his Thought. Every day a Mao Thought appeared in a special box at the top right of the front page of the *People's Daily*. Portraits or white plaster statues of him were in every public building. Airports, railway stations, main roads, and major intersections had murals depicting the Chairman in one role or another. In some he was surrounded by admiring representatives of all the peoples of China and the world in their traditional costumes. (He was always the tallest figure in the scene.) In others, he was shown signaling the way forward to the serried ranks of anonymous revolutionary masses over whom he towered as a colossus commanding an army of diminutive mortals. Millions upon millions of walls and billboards displayed his Thought. A pair of young people turned a corner in a park and there on a concrete screen was another Thought to greet them. On the radio day after day there were dramas in which the power of his Thought brought salvation to some community. As the drama built to its climax a worker or peasant would utter his name with the exaltation I had once heard used by the followers of Jesus in Sunday-School films. News readers spoke his Thought with a special tone of voice, filled with awe and reverence.

Other Chinese leaders had displayed a talent for poetry but the bookstores did not sell collected editions of their works, and *Red Flag* would certainly not use their poems to inspire the nation. The display in the Mao section of the bookstore in the heart of Peking resembled a shrine.

All achievements were ascribed to the illuminating power of his Thought. To have ascribed a success—say in nuclear physics—to any other Politburo member's writing, let alone to that of a nuclear physicist, would have been a flagrant act of political disloyalty. The history of the revolution became the history of Mao's triumphs, and the contributions of everyone else were belittled or effaced entirely.

As I looked around me at Chinese society in 1976 and looked back over the years since 1949, it seemed to me that, for many people, the spontaneity and sincerity must have gone out of their reverence for Mao. Surely they must resent being bombarded with his quotations and his image at every turn. Surely they must resent the lack of freedom and the absence of democracy. Surely they must have found it offensive that the left based its judgment as to whether or not a policy was "correct" solely on doctrinal grounds, irrespective of the wishes and the immediate material interests of the broad mass of the people. Although I recognized that the massive propaganda, backed by the stiff penalties for criticizing Mao, must hold many minds in thrall to him, I believed that there would be strong spirits who rebelled against it.

On the bottom line, the suppression of history and the sterility of art and politics were strong proof that the dogma of the ultraleft had not taken root in men's minds. One was not witnessing a ferment of lively leftist thought and art threatened by repressive rightist conservatism. On the contrary, a conservative left was using every means to suppress what it described as spontaneous capitalism and new bourgeois elements being born every hour and every minute.

To draw attention to such realities was, of course, very unfashionable, and quickly brought down on one's head the charge of being anti-Chinese. At an international seminar on China in the early 1970s I had been reproved by European sinologists for saying that the suppression of Western culture and Western-style intellectuals was damaging China. I was told that it was faintly ridiculous to assert the value to China of Western culture and thought at the very moment students in the West were questioning their own cultural heritage. It was put to me by a senior sinologist that perhaps the greatest contribution a

Chinese intellectual could make to his country was to commit suicide.

But one could not just sweep aside the evidence of popular dissatisfaction and alienation in China. More persuasive to me than the testimony of my eyes and ears and the conclusions I drew, guided by a belief in a bedrock of universal values, was a wall poster that had appeared in the southern city of Canton, first in 1973 and then in longer form in 1974. The 1974 version was twenty thousand Chinese characters long. It was written on sixty-seven sheets of newsprint and extended along one hundred yards of wall. Day after day, crowds flocked to read it in attentive silence. It expressed deep anger at the sufferings inflicted on China by some of its rulers in recent years and called for far-reaching reforms. Compared to this poster, the most outspoken criticisms made by foreigners seemed pale.

Its title was matter-of-fact: "Concerning Socialist Democracy and the Legal System," but its Chinese readers knew that these topics were highly controversial. The poster was the work of three young men. It was signed Li Yizhe, a pen name composed of one part of the names of each: *Li* Zhengtian, Chen *Yi* yang, and Huang Xi*zhe*. Li Zhengtian, a former Red Guard and a graduate of the Canton Fine Arts College, was their leader. They wrote that other people had called them "youths who are not afraid of tigers, but know how savage and cruel tigers can be."

"We are," they said, "survivors; we were once bitten by the tiger but it failed to grind us small enough to swallow. Its claws left scars on our faces; so we are not handsome."

How had their views been formed? "It is obvious that we have read very little Marxism–Leninism. Chiefly, we have been educated by cruel reality." Li Yizhe's message is this: China has neither democracy nor law; its people want both, and if they do not achieve them they will be condemned to experience new tragedies like those they have undergone since 1966. They have not forgotten their sufferings, and they know what changes are needed, but they face fierce resistance from power-holders with a vested interest in dictatorship.

Li Yizhe does not criticize Mao directly. He lays all the

blame for all the mistakes on others. He casts Lin Biao in the role of the "Prince of Evil," alleging that he usurped power from Mao in the Cultural Revolution and then proceeded to establish the "Lin Biao System—a feudal fascist autocracy."

Freedoms granted to the people in 1966 were suddenly taken away. The weapon of "expensive people's democracy" was snatched from their hands and the socialist legal system was suddenly declared inoperative. This, for Li Yizhe, was the central failure of the Cultural Revolution.

It was, Li says, in the summer of 1968 that the great repression occurred (this was the time when the army was used to suppress disorder and round up millions of Red Guards to send them to the countryside):

> All across the land, there were arrests everywhere, suppressions everywhere, miscarriages of justice everywhere. Where did the socialist legal system go? Allegedly it was no longer of any use. . . . Now there was no law and no heaven![6]

The people had nowhere to turn for justice.

> I called on heaven for help but heaven did not answer;
> I called on earth for help but the earth did not
>   respond.
> This was a rehearsal of social fascism in our country.

The Prince of Evil is dead now, but Li Yizhe warns that his downfall does not mean the end of his system. The process of establishing the system created a force of officials who have a vested interest in maintaining it. These officials resent such measures as have been taken to dismantle some of the more objectionable features of the system and they long to turn back the political clock. They have distorted the campaign to criticize Lin Biao by changing his classification from ultraleftist to ultrarightist and by introducing the theme of praising Qin Shi Huang (the First Emperor of the Qin Dynasty), who ordered the Confucian classics to be burned, condemned Confucian scholars to be buried alive, and adopted the ideas of the authoritarian legalist philosophers. The reactionary officials have done this, claims Li Yizhe, "to prepare public opinion for social-fascism, in order to complete Lin Biao's unfinished business."

To alert people to the nature of the danger, Li Yizhe recalls "scenes from the time when the system was flourishing":

We have not forgotten the prominence that was given to empty politics, which rewarded the lazy and punished the diligent, the "daily reading" [of Mao's works] which resembled the incantation of spells, the "discussion-application" [of Mao's works] which became more and more hypocritical . . . the grotesque "loyalty dance,"* and the endless excruciating rituals of showing loyalty [to Mao]—the morning prayers and evening confessions†. . . which were invariably colored with religion and shrouded in an atmosphere of the supernatural. . . . The innumerable meetings of "representatives of active elements" were in fact exhibitions of hypocritical, evil and ugly behavior. . . . We have also not forgotten the "wind of public property" which jeopardized the basic interests of the workers and peasants, the style of Party management under which "when one man has found the Way, chickens and dogs go to heaven with him,"** the style of study with trumpeted "whatever is useful, that is the truth" . . . the new stereotyped writing which encouraged lying. . . .

We have not forgotten the formula preachings of class struggle, and the scumhole type of "cow pens" [improvised prisons set up within units—factories, universities, etc.—during the Cultural Revolution, particularly 1968]. . . . In Guangdong province alone nearly 40,000 revolutionary masses and cadres were massacred and more than a million were imprisoned, put under "control" and struggled against.

Li Yizhe condemns the repression of 1968 as more inhuman than the massacres of worker revolutionaries carried out by Chiang Kai-shek's Nationalists in 1927 and by British and

* Dances such as that of "the sunflowers seeking the rays of the sun" popularized in the musical extravaganza The East is Red had become a standard part of "cultural shows."

† As standard practice, workers would be assembled at the start of the working day before a portrait or bust of Mao to seek strength from his Thought for the day ahead. In the evening before leaving work, they would fall in again to "report back" to the image of Mao on how they had conducted themselves during the day. Anyone who refused to join this ritual was liable to severe punishment.

** When the leader of a faction was promoted, he could bring his followers to high office on his coattails.

French police and soldiers in 1925. The Nationalists killed about ten thousand and the foreign forces sixty-five.

> But [Li Yizhe continues] there are some people who shut their eyes to the fact that the Lin Biao system, which has been witnessed by 800 million people, was ever established as the orthodoxy of the day. These thick-skinned people maintain that Chairman Mao's revolutionary line has, at all times and in all places, occupied the ruling position. Is this not to say that all these bloody butcheries and unreversed cases of long standing are attributable to the "revolutionary line"?

Li Yizhe places the Lin Biao system in its historical context: "The feudal rule which lasted for more than two thousand years has left its ideology deeply rooted. . . . The bad habits of autocracy and despotism are deeply imbued in the minds of the masses, even in the minds of the Communists in general." At a Central Committee meeting a year before he fell, Lin Biao had put forward a "theory of genius" which asserted that men of genius appear very occasionally in history and play a decisive role. Of course, he implied that Mao was one of these. For two days the Central Committee discussed it and a majority seemed to accept it (to do otherwise would have looked like disloyalty to Mao as well as his chosen successor). Then suddenly Mao came out against it, and Lin began his slide to disgrace. Li Yizhe wants to attack the cult of Mao, which continues despite the formal rejection of Lin's "theory." He does not dare to attack it directly, so he must "point at the mulberry to upbraid the ash." Lin's theory of genius can serve very well as a mulberry:

> The theory says that a genius appears only once every several centuries or several millennia, so everyone must worship this "genius," be absolutely loyal to this "genius," and do everything in accordance with the will of this "genius." Furthermore, whoever opposes this "genius" will be struck down. Is this not an all-embracing ideological and political line? No one is allowed to think; no one is allowed to study; no one is allowed to do research; and no one is allowed to ask a single why on any question. The "historical concept of genius" has indeed liquidated 800 million brains.

As a result of the Lin Biao system, says Li Yizhe, "our Party has been molded into a ruler-vassal party, a father-son party; our

state has been molded into a state under a feudalistic social-
fascist autocracy; and our army has been molded into a band of
soldiers like that of Yuan Shikai's Northern Armies."*

Many young men like the writers of this poster had answered Mao's call to rebel in 1966 hoping to break the power
of those officials they believed were using their positions to appropriate public wealth for their private use. They considered
that they had failed. Li Yizhe alleges that the "new bourgeois
class" is still enjoying an excessive share of the wealth of society:
he acknowledges the need for differentials in a socialist society
but claims that the members of the "new bourgeois class" have
set up a whole system of political and economic privileges which
they have extended to their families, their relations, and their
friends. "They swap privileges among themselves, and ensure
that their children inherit them." To maintain them, "they must
attack those upright revolutionary comrades who insist on principle, and they must suppress the masses who rise against their
privileges."

Complaining of the decision to forbid any further criticism
of Lin as an ultraleftist and the orders to denounce him hence-
forward as an ultrarightist and a proponent of the conservative
doctrine of Confucianism, Li Yizhe asks:

> Where in newspapers or documents . . . can we find any instruc-
> tion issued by "the highest, highest" Vice-Chairman Lin which
> called on us to study the doctrine of Confucius? . . . What he and
> his associates wanted was for people to worship Mao Zedong
> Thought, as a kind of religion: Was it not the new principle,
> "Whoever opposes Mao Zedong Thought will be struck down,"
> which enabled us to see the feudal nature of Lin Biao? . . .
>   Oh theoreticians! . . .
>   We can cite a hundred or even a thousand illustrations of Lin
> Biao's leftist essence, but how many can you single out to show the
> rightist essence which was manifested in the Party by Lin Biao
> when he was leading the opportunist line?

---

* A force used to support the political ambitions of its commander rather
than the institutions and principles of party and state. Yuan Shikai was a
general who had himself proclaimed emperor in 1915 after helping to overthrow the Qing dynasty.

"When appearance is taken for reality, reality becomes appearance,
Where nothing is taken for something, something becomes nothing."*

The Lin Biao system reached its highest peak in the Great Proletarian Cultural Revolution. But this is only one of its aspects. More important is that it has created a reaction to itself, a new social force.

Since the downfall of Lin, there had been "an upsurge of the spirit of democracy" everywhere in China and, in Li Yizhe's eyes,

> The iceberg of the Lin Biao system is now melting away, thinking is beginning to be liberated, and questions have been posed to those who are willing to really study socialism. . . . The masses are not Adou [a prince whose innocent ignorance and good-for-nothing character are legendary in China]. They are fully aware of the source of their misfortune. . . . They demand democracy; they demand a socialist legal system; and they demand the revolutionary rights which protect the masses of the people.
>
> "What? You demand democracy? You are reactionaries! Because you are reactionaries, we shall give you no democracy."

The left had called on the people to "go against the tide" and to adopt the attitude of "five fear-nots," meaning they should not fear suffering the loss of their job, expulsion from the Party, imprisonment, divorce by their spouse, or execution for the sake of their principles. Of course, they did not intend that people should go against *their* tide. They repressed their opponents severely, and, according to Li Yizhe:

> Among the revolutionaries who truly fought against the Lin Biao system, not a few had their heads chopped off, and so they are headless; some were imprisoned, and they are still in prison; some were dismissed from office, and they are still suspended. . . . From ancient times to the present, there have always been some people in China who are not afraid of being executed for speaking

* A quotation from Chapter 1 of the *Dream of the Red Chamber.*

out. Lu Xun was naturally one of those.* But he could go to his
Japanese friends to get his articles published; and where can today's "five-fear-nots" people go to have their articles published?
. . . The Lin Biao system is still threatening them; the stern rites
saturated with "loyalty" are still fettering them; and shackles,
iron-barred windows, leather whips, and bullets are waiting for
them.

The poster was condemned at the highest level of the party
as thoroughly reactionary, the leader of the writing group found
himself behind bars, and a poster appeared refuting Li Yizhe's
arguments from the orthodox point of view. But the people of
Canton showed extraordinary reluctance to bow to the party
line, denounce Li Yizhe, and refute his views. This was a time of
great ferment in Canton. New posters appeared on the walls as
fast as the city's cleaners could scrub off the old ones. Canton
was a city with a long tradition of revolution and had been the
base for the Nationalists when they were launching their revolutionary efforts early in the century. But that was not a reason to
dismiss the Li Yizhe poster as a freak. More likely it was a sign
which way the wind of public opinion was blowing. What I had
learned of the rest of China led me to believe that Li Yizhe's
views were widely shared.

Deprived of material incentives, stifled in their social life,
starved of culture, repressed in their communication with other
Chinese, denied knowledge of the outside world, forbidden
contact with foreigners, bound in a web of controls, naked in the
face of the power of the state, prey to corrupt and bullying
officials, having no say in the major decisions of their factory or
shop, excluded from the choice of their national leaders and the
shaping of national policy, and obliged to treat an all-too-fallible
man as a demigod, there had to be many among the Chinese
people in 1976 ready to support a leader who promised sweeping changes.

If Deng's record from the 1950s and 1960s had not convinced the public that he was such a leader, then they were

---

* Lu Xun (1881–1936) wrote short stories and short essays of great power
which did much to awaken people in the 1920s and 1930s to the evils then
prevalent in society. He had his work published by a Japanese publisher in the
Japanese concession in Shanghai, thereby evading Nationalist censorship.

surely convinced of it when his opponents disclosed the full scope of what he had been doing and saying in 1975. This they began to do in February 1976. Few men can have owed so much to their opponents as Deng did. The campaign to discredit him brought home to the whole nation the force and daring of his thinking and the pungent earthiness of his style. Few campaign managers in liberal democracies have succeeded in putting across their candidate's views and personality so well as Deng's opponents did. In seven weeks of February and March 1976 they presented him so effectively that I was prompted to comment to my colleagues that in another society the anti-Deng campaign could have served to have a man elected president.

The record of Deng's opponents in the two and a half months since Zhou Enlai's death was remarkable. They had belittled Zhou Enlai and alleged that behind his goal of the Four Modernizations lay "a complete set of revisionist programs and lines." They had issued a reminder that they were opposed to material incentives and the trend to stability and unity, and that they favored instead the reopening of class struggle in pursuit of ideological purity. They had brought home to the public the human qualities of the man they were trying to strike down, and recalled the long list of pragmatic policies for which he and his associates had fought over twenty-five years.

Although the country was calm, there had already been some signs that the campaign was not working the way the left hoped it would. First there had been the massive spontaneous expression of grief for Zhou in the week after his death. Then at the end of January, stories began to circulate of a political testament left by Zhou. There were different versions, but all of them made clear Zhou's preference for pragmatic policies and people. Whether or not they were founded on fact, they gained credence through the length and breadth of China.

But Deng's more extreme opponents were not in a mood to show sensitivity to that kind of popular feeling. They were preoccupied with the possibility that there might be a reconciliation between Mao and Deng. To prevent that, they needed to polarize the situation. In the last week of March they took a step that inflamed public opinion and ensured that people approached the Qing Ming festival in a state of tension.

6

The Decisive Battle

ON 25 MARCH 1976 one of the two mass-circulation daily newspapers in the leftists' base city, Shanghai, published an article that alluded to Zhou Enlai as "capitalist-roader."

Popular reaction was immediate. In Shanghai people surrounded the offices of the newspaper *Wenhui Bao* demanding an explanation. It was in Nanjing, however, that the first of the demonstrations occurred, at this time of Qing Ming, when Chinese have traditionally honored their dead. Nanjing is a handsome city, proud of its history, a history that had made it even more resistant than other places to the cardboard simplicities of the propaganda of the extreme left. Its name means "southern capital," and it has served as the capital of China several times when North China has been unstable or under occupation. In modern times, Chiang Kai-shek made it the capital of the Republic of China and his government bequeathed handsome buildings in both modern and traditional styles, among them the mausoleum of Sun Yat-sen, the father of the Republic of China. This mausoleum, built of white marble with a blue-tiled roof, stands on the pine-clad hills east of the city. It is a symbol of the continuity of the Chinese revolution, and in its beauty and dignity it is a moving reminder of what the Republic of China at its best aspired to. It contains a reminder also of the extent to which the China of 1976 had failed to fulfill the aims of Sun Yat-sen. Inside the mausoleum the walls display, in letters of gold engraved in black marble, the hopes of Sun Yat-sen for the development of democracy in China. He looked forward to the time when the people would have the right to appoint and dismiss the state officials. In 1976, a rope barricade kept visitors at a safe distance from such dangerous thoughts so that the words could only be read if one peered at them intently.

The city had a special link with Zhou Enlai. He had been sent there after World War II to negotiate with the Nationalists in an attempt to avoid renewed civil war.

It may be that Deng's supporters planned that Nanjing should lead the nation into the Qing Ming demonstrations, or perhaps the city was spontaneously reasserting its historical role as the alternative capital. Either way, it was fitting that this city embodying the links between Communist present and Republican past—a link Zhou had worked to maintain—should have been the first city of China to rise in defense of his legacy.

Nanjing had been in a state of quiet anger even before the insult to Zhou was published, and many people were preparing wreaths dedicated to him. One, of pine branches and white magnolias, had already been laid at the memorial to revolutionary martyrs on a hillside south of the city. When the *Wenhui Bao* was published in Shanghai on 25 March, news of the offensive phrase quickly reached Nanjing, 250 miles away. The city ignited.[1]

On the campus of Nanjing University large slogans and wall posters were pasted up, censuring *Wenhui Bao* and conspirators who were trying to usurp power. The alleged conspirators were compared to Khrushchev—whose name had long since become for Chinese a byword for betrayal of the socialist revolution. One slogan read "Beware of the Khrushchev-type individual and conspirators wishing to usurp the supreme leadership power of the party and the state!" Other slogans blended the terminology of revolution with language traditionally used in China to stiffen resolve in times of danger: "We will defend with our

fresh blood the red mountains and rivers won by innumerable
revolutionary patriots and forefathers with their fresh blood!"

The words may sound strange to foreign ears. Some of the
language evoked the atmosphere of Chinese operas or traditional novels; it was the language of heroism that was alive in the
minds of young Chinese, and using it was one means they had to
pluck up the courage to face danger and prepare themselves for
the possibility of self-sacrifice. It took me a little while to attune
myself to the notion of self-sacrifice, since my generation had
grown up preoccupied with self-fulfillment rather than sacrifice.
We might take a few tips for our style of dress, speech, or walk
from television characters or film actors, but antiheroes rather
than heroes were in mode at our end of the world. As the next
few days would show, the young Chinese were not acting out
any theatrical fantasy but engaging in a deadly political struggle.
To accuse a leading member of the Communist Party of conspir-
ing to seize supreme power was a crime punishable by death.

Large crowds gathered and soon slogans and posters spread
through all the main streets of the city. Impassioned speeches
were made in public places and wreaths dedicated to Zhou
began to crowd the pavements on the streets of the city where
he had once lived and worked. Then people carrying the
wreaths flowed out of the side streets and the alleys to form a
great river on the six-mile route from the New Railway Station
to the Yuhuatai, south of the city.

The Yuhuatai is a hillside, blessed by springs, that has long
been held sacred; after their victory in the Civil War, the Communists built there a memorial to one hundred thousand revolutionaries killed by the Nationalists. The name means "Terrace of
the Rain of Flowers," in memory of a day long ago when the
monk Yun Guang preached with such eloquence that flowers
fell like rain upon his congregation. The flowers that the memory of Zhou Enlai brought to the hillside at Qing Ming in 1976
will no doubt be remembered as long as those produced by Yun
Guang's eloquence.

Much care had been lavished on the wreaths. The largest
stood no less than 7.8 meters high, to symbolize Zhou's
seventy-eight years at the time of death. Down the column of

marchers people shouted slogans denouncing the unnamed conspirators who had inspired the Shanghai paper to attack Zhou:
"Haul out the behind-the-scenes backers of *Wenhui Bao!*" "We
will knock down whoever opposes Premier Zhou!" To show that
they numbered Jiang Qing among the conspirators they shouted
"We remember Yang Kaihui [Mao's first love, killed by the
Nationalists]." Despite their anger and their sorrow, the procession moved forward slowly in an orderly manner until they
reached the Yuhuatai and placed the wreaths on the monument
to the martyrs of the revolution.

The rulers of the province of Jiangsu, of which Nanjing is
the capital, had no love for the leftists so they did not suppress
the demonstrators.

On 30 March an army officer earned fame by pasting up in
public places copies of a handbill in which he attacked Zhang
Chunqiao by name as a conspirator and compared him to
Khrushchev. The next day a truck drove into town carrying
twenty managers and workers from a suburban factory. It
stopped in front of an army barracks. A man and a woman got
out and began to paste up a big-character slogan. A crowd
gathered to watch. Each Chinese character was written on a
separate sheet of paper; the slogan began "Strike down the big
careerist and big conspirator . . ." When the character *Zhang*
appeared the people shouted "It is him! It is him!" When the
word *Chun* appeared they called out "That's right! We want to
strike him down! Turn it upside down! Upside down!" (To print
or write the characters of someone's name upside down is an
insult.) When the character *qiao* appeared they shouted "Cross
it out! Cross it out!" (That meant they wanted him to die.)
Three red Xs were slashed across the characters *Zhang Chunqiao.*

Six students from the Nanjing Postal and Telegraph College
went to the New Railway Station to spread their propaganda
among the travelers and to write slogans on the outside of the
railway carriages, so that the protests of Nanjing would be carried through China. Workers at the station opened the gates for
them. Shop assistants brought ink but they decided to paint
their slogans in tar, so they could not be washed off.

The Shanghai Gang was well aware of developments in Nanjing, on which they were receiving daily reports. They blocked the news from the press, television, and radio but could not stop the tar on the railway carriages from carrying its message. When the train arrived in Peking its message spread fast, spurring on people in the capital. One of the Gang then condemned the Nanjing demonstrations as counter-revolutionary and the Nanjing authorities could stall no longer. As word spread that suppression was about to begin, a "Battle Song to Catch the Devil" appeared in Nanjing University, aimed at Jiang Qing and Zhang Chunqiao: "Where the evil wind blows, there is a devil . . . disrupting the party and the army; bringing calamity to the nation and misfortune to the people. . . . Originally named Li Jing, it was changed to Jiang Qing. . . . Its confederate possesses even more devilish tricks. . . . His name is Chunqiao."

The author of the poster was Li Xining; he had written a cogent denunciation of the leftists the preceding year and was already in trouble for that. Now he wrote in his diary: "Hereafter is the time when all sorts of tests will arrive. A revolutionary must face the storms with a smile, shed some blood, suffer some wrong in the interest of the people, and feel no terror of losing his life."

On 3 April, students of the Nanjing Postal and Telegraph College wrote many large slogans on the campus such as "Without fear of imprisonment or death, fight the Khrushchev-type figures to the final end!"

On 4 April, when the news spread that the large slogans on the campus would be removed, Zhang Xiayang, known as the warrior for truth, immediately said "It's all right to remove other slogans, but the one commemorating Premier Zhou must remain."

Just at the moment Nanjing was being silenced Peking was stirring into action. The Four were in the situation of "trying to use ten fingers to catch ten fleas." They might crush a flea here, but others were jumping all around. The Qing Ming festival was used as an occasion to demonstrate loyalty to Zhou and hostility toward the leftists in at least fourteen provinces and two cities with the status of provinces.[2] Some of these places reported demonstrations "throughout the province." Only the demonstration in Peking was widely reported abroad; it was the only one observed by foreign journalists and diplomats. How easily the world remains ignorant of major events in China!

In the last days of March my wife and I were in Jinan in Shandong province. On our last morning there we saw school children in the streets carrying huge wreaths. I asked our Chinese guide what the children were doing. His reply was bland: "They are preparing for the festival when we commemorate our revolutionary heroes and other dead." Only the next day, when I saw what was happening in Peking, did I realize that the Jinan children were probably starting their own commemoration of Zhou.

On 30 March the first wreath dedicated to Zhou was placed on the Heroes' Monument in Tiananmen Square. From then on, more and more groups came to the square to honor Zhou with wreaths and poems. At first they were just a trickle, but by Friday, 2 April, the trickle had grown to a stream and I estimated ten thousand people were on the square.

The Party leadership of Peking, under orders from the Four, sent an urgent notice to all units, civilian and military: "Don't go to Tiananmen to lay wreaths . . . Qing Ming is for ghosts. . . . Commemorating the dead is an outmoded custom." But all over Peking telephones were busy as people spread the news of the movement from office to office, factory to factory and school to school. "Are you going?" "Yes. Are you?" were words exchanged time and again. So as I drove back to Tiananmen on Saturday morning, I saw a great river of people flowing to the square. The Avenue of Eternal Peace was choked with columns of marchers, each column bearing its wreath dedicated to Zhou.

The wreaths were elaborately wrought of homemade flowers of silk paper. White, the traditional mourning color of China, predominated, but red and yellow, the colors in the national flag, were also much used. In the center of some wreaths a hammer and sickle, symbol of the Party, contrasted with a red background, but thousands more were formed around a portrait of the late Premier. Since the marchers were coming to the square in contravention of official instructions, the police did not deploy extra men to govern the flow of columns or to ensure that other traffic was not disrupted. But the very reason these men and women were marching was a longing for order, stability, and a return to those civilized values that Zhou Enlai embodied. Theirs was a counter-movement to the nihilism and violence of the Cultural Revolution. The disruption of traffic was kept to a minimum.

All day, an unbroken succession of columns numbering tens, hundreds, and even thousands of people entered the square and moved through the vast crowd until they came near to the Heroes' Monument. There, in the center of the square, they formed ranks, their wreaths on stands facing them, to hold brief but solemn ceremonies like those performed there in January, to dedicate their wreaths to Zhou and their lives to the defense of his ideas.*

From each wreath hung two broad ribbons of white silk on which were brushed in black ink words of homage to Zhou and the name of the unit that had made it. A few were dedicated to other dead heroes and heroines, among them the extrovert Chen Yi, the former Foreign Minister who had been very close to Zhou. (Chen, a man who loved life, wrote good poetry, and appreciated the ladies, had courageously denounced the excesses of the Cultural Revolution to Mao's face.) Others paid tribute to He Long, a handsome veteran marshal who had been a great guerilla fighter with a base independent of Mao's. He Long, it was widely believed, had attempted to organize a military opposition to the Cultural Revolution. Yang Kaihui, Mao's

* This account is based partly on my own observation during many hours spent on the Square over four days, partly on a very full account published by the New China News Agency on 22 November 1978, and partly on the observations of other foreign diplomats and journalists in Peking; my debt to my Japanese colleagues is especially great. The facts reported by NCNA coincided closely with the observation of foreign eyewitnesses, but the NCNA interpretation of those facts differed from mine in one major respect: NCNA said the crowds were opposed only to the Gang of Four and not to Mao. This of course was the official line at the time NCNA published its account. At that time all mistakes committed in the last ten years of Mao were officially attributed to Lin Biao and the Gang of Four. Statements made to me in November 1978 by dozens of young Chinese who took part in the demonstrations support my interpretation.

first love, was commemorated too—in an obvious slight to Jiang Qing.

These wreaths were the first things I had seen since my return to China that had been made with love and indeed reverence, the first things I had seen that were beautiful.

They were borne slowly down the avenue by columns of men and women dressed in their drab, dark cotton working clothes. They marched in silence except when they raised the strain of the *"Internationale"* or the national anthem. I was reminded of a Lenten procession I once saw in the Spanish town of Córdoba. There was the same alternation between silence and singing, the same contrast between the dark clothes of those who walked and the bright beauty of what they carried. But in Peking there was a tension I had not sensed in Spain, because these people were bearing their flowers as gentle arms to fight a battle that would decide how they would live for years to come. They were defying the will of their supreme ruler and could therefore expect, under the normal criteria for judgment, to be treated as counter-revolutionaries. That would mean a long term in a labor camp, or execution. (Indeed, Jiang Qing and her allies had already deemed the demonstrations counter-revolutionary.)

Standing beside the wreath brought by his column, a spokesman would deliver a eulogy to Zhou. Here is part of one:

> He left no inheritance, he had no children, he has no grave, he left no remains. His ashes were scattered over the mountains and rivers of our land. It seems he left us nothing, but he will live forever in our hearts. The whole land is his, he has hundreds of millions of children and grandchildren and all China's soil is his tomb. So he left us everything. He will live in our hearts for all time. Who is he? Who is he? He is our Premier!

Sometimes the eulogy would be a poem, and it was remarkable to find that, despite the years of suppression of China's literary and spiritual heritage, one poem after another fused social and political ideals of 1976 with traditional imagery, and expressed a conviction that a good man's spirit lives on after death.

Here is part of one poem, read by a young woman steel-worker:

> To the bitter cold wind which is rising, we ask,
> Do you suppose you can topple this mountain peak?
> To the river of time we say,
> You cannot sweep our thoughts of the Premier away. . . .

> For more than fifty years, to the end of your life
> You fought without rest, beloved Premier,
> Until today we see our country red as the Party's banner
> And you take your eternal sleep beneath the earth.

> No, you are still living,
> In the fields and in the factories.
> You are in the barracks and the sentry posts,
> Your ideals are written into the oath taken by your successors,
> Your spirit is dissolved in our blood,
> Your smile warms our heart like the spring breeze,
> The sound of your steps mingles with the tramp of our
>   revolutionary army.

The young woman who read the poem to the crowd took it to its climax, looking forward to the year set by Zhou as the target date for the modernization of China:

> Look at tomorrow's world,
> The wind unfurls the red flag.
> When the year 2000 comes, if we are still alive . . .

She paused and her audience chuckled, for they knew the risks they were running.

> . . . if we are still alive,
> We will cup our hands to raise up water
> From the rivers of this old land
> And we'll scoop up our Chinese earth.
> Then you will hear us shout
> Toward the past, toward the future,
> Toward the sea, toward the mountains,
> Beloved Premier Zhou, look!
> We have fulfilled your will!

The eulogy over, the group would raise their right fists, clenched in the Communist salute, and pledge to fight for

Zhou's honor and for his ideals, often mentioning the Four Modernizations. It was a fight that, for all they knew, might last years and claim many lives. During the ceremony there were tears in many eyes, young and old, but I saw no one break down. They brought the ceremony to a close by placing their wreaths in the lines of thousands of other wreaths. Then they broke ranks and moved around the square, taking in the spectacle.

The base of the Heroes' Monument was smothered with wreaths to a height of fifty feet. Baskets of flowers were hung from lamp posts and the evergreen hedges at the base of the monument bloomed again with white silk flowers people had taken from their lapels. Poems written on pages of exercise books were pasted to the base of the monument or to the marble balustrades around it. People crowded around the base of the monument to copy poems and the inscriptions on wreaths into notebooks. So dense was the press of bodies that those at the front had to read them out for those at the back. A poem that drew a large crowd was:

> The five great mountains and the forests of our country are sobbing and sighing.
> The bones of this loyal man still retain his warmth, although his soul has departed.
> The four seas, our rivers and our lakes shed tears. . . .
>
> Qing Ming is approaching,
> The whole nation's wound is throbbing again.
> Although it seems that darkness is spreading everywhere
> And wild ghosts whisper nervously to each other,
> The keeper of accounts in the spirit world declares your account to be cleared. . . .
>
> The golden cock flies up to the mountain peak to crow three times,
> The sun comes out again
> And the world sees
> That its hero lives forever.
> Take up Premier Zhou's heritage!

Most poems and inscriptions were simple eulogies for Zhou, but others expressed defiance and anger at those who were destroying his political legacy. There were numerous warnings against Khrushchev-type plotters maneuvering for power. Allegory, of course, was much used and the wealth of opportunity that Chinese offers for punning was fully exploited. The most striking of the allegorical poems was one written on four ten-foot-high placards which were given pride of place on the monument:

> The red heart has borne the fruits of victory,
> Loyal blood will make the flowers of revolution bloom again.
> If there are monsters who spit out poisonous fire
> There will be men who dare to seize them.

A reasonable paraphrase of this poem would be: Zhou Enlai won victories in his lifetime. His loyal successors will revive the revolution. If evil men and women try to sabotage the revolution, there will be people who dare to fight them. On the surface this was innocuous, but closer study reveals political barbs. The Chinese expression used for "loyal blood" in the second line was *bi xue*, literally "jade blood." This was a reference to a hero in Sichuan province in the Zhou dynasty who had been so loyal to his leader that, after his death, his blood turned into precious jade. These allusions to the Zhou dynasty and to Sichuan made one think of Deng Xiaoping, the designated successor in the Zhou dynasty and a native of Sichuan province. The character used for "monster" in the third line was pronounced *yao*, an obvious reference to Yao Wenyuan, one of the Shanghai gang. The same character had a female connotation; that pointed to the female member of the Gang of Four, Jiang Qing.

The four lines were so provocative a battle song that they were removed by the authorities when night fell. Just as provocative but much less prominently displayed were these lines by a young man who had been infuriated by the antirightist campaign of the preceding months:

> Devils howl as we pour out our grief,
> We weep but the wolves laugh,
> We shed our blood in memory of the hero,
> Raising our heads, we unsheath our swords.[3]

Another short poem reminded people that, even if their foes were invisible, they were close at hand:

Before the Monument at this Qing Ming the people form a real
   tide.
A mountain of flowers has been brought from all directions.
On every continent people are thinking of our Premier.
Children sob too: even they feel grief.
In their sadness, people call to the Premier.
But be watchful, for there are traitors about. . . .

A black wind is starting to blow again.
Angry eyes look to the northwest,
Where there are people who do not bring flowers.

The houses of the Chairman and members of the Politburo
lay just to the northwest of the square. What reports were reaching Mao? Was he being given a balanced account of what was
going on a few hundred yards from the little house where he
now spent all his days? Was his mind still clear enough to grasp
the true meaning of what he was told, and was he still capable of
giving coherent instructions for handling the dangerous situation that was developing? Did Acting Premier Hua Guofeng
have access to Mao, or was his way blocked by Jiang Qing and
her cohorts?

Deng was under house arrest; Li Xiannian and Ye Jianying,
the other two veterans of great authority, had stood aside, and
Hua could hardly challenge instructions brought supposedly
from the Chairman's bedside by Jiang Qing or push her aside if
she claimed the Chairman was too ill to see him. At this moment, when the government faced its greatest crisis of authority
since the Communists had come to power in 1949, there was
something close to a vacuum where supreme authority should
have been.

In the square, men and women were coming forward one
after another to warn of the dangers that menaced their country.
Some spoke or wrote in general terms:

"Who is trying to reverse the verdict on Premier Zhou?"

"We will fight a bloody battle against whoever attacks our
Premier Zhou or whoever wants to reverse the verdicts on him."

"Be on your guard, especially against Khrushchev-type
careerists and conspirators. We don't want people like that to
usurp leading power in Party and state."

"A generation of heroes created our world
Millions of people are worried
Who will succeed them?"

"For two weeks, we made wreaths, wrote poems, and prepared
to come to the Heroes' Memorial to mourn beloved Premier
Zhou. But on 3 April the Krushchev-style careerists in the Party,
with evil in their hearts, began to show their true colors. They
tried to stop us coming. These conspirators use Marxism as a guise
for their evil intention. These traitors will never be acceptable to
the people. They are attempting to change the direction of the
Party . . . and the people are dissatisfied. We are Premier Zhou's
successors."

Others identified their targets more sharply:
"Long live Chairman Mao! Down with Indira Gandhi!"
could only refer to one woman in China.
" 'Shining Bald' Zhang and Jiang are whipping up a counter-
current" was a plain enough reference to the bald pate of Yao
Wenyuan, to Zhang Chunqiao and Jiang Qing. Few people included Wang Hongwen in the group of targets for their anger.
In the popular mind the major villains numbered three, not four
as later: "Three people are but a small handful, but 800 million
are a mass" was a typical reference to the objects of popular
distrust. The Shanghai paper that had attacked Zhou on 25
March was the object of a denunciation really intended for those
leaders who must have given the order for its attack.
On the front of the monument was a poem titled "Call to
Arms at the Qing Ming Festival." It included this succinct
statement on the tactics of the Shanghai Gang and their allies in
Liaoning province who were led by Mao's nephew, Mao Yuanxin.

Today we respect our dear departed, but those people are worse
than ever.
They declare themselves against outmoded customs, but they are
really up to mischief. . . .
When you get to the root,
It's the cliques of Shanghai and Liaoning.
Consumed by thirst for fame and by avarice,
Burning to set up their own dynasty,

Abducting the Emperor to lead all the others,
"Better left than right," just like in Lin Biao's clique.

Wending my way through the crowd, reading inscription after inscription and poem after poem, I realized that I was watching not just the defense of Zhou or a protest against Jiang Qing and her allies, but defiance of Mao. The press had made it quite clear that he was the initiator of the campaign that had aroused the anger and anxiety of so many people, and he had not denied it. Had he wished to dissociate himself from Jiang Qing or Yao Wenyuan he could have done so with the greatest of ease—had he not dissociated himself from the far more substantial figure of Deng Xiaoping? The protestors made the Shanghai Gang the target of their attacks, knowing that if they swung the political balance against the left Mao would swing with it, the Shanghai Gang would be eclipsed and Deng restored to power. To bring down Jiang Qing and her friends, difficult and dangerous though it would be given Mao's backing for them, was less impossible than taking on Mao himself. She and her allies had neither his past achievements to fall back on nor a cult of deification to hold men's minds in thrall.

This defiance of Mao was not the work of "the masses" alone. Among the thousands of wreaths were ones sent by ministries of the central government, departments of the central command of the People's Liberation Army, and military units stationed on China's frontiers as well as factories, schools, stores, and communes in the Peking area.

Despite the anger that smoldered in the crowd of several hundred thousand that filled the square on that Saturday afternoon, order prevailed. In the turmoil of the 1960s I had watched students and workers in Europe and America resort to violence and obscenity to express their views, but here in Peking the Chinese used flowers and poetry. So orderly was the behavior that my wife and I decided to take our two daughters, aged two and four, to the square the next day.

On Sunday afternoon there were even larger crowds, but, seeing our daughters, they opened a path for us in whichever direction we pointed the girls.

For the first time at a Chinese political event I found I was allowed to be more than a mute spectator. People wanted to know how I felt about Zhou and accepted my respect for him as sincere. They helped me read inscriptions, although they would not interpret the political allusions into plain language for me or even for each other.

A young man in a flowing scholar's gown of an earlier era stood on a box and denounced *Yao* (demons), which he said were leading the country astray. He too was using *Yao* as a pun on the name of Yao Wenyuan. The crowd around him parted to let a Reuters correspondent, Peter Griffiths, hold up a microphone to record his speech attacking "the new Empress Dowager [Madame Mao]" and praising the Four Modernizations. An old man turned to Griffiths to ask if he had a good recording. He played back the last few passages, in which the speaker praised Zhou. As Griffiths left them to visit other parts of the square, the crowd cheered and clapped and roared approval for the British journalist.

Walking from one part of the vast square to another, I found a kaleidoscope of self-dramatization, humorous invention, pathos, and somber defiance.

A young railway worker wrote in his own blood on a piece of white brocade a pledge to defend Zhou's ideals: "Dear Premier Zhou, we shall defend you with our very lives!" He showed it to hundreds who gathered around him and became a hero instantly.

Overhead I watched balloons, filled with hydrogen and anchored to lamp posts, lift white streamers high above the square. Impudently they carried the messages "Remember our Premier" and "Carry the Revolution through to the End" over the ocher-red walls of the Imperial City to the residences of Mao, the Shanghai Gang, and other Politburo members inside the Zhongnanhai.

A young man taught several thousand people to sing a slow lament he had written for Zhou. He stood on a pedestal to be seen and heard by those around him, and I noticed he was wearing a jacket, not in the Mao style with turned-down collar and plastic buttons, but in the pre-1949 style with a stand-up collar and cloth buttons. Under his arm on the gray, drizzling afternoon was an umbrella: not one of the plastic ones now sold in Peking but one made in the old way, of oiled paper. He surely intended his archaic dress to recall that of the young men who had come to the original Tiananmen Square, a smaller place, on 4 May 1919 and, by their demonstration against the feudal rulers of their time, had launched the great movement of national renewal that came to be known as the May Fourth Movement. For years that movement had hardly been mentioned in public, since the Chinese revolution had been made synonymous with the history of the Communist Party. But Zhou Enlai's first political action had been in support of it. Now, almost fifty years later, this young man and many in his generation were evoking its spirit to struggle against what they saw as a new kind of feudal rule. Here was clear assurance that not all the young had lost their sense of historical perspective.

The hundreds of thousands on the square that afternoon came from all levels of society, ranging from high officials to the poorest of peasants. Senior cadres in their expensive woolen topcoats lined up to have their presence recorded by a photographer they had brought with them. A shabbily dressed, deeply tanned peasant woman breast-fed her baby on the steps of the monument as her husband gazed around in wonderment. An old woman with bound feet and clothes faded from many scrubbings tottered through the crowd to lay a plate of dumplings at the base of the monument as her offering to the memory of Zhou Enlai. There were people there from towns hundreds, even thousands of miles from Peking. Some of them no doubt were in Peking on official business, but others seemed to have come because they knew of preparations under way in their home towns for smaller demonstrations of a similar character and they expected that there would be a large-scale demonstration in Peking; they wanted to be part of it.

As a memorial for Zhou, this people's ceremony was more moving than any state funeral I have seen. As a political demonstration, it was utterly unlike anything I had ever seen in China. I had watched countless officially organized rallies and marches, complete with gongs and drums, slogans and banners—all carefully prepared under party orders—and usually they amounted to nothing more than ritual. But for Zhou the crowds were acting out of conviction, and their creative powers were working as I had never seen them work before. As the language and the imagery of the poems showed, streams of thought and feeling and ways of expressing these thoughts and feelings that had been flowing underground for years surfaced on Tiananmen Square on these days. I was watching not only a funeral and a demonstration but also a liberation of the Chinese spirit.

There was a mixture of emotions that I had never encountered before. There was anger at what had been done to the legacy of Zhou; there was a spirit of revolt against Mao for his part in that; there was apprehension for the future of China and defiance of those who would certainly seek to punish the demonstrators. But there were gentler feelings also. There was the affection the memory of Zhou evoked, the joy of realizing how widely shared their feelings were, delight and pride that they were freeing themselves from the worship of a demigod. An outsider could not but ask himself whether the people were not substituting a new demigod, Zhou, for the old one, Mao, but for the moment no one seemed worried by that.

A poem that conveyed better than most others the feelings interwoven in those days was "Cherish the Memory of Premier Zhou at Qing Ming." It begins with an apology to Zhou that his soul cannot yet rest in peace (because his enemies are trying to undo his work). But he should know that this is not because the people do not cherish his memory; on the contrary, their grief at his death is so deep that they can find no way of adequately expressing their feelings. The poem continues by castigating those who are maneuvering to gain control of the country and make Jiang Qing "Empress" (Chairman of the Communist Party). They are a ridiculous bunch of apes who overestimate their strength. The people can no longer be treated like feudal serfs: the day of Qin Shi Huang (Mao) has gone. If the apes persist in trying to turn the clock back and to emasculate Marxism–Leninism then those who are loyal to the memory of Zhou Enlai will, if need be, take to the hills again to raise a new guerrilla army, as Mao once did in the Jinggang Mountains:

Revered Premier Zhou
Your sons and daughters feel a sense of guilt that
Your noble soul cannot, to this day, rest in peace.

Even with our heart's blood
We could not show how we cherish your memory;
We could not fully express our sorrow and indignation
Even though we pour out all our tears.

History has placed its highest value on your life,
More brilliant than the sun and the moon are your
Meritorious deeds, and the heavens echo with your voice.
In the annals of international affairs,
There will always be a page for your image.
Every inch of the revolutionary road
Bears your footprints.
Winds and storms rose, and gods wept,
Heaven and earth were plunged into deep sorrow as the giant
     star fell.
Flags flew at half-mast everywhere across the five continents
     and four seas.

Despicable are the demons who, overrating themselves,
Once again attempt to stir up evil winds and bloody rains,
Talking glibly and carrying their mistress' train*
—what a ridiculous lot they are, a bunch of monkeys
Trying to crown themselves!
Ants on the locust tree assume a great-nation swagger
And Mayflies lightly plot to topple the giant tree.

Look around, you despicable lot:
Flowers blanket Tiananmen Square like snow
And tears fall in showers around the monument.
We cherish the memory of Premier Zhou; but you do not.
We offer our libation; but you do not.
China is no longer the China of the past,
And the people are no longer wrapped in utter ignorance,
Gone for good is Qin Shi Huang's feudal society,
We believe in Marxism–Leninism,
To hell with scholars who emasculate Marxism–Leninism!

What we want is genuine Marxism–Leninism,
For the sake of genuine Marxism–Leninism,
We don't fear to sh d our blood and lay down our lives,
And we will not he iitate to climb the Jinggang Mountains again,
     to rise in rebellion.

* The train of the dress Jiang Qing would wear if she were crowned
Empress.

We will carry forward Premier Zhou's behest.
The day the Four Modernizations are realized,
We will come to offer our libation and sacrifices.
Rest well,
Our respected and beloved Premier Zhou.

When I left the square in the late afternoon, new columns were still arriving with their wreaths. When I returned for a last look around at midnight most people had gone home and only a few small groups remained here and there, reading posters with the help of a flashlight or discussing the events of the day. But the huge square was far from empty. With the crowds gone I could see clearly the multitude of wreaths that had been brought there in the past few days. Row upon row of wreaths dedicated to Zhou, many bearing his portrait, were arrayed on their stands, facing the Gate of Heavenly Peace. They advanced northward from the monument to the very edge of the square, so that an army of Zhou Enlais confronted the portrait of Mao that hung on the Gate. Birnam Wood had come to Dunsinane. As men they had never clashed in public, but here the images of the dead Zhou and the dying Mao were arrayed against each other.

The political heart of China had been occupied by forces fighting for a vision that rivaled Mao's. The essential message of the flowers was simple: the Mandate of Heaven had been removed from Mao.

What was to be done? Should Hua Guofeng consult the Chairman, or was Mao too old and sick to be allowed to decide? Given the difficulty of communicating with him, was it fair to him or the country to put any responsibility upon him at this moment of crisis? And yet who would dare propose that the Chairman be excluded from the decision?

By a process that was not to be revealed to the public, a decision was made on how to react.

In the early hours of 5 April, before first light, two hundred trucks belonging to Peking Municipality drove onto the square. The wreaths were tossed unceremoniously into them and driven away. Some of those who had watched over them through the night protested; they were seized and thrown into prison. These were not the first arrests: in the preceding two days twenty-six people had already been arrested quietly, out of sight of the square. Others who saw the wreaths taken away ran to spread the word through the city. The news spread like wildfire, and as 5 April dawned people began streaming back to the square, this time as individuals rather than groups. They saw that the wreaths had indeed been taken away and the poems torn down. Pools of water lay on the ground where the poems had been scrubbed from the base of the monument. Three rings of guards surrounded the monument.

No attempt was made to defuse the situation by explaining, for instance on the radio or in the press, why the wreaths had been removed and why the usual Qing Ming practice of leaving them in place for a week would not be followed.

People were seething with anger at the way their homage to Zhou had been tossed aside. They saw the clearing of the square overnight as a massive insult to them and to Zhou Enlai. News of the arrests made in the past few days had also become widely known, adding fuel to the flames of popular anger.

In the first incident of the day, thirty teenagers from Peking Middle School 172 marched to the monument to present a wreath as a token replacement for those that had been taken away. Their way was blocked by the three lines of guards.

At about 8 A.M. I arrived at the square to find ten thousand people there already. Incongruously, this grim morning was bathed in spring sunlight whereas the days of flowers and poems had been overcast and rainy. The focus of attention was now the Great Hall of the People, because the crowd believed the wreaths had been taken there. Facing the east façade of the Great Hall, the crowd shouted "Give back our wreaths! Give back our comrades-in-arms!"

A police loudspeaker van appeared in the roadway on the east side of the hall and drove slowly through the crowd. From the van a young policewoman broadcast an appeal to the crowd to disperse and not to be led astray by "a handful of class enemies." Hundreds of people blocked the path and protested against the allegation that they were following class enemies. They pulled the police out and overturned the van that, for them, had become a symbol of the distortion and suppression of their homage to Zhou. They let the police go unharmed after forcing them to apologize for what they had said.

Massed on the steps and in the forecourt of the east entrance to the Great Hall, thousands of people continued to shout their demands for the return of their wreaths and the release of those arrested. "Long live the people!" the shout went up, and a cry of frustrated young people could be heard also: "Give us back our youth!" A student from Qinghua University called out that their demands were wrong and that there was no reason to present wreaths to Zhou Enlai: "He was the biggest capitalist-roader in the Party!"

The crowd rounded on him in fury. He was dragged over to the Heroes' Monument and forced to retract his words. According to one account, he was severely beaten.*

By contrast, the police, militia, and army deployed on the square that morning and afternoon were very restrained. They used no weapons and I was impressed by their patient efforts to minimize the confrontation. Some openly expressed sympathy with the demonstrators.

From about eleven o'clock the focus of attention shifted again, to a building in the southeast corner of the square that was being used as the tactical command post for the security forces. Thousands of demonstrators linked arms and marched toward the building singing the *"Internationale."* They halted before a human wall of militia. A group of four formed to negotiate with the commander for the release of the wreaths and those arrested. Among them were young students. The militia refused them entry to the command post, so they vaulted over the human wall and ran into the building. While they were inside some demonstrators urged the crowd to refrain from violence. But when the negotiators returned to report that neither the commander nor anyone else would negotiate with them, the anger of the crowd rose again. For two hours they did nothing,

* According to usually reliable sources in Peking, this student and eleven others were acting under orders from Vice-Chairman Wang Hongwen, who, together with the other members of the Shanghai Gang, was following developments from inside the Great Hall. Some of these alleged *agents provocateurs* who were rash enough to return to the Great Hall were reportedly sent away to be shot, to prevent them betraying Vice-Chairman Wang. (See also Section 7 of the NCNA account published on 22 November 1978.)

but then they turned to destruction to vent their feelings. Having left the square around midday I returned in the late afternoon to find that a car, two jeeps, and a minibus had been burned.

Now young men were storming the command post. They broke into it, damaged the ground floor and set it on fire; its occupants escaped by a back window. Smoke drifted across the square and the acrid smell of burnt rubber mingled with the sweeter scent of burning pinewood.

Still no counterattack was made by the security forces: they had passively prevented entry to the Great Hall and the Museum of Revolutionary History but had made no arrests. They had limited themselves to removing wreaths laid on the Heroes' Monument during the day.

Most of the crowd, which numbered tens of thousands in place of the hundreds of thousands of the days before, stood at a safe distance watching as a few score youths burned the building. They did not welcome foreigners as they had the day before. They were clearly saddened and angered that their peaceful demonstration had been turned to violence by the removal of the wreaths. Peter Griffiths, the Reuters correspondent who had been cheered by the crowd the day before, took some photographs and slipped the cassette of exposed film into his pocket. A few moments later he was surrounded by a group of angry young men demanding the film. He handed them an unused cassette and they ripped the film out, handing it back in a bundle. A Japanese correspondent was less fortunate: he was seized while trying to take pictures and was dragged into the crowd. He had his camera broken, his fountain pen and reporter's pad taken away, and was beaten until his eyes were swollen.

Undeterred by his earlier experience and ignorant of the fate of his Japanese colleague, Peter Griffiths returned to the square to make a sound recording. Again a crowd surged around him, someone tried to snatch the recorder, and he was swept from his feet. He was grabbed and frog-marched to a military post within the walls of the Forbidden City. After a long interrogation, during which security police listened to the tape several times, he was set free with the recording in his pocket.

At 6:30 P.M., the time Peking takes its evening meal, the loudspeakers on the square were switched on and the Mayor of Peking, Wu De, broadcast a somber appeal to the crowd to disperse and not to "fall into the trap which had been set for them." Most people then left the square, but about four thousand remained. They realized there was no hope now of recovering the wreaths, but they chose to continue their protest and face the consequences. As darkness fell they gathered around the Heroes' Monument. The city around them was silent; to strengthen their resolve for the long night ahead they sang the "Internationale" once again.

It was the last time they would sing together on the square. A young man recited in a hoarse voice one last poem for Zhou Enlai, "Farewell":

> How I wish, how I wish I had cloud-ascending wings,
> To soar to the Ninth Heaven and call on your loyal soul;
> To hear your words full of feeling
> And see your compassionate eyes.

> How I wish, how I wish I were Wu Gang the moondweller,
> And could serve you the mellowest wine;
> But all I can send to the Ninth Heaven are my laments,
> All I can offer you are these mourning lines.

Suddenly at 9:35 all the lights in the square were switched on, making it almost as bright as day, and loudspeakers blared a military song. Thousands of men with Workers Militia armbands and staves marched out of the Imperial City, where they had been gathered during the day. They began to clear the square, surrounding one section of the crowd at a time. They blocked the exits to prevent escape. Staves rose and fell. Bodies slumped on the ground. Men screamed in agony. Blood stained the paving stones. Young men drew pocket knives to defend themselves, to no avail. Hundreds, at least, were marched or dragged to the Imperial City, and thence to prison.*

---

* It has not been clearly established how many people were beaten and killed that night. All accounts, including that published three days later by the *People's Daily*, agree that there was violence. A Hong Kong magazine has published what it claims was a speech made by Yang Gui, a vice-minister of public security, a few weeks after the demonstrations. In it he is reported to have said that more than a hundred were killed on 5 April and three or four

For Mao, Qing Ming had been a tragedy tinged with irony. Through the mass movements to collectivize land in the Great Leap Forward and in the Cultural Revolution, he had done more than any other Chinese leader to awaken the political activism of "the masses," and now that activism had been turned against him. On Tiananmen Square in 1949 he had proclaimed the establishment of the Chinese People's Republic and told the people that they had "stood up." On Tiananmen Square in 1966 he had commissioned eleven million young people to fight for his vision. At Qing Ming 1976, many of those who had heard him in 1949, and many of those who had received his commission in 1966, came back to the square with a defiant message for him. Never before in this century had China seen so many of her workers, high officials, intellectuals, soldiers, and peasants join together without the leadership of any Party organization in defiance of the will of their supreme ruler. It was a terrible final act in Mao's political career, and those who claimed to be his most loyal disciples had goaded him into it.

For others, dismay was mixed with new hope. They had been part of a massive display of the ability of the human spirit to withstand long years of totalitarian rule and emerge strengthened. In Guiyang, Huang Xiang, the poet who had described that tyranny seven years before in *I See a War*, wrote "The idol of the past is now tied to the pillar of torture by fire," and on 8 April he composed a poem to express his conviction that the spirit of Tiananmen would rise again:

NO YOU HAVE NOT DIED

Why do you hide your face, Tiananmen Square?
Why do your pale lips quiver, Tiananmen?
Why is your chest bleeding, why does your body shake so violently?
Answer me, Tiananmen!

I know what burning flames and molten lava are hidden in your chest.

---

thousand arrested, of whom most were released the next day. According to a number of wall posters, about four hundred of those arrested continued in detention until November 1976.

I have heard you shake heaven and earth with your furious cries,
And I don't believe that you are just quietly dying,
I don't believe you are closing your eyes forever.
No, you will not die.
You have not died.

The whole world has seen the anger on your face.
Confronted by bayonets and rifle butts,
You did not shrink away.
Abused and trampled on by wild beasts
    without a weapon in your hand,
You held fast, you would not give in.
In a pool of blood, you lay like a hero.
No, you are not dead, Tiananmen.
And you must not die.

You did not lower your banner to surrender it.
Your silken ribbons bearing inscriptions were torn to shreds but
    their wings, red with fire, did not droop.
Your pamphlets and your poems have been gagged
But still they make their hoarse voices heard.
Your hammer-heavy fist still challenges and hits back, without a
    sound.
Your body, battered beyond recognition, still utters a silent ac-
    cusation.
Death has nothing to do with you.
You are invincible

Yes,
I believe freedom will not stop breathing.
Truth will not close its mouth.
There will be a day when you will rise again from the pool of
    blood.
Then you will be ten times, a hundred times, a thousand times
    stronger than today.
You will again raise the banner of awareness,
Win victory over those who once pointed their guns at you,
And you'll proclaim, with all your strength and majesty, the rights
    of man.

On the morning after the rioting, people gathered again on
Tiananmen Square. Groups discussed what should be done.
Some spoke in favor of a sit-down demonstration; others sug-

gested sending petitions to the leadership, and still others called
for parades. A worker from an electronics factory in the eastern
part of the city said "What's the use of a sit-down demonstration,
or petitions or parades? To have strength we have to organize."
He proposed that a "National Committee in Defense of Premier Zhou" be organized throughout the country; his idea was
immediately adopted, and a start was made in organizing provincial branches. But that kind of activity very soon became
impossible.

On 7 April the Politburo met to resolve the immediate
crisis. They approved unanimously a proposal by Mao that
Deng Xiaoping be stripped of all his offices and Hua Guofeng
be made First Vice-Chairman of the Party and continue in the
post of Premier. They condemned the Tiananmen demonstrations as counter-revolutionary. They declared that "the nature of the Deng Xiaoping problem had turned into one of
antagonistic contradiction"—that is, he had become an enemy of
the people. In an important concession to reality, the communiqué ended by saying that he would be allowed "to keep his
Party membership so as to see how he will behave in the future."
This concession showed how unsure was the basis for dismissing
him from office. Had there really been unanimity in the Politburo, Deng—as an "enemy of the people"—would have been
deprived of his Party membership.

This was the gravest crisis in the twenty-seven years of
Communist rule in China. In effect the Politburo had condemned as counter-revolutionaries not only millions of people
in the capital, but also countless thousands or millions who had
participated in similar demonstrations elsewhere. In such a crisis
the fate of all Party officials was engaged, and they stood together. Immediately, all over China, Party, state, and military
leaders organized massive demonstrations to acclaim the Politburo decisions. In Peking, in the middle of the night, scores of
thousands of people marched in procession around Tiananmen
Square banging gongs and drums and acclaiming Mao's name. It
seemed less like a counterdemonstration than an attempt to
drive Zhou's spirit from the square, but the hearts of the marchers were not in it. This was the most mechanical demonstra-

tion I had seen in China. The marchers did not even pretend to believe in the slogans. They mumbled them so that the words were indistinct and shambled along with a completely detached air.

In the weeks that followed Qing Ming, the press presented the Tiananmen Incident as masterminded by Deng to support his own cause, but gave no proof. So far as I could see, a remarkable feature of the demonstrations had been the absence of any mention of Deng.

A witchhunt was set in motion to track down and punish all who had been active in all the demonstrations in China. In Peking alone, according to a Hong Kong report of a speech by Yang Gui, Vice-Minister of Public Security, more than forty thousand were "charged," judged, and punished.* The security forces and the party attempted to suppress the "rumors" circulating about the demonstrations, but it was too late: travelers had spread the news by word of mouth and foreign radio stations received in China had broadcast the news in Chinese and English. (The BBC had broadcast an eyewitness account of the events of 5 April within half an hour of receiving it that day.)

If party officials, whatever their personal views, felt they must stand together, "the masses" also showed solidarity. In many places investigations ran into a wall of silence, there was sullen passivity at meetings to condemn the demonstrations, and many local officials did not press home the investigations. Some people who had copied down the poems and inscriptions preserved their copies by burying them, wrapped in plastic bags, in courtyards, flowerpots, or in caves in the Western Hills. Sixteen teachers from one of the language institutes in Peking collected and sorted hundreds of poems from Tiananmen Square. One of them was arrested, but they persevered. Other groups did likewise.

It became evident that the emotional shock of Qing Ming had weakened Mao physically. When he received the Laotian

* Reports published in the Chinese press in November and December 1978 indicate that in most cases the punishment took the form of public criticism rather than imprisonment. But some of those who had been most active were sentenced to jail for periods of up to twenty years.

prime minister in mid-April the meeting lasted only half an hour, in contrast to the hour and forty minutes Mao had spent with former President Nixon in February. At the end of April he received the New Zealand prime minister for only twenty minutes: Mr. Muldoon found him "frail." In May he met the prime ministers of Singapore and Pakistan. Neither meeting lasted more than twenty minutes and on both occasions the photographs showed Mao slumped in his armchair. Then it was announced he would meet no more foreigners. Perhaps Mao had read the Qing Ming demonstrations as confirmation of his worst fears about the course the country would follow after his death. But he still would not give up his fight against Deng. When Hua stayed behind at the end of the meeting with Prime Minister Muldoon on 30 April to brief him on the unrest in several provinces Mao was in no mood to capitulate. "With you in charge, I am at ease," he told Hua.

Jiang Qing and her allies were elated by Deng's dismissal. They strode the public stage as never before with the spotlight directed on Jiang Qing, as she congratulated those who had suppressed the Tiananmen demonstrations and presided over a May Day parade in the capital. Hua Guofeng was hardly in a position to enjoy his new eminence. To be promoted to First Vice-Chairman, and thereby designated at Mao's successor, over Deng's falling body was hardly an ideal way to climb the political ladder. As Minister of Public Security as well as Prime Minister he had to preside over the unenviable task of restoring discipline after the Qing Ming demonstrations. With Mao unrepentant over the campaign to criticize Deng, Hua had to persevere in leading the Party along that unpopular line. That was far from the end of his discomfort, for it was a year in which nature and man seemed to ally themselves to deliver blow after blow to the stability of society.

In January Zhou had died.

In February the anti-Deng campaign had begun, summoning the ghosts of the Cultural Revolution.

In March there had been a great shower of meteorites in the Northeast, a traditional sign of the approaching collapse of a dynasty.

In April there had been the Qing Ming demonstrations, then Mao's physical decline.

In May and June came reports that bad weather was affecting the harvest.

In early July came the death of Marshal Zhu De, the second great figure of the revolution to die in the year.

In late July the Tangshan earthquake claimed half a million victims, the worst natural disaster in the history of the world.* By Chinese tradition, earthquakes also presage the end of a dynasty.

The press published articles that reminded people of the signs presaging dynastic collapse and argued that no one should believe them, a sure sign that editors knew people were still voicing these old superstitions. All summer long respect for authority declined and social discipline weakened at an alarming pace. Strikes and labor unrest broke out in many places. For example, the heavy machinery plant in Wuhan, one of the largest in the country, shut down for four months; a motorcycle factory in Loyang had to close for four months also. The major tractor factory at Nanchang produced not one tractor from February onward. "Sabotage of production" was officially judged severe in twenty-one of twenty-nine province-level administrations. In Baoding—only a hundred miles southwest of Peking—workers came to many of the factories only once a month, to collect their pay; factory administrators desperately sold off trucks and other equipment to pay the striking workers.

The railway workers of China are a particularly close-knit and powerful group; in a country with a few trunk roads they learned to use their economic muscle long before the Communists came to power, and have never forgotten. In 1976 they drastically reduced the flow of goods through the national economy, and nowhere did they tighten their stranglehold more than in the strategic corridor from eastern China to the nation's far West, Xinjiang.

Peasants in many communes broke up collective landholdings to engage in individual farming.

* 240,000 dead and 164,000 seriously injured, according to official Chinese estimates published in November 1979.

The crime rate climbed steeply. For the first time one began to hear of bank robberies and the mass looting of goods depots at railway yards. Mobs broke into state granaries.

The rules laid down by the Central Committee for the conduct of the anti-Deng campaign were flouted in many places. "Fighting groups" were formed in violation of the rules and open attacks made on party offices and officials in a number of provinces. Official archives were robbed. Military armories were broken into and arms seized for factional warfare. Factions that had existed during the Cultural Revolution, but had then been disbanded, reformed under their old leaders and with the same membership. The commander of the armed forces on the front facing Taiwan died under mysterious circumstances and the Hong Kong press quoted travelers from that region as saying that he had been shot down by one of his own men while flying in a helicopter. Military barracks were attacked and military units fought pitched battles with armed groups.

In August, the top leaders of Shanxi province were kidnapped.* The incipient anarchy in the provinces was mirrored by signs of dissension at the center. In July the *People's Daily* published tentative allegorical attacks on Hua by writers who were clearly taking their orders from Jiang Qing and her friends. They accused Hua of having sold out to the right. Many ministers and senior officials feigned illness in hospital; others simply stayed home. This unofficial strike action was referred to privately as laying down the carrying pole (*liao tiao-zi*).

In late August and early September, the party leadership knew that Mao would not live long. As they waited for the death wind to blow they prepared the people psychologically, instructing them that when death came they should keep calm and "turn grief into strength."

When the news came that Mao had died in the early hours of 9 September people did keep calm. There were many who wept, but there was not the same stunned grief as there had been for Zhou. People were anxious for their future but put

* All this information is drawn from reports published by the official Chinese news media after October 1976, much of it confirmed by Chinese travelers arriving in Hong Kong.

much time into decorating shops, markets, cinemas, and other public places with yellow-and-black drapery and a profusion of white silk-paper flowers. The vehicles that brought "the masses" to the memorial ceremony at Tiananmen were decorated with huge white silk flowers—displays that struck more than one observer as ambivalent.

People in Peking were tense as they waited to see what would happen next. I thought often of something Jiang Qing's biographer, Roxane Witke, had told a gathering of American sinologists in 1975. She reported that Jiang Qing believed that, when Chairman Mao died, her enemies would move against her and would try to arrest her within a month of his death.* Jiang Qing's actions since her interviews with Witke had hardly diminished the hostility of her opponents toward her. Her chief opponent, Deng Xiaoping, was alive and well and in no mood for conciliation.

Soon after his dismissal he had been escorted from Peking to Canton by his supporter, General Xü Shiyu. Xü's command covered most of South China and he had strong influence over the armed forces of Central China, having served there as commander from 1954 to 1973. Deng remained in the South under he protection of General Xü and the leader of Guangdong province, W. i Guoqing. Deng received visitors but did not show himself in public. Two of his allies, Minister of Defense Ye Jianying and the economic technocrat Li Xiannian, returned to public life to prevent the launching of a mass movement of the type of the Cultural Revolution. Marshall Ye spent some of his time in Guangdong, his native province, and conferred with Deng while he was there. To meet Ye, Deng traveled discreetly in a police van with covered windows.

The deposed Vice-Premier strengthened the resolve of his allies to regain the leadership of the country. Speaking at the hot-springs resort of Conghua, Deng set out the choice for his friends and allies:

> Either we accept the fate of being slaughtered and let the Party and the country degenerate, let the country which was founded with

---

* This story was not included in Witke's biography of Jiang Qing.

the heart and soul of our proletarian revolutionaries of the old generation be destroyed by those four people, and let history retrogress one hundred years, or we should struggle against them as long as there is still any life in our body. If we win, everything can be solved. If we lose, we can take to the mountains for as long as we live or we can find a shield in other countries, to wait for another opportunity. At present, we can use at least the strength of the Canton Military Region, the Fuzhou Military Region, and the Nanjing Military Region to fight against them. Any procrastination and we will risk losing this, our only capital.[4]

After the death of Mao in September, Deng's allies were in no mood to procrastinate.

7

The Fall of
the Gang of Four

IN THE WEEKS after Mao's death on 9 September 1976 Hua Guofeng came under pressure from both ends of the political spectrum.

The leftists had to rely mainly on control of the media and redoubled efforts to create a climate of opinion that would support their claims to the succession or, at the very least, increase the risks inherent in any move to oust them from power.

Behind all the ideological justification, all the talk about the correct revolutionary line, the left's appeal, such as it was, rested on two down-to-earth motives: the fear of those who had climbed up the ladder during the Cultural Revolution that the rightists were getting ready to push them down again to make room for their own and the dissatisfaction felt by all who resented the privileges enjoyed by party officials and the controls imposed by the Party. In theory, this was a strategy with political appeal, but in practice the Jiang Qing faction was regarded by some as politically incompetent and by others as hypocritical, having itself become identified with the system of repression and privilege-seeking.

Since Qing Ming at least, the leftists must have realized how many of "the masses" did not regard them as the shining champions of their cause, but they had no alternative to challenging

Hua for the leadership and attempting to destroy a large number of their opponents on the right. They might be damned if they did, but they would certainly be damned if they did not. The position was desperate but, like gamblers with only one card left to play, they had better play it. That their tactics of the past nine months had caused increasing disorder in the nation worried them not at all. Chaos was their friend, order their enemy. Out of chaos they might somehow snatch victory.

During the summer months they had published a few articles designed to undermine Hua, but these had been low-key. After Mao's death they pulled out the stops and brought their biggest propaganda gun to bear: the team of writers whose articles were published under the pseudonym Liang Xiao. Articles appearing under this name were studied intently by millions of Chinese and combed for their open or encoded message. On 4 October, a major Liang Xiao article more clearly than anything published before denounced Hua as a new rightist figure who had emerged to succeed such older rightists as Deng Xiaoping. As soon as this appeared, another Liang Xiao article was prepared for publication. The second one would come within a hairbreadth of making an open call for an insurrection against Hua. It was written at a moment when the left saw its enemies closing in.

The right knew that the death of Mao had created the opportunity for which it had waited many years. The greatest antirightist of all was dead, and the events of 1976 had demonstrated the unpopularity of those who wanted to preserve his policies and his cult. Now, if ever, was the chance to implement the right's brand of pragmatism and exact revenge for the Cultural Revolution.

The Commander of the Canton Military Region, burly, gold-toothed General Xü Shiyu, was one of the right's most aggressive spokesmen. This came as no surprise to his colleagues. He was hot-blooded by temperament and his life had had the flavor of a traditional Chinese novel. The son of poor peasants in Hubei, he had dropped out of school at an early age and then wandered as a vagabond until he entered the Shaolin monastery. It was not religious faith so much as an adventurous temperament that took him there: the monastery was famous for teaching the martial arts. The monks instilled in Xü Shiyu the tradition of being ready "to draw the sword to help all who suffer injustice." In the Civil War against the Nationalists he had displayed extraordinary courage in battle, and he had been made a corps commander at twenty-seven. His troops called him Ironsides because he brooked no indiscipline. He had clashed with Mao on several occasions, starting in Yanan during the war against Japan, when he led four hundred military students in a protest against the way Mao was treating them. During the antirightist campaign of 1957–1958 he was demoted. In 1966, at the very moment Liu Shaoqi was coming under bombardment from Mao's forces, he encouraged his men to study a "heretical" book by Liu.[1] The following year he arrested two thousand Red Guards at a time the army had been ordered to support the left. When General Xü came from Canton to Peking for Mao's funeral, he is reported to have thumped the table at a meeting of high-level leaders, threatening "If you don't arrest that woman [Jiang Qing], I shall march north!"[2]

What kind of a leader now occupied the pivotal position in China?

Hua Guofeng was a relative newcomer to national leadership, having never held a post in Peking until he was fifty years old. He had grown up in the northern province of Shanxi, but from twenty-eight until he was fifty he worked in Mao's home province in Central China, Hunan.

He was born in Jiaocheng county of Shanxi province in 1921. He has described his family as "rather poor." Perhaps they were what the Communists call middle peasants rather than poor peasants, because they were able to send him to primary school, followed by two or three years of vocational school.[3]

In 1937, when he was sixteen, the Sino-Japanese war broke out. This had a decisive impact on his life, as it did on those of many in his generation.

The Communist Party recruited and led guerrillas in resistance to the Japanese occupation force in the province, using the mountains for their bases. In 1938, at eighteen, Hua helped mobilize support for the guerrillas and was accepted into the Party. He must have displayed unusual energy and ability, because before he was twenty-one he had been appointed county chairman of the ánti-Japanese League, county chairman of the armed forces committee of the Communist Party, and secretary of the county committee of the Communist Party. In these posts he was responsible for mobilizing and directing the local guerrilla force and for implementing party policies on land reform.*

When World War II ended and the Civil War between the Communist Party and the Nationalists resumed, Hua continued his military role. As the Communist armies advanced southward he moved with them, ending the Civil War in Hunan province. There he stayed for twenty-three years, from 1040 to 1971.

In 1951, something happened that was to shape his life as much as the war against Japan: he was appointed secretary of the Party Committee for the Hsiang-t'an district, in which Mao had been born. This brought him into contact with Mao Zedong in the early 1950s.

Under Hua's leadership the district outpaced others in rural organization, something that commended itself to Mao but not to those local leaders who shared the view of Liu Shaoqi and Deng Xiaoping that the cooperation movement was growing too rapidly and under too much pressure from party officials for its own good.†

In 1956 Hua was transferred to work in the provincial capital, Changsha, and two years later was promoted to Vice-Governor of the province and an alternate secretary of the province's Party Committee. This made him, at thirty-seven, one of the highest officials in a province with a population of thirty-six million.

In 1959, when Mao's Great Leap Forward policies were

---

* He became the local leader of the Anti-Japanese National Salvation Vanguard of China and in a guerrilla equivalent of baptism he chose the name Hua Guofeng from three of the Chinese characters that compose this title to replace the name he had been given at birth, Su Zhu.

† Mao showed his approval for Hua by having one of Hua's investigative reports on agricultural cooperatives included in a November 1955 special issue of a Central Committee journal which also carried one of his own articles on that subject. A month earlier Hua had been invited to make a presentation on the subject to an enlarged meeting of the Central Committee.

being criticized, Hua defended them. Mao again showed his approval, this time by personally nominating Hua to be appointed a full secretary of the provincial Party Committee.

From 1958 until 1972 Hua held a variety of appointments in the Hunan administration, gaining wide experience of provincial government. He was also able to continue to impress Mao, because in addition to his responsibilities at the provincial level he was put directly in charge of Mao's home district. Hua saw to it that the district was favored with a good share of capital-investment funds and projects in agriculture, transport, and industry. He also supervised the arrangements for putting Mao's family home on display to the public.

As a power-holder in Hunan, he automatically came under fire in the Cultural Revolution, but recovered much more quickly than provincial leaders senior to him. So in a matter of months Hua became in effect Number Two in the Hunan hierarchy in 1967, with the backing of Zhou Enlai and in the face of disapproval by Jiang Qing. In 1969 he succeeded to the top post in the province. Only a year later he was given a chance to prove himself in national politics, when he was appointed as chief of the Staff Office of the State Council. As such he was under the direct leadership of Zhou Enlai. He specialized in agriculture, finance, and commerce.

Zhou clearly approved of his performance; in 1973 he was promoted to the Politburo and eighteen months later, in January 1975, was made Minister of Public Security and a vice-premier. This was the time when Deng Xiaoping was put in day-to-day charge of the nation's affairs, and since Hua's star was rising also it seems Deng shared Zhou's good opinion of him. Together they dominated a very important conference on agriculture in September and October 1975, demonstrating to the whole country that Hua's responsibilities ranged well beyond security. He was clearly being groomed as a key member of the generation of men in their fifties and early sixties who would succeed the generation of Deng and Zhou. It was characteristic of Jiang Qing's approach to politics that Hua's long record of loyalty to Mao did not lead her to respect him. Indeed it is the conclusion of Ting Wang, author of the most detailed study of

Hua's career, that she and her allies opposed and attacked Hua for many years before Mao's death and were dismayed when Mao proposed Hua and not Zhang Chunqiao as Acting Premier in January 1976.

But Hua may have wished that greatness had not been thrust upon him quite so soon. Because he was so new to national politics, he had not had time to build much of a power base of his own outside Hunan. Nor had he acquired any experience of international affairs or indeed of military affairs at the national level. Fortunately for him and for the nation, his temperament enabled him to remain calm and balanced in a year of extraordinary stress. At no time were those qualities more needed than in the weeks following Mao's death.

On 18 September a mass rally was held on Tiananmen Square to commemorate Mao Zedong. One million people were assembled with military precision. The leadership was not arrayed on the Gate of Heavenly Peace, where Mao had so often stood to review "the masses," but on a lower rostrum specially built in front of the Gate. Mao's heirs were not yet ready to stand where he had stood.

For the third time that year the highest leaders of China assembled to commemorate the life and death of one of their number. Once again, as they filed to their places, they presented a tableau of the history of the revolution. The men and women who walked or hobbled across the stage spanned the whole life of the Communist Party and some, like the widow of Sun Yat-sen, were reminders of the revolution that had preceded the founding of the Party. The Minister of Defense walked with a nurse at his elbow; Sun Yat-sen's widow supported herself with sticks; Xü Deheng's flowing white beard evoked an era long past. Some who attended seemed no longer to have any function in public life other than to attend such occasions. One of these last was Zhou Jianren. This man of almost ninety evoked memories of his younger brother, the long-dead Lu Xun, a writer who had been the very incarnation of fearless truth-saying, one who would surely have abhorred the worship of any man as demigod. Standing grim-faced, gripping the handrail in front of him, determined to see out another ceremony, Zhou

Jianren was a symbol of the determination of many of his generation to outlast the darkness that had shrouded China and determination to remind the young that the revolution had once promised liberation, not enslavement, enlightenment, not idolatry. In the front rank stood Soong Ching Ling, the widow of Sun Yat-sen, still wonderfully good-looking at eighty-four, recalling for everyone a time long ago when to be beautiful, and to delight in it, was no crime.

Wang Hongwen, the senior person in the hierarchy of the National People's Congress since the death of Zhu De, presided over the ceremony and seemed uncertain of even the few acts he had to perform. Jiang Qing had come dressed with a theatrical touch. She had wrapped a large black scarf, almost the size of a shawl, around her head and thrown one end over her shoulder. If she had hopes of creating as moving an impression as Jacqueline Kennedy had made at her husband's funeral, she was unsuccessful: down on the square, the little grandson of a Chinese friend of mine whispered to the classmate standing next to him "Look at her! Do you suppose she has a cold?"

A few places along the line from Jiang Qing stood Yao Wenyuan, glowering, with a look of ill-defined fury on his face, like a thundercloud about to burst.

Hua Guofeng himself, who delivered the eulogy, was not a figure of much outward grace or authority. He shambled as he walked, he spoke with the slurred diction of his native Shanxi, his clothes hung baggily on his bulky frame, and his features would not have won him any hero's role in the Shanghai film studios where Jiang Qing had made her brief career.

But it was evident that he knew what he was doing. And some of what he was doing caused Wang Hongwen, who stood beside him, visible discomfort for reasons that were not far to seek. First, Hua failed to utter some words the left-controlled press was daily claiming to have been Mao's deathbed injunction to his successors: "Act according to the principles laid down." It was not immediately clear why Hua omitted them: surely he was not signaling an intention to go against the principles laid down (whatever they might be). Unless he was a very unusual political leader, he would proclaim his predecessor's principles all the more fervently if he were about to contravene them. But I assumed that the so-called deathbed injunction was seen as aiding the Jiang Qing faction in some way we could not yet fathom. The second feature of the speech that caused Wang Hongwen to arch his eyebrows even more anxiously, and to peer over Hua's shoulder at the text of the eulogy even more intently, was a passage in which Hua issued a warning against plotting. He gave no clues as to the identity of the plotters, but, as it later transpired, he couched his warning in the very words Mao had used to reprimand the Shanghai Gang for factional maneuvering on 3 May 1975. Wang Hongwen and his friends would have no doubt whom Hua had in mind.

From snatches of conversation with ordinary Chinese with whom I was in contact in these weeks I sensed a mixture of relief that death had put an end to the long-drawn-out agony of Mao's last years and anxiety as to what would happen next. One thing was clear: things could not go on as they were; something had to give. From a speech Hua had made a few days before Mao's death it was clear that he was well aware that, under the political deadlock of the past months, society had been crumbling. He had described the somber realities with refreshing candor and considerable courage.

Yet there were reasons for him to hestitate to resolve the deadlock. He had risen to the top just because left and right were in uneasy balance and he was a compromise candidate. If he moved against the left he would destroy the equilibrium that had worked to his favor. Also it would look as though he were going against the wishes of Mao, who had personally appointed him and whose benediction gave him his legitimacy. Personal considerations aside, no operation against the left would be risk-free. Unpopular though they might be, they had some following both among the elite and at the grass roots. They had also worked hard to build themselves political bases in Shanghai and Liaoning province. In Shanghai Wang Hongwen had devoted much effort to building up a civilian militia of a million workers. The commanders of the Peking and Shenyang military regions had both benefited greatly from the Cultural Revolution and the latter was believed to have been a close follower of Jiang Qing during that movement. How would they react to a move against the left?

The members of the Central Committee were guarded by a special military unit designated the 8341 Unit. The political commissar and de facto commander of this unit was Mao's former bodyguard Wang Dongxing. Would he defend Mao's widow and her allies?

On Friday 8 October came the first sign that the month-long delay in confirming Hua Guofeng as China's new leader might be at an end. It was announced in the name of the highest organs of party and state and the armed forces that a memorial hall would be built in Peking; here Chairman Mao's body would be placed in a crystal sarcophagus. It was announced at the same time that the Central Committee had decided that the work of editing and publishing the fifth and subsequent volumes of Mao's selected works and his collected works would be put under the leadership of the Politburo, headed by Comrade Hua Guofeng. This twin decision—immediately dubbed "The Box and the Books" by some irreverent foreigners—achieved two things: it wrapped the leadership in a mantle of loyalty to Mao and it established Hua as the supreme interpreter of Mao's Thought, a role that would sur ly go only to the highest political figure in China. He would be the high priest of Chinese Communism. This indicated that Hua had been acknowledged as Chairman of the Party but, if so, why did it not say so in clear terms? And, since the was no announcement of any of the supreme organs of party and state having met, how had they arrived at these decisions?

The next morning, Saturday, 9 October, I was watching the finals of the British Embassy tennis tournament when the car of the Reuters bureau chief, David Rogers, screeched into the embassy compound. Rogers had seen a poster on a nearby wall that was new and looked important, but he could not read it. He grabbed a Chinese-speaking First Secretary of the embassy and they roared off down the street, returning two minutes later with the news that Hua had been made Chairman of the Party and of its Military Affairs Commission. Since he was already Prime Minister he now held a trio of appointments (heading party, state, and army) that even Mao in all his glory had never held concurrently. Two hours later the poster disappeared. Had someone leaked an announcement that was supposed to be kept from foreign eyes or was the appointment being contested?

An editorial, one of the most authoritative kind, since it was published in the name of the three main publications of party and army, hailed the Box and Books decisions and warned that "anyone who betrays Marxism–Leninism–Mao Zedong Thought and tampers with Chairman Mao's directives and anyone who practicies revisionism and splittism and engages in conspiracies is bound to fail." It concluded with a call for unity and discipline under the leadership of the Central Committee "headed by Comrade Hua Guofeng." Ominously, it also called on the nation to "deepen the criticism of Deng Xiaoping."

The next day more posters appeared welcoming Hua's appointment as Chairman of the Party and its Military Commission, so that at least now looked firm. Three days later, on the morning of Tuesday, 12 October, we awoke to hear the BBC and other foreign radio stations report that Jiang Qing, Wang Hongwen, Zhang Chunqiao, and Yao Wenyuan had been arrested. At first many people were incredulous, and there was no confirmation from the Chinese news media or officials. We watched and waited.

Stories circulated that tended to confirm the reports but days went by without any official confirmation. On Friday a Japanese friend called to say that in Shanghai hundreds of thousands of people were pouring into the streets to denouce Jiang, Wang, Zhang, and Yao as a Gang of Four. Still there was no official confirmation of their arrests. Had something gone wrong?

On Sunday morning, 17 October, I went as usual to the Protestant church. I noticed that the English version of the order of service differed from the Chinese in one respect: in the Chinese version the reading from the New Testament was from Saint Paul's epistle to the Romans, and the English version showed another reading. My religious sentiments were overwhelmed by my China-watcher's habits. This was obviously a last-minute change, unique in my experience of that most meticulously planned church. It must be connected with the rumored change in China's leadership! I could hardly contain my curiosity to know which passage the Chinese minister would read. We reached that point in the service and he began. It was from Romans 3:

> None is righteous, no not one;
> no one understands, no one seeks for God.
> All have turned aside, together they have gone wrong;
> no one does good, not even one.
> Their throat is an open grave,
> they use their tongues to deceive.
> The venom of asps is under their lips.
> Their mouth is full of curses and bitterness,
> Their feet are swift to shed blood,
> in their paths are ruin and misery,
> and the way of peace they do not know.
> There is no fear of God before their eyes.

I was ready to wager one year's salary as a China-watcher that the ministers had chosen this as their first contribution to the denunciation of the Gang. After the service I remarked to one of them on my way out of church: "Well, in future there will be less danger of asps biting people." The only response I drew was one of those superbly controlled looks of puzzlement that Chinese give when they do not want to confirm or deny some piece of speculation. Two and a half years later, as I took my leave of the ministers at the end of my posting in Peking, I reminded them of the reading they had chosen that day and asked whether I had read their minds correctly. The response this time was more open: "You and we were one in the spirit of the Lord that day."

In fact, by the time the ministers read that passage on 17 October, the Gang of Four had been under arrest for ten days. The arrest had been planned by three leaders: Hua Guofeng, Minister of Defense Marshal Ye Jianying, and the security specialist Wang Dongxing. One of Hua's first moves had been to secure Wang's cooperation.[4] Hua and Ye had taken the views of several veteran marshals at the planning stage and had received unequivocal encouragement. Xü Xiangqian said "It should have been done long ago," and Nie Rongzhen fully supported the idea. This was important because the support of these highly respected veterans would be very valuable in influencing others after the arrests were disclosed and would stiffen the resolve of junior officers if the coup ran into opposition from other quarters.

Hua Guofeng issued a call for an emergency meeting of some or all of the Politburo members to be held on the night of 5–6 October, prompted perhaps by the publication of the inflammatory article by Liang Xiao on 4 October. At this meeting Jiang Qing proposed, not for the first time, that Hua support her for nomination as Chairman of the Communist Party. Hua declined, and there was an inconclusive discussion of the issue by those present. It was agreed that another meeting should be held to resolve the dispute. In line with this agreement, on 6 October the General Office of the Central Committee notified Wang Hongwen and Zhang Chunqiao that the Politburo's Standing Committee would meet at Conference Room No. 2 in the Huairen Hall in Zhongnanhai that evening to discuss issues concerning the convocation of a meeting of the full Politburo and the convocation of a plenum of the Central Committee. After the death of Mao, Zhou, and Zhu, the Politburo's Standing Committee had only four members: Hua Guofeng, Ye Jianying, Wang Hongwen, and Zhang Chunqiao.

On the evening of 6 October Wang Hongwen arrived at the Huairen Hall meeting place on time. He entered the conference room in high spirits, walked round a screen inside the door, and was surprised to find the room empty. As he turned to leave several security guards appeared from behind the screen and shouted "Hands up!" Wang attempted to resist but received a powerful kick on the shin and a heavy punch on the chin that sent him to the floor. The guards twisted his hands behind his back and handcuffed him. About the same time, Zhang's car pulled up outside Huairen Hall. As Zhang hurried into the conference room a guard shouted "Don't move!" Shocked, Zhang held up his hands to let the guards take him under arrest. The operation to round up Wang and Zhang had been completed in less than two minutes. Ye Jianying had personally directed it. He and Hua Guofeng had watched on closed-circuit television from another room in the hall.

Meanwhile, two operational squads from the 8341 Unit were carrying out the arrest of Jiang Qing and Yao Wenyuan at their homes. To avoid any misunderstandings or disagreements between the operational squads and the security guards of the two residences, officers senior to the security-guard commanders accompanied the squads making the arrests. According to one account, Yao was amazed at being arrested and, for the first time in years, the master propagandist found himself at a loss for words. Jiang Qing would change her sleeping place from night to night, but it was the duty of the 8341 Unit to know where she was at all times. On 6 October she was staying at her residence near the Temple of the White Pagoda in the western part of Peking. When the operational squad arrived, her security guards led them to arrest her. She was dressed in pajamas and reading on a sofa in her bedroom; the door was unlocked. As she heard someone open the door of her bedroom and enter, she called out "Who is it?" without looking up from her reading. The commander of the operational squad announced "On the orders of the First Vice-Chairman of the CPC Central Committee and Premier of the State Council, Comrade Hua Guofeng, we are here to arrest you and put you under examination in isolation."

Jiang Qing jumped from the sofa and shouted "Guards! Guards!" When she realized no one was coming to her rescue, she collapsed on the floor, rolling around and wailing "You people have started bullying me even before the Chairman's corpse is cold!"

Hearing the commotion, her female attendants came into the room. Reportedly they were delighted to discover what was going on and spat on her, saying "You stinking bitch! Now you have had it!"

In a separate incident, Mao's nephew Mao Yuanxin, who had acted as his secretary for the last months of his life, tried to escape from Peking to northeast China, where he was influential. He was caught as he tried to board an aircraft. He shot and wounded several of the security guards who tried to arrest him, but they returned the fire and he was wounded and arrested.

That night and the next day thirty close followers of the Four were arrested, including some members of the Liang Xiao writing group, whose last article, ironically, appeared after the arrest of the Four. Others arrested included the Minister of Culture, who had attempted to flee the country. The embassy of a country friendly to China had been surprised to receive a sudden proposal from him to visit their country, together with a request for the immediate issue of a visa for him and his party. Four of his vice-ministers were arrested with him. The ministers of sports, metallurgy, and public health all disappeared after the Four were arrested. On 7 and 8 October Hua summoned the most important members of the Central Committee to inform them of the action, but the plan for dealing with potential opposition in Shanghai and elsewhere called for keeping the arrests a secret from the public for the next few days. If Shanghai, whose eleven million people turned out one quarter of China's industrial product, rose in defense of the Gang of Four, Hua and Ye might be forced to compromise. The reaction of Shanghai could make the difference between a peaceful takeover and civil war. The story of how Hua and Ye dealt with Shanghai has elements of suspense and a stratagem worthy of China's long tradition of statecraft, in which deception, cajolery, and the buying of allegiance with half-promises have often played a role. Time and again cunning schemes have been devised to achieve the surrender of a city without a shot being fired. Of course, this kind of game can only be played if the rulers of the city are politically isolated from the citizens. The stratagem for Shanghai was based on a belief that if the leftist leaders of the city could be separated from each other, cut off from the Four, and confused by contradictory intelligence, then, knowing that the people were not with them and that their cause was quite half a fraud, they would have no stomach for a fight. If all went well, the leftist stronghold would end its days "not with a bang, but a whimper." But, without elections, opinion polls, or any substantial freedom of expression, there must have been great uncertainty about public opinion in the city.

At 9 A.M. on Thursday, 7 October 1976, Ma Tianshui, the senior Communist Party official resident in Shanghai, held an urgent meeting with Xü Jingxian and Wang Xiuzhen, his closest associates on the Municipal Revolutionary Committee, which ran the city's affairs. Xü was a highly intelligent politician in his early forties charged with maintaining radical control of the Shanghai media. Wang Xiuzhen was a short plump woman, also in her forties, whose responsibilities included the Shanghai militia. Ma told them that he had been wakened in the early hours of the morning by a telephone call from the General Office of the Communist Party's Central Committee, summoning him to a meeting in Peking that day. He said he was worried because when he was called to a meeting by the Center he would normally be warned of it and briefed by one of the Maoists in the Politburo on whose behalf he ran Shanghai. This time not only had none of them warned him or briefed him, but when he had telephoned for guidance he could not contact any of them.[5]

Xü and Wang were just as worried as Ma when they heard his news. Only three weeks before, just after Chairman Mao's death, the three of them had met with the political secretaries of Wang Hongwen and Zhang Chunqiao, who had told them that the rightists were gaining control at the Center but had added hopefully "Since there are so many good revolutionaries we'll win in the long run." Ma and his colleagues made a second attempt to contact their principals in the Politburo, again without success. So they tried telephoning fellow Shanghainese at the Center: the Minister of Culture, a Vice-Minister of Public Security, and a trade union leader. None could be reached. Ma would have to fly to Peking unbriefed on a situation he could only imagine with dread. As he and his colleagues waited in the airport lounge for his flight to be called, they agreed on a code he could use on the telephone with them. If, as they feared, the rightists had taken control, he would say "My old stomach trouble has come back."

As Ma flew the seven hundred miles to Peking, he must have reflected on the role Shanghai was cast to play in the drama of political struggle that seemed to be unfolding. He was not a romantic rebel but an experienced administrator in his early sixties who had thrown in his lot with the left and had seen enough of politics to make a shrewd and detached assessment.

Of course Shanghai was supposed to be the stronghold of the leftists. It had served as the springboard for Mao in the Cultural Revolution and had been the pace-setter for that time. Wang Hongwen, Zhang Chunqiao, and Yao Wenyuan still nominally held their posts on the city's party committee, even though they left day-to-day management to Ma. They had their people in key positions in the city, particularly in the mass media and the militia.

They had used the media most vigorously to propagate their views and support the leaders of their faction. On occasion they had even contravened Mao's own instructions and suppressed his views. They had tried to persuade public opinion that only through violent change could a better society be built. They had denigrated Zhou Enlai and had supported Zhang Chunqiao in his efforts to become premier. They had also prepared Shanghai physically to defend their cause. The one-million-strong militia in the city was supposed to be a counterbalance to the Garrison Command, which was not under their control. Wang Hongwen had had a fireproof, soundproof, and watertight bunker constructed. An automobile factory had been converted to make armaments and as a result seventy thousand semiautomatic rifles and two hundred machine guns had been distributed to the militia, in contravention of party policy. The same factory had been ordered to produce tommy guns, revolvers, handcuffs, and steel helmets. Ma himself had his own broadcasting facilities.

But Old Ma, as his younger colleagues called him, could not but be skeptical of the efficiency of all these preparations. The Politburo leftists were not exactly of a character to inspire self-sacrifice by others: Jiang Qing was widely detested and the seamy side of her life as a film actress in the 1930s was well known in Shanghai; Wang Hongwen was more popular but had a playboy reputation in the city because he showed as much interest in women and shooting and fishing as he did in politics; Zhang had more steel and more political savvy but was too much of an ideologue to have won a wide following in this most pragmatic of cities; Yao Wenyuan was a forceful and energetic propagandist but the part he and Jiang Qing had played in suppressing China's intellectuals and creative artists was intensely resented in Shanghai, where so many of them had lived and worked and found a public. Would the people of Shanghai, who had always seized every opportunity to advance their own power, defy the rest of China out of loyalty to the Four? Was sophisticated, materialistic Shanghai going to defend people who imposed an ascetic, egalitarian ethic on China? . . . Ma's plane flew on to Peking, the city which already, at Qing Ming, had declared that *its* loyalty was to Zhou Enlai's pragmatic vision for China.

Back in Shanghai Ma's associates waited anxiously. At midnight a telephone call came from Peking. Ma's secretary came on the line to say "Old Ma is having a bath, but I want to tell you that my old stomach trouble has attacked again." The rightists had taken control.

The next day, 8 October, Xü and Wang, having heard nothing from Ma himself, decided to take the initiative; they tried to telephone him, but could not reach him. Increasingly anxious, they dispatched a secretary of their ally, the Vice-Minister of Public Security, to Peking to find out what was happening. With him, they agreed on these telephone signals: if all was normal, he would say "The old stomach trouble has attacked again"; and if the worst had happened and the four Politburo leftists had been arrested he would speak of a heart attack. Their emissary left and then, at 4 P.M., Xü met with his closest collaborator in propaganda work in Shanghai, Zhu Yongjia. Together they sent out a call to the leaders of the Shanghai mass media to report to them what they knew of developments in Peking. At that moment their female colleague, Wang, joined them. She had been on the telephone to Shenyang to contact their friends among the military and civilian leadership like Mao Yuanxin, known as the overlord of the Northeast. Wang had asked her contacts in Shenyang "How's the weather in Peking?" They had either missed her meaning or pretended to. "How's Mao Yuanxin's health?" That too had drawn a blank.

The anxious trio soon had some news to digest. The voice of the emissary they had sent to Peking came on the line, saying "My mother has suffered a heart attack." That could mean only one thing: Jiang Qing had been arrested.

They went straight to a full meeting of the city's Revolutionary Committee at 5:00 P.M. and made their dispositions. Wang would summon the leaders of the city's militia to give them their orders, while Xü instructed the mass media.

In his instructions to the media, Xü said "If the New China News Agency reports the developments at the center, don't publish it without checking with me first. When the Soviets attacked China at Zhen Bao Island in 1969, the head of our national broadcasting service suppressed the news for twenty-four hours and became a hero. Follow his example." They did not have long to wait. At nine o'clock NCNA wire service reported the two decisions taken in the name of the Central Committee on the Box and the Books: the decision to build a memorial hall for Mao and to make Premier Hua Guofeng editor-in-chief of Mao's writings.

At midnight Zhu Yongjia, who had charge of propaganda work under Xü Jingxian, met with his subordinates and told them:

> Peking just now broadcast two decisions by the Center, to publish the fifth volume and build a Memorial Hall. This is a clever tactic of theirs to acquire some political capital. It's a smoke screen. We must get a move on, create public opinion for a counterattack, trade blow for blow. I want you to devise some slogans to arouse the masses, starting off with some "neutral ones," then move on to make our stand clear. I'm off to brief the newspapers and radio stations.

Zhu went to the editorial departments of the *Wenhui Bao* and the *Liberation Daily*, and ordered them: "They have seized [Mao's] banner by broadcasting these two decisions. We should disregard them; they have done it to get people on their side and it's aimed at us. Stand your ground. Print our material. If Peking puts out news about dragging out an anti-Party clique and NCNA distributes it, don't you publish it!"

When an editor asked what they should do about local printing of the Peking *People's Daily*, Zhu said: "If the paper is bad don't print it. If NCNA publishes a story about an anti-Party clique we will publish an 'Appeal to the whole Party and all the People.' We must rebel."

At the radio station he repeated what he had told the news-papers and ordered: "Don't relay the broadcasts from the Center." The director of the broadcasting station pointed out that even if he did not publish the two decisions of the Party Center people would pick up broadcasts from other stations that did announce them. Zhu shouted: "Jam the other stations! Use every bit of jamming equipment you've got!"

At one the next morning, Saturday 9 October, Wang held her meeting with the militia commanders. She arranged for a war headquarters to be set up and then ordered thirty thousand militia to be mobilized and issued with arms and ammunition in the next forty-eight hours. Their task would be to keep key installations in the city, such as the port, the premises of the two daily newspapers, and the broadcasting station, under leftist con-trol.

The trade-union leaders were summoned that night too. Those who represented factories manufacturing arms were told to increase shiftwork to turn out arms as fast as possible. The arms should be distributed immediately to worker militia. Militia armories in factories were to be opened and the weapons there distributed immediately. A close watch was to be kept on the regular army garrison. Subordinates were to be briefed at once on the crisis that had developed.

After the bombshells of the previous night, the rest of that day passed without any major development. At 4 P.M. Ma called from Peking for the first time since his arrival there two days earlier. His message seemed surprisingly reassuring: "I have seen our four bosses in the Politburo. Their health is quite good, but they are too busy working to meet me alone at this time. Comrades Wang and Xü are to come to Peking for a meeting tomorrow." Some of those who heard Old Ma's message were greatly relieved. They decided that the earlier coded message about Jiang Qing being arrested must have been a mistake. But Xü Jingxian was perturbed. Could it really be that the "revi-sionists" had been foiled in Peking and that the coded message and the other indications of an adverse trend of events were all wrong? Old Ma's call itself was full of contradictions: for in-stance, the Four were in good health but had not seen him privately. Finally, why were he and Wang ordered to Peking for a meeting? Old Ma had been unable to tell them anything about the meeting, and that alone made him suspicious. It was unprecedented. What should they do? To refuse to go would be an irrevocable act of defiance, but if they went they might be arrested as they stepped off the aircraft.

There was a heated debate. Zhu Yongjia, the propagandist, urged them to face the Party Center boldly. Thirty thousand militia would soon be mobilized in Shanghai and that would give them strength as they bargained with the leaders at the Center.

It was agreed they must go to Peking; before Wang and Xü set off the next day they gave instructions that the masses should be prepared psychologically and organizationally for a struggle. Xü's arrival in Peking led to another outwardly reassuring telephone call that evening, Sunday, 10 October. He said "We've arrived safely. Make a good job of the preparations. We'll be back in a day or two and all decisions can wait until then." But again the reassurance was at variance with other indicators, for that very day everyone in Shanghai had learned of Hua Guofeng's appointment as Chairman of the Central Committee and of the Party's Military Commission. Jiang Qing's bid for the party leadership had obviously failed. Moreover, the joint editorial published that day, instead of using the leftists' current slogan, had warned against plotting and splitting the party.

Monday the eleventh passed without any message from Ma, Xü, or Wang. Although it was now clear that the Politburo leftists were in deep trouble, those left to represent them in Shanghai lacked both guidance from their superiors and the authority (or daring) to act on their own initiative. They continued to mark time, doing no more than send more propaganda teams into workplaces to try to persuade people that their interests were threatened by developments at the Center. These teams met such a hostile reception that workers from ten districts telephoned the city administration protesting. The news of the arrest of the Gang of Four was being spread quietly in Peking and already a few people in Shanghai had heard of it. At least one poster appeared, demanding to know why the Shanghai leadership had not yet disseminated a Party Central document announcing Hua's appointment and the arrest of the Four.

The next day, Tuesday, 12 October, the secretaries of Wang Hongwen and Zhang Chunqiao came to see Zhu Yongjia, who was now in charge of Shanghai. They were growing desperate. Five days had passed since their bosses had been arrested; if Shanghai did not rise in protest now, there would be no possibility of forcing their release. They had tried in vain to contact Ma and Wang, so it looked as if they had been arrested. Even if they returned safely to Shanghai, it might be because they had capitulated to the rightists. "We should fight against the Center rather than wait for death," one of them shouted in a moment of melodrama. Zhu's response was more cautious—not surprisingly, since responsibility for mobilizing Shanghai had fallen onto his shoulders and his propaganda efforts were meeting strong popular resistance. He embarked on a long review of revolutionary history covering the two thousand years from the Qin and Han dynasties to the Paris Commune. Finally he ordered the drafting of two declarations: one to the people of China and another to the world, which would declare Shanghai's defiance of the Center. They were to be ready for broadcasting the next day—if the order was given.

That evening an official message came from Peking: "Ma, Wang, and Xü will arrive in Shanghai tomorrow at 10 A.M. Not too many people should meet them at the airport." This message also was read with suspicion. Why should only a few go to the airport? Perhaps an ambush was being prepared and soldiers would be hidden on the plane who would seize those now in charge of Shanghai when they greeted the aircraft. What should be done? There was a new dispute between those who said this was the last chance to launch an armed struggle and those who took a cooler view, questioning the value of thirty thousand militia pitted against several divisions of the PLA. The cooler heads prevailed, but, as a precaution, a medium truck was stationed near the aircraft parking place with two machine-gunners at the ready behind the flaps of its canvas top.

At 10 A.M. on Wednesday the thirteenth, Ma, Wang, and Xü walked down the ramp, their heads bowed. No soldiers emerged behind them. The trio was tight-lipped as well as disconsolate. Ma ordered the city leaders to meet him at three that afternoon. When they assembled the atmosphere was like a funeral. There were tears and curses as Ma confirmed their worst fears. Then he recounted how the Party leaders had said to them "The Gang of Four is the Gang of Four, and Shanghai is Shanghai. . . . We've already changed our direction. Haven't you changed yet? Of course there is evidence in Shanghai of criminal activities by the Gang of Four, but it doesn't matter much." Then the Central leaders had given them copies of the instructions Mao had written to Hua, expressing confidence in him as his successor and giving him guidance. Hua had also shown them something written by Zhang Chunqiao, entitled "My Feelings," which expressed his anger at Hua being promoted over his head to be Acting Premier after Zhou Enlai's death. Ma and the others had uneasily offered some explanation as to why they had mobilized the armed militia. Hua had listened to their explanation, laughed, and then said "We have trust in you."

It was obvious to their Shanghai colleagues that Ma, Xü, and Wang had surrendered, bought off with hints that their personal involvement in the treason and plotting of the Four would be overlooked. The meeting came to no formal conclusion on whether to defy Hua or hail him as Chairman. But it did decide to issue the next day, 14 October, a document containing Hua's speech to the Politburo of the seventh which announced and justified the action taken against the Four and the speeches of other central leaders the next day describing the alleged plot by the Four. They had capitulated, but in a last footling but face-saving gesture of defiance they did not refer to Hua in the document by his new title of Chairman and they excluded the speech by Wang Dongxing. They ordered the armed militia, who normally patrolled the streets in coordination with the army, to cease all activity for the next ten days. The resistance of the "revolutionary heroes" who had occupied the political stage of Shanghai for ten years had ended not with a bang but a whimper.

Hua Guofeng and Ye Jianying had not neglected military preparations in case persuasion failed. On 8 October they had ordered General Xü Shiyu to fly north from Canton to Nanjing to ensure that his old command supported the new Central leadership. According to a story told by people in Canton later, General Xü shot and killed the commander of the Nanjing troops in a dispute over army orders—certainly the Nanjing commander never appeared in public again.

That night at eleven o'clock the first posters went up in the city accusing the Four by name of forming an "anti-Party plot group." A crowd surrounded the headquarters of the Shanghai Revolutionary Committee and demanded that Xü and Wang come out and face them. They came out separately, and one at least was seized by the crowd and pushed onto the back of a truck to squat beside a group of exultant men and women who drove off with him, banging gongs and a big drum.

The next day, 15 October, posters appeared all over town attacking the Gang of Four, calling for them to be severely punished and for their local agents to be rooted out. That day hundreds of thousands of jubilant Shanghainese poured onto the streets. In the city they had hoped would rise in their defense the Four were hung in effigy.

In the week that followed Shanghai engaged in political activity on a scale it had not matched since the Cultural Revolution. The streets were choked with millions of people exulting in the Fall of the Four and acclaiming Hua. Posters plastered the outside of buildings like street wallpaper to the height of several stories along the riverside. This was a miniature Cultural Counter-Revolution which humbled the very people who had ridden to national prominence in 1966–1967. Such organization as was necessary for these largely spontaneous demonstrations was probably done by the army and a minority of the city leaders who sided with Hua and Ye. Just before midnight on 16 October, the Party Center telephoned the Shanghai leaders saying that "the rage of the masses" against the Gang of Four and them was well understood. The Center hoped that the leadership would work with the masses to expose the crimes of the Four. "The masses" must not be permitted to attack public buildings or interrupt communication and public transport. This order proved superfluous: the crowds were too united in their celebrations for there to be any disruption of public order. Mass rallies, one of more than a million people, held in perfect order, acclaimed the dramatic events of the past ten days. The isolation of the leftist leaders of the city from the people they ruled had proved greater than even their most optimistic opponents can have expected.

On 21 October the Party Center sent three high officials to act as its proconsuls in Shanghai.* They met Ma, Hua, and Wang for an hour that evening, and, in case there were any lingering thoughts of defiance, warned them: "Shanghai's implementation of the Center's decisions is of national importance. . . . Today eight hundred thousand demonstrated in Peking. Tomorrow another eight hundred thousand civilians and soldiers will march in the capital. The foreign press will be free to take photographs."

Early that morning I was driving down Peking's Changan Avenue with Nigel Wade of the London *Daily Telegraph*. We were looking for the start of Peking's demonstrations, which we believed must come soon, and we found it near the Peking Hotel: a column of marchers coming toward us with a banner that read "Warmly celebrate the great victory of the smashing of 'The Gang of Four' anti-party clique." As a slogan it was rather a mouthful, but it told us what we wanted to know: at last the Party had given the green light for Peking to celebrate. Nigel swung into the Peking Hotel parking lot and was on the line to his foreign desk in London within minutes.

No demonstrations in the thirty years of the People's Republic had been more eagerly awaited. Every column had equipped itself with firecrackers, drums, and cymbals. Men and women crowded onto the backs of trucks holding six-foot bamboo poles over the side with four-foot snakes of red firecrackers attached. They looked like fishermen landing wriggling, jumping, exploding eels. Where Changan Avenue passes the Gate of Heavenly Peace scores of thousands of marchers crowded in columns. Huge banners, each of a different color—pink, light

---

* Politburo members Su Zhenhua and Ni Zhifu and Jiangsu's first secretary, Peng Chong.

blue, light green, red, yellow—carried by the marchers clustered into forests of brilliance. The sound of firecrackers exploding never ceased.

In the evening as the sun was dropping behind the Great Hall of the People and its rays shone through the red banners carried above the marchers' heads, dancers and musicians from Korean, Thai, and other minority peoples of China brought their music and rhythm and bright costumes to the gate. Slim and graceful young women from Yunnan performed dances designed to please the senses and to express joy instead of the sterile "revolutionary militancy" imposed by Jiang Qing. Vitality had flowed back into the young men. The crowds around them delighted in being free, after so long, to enjoy grace and vitality for their own sake.

This was a celebration of victory, a victory that had been won by the people at Qing Ming as much as by the arrest of the Four. The gilded eaves and massive walls of the Gate of Heavenly Peace, which had watched the Red Guards being marched into battle in 1966 and seen them return with wreaths for Zhou in 1976, now heard them beat their victory drums with furious joy.

Friends old enough to remember World War II told me they had not experienced such a celebration since victory over the Nazis was won. But in China, they added, the crowds were more sober and better-mannered. According to NCNA, 5.8 million people took part in the demonstrations from 21 to 23 October.

The phenomenon of the Three Empties had appeared in Peking as in other cities: the liquor shops had been emptied for celebrations among families and friends; the firework shops had been bought out; and the hospital beds had emptied as one senior official after another, who had used a medical pretext to avoid the anti-Deng campaign, leaped from his bed shouting "The Gang of Four has been arrested! I am cured!" I had never before seen people in Peking laughing and smiling as they did that day.

Not all the faces were smiling, however. I saw a column of marchers from the Research Institute for Petroleum Exploration and Development. They had given pride of place to a formidable lady, about seventy years of age, tall for a Chinese and sturdy. She was dressed in black from head to foot: black scarf, black jacket and trousers, black cotton shoes. She moved at a measured pace. She and her colleagues were just the kind of technical people who had been harassed, rejected, and misused in the past decade. The waves of successive campaigns must have battered her but she had survived to march that day. As she led the shouting of the slogans against the Gang of Four, her fist in the air, her face was unsmiling. Perhaps because she knew too well the human and economic costs of the past two decades. Beside her must have walked ghosts of colleagues who had died under persecution or were toiling in labor camps or sitting in enforced idleness, their skills rejected by their own country. She would know too how much faster China's oil wealth could have been used to relieve the nation's poverty but for the follies of the ultraleft. Like the people of Europe under Nazi occupation, she and her colleagues must have wondered at times over the years whether a day like today would ever come. Now, with her voice and her fist and with every measured step, she was taking her solemn revenge.

8

Deng's Drive for Power

THE THREE DAYS of loosely organized but well-ordered marches in Peking by nearly six million people were followed by a rally on Tiananmen Square on 24 October in which one million people took part. This was an official celebration, and the national leadership made its first appearance since the arrest of the Four. Hua Guofeng, appearing in public for the first time as chairman of the Party, wore military uniform. Real excitement enlivened the drum-beating ritual. A new era was beginning.

The Mayor of Peking, Wú De, made the main speech. With his half-frame spectacles and beaming, avuncular features, he had the air of a Chinese Pickwick. But his speech had an important political purpose—to reinforce Hua's image as the worthy successor to Mao, chosen by Mao himself. He disclosed to the Chinese people the words Mao had used to give Hua his benediction: "With you in charge, I am at ease." The resolute action taken against the Gang of Four by "the Central Committe headed by Comrade Hua Guofeng" had demonstrated the wisdom of Mao's choice.

If the occasion was more than a convention for nominating a candidate for a U.S. presidential election, it was something less

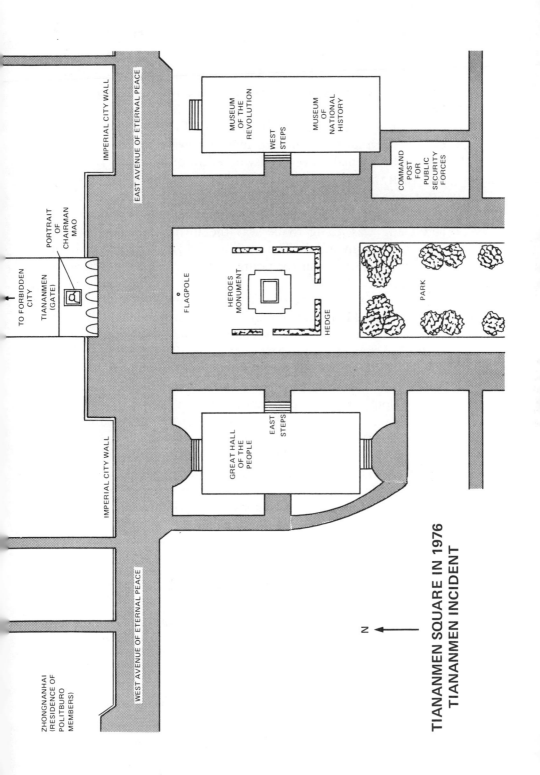

ZHONGNANHAI
(RESIDENCE OF
POLITBURO
MEMBERS)

TO FORBIDDEN
CITY

TIANANMEN
(GATE)

PORTRAIT
OF
CHAIRMAN
MAO

IMPERIAL CITY WALL

WEST AVENUE OF ETERNAL PEACE

EAST AVENUE OF ETERNAL PEACE

IMPERIAL CITY WALL

MUSEUM OF THE
REVOLUTION

MUSEUM OF
NATIONAL
HISTORY

WEST
STEPS

COMMAND
POST
FOR
PUBLIC
SECURITY
FORCES

FLAGPOLE

HEROES
MONUMENT

HEDGE

PARK

GREAT HALL
OF THE
PEOPLE

EAST
STEPS

N

**TIANANMEN SQUARE IN 1976
TIANANMEN INCIDENT**

definitive than a coronation. Despite all the genuine rejoicing, something was missing. Hua Guofeng did not speak, which was odd in view of his being proclaimed as the worthy successor. The rally was described as a municipal rally, not a national one, even though all the Politburo members were there—including those who normally lived and worked in other cities. But what was really missing was a man. Like the ghost of Banquo at Macbeth's celebration banquet, the image of Deng Xiaoping haunted Hua's victory rally. What the relationship between Hua and Deng was going to be was the unspoken question that dominated many minds. The settling of their relations would be a most important focus for political activity for the next two or three years.

Predicting the future of that relationship was especially difficult because Hua had been on the national stage for only a few years, and as a leader in the second rank. His personal views on major issues were a subject of uncertainty. True, one could look back to his record in Hunan, where he had consistently followed Mao's line in accelerating the collectivization of agriculture, but had he done so out of personal conviction or out of loyalty to Mao? True, he had made the major speech on agriculture at the Dazhai conference in 1975, but how far was he personally responsible for its content? Did he, for instance, really believe that Chinese agriculture could be mechanized in five years, as he had said it should be? After twenty-three years as a Hunan administrator, surely he must have known that this was unrealistic?* Perhaps he had not had the political status at that time to veto a target he knew could not be achieved. Almost certainly he was

* I would remember this target as I traveled through the Chinese countryside. Even twenty miles from Peking, in the Valley of the Ming Tombs, hardly a neglected area, some very primitive techniques were still in use, and when I went into the truly rural areas I saw only rare signs of mechanization: for every plow pulled by a tractor of any kind, I would see perhaps twenty pulled by bullocks or bullocks plus people; for every cart pulled by an engine, I would see perhaps thirty pulled by animals or people. Like others who travel around China, I was repeatedly struck by scenes that show no change from those painted by landscape artists a thousand years ago. This is not to deny the achievements of the last thirty years, but to see them in the perspective of the vast amount that remains to be done before China's agriculture can be said to be modernized.

too junior then to have brought into his speech, against all the fashion of the times, a realistic appreciation of how far agricultural technology in China had lagged behind that of other Third World countries in Asia and how unsatisfactory had been the rate of growth of Chinese agriculture compared to the growth of population.

Hua had delivered the euology at the memorial rally for Mao in September. Could one deduce from his call for continued criticism of Deng Xiaoping that he was opposed to the approach to government laid out by Deng in 1975 and that he intended that Deng should stay out in the cold? Or was this a short-term political tactic, dictated by the need to minimize the affront to Mao's memory in the first months after his death?

Now that Hua had been appointed chairman, was he his own master? As Chairman of the Party and Chairman of the Military Commission of the Party, he outranked Minister of Defense Ye Jianying, but I could not help noticing at his victory rally in October that as Hua moved back and forth along the balcony of the Gate of Heavenly Peace to acknowledge the cheers of the crowd two men moved behind him: Ye Jianying and Li Xiannian, with Ye very close behind indeed. Such moves are planned in China and signal messages that no one is prepared to put into print. Did it mean that Ye was playing the role of Warwick the Kingmaker?

If one thing was clear about the future relations between Hua and Deng it was that Hua would not try to exclude Deng from power as the Four had tried to do. Even with Mao alive and the Four in office, that had proved a recipe for political suicide, and Hua's career had shown that he was a political realist. He would have no difficulty calculating the approximate relation between his strength and Deng's.

It was far more than a difference of two political personalities: it was a difference of two generations.

Deng belonged to a generation of leaders of heroic stature. They had founded the Party, or joined it in its infancy. They had fought in every major phase of the revolution. They had earned the special aura that attached to men who had made the Long March. Then in 1949 they had brought order out of chaos: the

People's Republic was their personal creation. Few leaders in the world, let alone in China, had such long experience of governing hundreds of millions of people and of dealing with major international relations.

Deng himself had behind him twenty-one years' experience in the Politburo. In the Civil War, thirty years before, he had been political commissar to a front-line army of half a million and had organized some two million peasants in logistical support of that army. When victory was won, he became chief administrator of the whole of southwest China, one sixth of the country, with a population then of about a hundred million.

Deng's generation had experience of dealing with foreigners ranging back over more than fifty years to the time when they had gone to France and Germany as worker-students in their teens or early twenties. They had been dealing with the Soviet Union since the 1920s, when Stalin and his comrades had tried to call the shots for the Chinese revolution. They had managed the Sino-Soviet state-to-state relationship in good times and in bad. Deng himself had helped build the cooperation of the 1950s, had coped with tensions before the open break and had thereafter been in the forefront of the ideological struggle. His generation had thrown an army across the Yalu river into Korea to repulse the American army that seemed to threaten the three-year-old People's Republic. They had survived the years of blockade and isolation from the West, and in the 1970s had begun to build lines to Western Europe, Japan, and then the United States. In this phase also Deng had been prominent, after his restoration to power.

It was Deng's generation that had provided the most spectacular victims of the Cultural Revolution. They had made no abject self-criticism when struck down and they had not bought their restoration by surrendering their independence of judgment. That stood them in good stead now that people had grown tired of political trimmers and were putting a premium on integrity. The fact that Deng had shared the fate of millions of his fellow Party officials and fellow countrymen by being struck from power, and that his family had suffered like many others (one of his children, Deng Pufang, had been crippled during the Cultural Revolution) meant that many families across the land could identify with his professional and personal traumas.*

It was no reflection on Hua's personal qualities that he had only three years' experience in the Politburo, compared with Deng's twenty-one; or that he had moved up the political ladder during the years Deng was in disgrace; or that he had not had dealings with foreigners. By the standards of his generation he had a rich experience of government in an important province and had been promoted fast. Quite simply, his generation had grown up in the shadow of men who had been makers of history rather than administrators of an established regime, and they knew very well they had neither the political experience nor the national prestige of their elders.

The fact that elections played no part in Chinese political life meant that for Deng to translate the following he enjoyed among officials and "the masses" into political power he would have to use techniques unfamiliar to those who elect their governments. But a seasoned campaigner like him knew the ropes.

Hua would need a fine sense of balance and timing. He would have to abandon some of the people and policies most closely associated with Mao's last years. (He had made a start with the Gang of Four.) But if he went too far and too fast in this direction he would lose his political identity and become a figurehead and mouthpiece for the pragmatists: a Chinese equivalent of a constitutional monarch, making from the throne speeches that were written by others. He would have to diminish the cult of Mao, because it was becoming counter-

---

* Deng Pufang was about twenty-three when the Cultural Revolution was launched, and was studying physics at Peking University. He quickly became a target for the leftists. (The movement was supposed to destroy old ways of thinking but in fact multiplied rather than diminished such practices as visiting the sins of the parents on the children.) Pufang was imprisoned for a time in an unlighted room, then interrogated. One day, after interrogation, he fell from a high building, smashing his spine and paralyzing his lower limbs, which today are said to be shriveled "like hemp stalks." Pufang claims he was pushed; his interrogators said he jumped to commit suicide. (Cheng Ming, Hong Kong, No. 16, February 1979, pp. 30–31. Cheng Ming used a masculine pronoun when referring to Deng Pufang; other sources speak of Pufang as a daughter.

productive, but he must do so slowly so as not to undermine the force of his own claim to the succession.

The first move, a conciliatory one, came from Deng: on 10 October, four days after the arrest of the Four, he wrote a letter to Hua praising his level of ideological understanding and his political line and saying that his experience was rich, his age young, and his spirit vigorous. He commented that Hua's leadership in striking down the Gang of Four had shown him to be the Party's "wise leader." Therefore he, Deng, completely supported Hua as the leader of party and state and expressed the belief that, given his age, Hua could ensure that China would have at least fifteen to twenty years of stability and could march successfully into the twenty-first century.[1]

Hua's call at the memorial rally for Mao to deepen the criticism of Deng Xiaoping was not implemented. Indeed, the very opposite occurred: the slogan became a slogan without a campaign behind it. The last time it was pronounced by a high official was when Wu De made a speech to the Standing Committee of the National People's Congress at the end of November. By then the anti-Deng campaign was all over but the slogan-shouting; no specific criticisms of Deng had been heard for two months. At about that time the Politburo formally ruled that Deng was not a counter-revolutionary as the Gang of Four had alleged. This ruling became known to the world in a bizarre manner, like most important decisions that year. The change in Deng's status was disclosed in the magazine *Science News*, published in English for distribution abroad. The September issue did not appear until December, and when it did so two pages dealing with the criticism of Deng had been removed and a page of errata inserted. This deleted references to Deng as "the arch unrepentant capitalist-roader" and to his "revisionist line" as "counter-revolutionary," substituted "his erroneous remarks" for "his shameless lies," and stated that criticism of him should not be "deepened" but merely "continued." For the light relief brought by such gestures, China-watchers are duly thankful.

The first objective of Deng's supporters after the arrest of the Gang of Four was, of course, to get their leader returned to power. After that they could carry the attack into the camp of their opponents—those in the Politburo who resisted Deng's personal authority and his more radical ideas for reform, and those bosses of provinces and major cities who owed their promotion to the Cultural Revolution and were therefore less responsive to Deng than people he would appoint.

As *Science News* had so conscientiously informed its readers, Deng was now out of the counter-revolutionary doghouse but not yet returned to the Politburo palace: there was still no agreement on his public rehabilitation. Timing was important. The longer his return was delayed, the more firmly in the saddle those who had something to fear from it would be. These latter favored summoning a National People's Congress (NPC) at an early date, to consolidate their hold on power. Deng's supporters wanted an NPC only after his return to office, when he and they could exercise more influence over it; they won that battle. A poster campaign in favor of Deng's return sprang up in Shanghai, Canton, and elsewhere. The first anniversary of the death of Zhou Enlai, in January 1977, provided a golden opportunity to intensify this campaign. In Peking the Heroes' Monument on Tiananmen Square was no longer available as a focus of activity because almost the whole square had been taken over as the building site for constructing the Mao Memorial Hall and was surrounded by a wooden palisade. But of course the palisade provided inexhaustible display space for posters and the space in front of the Gate of Heavenly Peace, which is adorned with Ming-dynasty bridges and cloud-topped marble columns, provided a superb setting for a second great festival of the Chinese spirit. Again there was a great outpouring of emotion and creativity, but this occasion was smaller than that of April 1976—and happier, because the Gang of Four were now under arrest. Elegant baskets of artificial flowers, trailing ribbon, swung and bounced in the breeze, suspended from lamp posts. Pretty but prim young PLA women posed for their family photograph albums amid massive wreaths of a thousand brilliant flowers as if they were sitting on a carnival float. Factories, schools, and offices seemed to have engaged in a handicrafts competition and sightseers strolled around comparing the ingenuity of interwoven silk, tinsel, and tulle. Of course there was much serious political activity mixed with the handicrafts. The aims were now the return to power of Deng and the purge of what later would be known as the Whatever Faction.

Since homage to Zhou was no longer considered subversive, the official press was full of the kind of articles one might have expected at his death. Commemorative books, photos, and stamps were officially on sale. However, there were still undertones of confrontation between Zhou and Mao: a procession of thousands marched to the Gate of Heavenly Peace bearing a portrait of Zhou draped in black; there they halted and, having turned to face the huge portrait of Mao, they took an oath of fidelity—to Zhou. Their ceremony ended, they bowed low three times and marched away. Another column passed the Gate, shouting "Zhou is alive! He is among us!"

The posters that aroused most enthusiasm were those calling for the return of Deng. All day and late into the freezing nights, crowds gathered in front of the palisades to read posters praising Deng and calling for his restoration to office. "We want Chairman Hua Guofeng to give Comrade Deng Xiaoping a job!" often appeared. As at Qing Ming, the crowds were so dense that one man would read for the benefit of the others. I remember one evening struggling through a dense mass of bodies muffled in heavy topcoats and thick hats with ear flaps to hear a young man read out, by torchlight, a "bring back Deng" poster. When he came to a passage which said that morale had risen in 1975, when Deng was in charge of Party and state affairs, the young reader turned to the crowd and shouted "Is that right?" and they roared back as one man "That's right!"

From the carved cloud atop one marble column was suspended a small bottle of red glass with a label bearing the words *Very Good*. "Small bottle" in Chinese is *xiao ping*, so this was another vote of confidence in Deng Xiaoping. Symptomatic of the hope pinned on Deng to restore respect for Chinese culture were posters bearing tributes to him expressed in concise, classical language and traditional rhythm, written in elegant calligraphy. His merits were contrasted to the crimes of the Four: along the Avenue of Eternal Peace for twenty-eight yards stretched a series of cartoons attacking the Four; the series ended with a sketch of Deng which made him look like a handsome fifty-year-old, a Chinese Jeff Chandler. To read the series, people joined a queue at the start and shuffled along at a snail's pace until they reached the end. As a counterpoint to the little red bottle, some had hung the Gang of Four in effigy. The effigies were brilliant caricatures in papier mâché, showing Jiang Qing in a long black dress decorated with gold and Zhang Chunqiao complete with spectacles.

The praise for Deng did not claim infallibility for him: one poster-writer acknowledged that Deng had made mistakes after being restored to office in 1973, adding rhetorically "How can one work and not make mistakes?"

The more controversial posters were discreetly removed under cover of darkness, but one slogan painted on a wall was judged too inflammatory to be read at all. As soon as it was spotted two soldiers were ordered to cover it with their topcoats. The naked thought was thus shielded from the innocent eyes of the masses and the prurient eyes of foreigners until a detergent strong enough to remove it could be found.

Posters asked that the verdict be reversed on the Tiananmen demonstration of 5 April 1976, that its counter-revolutionary label be removed and it be recognized as a revolutionary action. One ran "We are asking that the bloody crimes and brutal suppression of the masses in Tiananmen be finally clarified." The Commander of Peking was attacked for his alleged role in that suppression; the Mayor, Wu De, who had called for the square to be cleared that violent Monday, was also attacked: "The people of Peking cannot be at ease while Wu De is in the capital." One evening a crowd gathered in front of the gate to the Zhongnanhai residences of the leaders to present a six-point appeal touching on the most sensitive issues of the hour: reinstate Deng; transfer Wu De; investigate the Tiananmen demonstrations; punish those responsible for their suppression; put the Gang of Four on public trial; and build memorial halls for Marshal Zhu De and Premier Zhou Enlai. An investigation was conducted and the core of the demonstrators traced to a Peking factory. They were arrested, to discourage others from following their unsettling example.

The Commander of Peking and the Mayor were not the only people attacked openly. So also were a Politburo member (Ni Zhifu) who was responsible for Peking's militia and a woman textile worker (Wu Guixian) who, like Wang Hongwen, had been swept upward by the Cultural Revolution to become an alternate member of the Politburo. The Minister of Health, who was the widow of a security minister assassinated while in office, a vice-foreign minister who was Mao's niece, and the head of the Peking security forces were also targets of open criticism. That ordinary citizens should dare to attack some of the most powerful people in the nation by name was a measure of the momentum the tide of demands for democracy had acquired.

For the first time we caught a glimpse of the deeper aspirations of many young people. Young men stood on walls or the luggage racks of their bicycles to make impromptu speeches calling for democratic freedoms in a sense that Montesquieu would have recognized and combining a general demand for democracy with statements of more immediate goals.

People writing posters and the young men standing on their bicycles were asking that truth be recognized, lies renounced, and democracy practiced. For the first time in years they found it worthwhile to create beauty in poetry, calligraphy, and banks of silk flowers. Watching the China that had revealed itself at Qing Ming and was revealing itself again in these days of January was like watching someone regain consciousness. The eyes showed a flicker of recognition, a smile moved the lips, and limbs began to stir. Seven years before, Huang Xiang, the poet of the Enlightenment Society, had written his poem about the attempt to enslave the spirit of the Chinese people and ended it with this irreducible expression of optimism:

> The people's freedom of the spirit never dies.
> Truth, Beauty and Goodness which live within the heart
> of man can never be uprooted, never be snatched away.

As news of events in Peking filtered to him in distant Guizhou province, Huang Xiang must have been excited to see these public signs that his faith had been justified.

The impression that hopes of far-reaching liberalization were being attached to the anticipated return of Deng Xiaoping was reinforced when there appeared in Canton late in January a poster that presented a devastating survey of the ills of the Chinese society and drove its points home with a comparison between the performance of the Japanese and Chinese economies since 1949. The writer attributed China's poor performance to her lack of economic democracy. His remedy lay in greater popular participation in economic decisions, and he quoted Engels to the effect that everyone who takes part in production in society should also take part in the decisions about investment and management of funds. The poster remained in place for several days and was guarded by soldiers. Clearly the Canton authorities, General Xü Shiyu and First Secretary Wei Guoqing, were in no hurry to suppress such thoughts, and it so happened that Deng Xiaoping was repeatedly sighted in Canton around this time.

In late January, one of Deng's allies, Tan Zhenlin,* told a group of Japanese visitors that Deng would be back by the end of the month. It was not to be. Instead, February saw a sharpening of tension between his opponents and supporters. On 7 February the *People's Daily* published an editorial that said that whatever Mao had said must be obeyed and whatever he had decided must be upheld. It described this as "Holding High Chairman Mao's Banner." The line of this editorial could not be reconciled with Deng's rehabilitation, unless he renounced publicly all his proposals for reform. His supporters in the Politburo labeled it the Two Whatevers. One of them, Geng Biao, commented: "If we follow this, we shall never do anything."[2] Deng's supporters in Canton expressed themselves more strongly. They sent a letter to Chairman Hua Guofeng and the members of the Central Committee urging them to review and criticize mistakes made by Mao Zedong: "The eyes of the people are wide open. Every one of them knows in his heart where Chairman Mao succeeded and where he failed." They warned that the Party Center would lose the respect of the people if it continued to

---

* A vice-chairman of the Standing Committee of the National People's Congress, formerly a Politburo member specializing in agriculture.

"paper over the faults and mistakes of Chairman Mao." They affirmed that the Party as a whole had made several mistakes and that the Cultural Revolution was one of them. They asked for a review of the cases of Deng Xiaoping and Marshal Peng Dehuai, the main critic of Mao's Great Leap Forward.[3]

At the beginning of March a high-level meeting was called to discuss the principal political issues facing the leadership, including the handling of the Gang of Four, the nature of the Tiananmen demonstrations, and the return of Deng to office. The meeting was not publicly announced, but as it drew to its close several well-informed sources gave accounts to foreign diplomats and journalists.[4] According to these, the meeting was attended by all the members of the Politburo and senior military and civilian figures from the Center and the provinces. One outward sign of the meeting was a cavalcade of some forty-five black Hong Qi cars (China's luxury limousine, reserved for the use of VIPs) that moved in and out of the center of Peking each day, carrying the participants to the meeting. Reportedly there was little or no outright opposition to the principle of returning Deng to office, but there was sharp disagreement on the position he should be offered. His strongest supporters, including Vice-Premier Li Xiannian, Wei Guoqing, the First Secretary of Guangdong province, and General Xü Shiyu of the Canton Military Region, were said to have proposed that Deng be made Premier and First Vice-Chairman of the Party. To this the Mayor of Peking responded by saying if the meeting was to listen to such a proposal, then the Gang of Four should be released from custody to address the meeting. Marshal Ye Jianying dissociated himself from the extreme position of Deng's supporters. A proposal that attracted much support was that Deng should simply be restored to his old posts. When he addressed the Deng issue Hua Guofeng reportedly began by dissociating him from the Tiananmen demonstrations.

That was slander spread by the Gang of Four, Hua was reported as saying. When Deng was leading the work of the State Council, his work had both successes and errors. Chairman Mao had raised criticisms of his errors, with the aim of helping him correct his mistakes and improve his work. But the slander and distortions of the Gang of Four caused him to be attacked. This was absolutely not Chairman Mao's original idea in criticizing comrades who had committed errors, which was to "learn from past mistakes" and "cure the sickness to save the patient." Deng's return to work required a certain procedure and a certain period of time—it must wait for the time to be ripe—but it would come, of course.

On the nature of the Tiananmen demonstrations, Hua said that they had started out as peaceful homage to Zhou Enlai but they had been infiltrated by a small number of counter-revolutionaries who had attacked party leaders and engaged in physical destruction. It had been absolutely necessary to suppress these counter-revolutionaries.

The meeting naturally had difficulty in reaching a decision on Deng, and according to some accounts actually ended without having decided the issue. But the anniversary of the Tiananmen demonstrations was drawing near and there was high risk of disorder if the question was left unsettled. The Minister of Defense, Marshal Ye, took on the role of arbiter and conciliator with the result that by the end of the month the Party was telling the masses (in briefings that were unpublicized and "for internal consumption only") that Deng would be restored to all his old posts of vice-chairman of the Party, vice-premier, and chief of staff of the PLA; in addition he would become a vice-chairman of the military affairs commission of the Central Committee. He would not assume his duties or reappear in public immediately, but after a delay of some three or four months, which would give time for the Central Committee to meet to confirm these decisions. Another most dangerous issue had been settled, and Qing Ming passed off peacefully.

At the end of December Hua showed that he was in tune with some of the pragmatists' ideas. Most striking was the use he made of a speech delivered by Mao twenty years before, in April 1956, under the title "On the Ten Great Relationships."[5] This was one of the most pragmatic statements with which Mao had associated himself after 1949. It was a synthesis of the views of the Politburo and thirty-four government departments on a number of key issues, expressed during an exchange of views that had lasted two months. By asking a national conference to study this speech, Hua signaled a return to the rational policy-making evident in most fields in 1956 and said something about the method of decision-making he preferred. Deng then wrote a second letter to Hua, on 10 April. He made four points, according to an account published in a reliable Hong Kong paper:

1. He had heard that, in his report to the meeting in March, Chairman Hua had said that the broad masses who went to Tiananmen Square to mourn Zhou Enlai were acting appropriately, and also that he [Deng] had no connection with the incident. This made him extremely happy, and he wished to express his thanks.

2. When he was leading the work of the State Council in 1975, Deng had done some beneficial work, but he recognized that his work also had some shortcomings and errors, and so he sincerely accepted Chairman Mao's instruction and criticism.

3. He hoped that Chairman Hua would correctly and completely follow Mao's line while leading the Party Central Committee.

4. He would fully obey the Central Committee's decisions as to when he would return to work, and what position he would assume.

The months of waiting for Deng's return were a time of considerable activity and some political movement. The three documents drafted under Deng's guidance in 1975, the "Three Poisonous Weeds," were pronounced to have been fragrant flowers. Scores of conferences were held to tackle urgent problems and above all to restore law and order. Numerous foreign leaders were received in Peking. But despite all this activity the country's return to normal working was slow, and the most thorny issues of ideology and policy were not grasped. Chinese I knew became a little more ready to express a view on politics and it was evident that they and many like them were impatient for Deng's return. They had to wait until July, when his rehabilitation was confirmed as one of the results of the Third Plenum of the Tenth Central Committee. When the decision was announced on radio and television at eight P.M. firecrackers and rockets shot into the air all over Peking. The next day there were jubilant processions in Peking, and throughout the country provincial leaders acclaimed his return to office. On 12 August he made his first public appearance at a soccer match in Peking's biggest stadium. There was an outside radio broadcast of the match and thunderous applause could be heard from the crowd of eighty thousand as his arrival was announced. At his side sat Mayor Wu De, who had been the last leader to issue a call to continue to criticize him. A few days later the Eleventh National Congress of the Party was held in the capital. The congress was a cautious mixture of continuity and change. In the words of the official commentary, it "held high the great banner of Chairman Mao." Indeed, it raised it to a safe height where the writing on the banner could be read selectively, with the aid of a telescope that remained in the custody of the Politburo.

Most of those who now marched beneath the banner of China's greatest visionary were hard-headed pragmatists. The Central Committee was purged of most of the Maoist "rebels," although many less radical people whose careers had prospered because of the Cultural Revolution retained their posts. Into the vacant seats came rehabilitated veterans and others. The Politburo changes, like those of the Central Committee as a whole, strengthened Deng's hand but did not put him in a dominant position. The changes had brought in some people who would give the leadership new vitality of thinking, but they were not young men. The average age of the new Politburo was sixty-eight. To outsiders the surprise appointment of the congress was the promotion of Wang Dongxing, Mao's former bodyguard, to be a vice-chairman of the Party.

China's three top leaders—Hua, Ye, and Deng—were presented as a triumvirate, and all made speeches to the congress. Deng's was a very brief but pithy closing address. He laid more stress on reviving the Party's lost traditions than on holding high Chairman Mao's banner. He made a striking call on the Party to "have faith in the masses and rely on them [and] listen to the voice of the people." Other thoughts he left with his audience that would have sounded as music in ears tired of doubletalk, hyperbole, and ideological wind were: "The minimum requirement for a Communist is to be an honest person, honest in word and honest in deed. . . . There must be less empty talk and more hard work."[7]

In the major speech to the congress, Hua publicized for the immediate future eight "fighting tasks" by no means unwelcome to the pragmatists and, in a theoretical passage, opened the way for structural change in the economy without announcing any specific decisions. But did they welcome his declaration that "Political revolutions in the nature of the Cultural Revolution will take place many times in the future"? Did they share his assessment of the Gang of Four as "typical representatives within our Party of landlords, rich peasants, counter-revolutionaries and . . . the old and new bourgeoisie"? The landlords, the rich peasants, and the bourgeoisie had rather gained the impression under persecution during the past ten years that the Gang of Four regarded them as vermin to be exterminated. The pragmatists among Hua's audience may also have been somewhat surprised to hear him say that the smashing of the Gang of Four was one of the great victories of the Cultural Revolution.

If the personnel appointments and policy line fell far short of what Deng might have wished, he had established a solid base from which to advance his forces.[8]

In the eighteen months that followed the Eleventh Congress, the pragmatists continued their offensive against both the ideology and personal power of their rivals and opponents, a very different struggle from that against the Gang of Four. This was not to be handled as a life-and-death affair in which the loser could expect to be driven from the Party and denounced as the root of all evil. One reason for the difference was a sense that the disagreements were now less fundamental; another was the recognition that yet another upheaval would not be understood abroad, and international opinion was becoming increasingly important to China. If the pragmatists could achieve their goals by discreet "salami tactics," they would do so. But whatever the means they chose, they were in dead earnest, believing that the drive to modernize would be aborted if they did not remove what they saw as fatal obstacles.

The pragmatists used the well-tried weapon of historical allegory. They used articles in the central press to identify a type of person to be attacked; these attacks on archetypes would then legitimize attacks on people who could be presented as fitting the description at different levels of society and in different localities. They leaked to a noncommunist paper in Hong Kong, known for its accuracy and objectivity, information favorable to them which in China was treated as classified—knowing that it would be fed back into China by foreign broadcasts in Chinese. They built up the credibility and prestige of political magazines in Hong Kong responsive to their guidance by giving their editors and writers access to sources in China better than any available to other journalists. These magazines then wrote in plain language the "inside story" of struggles that could be referred to only in veiled terms in the mainland press and, for a while at least, the magazines were available to senior officials.

With a nod and a wink they gave the signal for poster campaigns that brought the masses into the act in Chinese cities. Behind closed doors at gatherings of the top one hundred or so powerholders, they took their gloves off and leveled charges in the bluntest language. They devoted great energy to expounding the essence of their political philosophy and exposing the fallacies of the legacy of dogma. They chose a slogan, "Seek truth from facts," which was used as a banner around which people gathered to show where they stood in the contest for allegiances, and which became a new touchstone of political orthodoxy. On occasion, they used foreign travel as it is sometimes used by leaders in noncommunist states: to build a person's prestige by showing him or her in exotic surroundings or in the company of the great in foreign lands.

As I watched the events of 1977–1980 unfold, an image formed in my mind. The scene is a circus ring. In the center of the ring is one of those outsize balls acrobats move with their feet. The orchestra strikes up and a famous troupe of some twenty or so acrobats run across the sawdust to stand at attention around the ball. The orchestra plays a fanfare, the spotlights swoop back to the entrance, and on runs the leader of the troupe. He leaps nimbly onto the ball.

Drums roll and the troupe deploys itself around the ball. One group, whose costumes have the words TRUTH FROM FACTS emblazoned on them, stands to the right of the ball. To

its left stands a group with the words HOLD HIGH MAO'S BAN-
NER on their costumes. In a circle around them all stands a third
group. Their costumes are emblazoned with a single word,
TECHNOCRAT; they carry a fan in each hand. On one fan is
FOUR and on the other, MODERNIZATIONS. As the orchestra
launches into a march, those on the right put their shoulders to
the ball and start to push; and those on the left put *their* shoulders to the ball also, to resist. The Technocrats do not push one
way or the other: they circle around the others waving their
marked fans. When the ball moves, they move with it. The ball
always moves in the direction in which it is pushed by the
TRUTH FROM FACTS group. Sometimes it moves faster, sometimes slower, and sometimes the resistance is such that it comes
to a halt. The leader stays on top of the ball, displaying a sure
sense of balance. When the ball gathers such momentum that it
threatens the unity and stability of the different acrobats, he
uses his weight to slow it down.

In the public seats are the Masses. Many of them cheer for
the TRUTH FROM FACTS group and sometimes hurl invective at
the MAO'S BANNER people. When the noise from the Masses
grows too loud all the acrobats turn to them and tell them to
calm down.

A party of foreign visitors sits in a box marked CHINA
WATCHERS. They find the act hard to follow because the walls
of the box are made of thick glass that is deeply tinted and almost soundproof. Some of them spend a great deal of time
peering through the glass, trying to identify the acrobats in each
group. They compile elaborate charts and detailed name-lists.
Wiser ones among them content themselves with identifying
a few key individuals. Their box is air-conditioned and well
stocked with Scotch; so whenever the CHINA WATCHERS get
bored they hold a cocktail party.

It is not only foreign China Watchers who are intrigued by
what goes on in the ring. Hong Kong Chinese are, too. Hong
Kong political monthlies with privileged access to people and
information in China and a consistent ability to identify trends
there named Vice-Chairman Wang Dongxing as the chief
spokesman for the "Mao's Banner" group—identifying it as
the Whatever Faction, which had taken the line that whatever

Mao had said or decided must be upheld.[9] China-watchers everywhere, in a rare display of unanimity, identified Deng Xiaoping as the leader of those "Seeking Truth from Facts."

The most important issue facing China at the time of Deng's return to power in the summer of 1977 was the evaluation of Mao. Should the Communist Party continue to insist that Mao had been infallible, and that to suggest otherwise was not only blasphemy but a crime to be punished by law? This issue transcended all others at that time.

As the Eleventh Party Congress closed in August, the Chairman Mao Memorial Hall was being completed and the delegates were the first to enter. The anniversary of Mao's death was approaching, and this called for commemorative articles. The pragmatists seized the occasion to give their view of the proper way to approach Mao's Thought. It was to be taken as a model of how to apply the scientific method of Marxism–Leninism and was a development of that philosophy. It was a scientific system, to be viewed as a whole. The great crime of the Gang of Four had been to quote thoughts out of context and distort them. They had even forged some, according to a *People's Daily* editorial. Mao was quoted as having written that Marxism–Leninism was not to be regarded as "a dogma, but as a guide to action . . . as the science of revolution." This was an extremely important step forward by the pragmatists, but their arguments were couched in terms that, while they would be clear enough to intellectuals, would not send the blood coursing through the veins of the masses.

The pragmatists had no intention of letting matters rest there. In November they touched on the explosive issue of the deification of Mao, using again the safest device available, a quotation from the late Chairman himself: "It would be presumptuous for anyone to claim Godlike omniscience and omnipotence." But the writer shrank from actually saying that Mao had been deified, limiting himself to saying that the Four had treated Mao Thought as lifeless dogma.[10] A shock was sent through the system at the same time when the *People's Daily* printed an article entitled "Qin Shi Huang Did Not Belong to the Communist Party." To any sophisticated reader that could mean only one thing: Mao's credentials as a Communist were being questioned. The author, a soldier, wrote "As everybody knows, Qin Shi Huang was a feudal emperor. . . . As compared with the Communist Party, Qin Shi Huang was but a drop in the ocean, unworthy to be mentioned in the same breath."[11] It would theoretically be possible to interpret this article as a criticism of the treatment the Four gave Qin Shi Huang, but the editors of the *People's Daily* would never unintentionally publish an article open to grave misinterpretation. Articles like this are drafted with a little ambiguity simply to leave the writer and editor a defense if they are challenged, as this one might well have been. In April 1978 the Academy of Social Sciences was given space in the press to publish summaries of discussions its staff had been holding on topics taboo until then. Among the forbidden zones they had entered were the deification of historical figures in China, but still they shrank from saying outright that the Four had deified Mao. Mao had been dead nineteen months, but no one yet felt free in public to criticize his deification. Some China-watchers were wondering whether a torrent of criticism would be unleashed on him at some stage. Certainly the situation was not going to stand still, but no one would move before the highest leaders had spoken.

In June Deng seized the initiative on this issue, and in so doing gained the political leadership of the country. Oedipus was made king of Thebes because he outwitted the Sphinx, which had paralysed that city-state by fear; Khrushchev in his secret speech to the Twentieth Congress had seized the initiative in the Soviet Union by liberating it from the terror and the dogma of Stalin. In 1977 China was struggling to free itself from the paralysis induced by turning Mao into a demigod and his Thought into dogma. Deng did not make a frontal attack on Mao, as Khrushchev had done on Stalin. He had no wish to—and no need to, because by their actions on Tiananmen Square and hundreds of other places in April 1976 the Chinese people had gone far toward freeing themselves from the thrall of the demigod and his dogma. What was needed now was to complete that action and make sure that the Party's official position caught up with the people. This was still a task requiring courage and political skill, and the purpose was a very important one: to ensure that none among Mao's successors exploited his name and his writings to impose their own dictatorship on the people.

Deng displayed the bold intelligence of Oedipus rather than the bull-headed courage of Khrushchev: instead of attacking the demigod of the 1960s and 1970s he praised the human Mao, who had led the Communist Party to power in 1949. Instead of denouncing Mao's thinking of the later years he quoted the words of Mao's early years to put down those who were persisting in treating Mao's Thoughts as dogma. The end result he intended was death for Mao the demigod and revival for Mao the man.

Deng "captured" Mao for the pragmatic cause by reminding everyone in a speech at the All-Army Political Work Conference in June 1978 that the younger Mao's greatness had lain in the originality and courage he had shown in applying Marxist–Leninist principles to the actual conditions of China. "To seek truth from facts," he said, "is the starting point, the fundamental point in Chairman Mao's thought." He gave numerous quotations from Mao's earlier years to drive the point home. Mao, he said, had "advocated and practiced investigation and study of objective social conditions"; he had abhorred doing things from wishful thinking or strictly according to the book. In his 1930 article "Oppose Book Worship" he had written: "When we say Marxism is correct, it is certainly not because Marx was a 'prophet' but because his theory had been proved correct in our practice and our struggle." Deng told his audience that Mao had warned the Party not to take Marxist theory as lifeless dogma. He had discussed problems in the light of different times, places, and conditions and used quotations sparingly.

As they heard or read Deng's speech, people would remember only too well how Mao in later life had acted in accordance with how he thought people should be rather than were, how he had lost touch with the aspirations of ordinary citizens, and how he had allowed his followers to turn his Thought into dogma and worship his little red book. Deng had no need to make explicit the contrast between the younger Mao and the Mao who for instance forced the pace of collectivization in the mid-1950s, when he was already more than sixty years old.

Deng did, however, make a very explicit attack on those

who, contrary to the principles and practice which had made Mao great, now insisted that whatever he had said or decided should be upheld. "There are comrades who talk about Mao Zedong Thought every day, but often forget, abandon, or even oppose Chairman Mao's fundamental Marxist view and method of seeking truth from facts, proceeding from reality in doing everything and integrating theory with practice. Furthermore, some people even maintain that whoever persists in seeking truth from facts . . . is guilty of a heinous crime. In essence their view is that one may only copy straight from Marx, Engels, Lenin and Stalin, and from Chairman Mao and should rest content with mechanical copying, transmitting and reproduction. . . . What they raise is no minor issue!"[12]

His audience would know the leaders against whom these words were aimed. If the NCNA account is to be believed, the audience liked what they heard; NCNA reported "his speech was frequently punctuated by stormy applause." It did not claim as much for the speeches made earlier by Chairman Hua and Marshal Ye. The strength of what Deng said was that it was true. He had of course left the dogmatic Mao of the later years decently buried, but his opponents would have a hard time holding that against him. Even "Seek truth from facts," which Deng had used repeatedly in his speech and which was to become a rallying cry in the campaign for pragmatism, had its roots in Mao's own life: it had adorned the gateway to the teachers' training college in Changsha that he attended as a young man. There seemed no way in which Deng's rivals could counterattack, and yet if they did not the initiative would remain in his hands.

The pragmatists had by no means waited for this master stroke by Deng before starting to purge their opponents and implement their ideas. All through the autumn and early winter of 1977 provinces and cities had been holding their People's Congresses to elect new leaderships, and everywhere veteran officials who had been struck down by the Cultural Revolution were restored to power, replacing men who had less reason to give their allegiance to Deng. In late 1977, his close collaborator Hu Yaobang had been appointed Director of the Party's Organization Department, a key position for influencing promotions and demotions. In the spring of 1978 the Fifth National People's Congress had held back those Politburo members who were suspect in Deng's eyes and advanced the technocrats. A press campaign to denounce political trimmers had been launched in late 1977 and continued spasmodically through 1978; among its victims were one full and one alternate member of the Politburo. In the two years after Mao's death the leaders of twenty-six of the twenty-nine province-level governments were sacked and replaced by people favored by the pragmatists. An equally important remanning of the central ministries took place.

After his return to office Deng first turned his attention to education and science. Under his leadership, university entrance examinations were re-established, "key schools" were designated at primary, secondary, and college levels in which were concentrated the best resources and the brightest pupils, and an ambitious long-range program for science was drawn up. He had promised improved status and more academic freedom for intellectuals. Since July 1977, a general revision of wages had brought increases for 46 percent of industrial workers. Bonuses had been restored and the sinful taint removed from profits and from material incentives.

A start had been made on releasing from labor camp the victims of the 1957 antirightist drive.

In diplomacy some progress had been made also. In September 1977, Marshal Tito had paid a very successful visit to China—something he could not or would not do while Mao was alive. To signal the new relationship between the countries, he was the first foreigner to enter Mao's Memorial Hall, which must have been a piquant occasion since it was Mao who had turned China aside from serious consideration of the Yugoslav model of development in the late 1950s and had caused Tito to be denounced as a "paid agent of imperialism."

The cultural scene had also been enlivened between Deng's return to office in mid-1977 and his speech on Mao to the All-Army Political Work Conference in mid-1978: traditional art forms were respectable again and the many good films made before the Cultural Revolution could be shown again. Foreign works were no longer taboo.

But Deng's speech on Mao was a watershed. After it, there came an acceleration in the pace of change. In July 1978, to mark the anniversary of the Communist Party he had helped establish and bring to national power, the *People's Daily* published a speech by Mao in which he himself declared that he had made mistakes and that the people should know that he acknowledged as much (he was speaking in 1962 at a time when his Great Leap Forward had been criticized in high party circles). The speech had never been published in China in the sixteen years since he had delivered it. A week or so later, Hu Qiaomu, president of the Academy of Social Sciences (the pragmatists' think tank), delivered a speech to the state council setting out the pragmatists' economic philosophy, in which he made it clear that Mao's subjectivism in the 1950s and 1960s had brought disaster to China's economy.[13]

In diplomacy China became more active than ever before in her history. An unprecedented number of Chinese leaders visited foreign countries and China received more foreign leaders and delegations of every kind than ever before. Deng stripped away the ambiguities surrounding China's relations with the West and Japan: he wanted alignment of strategy to oppose the Soviet Union. This was not at all in accordance with Mao's "Theory of the Three Worlds," which called for China to join with other developing countries and middle-ranking powers to oppose the two superpowers. Now that Deng was in the ascendant, policy could be developed in accordance with changing realities, just as he had argued in his speech on Mao. Deng personally grasped the thorny issues involved in concluding a China–Japan Treaty of Peace and Friendship and in normalizing Sino–U.S. relations. Hua visited Eastern Europe, tweaking the Soviet bear's tail. Deng went to Japan and to Southeast Asia. Both went to Korea. Aid to Albania and Vietnam was cut off.

In foreign economic relations, taboo after taboo was eliminated: foreign long-term credits, foreign direct investment, payment with product for imported plant, and technical consultancy were all declared permissible.

The pace at which developments followed one another was breathtaking, faster than before Deng's June speech and much faster than before his return to power.

From time to time it became evident that there were differences of view among the leaders on matters of considerable importance. For example, at the conferences on science and education held in the spring of 1978, while both paid tribute to the importance of learning in a way Mao had not done in public in his later years, Deng's speech showed that he was prepared to go further than Hua in freeing the intellectuals from an obligation to study and conform to political orthodoxy. He said:

> Our scientific undertakings are an important part of our socialist cause. To devote oneself to our socialist science and contribute to it is an important manifestation of being red, the integration of being red with being expert.

Hua gave much more emphasis to politics. He told the national conference on science that "politics is the commander, the soul of everything."

Deng emphasized the need for "a large number of scientists and experts in engineering and technology who are first-rate by world standards."

Hua emphasized the need to spread scientific and cultural knowledge "to raise the level of the entire nation," a position much closer to Mao's thinking.

Hua praised the Cultural Revolution publicly, but Deng never did so. Hua looked forward to future movements of the same type; Deng understandably did not.

When the Mayor of Peking and others were coming under pressure in the autumn of 1978, Hua and Marshal Ye called for "unity and stability," a phrase Deng avoided.

Hua played the leading role at the Fifth National People's Congress in March 1978. This was natural since he was premier, but Deng kept a strangely low profile.

None of this amounted to a split in the Politburo such as to threaten the stability of the leadership. Each side seemed concerned to handle the differences of view with sufficient restraint to avoid a crisis. However, there was no mistaking the determination of the reformers led by Deng to press ahead, and they usually had the strength to prevail.

Popular dissatisfaction over the suppression of the Tiananmen demonstrations also caused Hua some difficulty. For instance in July 1978, on the anniversary of Deng's return to office, someone pasted up outside the offices of the *People's Daily* in the heart of Peking an open letter to Hua saying "21 months after the smashing of the Gang of Four the full truth about Tiananmen has not yet been made known. . . . Perhaps it is because you are too busy." He attached a copy of the *People's Daily* editorial of 10 April 1976 entitled "A Great Victory." He called for criticism of such articles and the opening of the columns of the official press to accounts of what really happened on the square at that time.

At no time was Hua the object of a concerted campaign of criticism, veiled or open. The same could not be said of the Peking Mayor, Wu De, who had become a focus of the resentment caused by the Tiananmen affair. This may have been unfair to some extent, because Wu De could not have been responsible for the decisions to take away the wreaths and arrest demonstrators. But apparently he had not taken the opportunity to extricate himself from his difficult position once the death of Mao made that possible. And, as they piled on the pressure in the autumn, the Deng group made it a major objective to gain control of Peking's city council.

Hua had discussed Wu De's political problems with him during the summer and straightened him out on one or two matters; the word went out that Wu De was now lined up in the right direction and would survive. But it was not to be, and the way he lost Peking is a good illustration of the way Chinese politics worked in 1977 and 1978.

In January 1977 Wu De had been attacked in posters for his part in the Tiananmen affair. According to Hong Kong magazines, it was excessive zeal in the investigations that followed the demonstrations which first made him so unpopular. He might have recovered from this if, after the fall of the Four, he had responded to popular demand to recognize the Tiananmen demonstrations as a great blow against the Four. But he stuck to the view that they had been a counter-revolutionary incident and he was alleged to have defended this position on the simple ground that the Four held high offices of party and state at the time. In the winter of 1977–1978 he came under pressure when the press denounced the "cover-up faction," the

Chinese for which contained a clear pun on his name. During that winter posters critical of him appeared in Peking University. In April he was criticized in posters again, this time on Tiananmen Square on the second anniversary of the demonstrations. His authority was being flouted: editors of an anthology of Tiananmen poems requested his approval for publication and, having received no reply after repeated applications, went ahead without it, an act unprecedented since 1949.

On 9 August 1978 a meeting was organized in Peking at which young people who had taken the lead in opposing the Maoists in 1976 were invited to describe their experiences. A shy young man named Han Zhixiong stepped up to the rostrum amid applause. He glanced at his prepared script. Then, obviously embarrassed, he put it down, and began to tell his story in his own words instead of those that had been written for him. First, he said that there were young people at the meeting who were more worthy of attention than he and who were still subject to discrimination by the city authorities. Then he gave his report. It was evident from his story that he had been brave, but what was noteworthy was the admiration he had reportedly expressed for Deng Xiaoping at the time of Qing Ming and the criticism he made of the way the Peking security forces continued to persecute him into the summer of 1978. This reflected very badly on the mayor, Wu De. The *People's Daily* account of Han Zhixiong's remarks tells of the encouragement and support Han was given by "leading comrades of the department of the central authorities concerned" before the meeting.[14]

Also in August 1978, the *People's Daily* started to publish letters from readers complaining about the city administration. One protested that the security forces had held a man in detention, after the fall of the Four, for reading *Anna Karenina*;[15] another complained of the rising cost of food in the capital and criticized the poor performance of the city's administrators compared with the improvements made in other cities. Other letters in September complained of bad sanitation work and noise pollution—complaints common enough in most cities but in China such complaints had not, until then, been published in papers available to foreigners. Ten days later the English-language service of NCNA sent the story of these letters around

the world on the day Jacques Chirac, the Mayor of Paris, returned home from Peking,[16] where Wu De had been his host.
Publication coincided with the appearance of a twenty-yard
poster complaining of Wu De's continued suppression of civil
liberties.[17] The writing was on the wall for Wu De, quite literally.

Any lingering doubts that he was under concerted attack
were removed when the *People's Daily* used as its lead story on
5 October a vivid account of how the neighboring city of Tianjin, only ninety miles away, had rid itself of its Mayor four
months earlier and the headline contained a pun on "exposing
Wu." Four days later the official notice went out: Wu De had
been replaced as mayor by the victor of the Tianjin struggle.[18]
Wu De was the first full member of the Politburo to suffer a loss
of power since the Eleventh Congress in 1977. Everyone was
intrigued to see what would happen to him. He was retained in
the Politburo and continued to make appearances in public
when all the leadership turned out, but for the time being he
seemed to have no specific duties.

An even more important target of criticism was the Party
vice-chairman and security expert Wang Dongxing. After the
Eleventh Congress closed in August 1977, the *People's Daily*
had quickly published an article about the palace guard, the
8341 Unit, which had carried out the arrests of the Four and was
under Wang's control. The article presented the guards and, by
association, Wang Dongxing as pillars of Maoist orthodoxy,
guardians of the true faith.[19] Ten days later the same paper
published a reminder of the need for collective leaderhip and
the dangers of any leader building himself an independent
power base by relying on people who would "replace ideological
and political work with punishment"—that is, would use the security forces to compensate for lack of political support.[20] Some
observers saw the second article as a counterblow to the first.

Since the arrest of the Gang of Four, Wang had held some
responsibility for the press. In September 1978 the first issue of
the *China Youth* monthly magazine to be published since 1966
was printed and ready for distribution. One of the articles in it
spoke positively of the Tiananmen demonstrations, another
compared the creation of the cult of Mao with religious "blind

faith"; a third was entitled "Why 'Every Word Is Truth' Is Ridiculous." To Wang, all must have been heresy and, according to the Hong Kong left-wing press, he ordered distribution suspended.[21] The Politburo considered the issue later in September and Wang was overruled: the magazine went out with the addition of an inscription by Chairman Hua.

According to well-informed political magazines in Hong Kong, Wang enjoyed considerable influence over the Party's theoretical monthly, *Red Flag*. When the pragmatists took up the cry "Seek truth from facts" in May 1978 and declared, quoting Mao, that "practice is the sole criterion for truth," *Red Flag* remained silent on the issue. It maintained this silence as one leader after another identified himself with the slogans and one publication after another printed articles in support of them. *Red Flag* never even mentioned "practice is the sole criterion for truth" until October. Deng Xiaoping's warnings at the All-Army Work Conference in June to those "comrades who talk about Mao Zedong Thought every day, but often forget, abandon, or even oppose Chairman Mao's . . . method of seeking truth from facts" had apparently not impressed Vice-Chairman Wang.

In October a Hong Kong magazine pointed out *Red Flag*'s failure to endorse the campaign for a pragmatist philosophy, and in mid-November a wall poster in Peking did the same.[22]

More sinister, on 12 November, the *Guang Ming Daily* reminded its readers that Stalin had condemned Zinoviev in 1926 for insisting that the Soviet leaders follow strictly the texts of the teachings of their Marxist predecessors. *Guang Ming* commented that the story was precisely applicable to China in November 1978, where someone was saying that it was impermissible to change even one word of Mao's sayings and writings. The paper labeled Zinoviev "a chieftain of revisionism" and condemned him for forming a "New Opposition." The Hong Kong left-wing journals interpreted this as another attack on Wang Dongxing. That the official press in China should claim that there was a latter-day Zinoviev in the Party leadership was a clear sign that politics had entered a new phase. The pragmatists were intensifying their offensive.

9

Capturing the Heights

As THE AUTUMN OF 1978 turned to early winter and the persimmons ripened in the Valley of the Ming Tombs, spheres of brilliant orange on bare gray branches, the pragmatists brought the political situation to maturity also. In November and December they would pluck a whole basketful of victories from the branches of the Central Work Conference.

In the weeks before the conference opened they orchestrated massive pressure for a large number of major decisions and did everything possible to ensure that when the conference took place the city of Peking would be in a state of political ferment, their forces would have gained the leadership of one province after another, and high expectations of change would have been aroused throughout the country.

In the autumn six of the remaining provincial and city bosses appointed before Deng's 1977 rehabilitation were sacked, including Wu De in Peking. The *People's Daily* began to write about the lack of proper democracy in China[1] and to say loud and clear that when socialist bureaucracy is unchecked Communist Party officials degenerate into feudal tyrants.[2] It argued that it was the lack of democratic institutions[3] and elections that had made it possible for socialist China to sink into "feudal fascism" in Mao's last ten years. As part of its campaign for democracy the *People's Daily* published a 1956 speech by Dong

Biwu on the need for constitutional government and an end to rule by mass movements.[4]

In his crucial speech to the army political conference in June, Deng had said that there could be no construction without destruction, a phrase he must have pronounced with sense of sweet irony since Mao's followers had used it constantly against the pragmatists during the Cultural Revolution. The destruction Deng insisted on in June 1978 was criticism of the late Marshal Lin Biao. In 1970 and 1971 a campaign of criticism had been launched against Lin but was quickly suppressed by the Four because they were too closely associated with him. Even in 1978 a powerful group in the party leadership opposed criticizing him and declared publicly that criticism of the Gang of Four should not go back before 1973.

The issue at stake was not so much whether criticism of Lin Biao was to be permitted but whether the Cultural Revolution should be criticized. If there was a ban on criticizing Lin and criticizing the Four before 1973 no one could use the device of criticizing what Lin and the Four had done in the Cultural Revolution to expose the folly and trauma of the Cultural Revolution itself. In the autumn offensive the pragmatists broke through this roadblock.

Then we spotted two of those announcements cloaked in allegory that make China-watchers comb newspaper articles with extra care and set them searching through their memories and files to nail down references: the *People's Daily* published a veiled and tentative call for the rehabilitation of Marshal Peng Dehuai, whom Mao had dismissed in 1959 for criticizing his leadership of the Great Leap Forward;[5] a day or so later, my eyes lighted on a reference to an opera called *Three Times up Peach Mountain*. Surely that opera had been condemned in the Cultural Revolution because it had (in allegory, naturally) promoted Liu Shaoqi's views and criticized Mao? Now the *People's Daily* was arguing for the rehabilitation of this banned opera. If *Peach Mountain* was coming back, could Liu Shaoqi (dead or alive) be far behind? In the eyes of the pragmatists, Peng Dehuai and Liu Shaoqi were the two greatest victims of injustice wrought by Mao, and the *People's Daily* had shown us that a move was afoot to clear their names. It was one of the those moments that compensate for hours of arid reading.

Day after day in October and early November the *People's Daily* published outspoken articles on the most sensitive subjects. The cult of Mao worship was condemned. Lau She, a playwright who had committed suicide in the Cultural Revolution, had his work performed again. Alluding to the Cultural Revolution, one writer said "this bloodstained picture is still in our mind." A *People's Daily* commentator condemned discrimination against people because of their parents' record, and to dramatize this message twenty-one sons and daughters of high officials who had been attacked during the Cultural Revolution because of their parents' deeds (including Deng's crippled eldest child, Pufang) were rehabilitated in a public ceremony at Peking University.

Readers' letters were published complaining of the way officials exacted revenge through physical violence or administrative discrimination on those who exposed their corruption. A "Specially Invited Commentator" issued a call to "break through all spiritual shackles," and "emancipation of the mind" became a frequently used phrase.

The pragmatists made a special effort to mobilize youth: the Communist Youth League Congress praised the heroes of Tiananmen, and two groups of young Peking people who had been arrested for their part in those demonstrations were completely rehabilitated, having suffered discrimination after their release from camp. Television as well as the press publicized the young Peking hero Han Zhixiong.

November fifteenth was an extraordinary day. *Guang Ming Daily* announced that a hundred thousand victims of the antirightist campaign of 1957 were to be rehabilitated by decision of the Central Committee and reported that the Peking party committee had declared the Tiananmen demonstrations to have been "completely revolutionary." *Guang Ming* also published a vehement denunciation of the very article by Yao Wenyuan that had been the first salvo of the Cultural Revolution and described it as a "counter-revolutionary signal," a signal "of fascist dictatorship aimed at shackling people's minds." This was the article that, as everyone knew, Mao had personally approved and had so eagerly published. Yao was prompted in his writing, it was alleged, "by a political conspiracy." The purges by the Gang of Four of officials, intellectuals, and workers in the Cultural Revolution were part of a "criminal plot to frame the innocent. This brought disaster to the intellectuals. Countless numbers of them were given hell on various false charges. . . . The Motherland's culture of several thousand years was thrown to the winds. The vast land of China knew only the 'all-round dictatorship' of the Gang of Four and not the least semblance of democracy."[6]

I cannot recall any noncommunist commentator outside China using such vehement language to denounce the Cultural Revolution. Such violence against a movement to which Chairman Hua had paid tribute at great length at the Eleventh Party Congress only the year before must have had an electrifying impact on those who read it.

The next day it was announced that Chairman Hua had written an inscription for the first anthology of Tiananmen poems to be published with official approval. This was another instance of Hua's flexibility and his sure sense of political timing. At the March 1977 Central Work Conference he had maintained that the suppression of the Tiananmen demonstrations had been justified. Now he associated himself very personally with the declaration that the demonstrations had been "entirely revolutionary." According to Peking Broadcasting Station, when one of the compilers saw Hua's handwriting "he said exultantly: 'Chairman Hua is really of one mind with the hundreds of millions of people.' And immediately telephoned the Party Committee, where he worked, to report this 'good news.' "[7] To appreciate the impact these weeks of dramatic political developments had on the Chinese public one had to remember that the issues at stake had never been discussed openly in official Chinese publications.

Ever since the start of the Cultural Revolution foreign newspapers had carried news and comment on all the themes now filling the Chinese press, such as the dark side of that upheaval, the fallibility of Mao, the careers of the Shanghai Gang, and the lack of democracy in China; we could walk into a bookshop and buy a collection of many of the unpublished speeches of Mao or accounts of what he had said to Edgar Snow about the need for deification of leaders. But Chinese had read such things only in illegal pamphlets or in "counter-revolutionary" posters by people like Li Yizhe. For them, to see the press acknowledge for the first time the damage done by the Cultural Revolution was to have a heavy weight removed from their backs or to see dark clouds swept away to reveal a patch of blue. Those images may seem banal, but they were ones which would be used by Chinese time and again in the weeks to come to describe their feelings. Watching old friends begin to share with me thoughts and feelings they had repressed for years was to watch them straighten their backs and stand erect. This was a time when those of us who had grown up in societies where the diversity of opinion is bewildering, the flow of information threatens to swamp us, and human rights are just another news story came to appreciate more fully the freedoms we had too often taken for granted.

The Central Work Conference opened on 10 November, bringing together the few hundred most powerful men and women in the land. As they came, the delegates must have been impressed by the political tide the pragmatists had whipped up, one so strong it could carry Chairman Hua with it to write the inscription for the Tiananmen poems. The high tide had been well timed to impress them and to give them courage to speak their minds on the major issues of the past twenty years and for the years ahead. The conference was to last until mid-December, a full month. That was not unprecedented, but this conference covered more ground and heard more frank speaking than any in two decades. It took on the character of a primitive parliament, but with the proceedings closed to the public. We foreigners would have to wait for the official communiqué of the Central Committee meeting (which followed the Work Conference), for the carefully managed leaks in Peking and the "inside stories" in the Hong Kong press. In the meantime we could observe with our own eyes and ears the ferment of the young people. News of the Work Conference leaked to them through the children and the grandchildren of the delegates to the conference. Like the older generation, they were convinced that now if ever was the time to speak, the chance to influence the course of events. Although not physically present, they could make their message reach the conference hall.

"Shout, for the Lord has given you the city," Joshua had told his troops before the walls of Jericho. Young voices shouted from Democracy Wall and from the impromptu tribunes on Tiananmen Square, and older voices heavy with the repressed scorn and fury of decades rang out at the Work Conference. Down tumbled political walls that could not be rebuilt easily, if at all.

The Work Conference was the greatest concentration of political energy the People's Republic had seen. Within the space of a month it tackled the issues of agriculture, cadre training, industrial organization, class struggle, emancipation of the mind, leadership style, the history of economic development since 1949, the status of leaders dead and alive, the history of the Cultural Revolution, and—of course—the role of Mao and his Thought.

The Whatever Faction took a hiding, and the pragmatists achieved a fundamental reorientation of Chinese politics.

The Central Work Conference was followed almost immediately by a plenum of the Central Committee. The communiqué issued by this plenum showed how much the pragmatists had gained at the conference and the plenum but did not reveal the content of the speeches at either meeting, nor did it list who had spoken and who had not. That kind of information was leaked to the Hong Kong press. Information in both the left-wing press and the liberal *Ming Pao* gave vivid accounts of what had been said which had the ring of truth and were supported by developments in China in the following months. But one had to bear in mind as one read that they came from sources sympathetic to the pragmatists.

The Hong Kong press reported that at the Work Conference the most damaging charges were laid against Party Vice-Chairman Wang Dongxing, the Commander of the Peking Military Region, General Chen Xilian, the Mayor of Peking, Wu De, and another Politburo member, Ji Dengkui.[8] General Xü Shiyu, the Commander of the Canton Military Region and one of Deng's strongest supporters, was reported to have drawn attention to the advanced age of Marshal Ye and Vice-Premier

Deng and to have warned: "There is a Khruschchev waiting right beside them with evil intentions. Given a chance, he will stage a counterattack and follow the old road . . . of the Gang of Four."[9] According to *Ming Pao*, General Xü made it clear that he was referring to Wang Dongxing. Wang was accused to his face of being the leader of the Whatever Faction. He was also accused of having been dilatory in investigating the Gang of Four and in rehabilitating senior veteran officials who had been struck down by the Cultural Revolution. Chen Yun, the veteran economic expert who had been forced to take a back seat for many years because of his opposition to Mao's economic policies, reportedly asked Wang, "People say that you earned merit by arresting the Gang of Four and performed meritorious services. Do you feel this way? What kind of great meritorious service is this? To arrest the Gang of Four was a duty for any member of the Communist Party. . . . You have not explained clearly your relations with the Gang of Four."

The charges made against the Commander of Peking, Chen Xilian, were of staggering proportions. It was alleged when he was Commander of Northeast China and First Secretary of Liaoning province, before his 1973 transfer to Peking, he had ᵗbeen responsible for thirteen thousand miscarriages of justice relating to political groups. These thirteen thousand cases, it was charged, involved some forty-four thousand people, of whom twenty thousand had been "persecuted to death." He was further accused of sixty-two thousand individual cases of miscarriages of justice.*

Vice-Premier Ji Dengkui was criticized for displaying gross complacency about the state of Chinese agriculture in a report he had written for the meeting. He was also denounced as a "careerist" and "a time-bomb in the Politburo." Allowing him to continue as the leader of the central political and legal group "might result in lives being forfeited," it was said. During the Cultural Revolution he had allegedly been the "root" of fighting and looting in Henan province.

---

* "Tiger" Chen was commander of the Shenyang military region from 1959 until 1973 and first secretary of Liaoning province from 1971 to 1973. Throughout the period from the start of the Cultural Revolution until his departure from the region, he played an important role in the maintenance of law and order in addition to his military duties.

Vice-Chairman Wang and the Commander and the Mayor of Peking all made self-criticisms. One leading pragmatist rejected them as utterly insincere, likening them to a self-criticism made by Zhang Guotao, the most famous turncoat in the Party's history.[10] Hua Guofeng did not defend the record of Wang and the other politburo members who came under attack. He refused a request by Wang to speak at the closing ceremony in his capacity of Vice-Chairman of the Party, restricting him to a general speech. When Ji Dengkui made a report to Hua about the nature of his mistakes, Hua ordered that the report be circulated to everyone at the conference. Hua told the conference that he himself had made mistakes. He said that he had failed to criticize the wrong done by Mao and had failed to endorse the philosophy of "seeking truth from facts" that had been the foundation of Deng's strategy for government and of his drive to achieve dominance in the leadership. Hua also admitted that he had treated friends as enemies at the time of the Tiananmen demonstrations.

Hua renounced the status of supreme leader that had been given him when he first succeeded Mao. "The Party Central Committee constitutes a collective leadership," he said. When lower levels sent in reports they should no longer be addressed "To Chairman Hua and the Central Committee" but simply "To the Central Committee." From now on he was to be referred to as "comrade" instead of "wise leader."[11]

Hua's self-criticism and his acceptance of his position as one member of a collective leadership cannot have been easy for him but they probably strengthened his position for the long run, because they accorded with the realities of the time. He had again displayed a capacity for sensing the mood of the Party and a readiness to adjust to it.

In his speech to the conference Deng emphasized the need for officials to emancipate their minds, saying that democracy was essential to accomplish this. He said that the Party was looking to the future and was addressing problems which the founding fathers of Marxism–Leninism and Mao Zedong himself had not faced and therefore had not solved. New problems could not be solved by old formulae: "Some people said that we must do what Chairman Mao said. Actually, there are many things which the Chairman did not say. Engels never rode in a plane. Stalin never wore Dacron. Practice is developing. We must study the new situation and solve new problems."[12]

Marshal Ye Jianying, who had relinquished the post of Minister of Defense earlier in the year and was now Chairman of the Standing Committee of the National People's Congress and therefore China's nearest equivalent to a head of state, stressed the need for democracy, as Deng had done, and also called for strengthening the legal system.

The conference looked backward before looking forward. The Great Leap Forward and the Cultural Revolution were blamed for China's economic setbacks. Both had "sabotaged" the economy. The latter had "repeated and expanded" the mistakes of the former.

The conference reviewed and revised the Party's official evaluation of ten other historical events and personalities, beginning with Peng Dehuai and ending with the Tiananmen demonstrations.* Most of these concerned the Cultural Revolution. No overall re-evaluation of the Cultural Revolution or of Mao was undertaken because the issues were considered still too divisive, but the review of economic policy in the past and the "reversal of verdict" on the ten historical questions were a devastating piecemeal act of criticism of both Mao and his mass movements.

Chen Yun did permit himself this judgment on Mao's career: "Had Chairman Mao died in 1956, there would have been no doubt that he was a great leader of the Chinese people. . . . Had he died in 1966, his meritorious achievements would have been somewhat tarnished, but his overall record still very good. Since he actually died in 1976, there is nothing we can do about it."[13]

When it turned to discuss policies for the future, the conference considered a wide range of questions and approved a multitude of documents. Some of its decisions were disclosed at the plenum of the Central Committee in December, some would only be revealed later.

The highest leaders disappeared from public view in the

---

* The ten were the "January storm," the "February adverse current," "the clique of 61 renegades," Peng Dehuai, Tao Zhu, Kang Sheng, Xie Fuzhih, Yang Shangkun, the army's support for the left during the Cultural Revolution, and the Tiananmen demonstrations.

middle of November and stayed out of sight for about ten days while the Work Conference proceeded. The first to reappear was Deng Xiaoping, speaking with the authority of the Central Committee. Obviously things had gone well for him. In a meeting with a delegation of the Japanese Democratic Socialist Party, on 26 November, he dealt with the sensitive issue of Mao's decisions, approved by the Politburo on 7 April 1976, to dismiss him and appoint Hua as premier. He told the Japanese that at the time Hua had not been able to meet Mao, who had been briefed on the events of Qing Ming only by a member of the Gang of Four.[14] He went on to say that Mao was seriously ill at the time, could not speak clearly, and had failed to grasp the actual situation.

Referring only to the decisions to dismiss him and condemn the Tiananmen demonstrations, Deng said: "If Chairman Mao had been in good health, if he had been capable of making up his own mind, he would not have made such decisions." He said the decision to appoint Hua premier had been proved a good one by the way Hua had led the Central Committee in smashing the Gang of Four.[15]

China had waited a little over two years since Mao's death to hear a plausible account of Deng's dismissal and to hear one of its leaders admit that Mao had been senile. By treating the Chinese people as adults who deserved to be told the truth instead of feeding them fantasies that a child would question, Deng did more than earn himself respect; he gave them an implicit pledge that two plus two would once more be held to equal four in China, and that they might say so without being sent to jail. For years they had been expected to behave like the Queen in *Through the Looking-Glass*, who on some days believed six impossible things before breakfast. Now they heaved a collective sigh of relief that was almost audible.

On 27 November Deng received the American columnist Robert Novak and answered questions on both foreign and domestic issues. On domestic affairs he showed a willingness unprecedented in an interview by a Chinese leader to discuss internal differences in the leadership and accepted that there were differences between himself and Hua, adding with a grin "Even Marx and Engels were different." But he denied that there was any power struggle between them.

In mid-December the Central Committee met and on 23 December issued its communiqué, a document of great scope that summed up the revised version of history approved by the Work Conference and erected signposts to the future. The communiqué formally vindicated Deng's record in 1975, canceled the party documents that had been issued in the anti-Deng campaign, and expressed its "high appreciation" of the campaign in which Deng's pragmatism had been propagated.

On economic policy, it called for a bold shift in decision-making power from party to state and from state to economic enterprises. It announced measures to increase the income of the peasants by fixing higher prices for grain and other agricultural products and lower prices for the industrial goods the peasants purchase. It indicated that the plenum had authorized the issue of two draft documents on agricultural production and the people's communes.

The plenum approved the establishment of a Central Committee Disciplinary Investigation Commission. This body would investigate political cases against party members, rehabilitating those who had in its view been wrongly struck down and disciplining those who had breached party discipline. The plenum renounced government by mass movements, as the pragmatists had advocated for nearly twenty-five years. It also made clear that in future class struggle would take the form of the "struggle for production." There would be no more "empty politics" or class struggle "for its own sake." The decisions taken by the plenum on personnel matters strengthened the hand of the pragmatists and weakened the Whatever Faction. No one was dismissed from the Politburo, but a number of people appear to have been stripped of their specific responsibilities and powers. According to numerous accounts in reliable Hong Kong papers, confirmed by the pattern of leadership activities in the months that followed, this group included Wang Dongxing, Ji Dengkui, Chen Xilian, Wu De, and Chen Yonggui. Chen Yonggui was in a separate category from the others. He was not accused of political crimes; he seems to have been eclipsed because the model agricultural brigade where he had made his name as a peasant leader had lost its role as a national model and he did not have the technical knowledge to hold his own in the new age that was beginning.

The economic specialist Chen Yun was made a vice-chairman of the Party and put in charge of the Discipline Commission. Three other Deng supporters were appointed to the Politburo: Zhou Enlai's widow; an overlord on the industrial front, Wang Zhen; and Hu Yaobang, who had assisted Deng in 1975 by working on the "Poisonous Weed" that dealt with science and technology. Hu was also made Secretary-General of the Party. Since he was in his mid-sixties, this put him in a potentially strong position for the time when Deng, Ye, and Chen Yun would pass from the scene. During the Cultural Revolution Red Guards had denounced him as a "loyal veteran fighter" of the "Liu–Deng command." He had served with Deng in Southwest China in 1950 to 1952. He had then moved to Peking with Deng and had become active in the Communist Youth League, becoming its First Secretary in 1957. If the Red Guards are to be believed, he had encouraged young people in skepticism toward the cult of Mao long before the Cultural Revolution. One day in November 1955, he was with a crowd of young people at the Meishan Reservoir in Anhui province. They had worked on constructing the reservoir and were taking part in the dedication ceremony. At the end they shouted the standard slogan, "Boundless life to Chairman Mao!" Hu cut short the ritual, saying

Well! Ten thousand years! They say it is rather rare to live to seventy. Can the Chairman live to ten thousand? You workers have sweated away with hardly a break, so we can wish you a life of ten thousand years. I, Hu Yaobang, am an X grade official. May I not be wished a life of ten thousand years also? I think all of us might be wished a life of ten thousand years, except of course that hut over there with a thatched roof. There's no way it would last ten thousand years.

Hu had displayed less than total faith in the omnipotence of Chairman Mao's thought. He remarked to an audience of Communist Youth League secretaries from schools in July 1956:

The Chairman is only sixty-three. The human race has a history of one million years. It has accumulated immense scientific knowledge and encountered innumerable problems, such as no single individual can possibly grasp fully or can ever cope with. . . . If we think that the greater the responsibility an individual shoulders the more capable he is of solving any problem, that is nothing but superstition.

Speaking to staff of *China Youth*, the magazine of the Communist Youth League, in November 1955, he had said "If we have to speak as though we were reciting classical texts, then language and words would eventually become obsolete and dead. That is the way thinking becomes ossified, rigid, and stagnant."[16] If he thought that way in 1955, what can he have thought twenty years later reading the *People's Daily* under the control of Yao Wenyuan, when the language struck even a foreigner as dead?

Little wonder that when *China Youth* published its article in September 1978 denouncing the deification of Mao, many people believed that Hu Yaobang had inspired or even written that article.

The skeptical spirit manifest in Hu's remarks from the mid-1950s was very much in tune with the spirit of the young people who in November 1978 took courage when they read the spate of iconoclastic articles in *China Youth* and other papers and heard that the Central Work Conference was under way.

This, if ever, was the moment for them to speak out. Huang Xiang, the poet of the Enlightenment Society, had not even waited that long. In October he and a group of friends had brought his poetry face to face with the man in the Peking street. On 11 October they pasted up Huang Xiang's *God of Fire Symphonic Poems* in an alleyway next to the offices of the *People's Daily*, in the center of town. For days on end the alley was choked with readers. The day after helping Huang Xiang paste up his poems there, Li Jiahua, one of the group from Guizhou, went to Tiananmen Square. Under a brilliant clear sky, the great square was very quiet. He look around and recalled the events which had moved Huang to write his poem "No You Have Not Died" in April 1976. Li listened carefully and suddenly he heard the voices of those who had died two years before. The voices thundered out a call for vengeance:[17]

Arise, victims of injustice and humiliation,
Today is the day of your rehabilitation.
Let us rally together once again!
Hold the banner higher still.
Clench our fists tighter still, and
Boldly sing the song of vengeance
To mourn our brothers who fell for the cause of truth.

Arise, victims of long, long suppression,
Let us quickly assemble from every direction,
With a common hatred of the enemy and with all united as one,
Hold high the torch of enlightenment,
Pull down all idols from their gilded niches
And destroy the palace of autocracy!

Arise, those who have been benumbed,
Stop muttering in the streets and lanes.
If throughout our whole life
We cannot be sure of ourselves, and
Can only live in fear and anxiety, and
Die without the courage to air our grievances,
Then our offspring in the future
Will laugh at our weakness.

Arise, you who have been fooled,
Do not wait or hesitate.
Take up truth as your weapon,
Arise amid the whirlwind of the age.
For the sake of China's future,
And for the children's beautiful tomorrow,
Let us fight a war to determine right or wrong and good or evil.

A little over a month after Li Jiahua wrote this poem young people did turn from "muttering in the streets and lanes" and began to speak out in wall posters that they pasted up on a stretch of wall about a mile from Tiananmen Square. Their voices were no less heavy with anger over the past than those of older men who were speaking at the Central Work Conference. The people they criticized were often the very ones who were being criticized at the conference. But the radical nature of their demands for change would startle even those of us who had watched the events of the preceding two years.

10

"Human Rights over Here!"

IT IS AN UNIMPRESSIVE stretch of wall about two hundred yards long and twelve feet high, made of an acid yellow-gray brick. In front of its runs the Avenue of Eternal Peace and behind it is a municipal bus depot. The Avenue's sidewalk is very broad here and consists largely of hard-trodden dusty earth. Sparse trees grow at intervals along the wall, and a low, ragged evergreen hedge runs parallel to it a few feet away. For four months in the winter of 1978–1979 voices came from that wall which were heard around the world and earned it the name Democracy Wall.

On this drab stretch of brickwork over the weekend of 17–19 November a poster appeared criticizing Mao by name. In a total of four and a half years in China I had never seen or heard Mao criticized by name in public, nor had any other foreigner in Peking. Yet here in the heart of the capital in a most public place someone had displayed a poster that, commenting on a recent play about the Tiananmen demonstrations, dared to say "In 1976 after the Tiananmen incident, the Gang of Four made use of the prestige and power of *Chairman Mao Zedong's mistaken judgment on class struggle* and launched an all-out attack on the cause of revolution in China."[1]

Chairman Mao had made a mistake about class struggle?

Surely he was the world's greatest expert on class struggle? He might not have known much about economics or science, but endless paeans had been sung to his brilliance and originality in this field—not least by some people in Western nations who prided themselves on their understanding of China. Yet here was someone identifying himself or herself as a motor mechanic, holding Work Permit Number 0538, employed at the motor repair shop at 57 Wangfujing Street, Peking, who said that the Chairman got it wrong. And so badly had Mao blundered that the Four had exploited it to engage in counter-revolution. This motor mechanic had come within an ace of calling Mao himself a counter-revolutionary!

And that was not all. Work Permit No. 0538 went on to say

> Because Chairman Mao's thinking had become metaphysical in his old age, and for all sorts of other reasons, he supported the Gang of Four in raising their hands to strike down Comrade Deng Xiaoping, and suppressed the Tiananmen incident which had shaken the whole world like an earthquake and showed that the Chinese people wanted liberation, progress, and revolution. The broad masses of people experienced a great contradiction between the current political theory and harsh reality. . . . On the other hand there were people who disbelieved official propaganda, who did link together all the different events at that time and analyzed them. These few cadres and other people suffered in consequence and were suspected of being counter-revolutionary. As for those who held high the principle of practice being the only criterion of truth,* these were the real heroes.

I knew of someone who had been sentenced to fifteen years in labor camp merely because, in a moment of boredom at some interminable meeting during the Cultural Revolution, he had absentmindedly scratched his back with a copy of the little red book. The poster we now saw could earn the writer execution by firing squad if he had misjudged the political climate. We watched to see if it would be torn down by official order or by some outraged citizen.

* The central principle of the pragmatic philosophy propagated by Deng Xiaoping and his followers beginning in May 1978.

Twenty-four hours passed. It was still there. Forty-eight hours passed and it was still there. We were in a new era.

On Monday, 20 November, came a poster (titled *Democracy Must Judge Despotism*) that said "the history of the last ten years, from first to last, has been shot through with the struggle between the scientific socialist line represented by Comrade Zhou Enlai and the feudal fascist dictatorship line of the Jiang Qing–Lin Biao clan." The author, signing himself Wu Wen, mourned those who had been persecuted to death for the cause of scientific socialism and democracy, naming Zhou and five of the best-known of Mao's Cultural Revolution victims. He described Deng Xiaoping as "the living Zhou Enlai." He denounced the suppression of the Tiananmen demonstrations as a "bloody incident" created by the "feudal fascist dictatorship" and called for full public exposure of those responsible. He called for a joint investigation committee to bring the facts to light and for trials and public meetings on a national scale for the "principal criminal, the general director, and the planners of the incident." That would make the Watergate hearings look like a vicarage tea party. Wu Wen's silence on the role of Mao was eloquent.

"Feudal fascist dictatorship" was the term Li Yizhe had used in his poster in Canton four years before, and the *People's Daily* had used only a few days ago.

The next day, Tuesday, someone signing himself "Interests of the people" wrote in another poster:

> Under great pressure from the people, the Tiananmen incident has been cleared up. The original judgment of its place in history has been reversed. This victory belongs to the people, but the revolutionary struggle has not finished. . . . Why has it taken two years since the smashing of the Gang of Four to clear the name of the April Fifth revolutionary movement? Why have the executioners who suppressed the revolutionary masses movement not been publicly brought to justice? . . . Why are there people who are so afraid of democracy and are oppressing the revolutionary masses? . . . The reason is that even now there is still a small group of highly placed people who are holding leadership power . . . a small group of feudal fascist despots. In April 1976 they waved the

big stick of "power is truth" just like the Gang of Four and blood-
ily suppressed the masses who were commemorating Premier
Zhou Enlai. After the Gang of Four were smashed, they continued
to oppress the masses.

Wu Wen returned to the wall that day to put up part two of
Democracy Must Judge Despotism. He began by recalling the
history of China's revolution:

> The Revolution of 1911 put an end to the cruel, barbaric feudal
> despotic rule established in China by Qin Shi Huang several thou-
> sand years ago, and established the Republic of China with a
> republican-type government; that is, one in which the people exer-
> cise state power. However, on March 18 of the fifteenth year of
> the Republic [1926], the reactionary government of Duan Qirui
> bayoneted to death several hundred young people, who had come
> to present a petition, in the Tiananmen Square. Lu Xun said of the
> bloody March 18 incident "such cruel and barbaric behavior is not
> only not to be found among wild beasts, it is seldom found even
> amongst mankind. There is only the case of Nicholas II sending in
> the Cossacks to kill the people which bears any resemblance."
>
> On October 1, 1949, the People's Republic was established.
> This means that the people exercise state power. Premier Zhou
> spent 28 years administering it; Deng Xiaoping was appointed
> Acting Premier twice. Tiananmen Square was always peaceful and
> happy; it was a symbol of national unity.
>
> But not long after Premier Zhou left us, several thou-
> sand people went to Tiananmen Square to commemorate him. A
> democratic discussion arose, and was met with a massacre one
> hundred times more barbaric than that of the reactionary Duan
> Qirui government or Czar Nicholas II. The feudal, fascist, despo-
> tic government sent in one hundred thousand armed Public Secu-
> rity Police to kill defenseless citizens. . . . The socialist People's
> Republic had become an empty name. The lives of people, democ-
> racy, human rights—had all become nothing. The law had be-
> come a scrap of paper used to cheat and bully the people.
>
> After the fall of the Gang of Four, the first thing the Chinese
> people wanted was to reverse the verdict on the Tiananmen inci-
> dent. This was ordinary common sense, and did not need any talk
> about "wise" decisions. But contrary to their expectations, the
> Chinese were blamed for the Tiananmen incident for the next two
> years. And, strangest of all, around 8 January 1977, many people

were secretly jailed*. . . . Should not the People's Republic live up to its name? If not, we may just as well call the country the Feudal Fascists' Great Chinese Empire. . . . It is incredible that in a People's Republic there should still be among the officials to whom the people have entrusted national sovereignty executioners and murderers whose hands are stained with the blood of the people. . . . In capitalist society, there are cases like the Watergate Affair, the Lockheed Scandal, and the Guillaume Gerhard Spy Scandal in West Germany. Capitalist laws are very strict in their punishment. But as for the Tiananmen incident in China . . . a country of proletarian dictatorship armed with the Great Thought of the Era, we certainly do not measure up to the people of ancient times or foreign countries. . . .

Whoever organized and directed the crushing of the Tiananmen demonstrations must be handed over to the judgment of a people's court. Democracy must judge despotism.

On 22 November a worker in a radio factory supported the calls for inquiries into the suppression of the Tiananmen demonstrations and claimed: "This request cannot but be supported by all who remember the fascist dictatorship of the time before the fall of the Gang of Four. . . . To make people think that democracy and human rights are only slogans of the Western bourgeoisie, and that the Eastern proletariat needs only dictatorship, and especially all-round dictatorship in all spheres of the superstructure, is something that cannot be tolerated any more.

On Wednesday a railway worker asked some searching questions about Mao's responsibility for the events of the last ten years of his life. (The official line until November 1978 had been that the Cultural Revolution had been a great and good thing and any subsequent wrongdoing was the fault of the Gang of Four.) The railworker wrote:

Mao's great merits do not mean that he did not make mistakes.

Just ask yourself: Without Mao's support could Lin Biao have achieved power?

Just ask yourself: Didn't Chairman Mao know that Jiang Qing was a traitor? . . .

---

* Presumably a reference to those who were arrested for having gone to the Zhongnanhai to present six demands, including one for reversing the verdict on the Tiananmen incident (see Chapter 8).

If Chairman Mao had not agreed would the Gang of Four have been able to achieve their aim of . . . striking down Deng Xiaoping?

Just ask yourself: If Chairman Mao had not nodded his head, would the Tiananmen incident have been regarded as a counter-revolutionary incident? . . . We say Chairman Mao was a man, not a god. . . . If we do not permit the masses to express their own opinions of Chairman Mao, then freedom of speech and democracy are only empty words.

There were six posters by railway workers and all, in effect, accused Mao of having been in collusion with Lin Biao and the Gang of Four.

A poster signed "Peking Xidan Hyde Park Observer"* contained an appeal for equality before the law:

Don't only judge grass-roots criminals, but also those who sneaked into senior party positions. Denounce them and punish them according to law! This would be a pioneering event in our socialist country, something unprecedented throughout the whole country. It would guarantee democracy and law and order. Democracy and law and order are two powerful weapons against revisionism and changing the political color. Carry on the April 5 revolutionary movement and continue the struggle for generations to come!

On 23 November there finally appeared a poster defending Mao—and indeed Hua Guofeng, although there had been no criticism of Hua by name. It was signed with a pen name, Yao Hanwei (meaning: we must be on our guard!), rather than a job description:

Chairman Mao was great [Yao wrote], Premier Zhou was honest and open, Chairman Hua Guofeng is wise. He who opposes Chairman Mao will come to a bad end, he who opposes Premier Zhou will come to a bad end, and so will he who opposes Chairman Hua. We must protect them.

Unlike most of the writers, Yao Hanwei gave no reason for his position. And someone wrote on his poster: "This is just

* The Democracy Wall was situated at the junction of Xidan Street and the Avenue of Eternal Peace; poster-writers saw a link with the tradition of speaker's corner in London's Hyde Park.

sloganeering. Where is your argument?" Another reader was
more blunt: "Dog fart!"

Friday, 24 November, brought a startling sight to Tiananmen Square. Huang Xiang, the poet from Guiyang, had—with a
little help from hometown friends—pasted up on a tall fence at
one side of the square no fewer than ninety-four panels of
big-character posters bearing his *God of Fire Symphonic
Poems*. High on an embankment they stretched for seventy
yards along the fence. Hundreds of people gathered to read
them, and for once the display had been so well planned that
there was no crush; all could read at leisure. At twelve noon
precisely, Huang Xiang and his seven companions founded the
Enlightenment Society, dedicated to the goal of "ideological
modernization." They pasted up a poster formally announcing
the founding of the society, declaring that its emblem was a
burning torch, and signed their names. They distributed copies
of their society's journal, called simply *Qimeng* (*Enlightenment*). The young men in the group had been friends for many
years, having first come together in the years of darkest oppression after the Cultural Revolution. One, Li Jiahua, had written an introduction to and commentary on Huang Xiang's
poems, published in the 24 November issue of *Enlightenment*.[2]

Li claimed that "A great ideological revolutionary movement to distinguish truth from falsehood is now sweeping the
country. . . . In the face of this great revolution, all reactionary
idols who went against history have fallen, one after another,
from their so-called summits.* Those high-and-mighty superstitions which fooled the people have been exposed one by one."
But he called for the struggle to go on, under the leadership of
the Party, "until the influence of Lin Biao and the Gang of Four
is completely eliminated," and described the goals in these
words:

---

* During the Cultural Revolution, Lin Biao ensured that Mao Zedong
Thought was hailed as the summit of ideology in our era.

> We must free ourselves from the patriarchal rule of the past thousands of years, free ourselves from the enslavement of feudal despotism and superstitions, smash the spiritual shackles imposed by Lin Biao and the "Gang of Four," appeal for democracy, safeguard great socialist democracy and speed up the rate of development of the national economy—these are the important things we have to do today.

These goals, he believed, were consistent with the state constitution and should be attained by insisting on the constitutional rights of the citizen.

At Democracy Wall a poster went up calling for the rehabilitation of Marshal Peng Dehuai and of Tao Zhu, the pre-1966 overlord of South China who had fallen and died in the Cultural Revolution. Even more dramatic, a notice appeared announcing that some activists had held a meeting at the wall and had founded an Action Group "to fight the feudal fascism [that has been practiced] since the Cultural Revolution."

That evening Wu Wen put up the third and last part of *Democracy Must Judge Despotism*. This time his pen had really run away with him. In reviewing the ups and downs of Deng Xiaoping since 1975, he wrote that after being put in day-to-day charge of party and state affairs in 1975, Deng "took drastic measures and was able to turn the tide rapidly against the terrible mess that looked like a face with a thousand scars," clashed with the theory of the "God of the Heavenly Court," and incurred the opposition of the "despotic dictators."

On the afternoon of Saturday, 25 November, I went to see what was new at the Wall. It was a sunny winter's afternoon, and the crowd there was even larger than usual. I paced a hundred yards along the Wall, surveying the old as well as the new; it was always interesting to see how some posters that had said nothing very original were soon covered over while the strong and articulate ones remained visible. They gathered comments scratched in ballpoint pen, and sometimes when they were torn by accident they would be glued together again by considerate visitors.

There were small-character posters (*xiao-zi bao*), written with pen or pencil on pages torn from notebooks, and there were big-character posters (*da-zi bao*), sheets of paper three feet high on which the characters were written with a brush and black ink. Some messages were elegantly presented on pink, yellow, or green paper to bid for attention. Many more were plainly done.

Most of the readers were under thirty-five and workers rather than students. They stood reading with rapt attention, many of them copying texts as they had begun to do at Qing Ming in April 1976. Silence reigned except when someone read out a text for a group to hear, or two friends muttered comments to each other.

I decided on a place to begin and approached the Wall with keen anticipation of learning more about the political views of young Chinese. As on the previous days, I could not predict what I would find but felt sure it would teach me something of how the young of China saw their country and their future. After a week of daring and exuberance unreproved from on high, I sensed a little more openness among the crowd toward each other and toward foreigners, and decided to test whether people were now ready to talk to foreigners in public about politics. After reading some posters, I turned my back on the Wall, walked a few feet, and addressed a bland and general question to a small group nearby. Immediately I was surrounded by twenty people and a discussion began. It was as if a frieze had come to life. Invisible forces that had held these people mute if not immobile in the presence of foreigners all their young lives seemed suddenly to have relaxed their grip. From twenty the crowd grew to fifty and then a hundred.

They were eager to know what I thought about the Four Modernizations, then someone said: "What did you think of the Chinese people two years ago? Did you think we were empty-headed? Now you can see we are not!" They cheered when I told them I had never thought them empty-headed, only restrained in what they could say.

They wanted to know about how countries like Britain really work. They bombarded me with questions on democracy and human rights: "Can you really criticize your Prime Minister? Who owns the newspapers in Britain? How do they decide their editorial policy? How is the BBC controlled? How are elections organized?"

Some were by no means ignorant but wanted to check out the information they had acquired one way or another; others were simply thirsty for knowledge. As one who had seen something of the xenophobia of the Cultural Revolution in China at first hand, and had walked through the charred shell of the British Embassy after it was burned by Red Guards, it was exhilarating to talk with these young Chinese who cared intensely about their own country but were also interested in and indeed admired the political system in Britain.

I looked around me and saw Chinese-speaking American and Australian diplomats surrounded by groups of young people. I heard one of the Americans telling the Chinese around him that some people in the West wondered whether the pace of change in China was not now too fast, and voices shouted back: "Not too fast! Too slow! Too slow!" An Australian was asked what he thought was the state of democracy and human rights in China. His circumspect answer was greeted with obvious disappointment. so he turned the questioning around and asked young men at his side what they wanted for China. One of them replied: "A prosperous nation, with a strong army [fu-guo qiang-bing]."

"What do you others think?" asked the Australian, "Do you agree or disagree?"

"Agree! Agree!" other voices called out. As I heard this exchange I could not help wondering where the ideal of Communism fitted in. What we were hearing was the nationalist strain to which Zhou Enlai's Four Modernization formulation appealed so strongly.

Earlier in the week, a wall poster had mentioned Hua Guofeng by name. It had been written by someone whose poems had been included in the anthology of poetry from Tiananmen for which Hua had recently inscribed the title in his own handwriting. The author said that Deng, not Hua, should have written the inscription and threatened to withdraw his poems from the collection if this change was not made. (The poster disappeared within twenty-four hours and not surprisingly its threat was ignored.) Following on from this, the denunciation of the suppression of the Tiananmen demonstrations and the calls for revoking the two resolutions of 8 April 1976 had fueled speculation in the foreign press that Hua Guofeng was under oblique attack from Deng's supporters—who, it was suggested, wanted Deng to replace Hua as premier. But at the Wall that afternoon people spoke respectfully of Hua, seeming to make a distinction between the man himself and the circumstances under which he reached the position of premier.

I spotted Philip Short, the BBC's Peking correspondent, approaching the Wall. When the crowd heard who he was they cheered him, knowing that he had been sending the message of the Wall around the world.

Nigel Wade, the London *Daily Telegraph* correspondent, was locked into a group like mine a few yards away. When we had both extricated ourselves, we compared notes. One young man had told him "We are speaking what has been in our hearts for years," and others had thanked him for taking an interest in Chinese affairs.

I returned to the Wall that evening and was surrounded by a group who plied me with questions until my voice threatened to give out. The press of the crowd kept me warm on the windswept street, and so tightly did they pack around me that I had to lean outward to keep a breathing space. The crowd was drawn not by any personal magnetism of mine but by those concepts of "democracy" and "human rights" which I had often been told were irrelevant to these people.

Driving home along the broad and empty expanse of the Avenue of Eternal Peace, I looked back on an extraordinary fortnight, which had begun with those articles in the *People's Daily* that had dynamited positions held rigidly for years—on Mao, the Cultural Revolution, political democracy. It was as if the official press had blown breaches in the wall of a citadel through which young poster-writers, poets, and pamphleteers were now pouring. The foreign community in Peking was watching in amazement, and the fact that posters dealing with the most controversial issues of the hour had been allowed to remain on display for a week convinced me that there had been

a decision at the highest level in favor of tolerance—at least for
the time being.

The next day—Sunday, 26 November—Deng told a
Japanese visitor that the decision had been made this way: "In
the beginning we made an attempt to stop the campaign. We
thought the masses would oppose attempts to use Mao's name.
The leaders were opposed to it and I am not supporting it. But
we should not check the demands of the masses to speak."[3]

There were so many people in Peking—indeed, all over
China—who had a good deal that they were burning to say
about Mao, democracy, Deng's opponents in the Politburo, and
the shortcomings of China's political and economic system that
there was no need for Deng's people to give instructions on
what to write: they just had to ensure that the city authorities
did not tear down posters that broke new ground, that dared to
say what had not been said before.

The judgment on what was the permitted area of freedom
had to be made first by the writer. There was no guarantee that
he would not be arrested immediately, or months or years later.
The writer ran the risk that the political pendulum would swing
back and the men who were lifting the lid now might be forced
to retreat, to permit arrests.

The risks of associating with this movement were glaringly
obvious and deterred millions of people in Peking from even
coming to the Wall to read the posters, let alone write one or
speak at a meeting. To do that required nerve. It was a degree of
testing and forging that most of us who had grown up in established democracies had never experienced.

On Sunday afternoon, John Fraser of the Toronto *Globe and
Mail* took American syndicated columnist Robert Novak,
who was visiting Peking, to see the Wall.

When people there heard Novak might see Deng the next
day, hundreds crowded around and poured out suggestions as
to the questions he should ask and the views he should transmit.
Fraser had them write down their suggestions on scraps of paper. He had them translated and then made a selection. Novak
was of two minds as to whether it would be proper for him to
act as an intermediary between the people and Deng, but de-

cided to go ahead. At the end of an unusually long two-hour interview Novak brought up the "Thoughts from the Wall," and Deng rose to the occasion. By previous arrangement, Fraser returned to the Wall the next evening to report back to the crowd on behalf of Novak, who had left for a tour of Northeast China. Friends had warned him that he might find himself under pressure to cross the line between observer of and participant in Chinese politics, but he said he must go: "So many promises have been made to these people and so many broken. I don't want to add to the total."

I arrived at the Wall just before 7:00 P.M. to find several thousand people gathered around Fraser and the organizers of the meeting. Every minute hundreds more arrived. I made my way through the crowd and squatted on the ground among the young men and women of the audience, not too far from Fraser. The crowd was buzzing with excitement. Here and there I spotted the familiar faces of other foreigners who came regularly to the Wall.

Nothing quite like this had happened before in modern China. These people had sent their message and questions to Deng yesterday and today they would get his reply. For once, they had bypassed the bureaucracy. (Some in the crowd could remember how they had once thrilled when Mao had made his end runs around the bureaucracy to appeal to them directly. But then it was always he who sent the message; now there was a dialogue.)

People perched in trees and on top of the Wall. Most squatted on the ground. There was not a policeman or a voluntary marshal to be seen, but the crowd kept order in the best tradition of Chinese self-discipline.

The organizers included one or two well-groomed, intelligent-looking young men in smart jackets that were not seen on the backs of ordinary citizens, and they carried cassette tape recorders in shoulder satchels. They had the self-confident air of the sons of high officials, and later I learned that a number of such young men were active in the movement.

Fraser began his report, telling the crowd that Deng had said the Wall was a fine thing. This brought roars of appreciation. As Fraser continued, the crowd reacted without inhibitions to

Deng's free-ranging comments on the hot topics of the hour. What surprised me was the cheer that went up when Fraser broke the news that Deng had indicated that the late Marshal Peng Dehuai would soon be rehabilitated. In 1959, when Peng had bitterly attacked the damage done by Mao's leadership of the Great Leap Forward, blasting the headlong rush to Communism and defying the revered leader, some of these young people had not been born and the rest had been at their mother's knee, and yet Peng was a hero to them. When they heard that Deng had avoided answering the question whether the deposed head of state, Liu Shaoqi, would also be given a posthumous restoration, they chuckled. They drew hope from the fact that Deng had neither excluded the possibility nor applied to Liu the usual damning epithet "bourgeois revisionist."

At the end of his report, Fraser was able to slip away without any fuss. He had succeeded in limiting his role to that of a reporter. His place was taken by a young Chinese man who made a speech calling for democracy and human rights. He spelled out the advantages of American-style separation of powers and called for removal of the obstacles to unity, stability, and democracy that he said were posed by leaders whose minds were deeply influenced by the Gang of Four.

In their laughter, their cheers, their hopes and anger, these young people showed themselves united and remarkably free that evening. Here at the Wall they were in a place of their own, and joined with kindred spirits.

When the Chinese speaker finished, the organizers dispersed the meeting because there were now more than five thousand people present and without a public address system those at the back could not hear. Some two thousand began a march to Tiananmen Square, walking thirty abreast down the vast Avenue of Eternal Peace, arms linked and singing. When they reached the Great Hall of the People they saw that lights were burning on upper floors. Perhaps this was where the Central Work Conference was meeting. They halted, gathered in front of the Great Hall, and sang the *"Internationale"* and the National Anthem. The singing brought people to the windows on the lighted floors, so they shouted slogans for freedom and democracy and sang the *"Internationale"* again. Then they entered the square and divided into three groups to discuss what to do next. After ten minutes most of them gathered around the Heroes' Monument to hear more speakers and to give more people a chance to hear what message Deng had sent them. Others formed small groups around foreigners to talk again of elections, law, human rights, and world affairs.

Speakers at the Heroes' Monument called for learning from the Yugoslav form of socialism, saying it gave more individual freedom and more democracy. There was more talk of learning from the good side of U.S. democracy, including the separation of powers. One speaker started off "I want to talk to you about Liu Shaoqi" and the crowd roared back: "Comrade Liu Shaoqi! Comrade!"—for them, he was still a Communist in good standing. The speaker resumed. "All right, I'll talk to you about Comrade Liu Shaoqi." Recalling a 1958 speech made by Liu praising Yugoslavia's agricultural ownership policies, he said "Today, twenty years later, Chairman Hua also wants us to follow the Yugoslav example. Twenty years, comrades! We've lost twenty years!"[4]

On the following two nights there were again meetings on Tiananmen Square. On 28 November the crowd heard a fifty-year-old man with the air and eloquence of a high party official criticize Mao for his choice in 1949 of the "Soviet Model" and for the policy of "leaning to one side" (the Soviet side) which, he claimed, had prevented China from responding to a possible U.S. State Department willingness to establish diplomatic links. "Twenty years lost" was his refrain also. He maintained that leaders should be critized in their lifetime: "We must not wait until emperors are dead to judge them."[5] At the Wall a separate meeting heard a hoarse-voiced orator shout "This Wall is the base which supports democracy in China. It is the Yanan* of our day." But already there was a new tone to the speeches, a greater concern with orthodoxy, because a Central Document issued

---

* Yanan, in Shaanxi province, had served as the headquarters of the Communist Party for a decade from 1936.

by the Party was passing on a warning from Deng that some speakers and writers had gone too far.

So the next night the speeches were tamer, but this was interesting too. The crowd grew restless as the speakers failed to break new ground, and speaker after speaker gave way in the face of catcalls deriding his lack of nerve. When one speaker said "We must not accept emasculated Marxism–Leninism. We must go back to study the original words of Marx, Engels, and Lenin," a young man standing near me muttered "Why must we go back? We should go forward." The only time the crowd showed interest was when speakers entered the dangerous zone of learning from foreign countries. "We should ask ourselves why the U.S., Japan, and Western Europe have such advanced economies. Is it a result of the kind of constitutional systems they have?" "Now we are getting somewhere," a voice called out. But the speaker took it no further and people began to talk among themselves and drift away. There were no more public meetings on the square for a long time.

But the poster-writers soon regained their former nerve. In the weeks that followed, opinions were expressed on a great variety of topics and new forms of poster emerged. One night there appeared an open letter to President Carter, written on 8 December, the day after the American president had made a major speech on the place of human rights in diplomacy; it began:

> Your speech yesterday "Human rights is the soul of American foreign policy" has moved the conscience of the world. As Chinese citizens, we think that truth is universal and that the soul of mankind—human rights—is not limited by national boundaries, geography, or borders. On this small planet on which we all live there are people of different races, countries with different historical traditions, and people with different languages and cultures. But the demand for basic human rights is common to all. Your concern for Sakharov, Shcharansky, and Ginsburg was very moving but . . . you should not only protest against unsuccessful oppression, because successful oppression is even more fearful. . . . In a country which regards Marxism as a new religion and in the

name of the proletariat uses oppressive methods, it can happen to any citizen who expresses a different opinion that this will be considered a counter-revolutionary crime and he can be arrested, imprisoned, punished, or sent into exile and even executed. Any citizen can be cruelly harmed and oppressed in a political movement about which he knows nothing. We would like to ask you to pay attention to the state of human rights in China. The Chinese people do not want to repeat the tragic life of the Soviet people in the Gulag Archipelago.

A poster signed Yi Yan denounced the "cultural bureaucrats who review all foreign literature and films and whose whims decide what the people can see and read. If literature and art are not free, there will be no hope for the nation."[6]

A demand for sexual freedom was pasted up by a group of earnest young men of sober appearance. Their poster included the assertion that "Chinese should be free to have sexual relations when and with whom they like."

When Deng expressed his disapproval of criticizing Mao by name in posters, adding that "the masses have their doubts on some questions—some utterances are not in the interest of stability and unity," there were strong protests—the first occasion on which public criticism was made of Deng. Li Ping wrote: "Vice-Premier Deng, you are wrong, completely wrong . . . for you did not conduct any opinion poll on this subject. There is no doubt that, a long time ago, the Chinese people took note of Chairman Mao's mistakes. Those who hate the Gang of Four cannot fail to have grievances against Chairman Mao." (While Li Ping may have been correct in his assessment of opinion among those too young to have known Mao in the time of his greatness, he probably underestimated the degree of residual loyalty and respect for Mao among those who, like Deng, had come to power under his leadership. As to "stability and unity," Li Ping, like writers in the People's Daily and other publications, failed to see how the heady atmosphere produced by the posters—and the tolerance given them—would encourage some people to acts of "civil disobedience.")

One writer saw the link between political and economic development this way: "China's system of government is modeled

on the Russian system. This is a system that produces bureaucracy and a privileged stratum. Without changes in this system,
the Four Modernizations will stop at the halfway point or just
beyond, as in Russia where the state is strong and the people are
poor. The Russians are better off than we Chinese but they are
still poor compared to people in advanced Western countries.
We need a state where all delegates are elected and responsible
to the people."

Mao's words of blessing to Hua—"With you in charge, I am
at ease"—came in for criticism in a forty-eight-page unsigned
poster that appeared on 17 December and was widely reported
abroad the next day. The anonymous writer complained that the
words "I am at ease" showed that Mao was motivated by personal considerations and concern for his role in history rather
than the will of the people. Was he concerned whether the
people were at ease?

This writer quoted a letter that he said Mao had sent to Jiang
Qing in 1976 as death approached:

> These will be the final words that I shall write to you. Today we are
> separating into two worlds. May each keep his peace. Man's life is
> limited but the revolution knows no bounds. In the last ten years, I
> tried to teach the Chinese about revolution, but I was not success-
> ful. If you reach for the top and fail, you will fall into an abyss.
> Your body will shatter, and your bones will be smashed.

(Despite the letter's poignance, it must be doubted that Mao
was capable of writing anything so coherent in the summer of
1976.) The author of the poster asked "Comrades, how are we
to interpret this letter? People should know the facts. Are we
not entitled to request publication of all Chairman Mao's
speeches and articles since the Cultural Revolution so that the
masses may know the facts, and can no longer be taken in?"
Denied for so long the right to criticize their leaders, people
lashed out ferociously now. Ni Zhifu, a former worker who had
been responsible for Peking's militia at the time of the Tiananmen incident, was the target of an accusation of having wanted
to take part in an armed coup in support of Jiang Qing after
Mao's death. The poster called him a criminal butcher who re-

pressed the Tiananmen revolution and said "he wanted to set up an armed battalion for the empress' coup!"[7] A law of libel could probably have prevented such poorly substantiated accusations from being published, but China had no law of libel. How long, one wondered, could *any* political system tolerate attacks like this on incumbent leaders? The writer undoubtedly believed Ni Zhifu to be an obstacle to democratic reforms, but this kind of poorly substantiated attack was more likely to bring retribution than reform.

Another target of criticism was Kang Sheng—the man who had introduced Jiang Qing to Mao in Yanan and had served him as a theoretician, but more especially as a domestic security expert. He had made a detailed study of the files of the Chinese leadership and knew where the bodies were buried. Kang Sheng had died in 1975, but there were people who were eager to see his named dragged through the mud and others equally anxious to prevent this. On Democracy Wall, Kang Sheng was caricatured wearing Nazi uniform and giving a Nazi salute with blood dripping from his upraised hand. After Mao's death but before Deng's rehabilitation, photographs of this sinister figure who had been a leading hatchet man in the Cultural Revolution were given a prominence surprising at a time when the people were being assured that the "hearts of Chairman Hua and the Central Committee beat as one with the hearts of the people." This may have reflected the influence at that time of Wang Dongxing, who had worked closely with Kang.

People like Kang Sheng are virtually unknown outside China except to those who have a personal or professional interest in the country. But their names are rich in resonance to citizens of the People's Republic. There was therefore no need for Deng's subordinates to drop specific hints to poster-writers to attack them: they could see for themselves that to do so would advance their cause. Even if hints *were* dropped (and there is no evidence one way or the other), it does not alter the fact that the young at Democracy Wall showed by their scrawled or oral comments and their numerous posters that Kang Sheng and others like him were widely hated.

Disillusion and skepticism were much in evidence in the posters, but little or no cynicism. Even the angriest of writers

believed there was a better way of living and that evil would be
punished. One poster recounted the thoughts that ran through
the mind of a worker as he walked to his home in the outskirts
of Peking late one night after going to the cinema. In his imagination he talked to the villain in the film he had just seen. "If you
learn how to change faces and twist your head, follow others and
flatter others, you can survive. Let me introduce you to another
way of surviving: you can abandon truth. Is this not noble
power? Nothing of the sort. . . . If you go too high you will
stumble. . . . If you want to be saved from that, you must be
quick to renounce that goal. Remember that the owl sees the rat
in the dark—the rat who harmed the people."

The fiercest skepticism came from Wei Jingsheng in his
poster *The Fifth Modernization—Democracy*. While many
poster-writers had attacked Mao, the Gang of Four, and those in
the current leadership most closely associated with them, and
had called for fundamental reforms of the system, Wei
Jingsheng was almost alone in calling into question the good
faith of the pragmatic reformers and in claiming that the slogan
"The Four Modernizations" was being used to dupe the people.
Everything he wrote was read with intense interest but it was
hard to know how far his readers shared the extreme skepticism
expressed, for instance, in these passages from *The Fifth Modernization:*

> We have not heard so much about the "class struggle" on television
> or the radio or in our newspapers and magazines recently; this is
> because people are thoroughly sick of hearing about it. But, as the
> old goes, it is replaced by the new. So they have dreamed up a new
> promise: the Four Modernizations.
>
>   There is an old Chinese saying "to paint a picture of a cake in
> order to satisfy one's hunger." This shows that the ordinary people
> of ancient times humorously saw through this fallacy. But there
> are still some people who believe it. For several decades the
> Chinese people, following the "communist ideal" of the "Great
> Helmsman," went through the "Great Leap Forward" and the
> "Three Red Flags,"* always marching onward. Thirty years passed
> like a day, and gave us this lesson: the people are like the monkey

---

* I.e., the General Line of the Communist Party, the Great Leap Forward,
and the People's Commune.

grasping at the reflection of the moon in a pond: don't they realize there is nothing there?

So, when Deng Xiaoping raised the slogan of "getting down to business," the people cried out over and over again for him to be restored to power. The people wanted to "seek truth from facts" to investigate the past. . . . But "some people" warned us . . . Chairman Mao is the great savior of the Chinese people, if there were no Communist Party there would be no "New China," if there were no Chairman Mao there would be no "New China." If you don't agree with this you will come to no good end! "Some people" also reminded us "The Chinese people need dictatorship; they have passed the feudal state, and that shows what a great people they are; the Chinese people do not want democracy, what they need is a 'democracy' under a 'collective leadership' or they are not worth a penny. You can believe this or not as you like: jail will prove the point." But then they left us a way out. With the Four Modernizations as the key link, and with "unity and stability," go on, old yellow oxen, continue the revolution: you will reach your heaven in the end: Communism and the Four Modernizations. . . .

Do the people enjoy democracy nowadays? No. Is it that the people do not want to be their own masters? Of course they do. This was the very reason the Communist Party defeated the KMT. After their victory, did they do what they promised to do? The slogan of People's Democracy was replaced by the Dictatorship of the Proletariat, making a very small percentage of the hundreds of millions of people the leaders. Then even this was canceled and the despotism of the "Great Helmsman" took over. Then came another promise: because our Great Leader was just so great, the superstitious belief in a great leader could bring the people far more happiness than democracy. The people have been forced against their will to accept these "promises" time and again right up till the present day. But are they happy? Are they prosperous? We cannot hide the fact that they are more restricted, more unhappy, and the society is more backward than ever.

According to the founding fathers of Marxism–Leninism, the people should control the means of production. Just ask yourself, Chinese workers and peasants, apart from the little bit of salary you get each month to stop you from starving, whose masters are you? Or what do you own? To spell it out is pitiful: others are your masters; even marriage is not an exception. In a socialist society the workers are supposed to enjoy the fruits of their labor. But what do you get? All you get is a bit of salary to maintain your power to produce.

Toward the end of his poster he affirmed: "The people have finally learned where their goal is. They have a clear orientation and a real leader—the democratic banner."

People were free to comment on posters, and some writers thoughtfully provided sheets for comments. Usually writers spurred each other on and the scrawled comments encouraged rather than criticized. But dissenting posters did occasionally appear, defending Mao or, once, drawing attention to some of the uglier features of U.S. society. Those who wrote in defense of Mao were liable to see someone scrawl "Gang of Four-type thinking" or "People should dare to make comments on their emperor," but ran no more serious risk. In early December, a few days after Deng's disapproval of people criticizing Mao had been conveyed to the nation by Central Document, a poster appeared in central Peking saying "If people who want to put up posters criticizing Chairman Mao would give us their names we would smash their dogs' heads. Chairman Mao is the red sun in our hearts." This kind of language was reminiscent of the Cultural Revolution. It was the only poster of its kind that I heard of.

A few of the posters may have been inspired by hints from highly placed officials. Sometimes the themes of posters so closely paralleled what was being said inside the Work Conference as to suggest coordination. For instance, there was a poem that aimed at Wang Dongxing all the same charges that were being leveled at him at the Work Conference, according to reports published later in the Hong Kong press. Others appeared under circumstances that were a little mysterious: An inquiry to the motor repair shop where the writer of the first poster criticizing Mao by name had stated that he worked was met by a good-natured denial that anyone with Work Permit 0538 was employed there. At the same time, such a diversity of opinions developed and such a multitude of posters appeared that it was utterly implausible to suggest that the whole thing was a product of manipulation. Besides, when we came to know a number of those who put up posters it was very evident that they were not under remote control from any command headquarters.

The activists at the Wall took pains to make sure that journalists and diplomats did not miss the important posters. On one occasion a friend of mine started to edge his way through a crowd toward an "Open Letter to Brzezinski" but became discouraged by the throng and gave up. He was about to turn away when he felt a pair of hands clasp his hips from behind and start to push him forward again politely but firmly. He was grateful to his guide: the poster was of interest. Journalists would be summoned to the Wall by telephone. Late one night Nigel Wade of the *Daily Telegraph* was wakened from his sleep by a familiar voice on the telephone that told him of an important new poster on human rights. When he reached the Wall he began to search for it, not knowing quite where to begin. Then a voice rang out in the darkness, "Human rights over here!" It was his guide and self-appointed interpreter, ready to help him get the story out.

Posters would go up one day, be reported immediately by agencies and be broadcast back to China, in Chinese, by foreign radio stations within hours. By late November, many people in China were prepared to listen to radio stations like the Voice of America, Radio Japan, Radio Australia, and the BBC (when it was audible) either in Chinese or English. China had joined the "global village." Denied access to their own press, the activists used foreign media as their megaphone to talk to their compatriots. But at no time did any foreigner to my knowledge make any suggestion as to what a poster-writer should say or any activist do by way of organizing the democracy movement.

Were foreign journalists and broadcasting services interfering in China's internal affairs, or just performing a legitimate newsgathering and dissemination function? It would be idle to pretend that the dissemination of news from Peking across China by foreign broadcasts had no effect but, over the years, Peking-based Western journalists and diplomats have shown themselves ready to report news and views from all parts of the political spectrum. There are people in the West who simply cannot accept that in China or anywhere else in the Third World there can be respect for the values and institutions of liberal democracy. They find it shocking when Western news media report objectively on evidence to the contrary, and they search wildly for some way of discrediting those who report that evidence. But in the winter of 1978 no Chinese made any criticism or protest, official or unofficial, to any Western journalist or diplomat in Peking about his or her news-gathering.

Later, it became very evident that there was resentment in some parts of the Chinese bureaucracy. In April 1979, the Peking Public Security Bureau (police department) classified the four foreign journalists who had been most active in covering the democracy movement story as "international spies." A rally was held to denounce them in their absence. The four were never officially informed of the classification; their relations with the Information Department of the Foreign Ministry were not affected, and they were not impeded in any way from doing their work. The Chinese contacts who unofficially informed them of the classification told them it had been done for "internal purposes only"—i.e., for use in China's domestic apparatus—and not to affect China's external relations. Among journalists it became something of a professional joke. Richard Thwaites of the Australian Broadcasting Corporation, who had worked hard on the democracy movement, said he was insulted and outraged that he had not been included in the list of spies and told his colleagues he was considering writing a letter to the police to protest the insult to his professional integrity.

This classification story figured in an article in the Hong Kong left-wing monthly *Cheng Ming*, which praised the work of these journalists—who, it said, were "trying to do a proper job." The author of the article pointed out that among the foreign journalists there were two different attitudes prevailing. The first attitude was fear that too much contact with unofficial Chinese and too many visits to Democracy Wall would attract unwelcome attention from the authorities. These journalists preferred to spend their day in their offices relying on the officially provided translations of the Chinese news service as their main source. The second attitude was one of seeing the democracy movement as an opportunity to gather firsthand news. The journalists with this approach to their work would go down to the Wall, said the author, in all kinds of weather and at all times of the day or night. John Fraser of the Toronto *Globe and Mail*, Georges Biannic and Francis Deron of the Agence France Presse, and Nigel Wade of the London *Daily Telegraph* were cited as examples of this active journalism. Thanks to them, the author continued, the democracy movement had been covered more fully in the Western press than any political movement in China since 1949. That these four, "who had shown a genuine concern for the Chinese people," should have been dubbed international spies showed, according to the author, that there was a real need for "serious re-education" within the ranks of the police.[8]

The reaction of the citizens of Peking to the posters on the Wall was in strong contrast to that of Muscovites to demonstrations by Soviet dissidents. No group of "enraged citizens" ever came to tear down a poster. On the very few occasions an individual did so, he was usually suspected of being a plainclothes policeman and met angry resistance from readers who would say: "We do not necessarily agree with what is written here, but you have no right to stop us from reading it." From numerous conversations foreigners had with ordinary workers who themselves had no part in the activities at the Wall, it emerged tha people had mixed feelings about the Wall and those who expressed themselves on it. There was widespread hope that the frontiers of freedom would be pushed forward, but people with responsible jobs and families to look after preferred not to participate themselves, and some older intellectuals found the young utopian in their calls for sweeping away the system of controls. There was anxiety lest the young should cause society to become unstable again.

When the communiqué of the Third Plenum of the Eleventh Central Committee was published at the end of December 1978, Democracy Wall had been alive for five weeks—the life span of the entire 1957 period of free speech, the Hundred Flowers campaign—but the December communiqué certainly did not signal an end to the thaw of 1978. On the contrary, it seemed likely to encourage further developments in the democracy movement.

It was time to step back for a moment from the hectic task of keeping abreast of day-to-day news and review what we had seen in the five weeks of looking through the best window into the thinking of young Chinese that had opened up since 1949.

As they reviewed the texts of posters and speeches, foreign journalists and diplomats agreed that a fundamental characteristic of all the young writers and speakers was that they did not view the world as Marxist–Leninists. Some professed to keep faith in Marx, but Lenin's system of dictatorship was anathema to them. Of the three panels of the Marxism–Leninism–Mao Zedong Thought triptych, they had rejected not only Mao's thoughts but also Lenin's, and the nature of their allegiance to Marx had been left very vague.

The fact that the dictatorship to which they had been subjected had been called "the dictatorship of the proletariat" impressed them not at all. The fact that Mao, Lin Biao, and the Gang of Four had been leaders of a party named the Communist Party had not impressed them either—they still described the last ten years of Mao's rule as "feudal fascist dictatorship."

They were asserting the rights of the individual against the state and against the collective. They had been careful to say that of course they did not want to turn China into a bourgeois society but only to adopt "the best features of bourgeois democracy." Then they had specified all the fundamental features— political and social—of liberal societies. They had called for constitutional government, the election and recall of state officials by popular suffrage, the rule of law, civil liberties as known in the West, a free labor market, cultural freedom as we know it, the free movement of peoples and ideas, and sexual freedom.

It was not only Western observers who were struck by this interest in Western values and institutions. The Hong Kong left-wing monthly *Dong Xiang* published an article "Why Do They Advocate Western Democracy?" that described and analyzed this trend.[9]

The young showed no sign of accepting the claims once made for socialism on the grounds of justice and efficiency. They were appalled by what they knew of poverty in some parts of the Chinese countryside but they saw dictatorship—not poverty—as the immediate enemy, believing that only through greater democracy and freedom could China escape from poverty. Wei Jingsheng had summed up that view when he called democracy the Fifth Modernization. Insofar as the socialist tradition applied, it was brought in to support the calls for democracy. There was some support for egalitarianism, but no interest at all in the ultimate goal of communism—the common ownership of all property. The countries that attracted them were capitalist countries—and Yugoslavia, because it enjoys more freedom and democracy than other states claiming to be socialist. They acknowledged both the material achievements and the high level of freedom of capitalist societies.

Did they want capitalism in place of Marxism–Leninism?

The demands for political and civil liberty were not matched by an equal volume of demands for economic reform, but some voices were heard on the subject. The declaration of the China Human Rights League called for a gradual total transition from state ownership to social ownership (the Yugoslav system of worker control). In *Fifth Modernization—Democracy*, Wei Jingsheng had seemed to hint that capitalism had a wide appeal when he wrote "After the fall of the Gang of Four, the people eagerly looked forward to the reappearance of Deng Xiaoping, of whom it was said, at one stage, that he would 'restore capitalism.' At last he came back, and the people were full of excitement and hope. But unfortunately the old power system oppressing the people is still with us!" But that was a statement about popular attitudes, not a call for capitalism.

One of Wei Jingsheng's fellow editors of *Exploration*, a slightly built thoughtful young man named Yang Guang, remarked one day: "What is happening now is that many young people who used to accept the whole theory of communism as they accept that the sun is red and the table is made of wood are now studying and observing in a spirit of skepticism. This is a very good beginning. Whether Marxism–Leninism is good or bad cannot be known from force-fed propaganda. We must study and explore for ourselves. We shall probably end up with a system which is neither Marxism–Leninism nor capitalism. The important thing is not to make a choice now but to explore."

From conversations such as this, and from the posters and speeches of November and December 1978, two modest conclusions could be drawn: First, Marxism–Leninism has little hold on the mind of some of the more daring and articulate of the younger generation in China and, second, the capitalist and mixed-economy societies have no devil image in their eyes.

11

Blooming and Scything

THE VOICES we heard at Democracy Wall be-
longed to the generation in its twenties and thirties. Many had
been in their teens when Mao mobilized them into the Red
Guards in 1966, releasing them from the routine of study and
the constraints of school, family, and neighborhood. They had
responded with enthusiasm to his call to smash the old bureaucratic order. They had been fanatically loyal to Mao because
they thought he could lead them to a new society where there
would be democracy, freedom, and purity. One Peking middle-
school student had written then: "We turn the old world upside
down, smash it to pieces, pulverize it, create chaos and make a
tremendous mess, the bigger the better. . . . We are bent on
creating a tremendous proletarian uproar, and hewing out a
new, proletarian world!"[1]

They had indeed created chaos, but neither they nor Mao
had known how to hew out a new proletarian order. So, two
years later, instead of becoming builders of a new world, they
had been rounded up by the army and marched off to the local
railway station, bands playing, banners waving, to board a train
for some remote area where they were to spend the next few
years—or the rest of their days—working as peasants or lumber-

jacks. Many had ended up in the frozen forests of the North-east.

What they had seen of China as they roamed the country at the height of the Cultural Revolution, or afterward when they were forced to settle there, had shocked them. These city-bred youths had not realized what depths of poverty still existed in parts of the Chinese countryside. Their life in the cities had not been luxurious or highly civilized, but the country was far more primitive. They now learned for themselves what it was like to live without any of the amenities of town life—books, informa-tion, passable health care and education, and professional enter-tainment. They were not welcomed by the peasants, who re-garded them as a burden on the local economy. Most of them found the cultural gap unbridgeable.[2]

Of the seventeen million youths sent to the countryside since 1967, about seven million had been allowed to return. They had brought back with them a harsh view of reality, and their prospects in the cities were not so bright as to erase that view. Their academic education had been truncated. All had lost two years of school, and those who had completed their school-ing found the universities and technical institutes closed until 1971. Thereafter the few who managed to extricate themselves from the villages and obtain a place received a caricature of a higher education. They knew this, and knew that society was not going to rush to put them in positions where they would enjoy such rewards as were available, so they had little to lose in a material sense by challenging the powers that be. Their position was remarkably like that of Mao in 1917 when he played a leading role in the formation of the New People's Study Soci-ety, which sought radical changes in the China of his day.

They had learned to take nothing on trust. They had seen not only the poverty of the countryside, but in some places corruption and bullying by local officials as well. Their eyes had been opened to the fallibility of Mao and the system by which they were governed. Instead of a generation of loyal successors, Mao had bred a generation determined to revenge itself on him. Steeled by ten years of arduous life, they came back to Tianan-men Square in April 1976 to tell him his day had gone; driven by their personal disillusion and suffering, they went beyond the traditional Chinese preoccupation with the character of the leader to question the system itself. That was what they had been doing at Democracy Wall.

The demonstrations in April 1976 had proved to them how deep and widespread was support for Zhou Enlai's legacy, and how strong the opposition to Mao and the Shanghai Gang. Although the repression was fierce, they had felt the strength of their own arm and the strength of older people who shared their views. The arrest of the Shanghai Gang in October and the way Chairman Hua and Marshal Ye pointed the regime afterward encouraged them to think that the message of Qing Ming had been heard and heeded. To take risks in the struggle was no longer to invite certain disaster.

Deng and his associates had understood their mood and encouraged them to speak out at key moments on key issues. They had responded with alacrity. Here at last was someone going in the right direction. They worked to restore Deng to office, purge the Mayor of Peking, reverse the verdict on the Tiananmen demonstrations, and undermine the Whatever Faction. They saw themselves as successors to the participants in the May Fourth Movement that began in 1919 and lasted into the 1920s. One of the goals of that movement was the emancipation of the individual from feudal ideas and controls. The young democrats of 1978 regarded the deification of Mao and the control system instituted in his time as feudal. Ideological and political struggle went hand in hand for them, as for the activists of the 1920s. The name they often used, the April Fifth Movement, pointed to the parallel between the two movements. So did the fact that demonstrations on Tiananmen Square had given momentum to both of them. Huang Xiang wrote in a poster that appeared on Democracy Wall on 30 November 1978:

> The April Fifth Movement is the successor to the May Fourth Movement, its deepening and development. If the May Fourth Movement's banner was against feudalism, then the banner of the April Fifth Movement was that of socialist China against dictatorship, a demand for fundamental human rights and democracy. . . .
> [It] is an awakening of the Chinese people who have been kept in the dark and kept ignorant. . . . The frozen feudal system in

China is slowly melting away. . . . *However, this is happening too slowly.* . . .

Curious to know to what extent outside influences had shaped the thinking of the young activists, foreigners asked a number of them—like Wei Jingsheng and Ren Wanding, the organizer of the Human Rights Alliance—about the reading they had done. They had read very few foreign books either in translation or the original. Neither Wei nor Ren speaks English or French. They were eager to read foreign authors and political magazines, but they had little or no access to such publications. They listened to foreign radio broadcasts in Chinese and they read *Reference News*, the daily digest of foreign news reports that has a circulation of about ten million. The Democracy Wall references to foreign constitutions, Russian dissidents; the Watergate, Lockheed, and Guillaume Gerhardt scandals; and the standard of living in Taiwan showed they had gleaned considerable knowledge of foreign countries and that a minority had even gained access to foreign works of philosophy and history; the founders of the Enlightenment Society succeeded in making the acquaintance of the Greek god Prometheus and Sir Thomas More's *Utopia* in remote Guizhou province. An even smaller minority had seen something of liberal democracies when overseas with their parents. (The activists included children of high-level diplomats and of researchers in the Academy of Social Sciences.) But the main forces shaping their thinking had been their own experiences and their analysis of them in the light of their basic knowledge of other systems.

They were open to foreigners to a degree that shocked conservative veteran cadres. Young men and women found it entirely natural to come to my flat for a meal, or even for a very chaste dance party. One, at his own suggestion, cooked a splendid meal for my family in our home at the Spring Festival, and others invited me out for a meal. To produce a fistful of business cards at Democracy Wall was to risk being mobbed. People to whom we gave cards would telephone to suggest meetings—not to betray state secrets but to have normal relations with a foreigner shared their interest in the big questions about the future of their country.

In January 1979, the spirit of a Peking Municipal Party

Committee conference was conveyed to the people of the city. The committee voiced numerous criticisms of the democracy movement, including these: "foreign embassies have frequently carried out activities, some foreigners have used money to buy big-character posters, some Chinese have asked foreigners for mimeographs, some Chinese have dined in restaurants at the invitation of foreigners, and all this has impaired the state system." Wei Jingsheng's comment was "How pompous the state system looks! This isn't the spirit of the 1970s, it's the closed-door spirit of the Qing dynasty. How about Deng Xiaoping accepting the Japanese emperor's invitation to dinner? Did this 'impair the state system'?"

One activist did indeed go to several foreign diplomats and journalists to ask for a mimeograph machine to enable him to improve the legibility of the journal he and his friends were putting out. All refused. With my refusal I explained that this would be interference in China's internal politics and asked what he thought the reaction of his readers would be if they learned that he had obtained this kind of foreign assistance. Without a moment's hesitation he replied: "They would be delighted that foreign money was at last going to a good cause, to help them struggle for something worthwhile. They have seen our leaders go around the world seeking billions of dollars of foreign loans and imports for large-scale projects and they would be glad to see one mimeograph put to work for democracy."

The young had been taught to suspect foreigners. They had been bred on a diet of illustrated booklets that generally painted Westerners in a bad light, such as U.S. soldiers maltreating Chinese captives in the Korean war, but the people we came to know seemed untouched by these attempts to generate hate. They saw nothing unpatriotic in making friends with foreigners, and as for those who were politically motivated, it was concern for their country that impelled them to seek out foreigners. When the Peking Party Committee issued its warning about contacts with foreigners, *Exploration*, the journal edited by Wei Jingsheng and his friends, put up a poster that included this passage: "The foreign diplomats and journalists from democratic countries show by their concern and support for our democratic movement that they are not letting down their own people. They are promoting relations between countries. It shows they have not forgotten China. Their inviting Chinese for conversation and meals shows they respect the Chinese people."

My guess—and in the absence of opinion polls or other "scientific" evidence one can only guess—is that the attitude of most Peking citizens would lie somewhere between those of the city fathers and the man who asked for the mimeograph.

In late December 1978, encouraged by the continued tolerance of the airing of controversial views on Democracy Wall, a number of young activists took two steps beyond writing posters: they launched nonofficial publications and formed organizations to promote their cause. The first of a dozen nonofficial publications appeared in Peking and were greeted with great enthusiasm. To avoid being crushed by would-be buyers, those who brought the journals for sale quickly adopted the tactic of sitting astride the Wall and handing them down one at a time. This prompted the Enlightenment Society to write in its journal: "We invite the editors of certain official publications to go to Xidan's Democracy Wall to take a look at the enthusiasm with which people buy nonofficial publications. Only when a newspaper is rooted among the people can it possess vitality." (The themes of the journal articles were very similar to those of the posters.)

The largest of the organizations was the Enlightenment Society, which had headquarters in Guiyang and set up offices in Peking and several other cities to form local branches and recruit members. Another important one was the China Human Rights Alliance, formed in Peking on 1 January 1979. It brought together the leaders of other groups and the editors of a number of nonofficial journals to draw up a declaration on human rights which became one of the most widely read documents of the movement (see appendix).

These organizations and journals committed themselves to observing the state Constitution, and one of their main aims was to generate pressure on the organs of party and state to observe it also. In the hundreds of posters and articles from the movement for democracy and human rights I read I never saw a call to violence or to civil disobedience.

On 28 January 1979, several groups of young democrats joined together to hold a public meeting at the Wall. One purpose was to publicize the fact that the groups were not operating underground but openly, and were exercising rights stipulated by the Constitution. They stood on an embankment with their backs to the Wall. Behind them stretched a long banner with black lettering on pink paper: DEMOCRACY DISCUSSION MEETING. Beside it were two smaller signs proclaiming two constitutional freedoms, freedom of speech and freedom of assembly. Each speaker announced his name and the name of the organization to which he belonged before he began to speak. One invited any plainclothes policemen in the crowd to make a tape recording of everything that was said.

The meeting drew a crowd of about seven hundred. This was much smaller than the crowds at the Tiananmen Square rallies two months before, and there was a tension that had not been present earlier. Some speakers struck a note of defiance. "We must not stop the struggle for democracy," one urged. "If some people try to stop us, then we are ready to pour out our blood." The crowd, who had been very quiet, almost impassive, until this point, roared their approval. But the loudest cheer of the day was earned by Yang Guang of *Exploration* when he said that since China's leaders were free to teach Marxism he should be free to speak from a non-Marxist viewpoint.

Another young man spoke bitterly of inequalities in Chinese society, arguing that China would never modernize itself until people were given basic rights. He drew ironic chuckles from the crowd when he said that one problem was that "the high-ranking officials have already modernized their style of living so they are not really concerned about the rest of us." He complained that high officials enjoyed comfortable houses while some young women who had been sent to the countryside after leaving school were forced into prostitution to get food.

The steps taken to consolidate the movement for freedom of expression appeared to be in line with the thinking of some senior leaders. On 1 January 1979, the three members of the Li Yizhe group were released from detention on orders from the Central Committee itself, a triumphant vindication of their Canton poster.* The preceding six weeks had seen the official press and the democracy movement echo the essence of their 1973–1974 call for democracy and legality, so it was only natural that they should now be restored to honor. When they were interviewed by Agence France Presse correspondent Francis Deron a fourth man emerged as a member of the group. He was Guo Hongzhi, who was twenty years older than the others and had been a high-ranking employee of the provincial Radio Guangzhou when the poster was written. He had served as the patron for the poster manifesto but gave no indication that the ideas in the poster had been handed down from anyone above him. The release of these folk heroes of the younger generation had been interpreted as an encouraging sign by the young activists.

So too had a *People's Daily* editorial on 3 January:

Let the people say what they wish. The heavens will not fall. . . . A range of opinions from people are good for a revolutionary party leading the government. If people become unwilling to say anything, that would be too bad. When people are free to speak, it means the Party and the Government have strength and confidence. . . . If a person is to be punished for saying wrong things, no one will say what he thinks. . . . The suffocation of democracy produces bad results.

Ten days before, another editorial in the same paper had said (and must have had the authority of members of the Politburo to say it): "Some comrades, when they see people putting up wall posters expressing opinions about the leadership, or see that some of the posters raise improper questions, dismiss these methods as detrimental to stability and unity. This is entirely wrong."

These editorials were written in the spirit of Deng Xiaoping's remarks of 26 November to the chairman of the Democratic Socialist Party of Japan. As reported by the official New China News Agency, he had made this comment about the upsurge in poster-writing:

This is a normal phenomenon, a manifestation of the stable situation in our country. . . . The writing of big-character posters is

* See Chapter 5.

permitted by our constitution. We have no right to negate or criticize the masses for promoting democracy and putting up big-character posters. The masses should be allowed to vent their grievances. Not all of the opinions of the masses are well considered and it is impossible that all their demands are completely correct, but this is not to be feared. Tempered through the Great Cultural Revolution, the overwhelming majority of our people are exceptionally great in their ability to distinguish between right and wrong and in their concern for the destiny of the country. The broad masses demand stability and unity and take the whole situation into consideration. The masses have doubts on some questions and there are words that are not conducive to stability and unity and the achievements of the Four Modernizations. We must make things clear to the masses and be good in leading them.[3]

On 22 January 1979 the *People's Daily* published an article which said that democracy was not a handout which could be withdrawn. Extensive socialist democracy was of the essence of a proletarian state, in which the people were the masters. Absence of such democracy indicated a failure to bring this essence into being. It could even mean the degeneration of a proletarian state: "When we say we must adhere to socialist principles, we refer not just to the style and methods of work of cadres. Fundamentally, we mean we must adhere to the proletarian state system, the proletarian democratic system that guarantees the people's participation in running the state, managing economic and cultural undertakings and supervising state organs and functionaries."

If leading cadres were not democratic in managing state affairs, they would become overlords rather than public servants and the people would become slaves rather than masters of the state. The solution to this problem, in the final analysis, depended on the improvement and development of the democratic system: The question of democracy is closely related to the question of law. Problems concerning cadres' styles and methods of work cannot be truly solved unless efforts are made step by step to form a comprehensive system that guarantees the people's right to act as masters of the country, to elect, supervise, and remove cadres of state organs.

"If we had had a complete system of proletarian democracy,

it would have been impossible for Lin Biao and the Gang of Four to rule the roost for a decade and to cause such havoc to the state. This is a profound lesson." The article had concluded that the proletarian state meant both proletarian dictatorship and proletarian democracy, that is, dictatorship over the bourgeoisie and democracy among the people. Without extensive democracy, the dictatorship could not be consolidated.[4]

The note of defiance struck by some speakers at the Xidan meeting showed that they did not believe that Deng's public pronouncements and the editorials of the *People's Daily* represented the unanimous view of a united leadership. They had to balance the reassuring tone of those words against the disapproving noises coming from the Peking city council. They balanced it also against the arrest of Fu Yuehua, a thirty-two-year-old city-born woman who had helped peasants organize a demonstration march in Peking on 8 January, the second anniversary of Zhou Enlai's. Posters in Peking on 25 January had claimed that Mrs. Fu had been arrested in violation of Article 47 of the Constitution, which stated that "the liberty of the individual and the sanctity of his home are inviolable. No citizen may be arrested without the ruling of a People's Court or the recommendation of a People's Prosecutor. The arrest must be carried out by the public security services." The poster charged that Mrs. Fu had been arrested without a warrant.

By this time the activist movement had spread well beyond Peking.

When they heard about Democracy Wall in Peking and the kind of posters that were being tolerated there, people in other cities had followed the example set by the capital. The same large themes of human rights and democracy were taken up first in Shanghai. On 10 December ten thousand people gathered on the Shanghai waterfront to demand more democratic government and the full panoply of human rights, including the right to choose work assignments. Posters appeared making the same demands on People's Square and on the streets. One poster gave the opening text of the American Declaration of Independence, and after this catalogue of basic human rights declared "In China we do not have these rights." Travelers reported democracy walls in Wuhan, Hangzhou, Tianjin, Xian, and other provincial centers.

The poster-writers worked in a twilight zone between official approval and disapproval. At no time did the official Chinese news media accessible to foreigners report the contents of posters or describe the spread of the democracy movement. But the *People's Daily* continued to give encouragement in general terms:

> If the people could not air their views on State affairs, and could not criticize Party and Government officials, including leaders, would not socialist democracy be empty talk? . . . Of course some people's opinions are going to be wrong. But the method of suppressing criticism is a foolish one, used by those who lack confidence in the truth. Such is the foolish tendency of some comrades who want to call in the Public Security Department whenever someone puts up a big-character wall poster criticizing leading comrades. . . . As for the method of giving someone enough rope to hang himself, letting people's errors grow until they give rise to grave consequences and then cracking down on them, that is a tactic used against the enemy and cannot be applied to the people.

In cities where people did not address the general themes there were still many posters expressing personal grievances. The hard lot of the young city-bred people living in what they saw as rural exile was one of the most persistent subjects. In one center of the Southwest there appeared a huge painting of a mother stretching out her arms to a young man and woman laboring in the sun in distant fields. The caption was simple: "Give me back my children."

The young in the countryside were not content to use words alone to express their hopes and discontent. Many took the law into their own hands. Driving past the Gate of Heavenly Peace in Peking one afternoon between Christmas and the New Year, I came across the representatives of one group engaged in a major protest. Snow was falling from a leaden sky, adding a touch of white to the golden tiles of the Gate, and in the open space beneath the Gate squatted twenty-four young men and women with their bedding rolls strapped to their backs. They were tough and lean, their clothes were worn and rough but just adequate to protect them against the cold of that gray afternoon.

They held a banner announcing that they were a group from Yunnan, a province in the Southwest, who had come to Peking to present a petition. A young man got up to distribute leaflets to the crowd of onlookers. The crowd surged toward him, so he tossed them into the air and upstretched arms grabbed them as they floated down. It was a "message to the whole nation" that set out the grievances his group had come to present to Chairman Hua and Vice-Premier Deng on behalf of fifty thousand city-born youths who had been working for years in the plantations of Yunnan.

The message claimed they had been maltreated for years and had failed to gain redress from the local authorities through peaceful representations. So they had mounted a demonstration, chanting "We want human rights! We want dignity! We want our status in society!" This had not moved the local authorities. "Being driven beyond the limits of endurance, we have taken the last road—strike." The right to strike was guaranteed by the Constitution, but they would call it off as soon as the Central Committee declared their petition legal. A few days later they were received by a vice-premier who told them to return to their plantations and confess they ought not to have come to Peking without official permission. But he also assured them that he would see to it that their conditions were improved.

In the capital of Hunan, workers and students danced in the streets all night long, brawling increased, and fortune tellers became active.[5] In Shaanxi province thirty-one young people, who had been assigned to the countryside twelve years before, staged a hunger strike with the support of their parents, to press their demand to be allowed back to the city.[6]

Some of the Down-to-the-Countryside Youth, as they are called, disrupted public order to force attention to their demands, and others used violence. In Shanghai and a number of other cities, young people allowed home for the Spring Festival at the end of January refused to go back afterward. They organized demonstration marches and campaigns of civil disobedience that, in Shanghai, included blocking the railway tracks, occupying the station, smashing carriages, cutting trolleybus power lines, and invading public offices. Many of the Shanghai demonstrators were not youths but older people who had been sent to the countryside in the early 1960s when there was no longer food or work for them in Shanghai as a result of the Great Leap Forward. As they blocked the trolley lines and railway tracks they shouted "We want democracy!"[7] When their leaders were arrested, they shouted "Give back our comrades-in-arms" and accused the city's party committee of "bloody suppression of the masses."[8]

In Anhui province there were official reports of groups breaking into party and government offices in the provincial capital. The local officials dared not stop them. In the capital of Sichuan, the labor office was attacked and officials dragged out in the name of freedom and democracy. Such actions were earning the democracy movement a bad name.

Encouraged by the calls in the official press to redress past wrongs, tens of thousands of people began to converge on Peking to lay their stories of personal tragedy before the Central Committee, to present their petition as it is traditionally described. Many of them came without the travel permission that is obligatory for all movement in China. They had no money to buy train tickets, but the railway staff did not turn them off the trains. Some walked hundreds of miles to reach the capital. When they reached Peking, they filled to overflowing the reception stations, simple quarters where they were supposed to lodge; latecomers camped in front of the railway station. We saw them lying or sitting on the pavement outside the gates of the central government offices, day after day. Some earned a livelihood by simple handicrafts, others begged on the streets. On the eve of the Spring Festival, the *People's Daily*'s own commentator wrote sympathetically of their plight, saying that even if people insisted on exaggerating their troubles, this should not be treated as "unjustified clamoring."

A group of petitioners from Jilin province put up a long poster that began

> From the majestic Himalayas to the shores of the surging Eastern Sea, from the villages surrounded by ice for a thousand miles in the northern border areas to the luxuriant growth of coconut trees

of the south, a battlefield of cries of anguish against the Gang of Four is everywhere, people who have been cruelly oppressed are everywhere. If you want to talk reason, where can you go? If you have suffered injustice, where can you appeal? Those who have suffered, their breasts full of anger, follow the voice of the Central Committee, and, full of love for the Central Committee, come to the city of Peking, carrying their sons and their daughters, and with their appeals on their backs!

The Party Central Committee is located here; Chairman Hua is here. The heart of the revolution is here: this is the hometown of the theory of Marxism–Leninism. Coming here, what cases of injustice cannot be overturned? They come with deep feeling, with solid hope!

But the reception they get is a dish of cold water, a piece of ice. No one cares about these enormous, strange injustices, there is no place for them to spill out their thousands of words! . . .

How many people, who worked hard for the revolution for decades, were suddenly confronted with a terrible lack of pity?

How many people, injured at work and driven out of their jobs, now have no way to make a living? Their limbs broken, their bodies crippled, they find it difficult to pass their days.

How many families have been split up, the wife leaving and the children scattered? How many people have met with disaster and carry a sea of bitterness in their hearts? Their tears roll down one after the other. . .

Where to appeal? Where to complain?
Who reads the tens of thousands of letters?
Central Committee, Central Committee!
How can you know about the thousands of injustices and the tens of thousands of bitternesses?
Chairman Hua, Chairman Hua!
How can you hear the sorrowful voices and appeals for help?
At the Xinhua Gate the walls are high and the courtyards deep.
The people cannot see inside.
At Zhongnanhai,
The ordinary people cannot enter.
Where can they go to talk about their thousand bitternesses and ten thousand injustices?
Heaven! Can you not lower your head to listen to the people?
Earth! How can you be silent, making no answer? . . .

Another angry poster took a swipe at the relatively well-fed young democrats of Peking as well as party and government officials:

TO THE LORDS AND LADIES AND
YOUNG MISSES OF PEKING

Tens of thousands of people don't have enough to feed or nourish themselves. That's a fact, so where's your communist humanitarianism gone? You continue to wrong the ordinary people. Go fuck yourself with your "socialism" and "communism" in a society where people don't have enough to eat or clothe themselves decently. Since the Fall of the Gang of Four a lot of people are still waiting to be rehabilitated. My miserable comrades, unite! We want to take in hand our own destiny. We want to be masters in our own country. Go to the devil all you who fatten yourselves on the blood and tears of the people and who do nothing for the people. The people want loaves to stave off hunger, Lords and Ladies.

—The Little People

One petitioner alone put up ninety wall posters to publish his grievances. Many were not content with putting up posters and waiting to be received by officials. On the anniversary of Zhou Enlai's death in January, they marched to Tiananmen Square. Onto the square that day there came columns of older men and women, their faces sunburnt darker than those of city people, their clothes far more patched and ragged, insurgents from an underworld of darkness that had been screened from the eyes of Peking for the thirty years since liberation. In earlier times, official propaganda had insisted that such misery had been eliminated from the New China. Now foreigners could see what the city-bred Red Guards had discovered in their travels during the Cultural Revolution: the misery had only partly been eliminated; much of it had simply been shut out from major cities by rigid controls over movement. To see it erupt now was no cause for gloating. Rather, it was to the credit of those leaders who sought to make party officials face facts that such people now felt emboldened to come to Peking and were allowed to do so. It was these petitioners the young intellectual Fu Yuehua had reportedly helped to organize themselves. So far as is known, she was the first of the new generation of young democrats to try to aid this substratum of peasants and urban unemployed—an echo of Mao Zedong's own pioneering attempts to focus peasant grievances in Hunan in 1927. And, on 18 January 1979, she became the first young activist to be arrested.

On 14 January a group of petitioners decided to march to the gates of the Zhongnanhai. They formed a column one hundred strong on Tiananmen Square, behind banners: "Persecuted People from All Over China," "We Want Democracy and Human Rights," "A Plea for Help from Deng Xiaoping." They set off for the Zhongnanhai shouting "We're tired of being hungry" and "Down with oppression." In the front walked a man of perhaps fifty carrying on his back a crippled woman who could have been his mother. He had already carried her for half an hour and would carry her for much longer. They were the angriest group of people I have ever met. They tried to go through the gates of the Zhongnanhai to present a letter to Chairman Hua. Unarmed soldiers gently but firmly barred their way.

One petitioner, a man of about sixty, broke away from the group to pour out his story to me. He spluttered out words of sorrow mingled with saliva that dribbled through the gaps in his rotting teeth. Not heeding the cold winter air, he opened layer upon layer of thin cotton garments, then tore shreds from the rotting innermost undershirt and thrust them in my hand. From a small worn satchel he produced tattered papers that told me that in the hungry aftermath of the Great Leap Forward he had been sent from the city, where he had a factory job, to seek food and shelter in his ancestral village. There he had barely subsisted ever since, earning an absolute pittance. For years he had asked to be reinstated to his factory job, to no avail. Now he had walked almost one thousand miles from Changzhou, near Shanghai, to Peking. Tears streaming down his cheeks, he said "We won't leave Peking until we've seen Chairman Hua and given him our petition, or the authorities solve our problems." The soldiers continued to bar the way for the petitioners. Eventually the peasants gave up, but not without a second demonstration a week later. A dramatic photograph of the marchers was published by newspapers around the world and given prominent play by *Newsweek* on the eve of Deng Xiaoping's arrival in the U.S.

While Deng was touring the U.S. in February, those favoring suppression were inhibited. However, on 16 March, in an unpublished speech to senior officials of central ministries and departments, Deng reluctantly acceded to pressure for action against the activists. A military intelligence report from Taiwan later published these purported extracts from Deng's speech:

> You say you want to dissolve the human rights organization, to ban the masses from storming government offices, to suppress counter-revolutionaries and even to close down Democracy Wall.
>
> If you all want it I will go along with the majority opinion. . . . The worst that might happen is that the masses might speak badly of me if they decide I've shown both a "white face" [a good mien] and a "black face." But I have to make clear that although the central government may have its reasons to ask me to do that, the result will definitely be unfavorable. Counter-revolution can be suppressed, sabotage can be restricted, but to walk back down the old road of suppressing differing opinion and not listening to criticism will make the trust and support of the masses disappear. Therefore, in my view, let the people post some big-character posters, catch a few proven evil-doers in the human rights organization, and let the others do whatever they want to.[9]

Unofficial accounts of Deng's speech circulated quickly in Peking. On 25 March, Wei Jingsheng and his fellow editors of *Exploration* brought out a special issue that consisted of an editorial written by Wei. He accused Deng Xiaoping of having "laid aside the mask of protector of democracy."

The long editorial ignored important evidence and arguments that did not fit its thesis. It made no attempt to explain why the official press had continued to encourage free speech after Deng had achieved a dominant position in the Politburo or why the encouragement was couched in such unequivocal terms. Nor did it consider the long-term impact of the gradual liberalization already announced and under way in the fields of judicial work, the economy, culture, education, demythification of Mao, and the press. But it was a clear and forceful statement on a key issue by a man who aroused, at the least, great interest whenever he expressed himself in public.

Three days later regulations designed to suppress disorder and curb the activist movement were issued in Peking. Similar but less restrictive regulations had already been issued in Shang-hai. The regulations included this passage: "Slogans, posters, books, magazines, photographs, and other materials which op-pose socialism, the dictatorship of the proletariat, the leadership of the Communist Party, Marxism–Leninism, and Mao Zedong Thought are formally prohibited." The press began (and con-tinued for months) to insist on the need to observe the Four Principles of "keeping to the socialist road and upholding the dictatorship of the proletariat, the leadership of the Commu-nist Party of China, and Marxism–Leninism–Mao Zedong Thought." At the same time it asserted that there was a continu-ing need for the "emancipation of thinking" and for upholding "practice as the sole criterion of truth." The Four Principles could be used for suppressing any criticism of established phi-losophy, policies, and the current leadership. Anyone who said that in practice socialism, the dictatorship of the prole-tariat, and so on had worked badly in China and should be dras-tically reformed or even abandoned could now be treated as a criminal.

Wei Jingsheng's writings amounted to a sweeping condem-nation of Chinese Communism; he was arrested on 29 March, the day after the regulations were issued in Peking. In the days that followed, newspapers in the capital unleashed strong attacks on the democracy activists. The leader of the Human Rights Al-liance, Ren Wanding, was arrested with three of his associates while hanging on Democracy Wall a poster criticizing the new trend of articles in the official press—*The Enemies of Democ-racy Have Begun Their Attack*. Other arrests followed until, at the end of May, the Agence France Presse, the news agency in Peking best informed on the movement, reported an estimate of thirty arrests in Peking alone since mid-March. The conflict between the current repression and the longer-term measures of liberalization, the contradiction between the Four Principles and "emancipation of the mind," and the inconsistency between the encouragement of free expression in past months and its dis-couragement from the middle of March was glaring. They are not convincingly accounted for by Wei Jingsheng's allegation that Deng Xaioping had simply used the democracy issue to gain power and had thereafter cynically abandoned "the mask."

One explanation that better fits the facts is that Deng and his associates were resolved to introduce a measure of democracy into the Chinese system and enlarge somewhat the area of freedom but were forced to beat a tactical retreat on the issue of free expression. The threat of anarchy, doubtless exaggerated by those opposed to liberalization but not negligible, was a political fact of which Deng had to take account.

Wei's co-editors of *Exploration* stood by the editorial he had written and issued a statement through foreign journalists:

> For the past four months Wei has been active in the spontaneous democracy movement. He has fiercely criticized all backward factors which he thought prevented China's modernization, including the obstructive role which he thought was played by Marxism and the Thought of Mao Zedong.
>
> Because of that, the Chinese government has arrested him for the crime of counter-revolution. Where is freedom of speech in China? . . . the Chinese government does not want any democratic freedom and the so-called "genuine democracy and freedom" that it talks about only compels the Chinese people to bolster the prestige of the authorities in power.
>
> All criticism is fiercely suppressed as contrary to socialism and to the dictatorship of the proletariat. So much for democratic freedom under the Chinese Government. What brutal hypocrisy![10]

In the weeks that followed province after province issued tough regulations designed to suppress the wave of civil disorder and crime which, it was claimed, was sweeping the country, and also to restrict the activities of the young democrats. From now on posters could only be put up in specially designated places, normally small bits of wall in obscure parts of town. Democracy Wall in Peking survived a few more months, perhaps because of foreign interest in it.

The measures taken were sufficient to halt the trend to free expression and to roll it back somewhat. But there was nothing like the wave of arrests of hundreds of thousands of people such as had scythed down the Hundred Flowers of 1957. This was partly because the critics of 1979 were young people without official positions, whereas those of 1957 had included many in positions of influence. Another reason was that in 1979 there was a strong group in the leadership who had recognized the waste caused by the antirightist purge of 1957 and wanted to lead rather than repress the younger generation of 1979. I am convinced that some of the leaders acknowledge the truth of many of the criticisms made by the young, and agree on the need for more democracy and freedom, but believe that the young want too much too soon, that the speed and the degree of change desired by them would be politically suicidal.

One of the young democrats wrote an essay analyzing the reasons for the failure of the "Peking Spring." He attributed the failure to the absence of a theoretical platform and a model of a new society to counter the Marxist system, the imprudence of inexperienced activists unprepared for police repression, and the preferential treatment given to intellectuals by the regime that deters them from joining a "dissident" movement.[11]

Not all of the activists would judge the "Peking Spring" a failure. Some of them went into it with their eyes open, living from day to day, expecting repression sooner or later, and treasuring their chance to speak. They made their thoughts known to a wide audience and won some support. They may believe that they have advanced their cause.

The clampdown on free expression evoked protests from the young activists but little from the general public. The leadership had won support by the decisions, announced in the preceding months, on the economy, on reassessment of the history of the past twenty years, on foreign relations, and on collective rather than individual leadership. The announcement of a program of legislation to give China its first post-1949 codes of civil and criminal law had also given people an assurance about the underlying trend toward constitutional government. Deng Xiaoping, although under pressure, was still the predominant leader and held the confidence of the country. People had seen not only the emergence of free expression but also some disruption of public order. There was therefore no reason to believe that these arrests heralded a wholesale abandonment of pragmatic reforms, and a massive lurch to the left as had happened when the Hundred Flowers were scythed in 1957. The silence of the older generation during the period of thaw had shown they were not convinced it would last forever. The surprising thing for most people was probably that free expression had ever been allowed to develop as far as it did, not that it was now being limited again.

The measures taken to curb the expression of unorthodox views were not carried so far as to turn the clock back to where it had stood before the Central Work Conference of November 1978. In the official press, a debate about the limits of freedom emerged and went on through the summer and early autumn. In the course of this, the learned journal *Historical Research* published an article that flatly contradicted the line then taken by most official publications. It said that although the concepts of human rights, freedom, and equality had been developed by the European bourgeoisie, they had "very real meaning for [China's] struggle against feudalism and for the development of socialist democracy."[12] The Enlightenment Society published a further issue of *Qimeng* after the arrests began. Another unofficial paper, *April 5 Tribune*, continued to publish, devoting an entire issue to a discussion of what "proletarian democracy should be" and calling for the introduction of a two-party system. Posters on major themes appeared on Democracy Wall from time to time; they were torn down more often than in the past, but the tearing down sometimes gave rise to protests on the spot. Peasants continued to demonstrate in front of the Zhongnanhai, and other groups used demonstration marches to support constitutional demands, sometimes with success. There were repeated calls for the release of the arrested activists.

Exploration appeared again in September, when six hundred copies were sold in forty minutes at Democracy Wall. Also in September, a rally organized on Tiananmen Square by a group calling itself the Society for the Study of Democracy and Scientific Socialism was attended by more than a thousand people. Several speakers complained that the authorities were neglecting the grievances of the petitioners who came to Peking; others called for the release of the activists who had been arrested in the capital and disclosed that others had been arrested in Shanghai, Hangzhou, and Qingdao for unofficial publishing. For the first time at a rally, speakers included a peasant woman and a former soldier, and workers and peasants stood side by side in the crowd.

There were occasional criticisms of leaders by name. Vice-Chairman Wang Dongxing was accused of building himself a luxurious residence in the Zhongnanhai. A farm worker from Shaanxi, Zhang Xifeng, put up on Democracy Wall a seven-thousand-word poster attacking Hua Guofeng and Deng Xiaoping for sending petitioners back from Peking to their home provinces to pursue their demands for redress of grievances there. "What sense does it make to hand over a petition to the very same person who is being accused of misdeeds?," he asked. "How in heaven can the accused persons be expected to solve the problem and punish themselves?" Zhang claimed that when the petitioners went home they were harassed, mistreated, and often branded as counter-revolutionary troublemakers.

The Party had in fact taken some steps to deal with these problems. It had sent a thousand inspectors-general to the provinces to improve the handling of grievances. The official press had threatened that local officials who refused to follow Party policy on the redress of grievances would be severely punished. There were far too many grievances to be dealt with by any central institution. The New China News Agency had reported that, according to statistics from seventeen of China's twenty-nine province-level administrations, 3,850,000 cases of persecution from the Cultural Revolution had been heard by party, government, and judicial organs. Eighty-five percent of them had been resolved, it said.[13] There was no practical alternative to leaving responsibility in the hands of the provinces. As some party leaders undoubtedly realized, the lack of a proper judicial system that in the past had greatly contributed to the number of grievances, now severely hampered the drive to redress them.

The morale of democracy activists must have been somewhat revived by developments around 1 October, National Day. One of the objectives for which a number of them had been working—official recognition that the Cultural Revolution had been a disaster—was attained when Marshal Ye Jianying, speaking with the approval of the Central Committee, declared the Cultural Revolution to have been "an appalling catastrophe suffered by all our people." Indeed, Marshal Ye's speech contained numerous passages which gave satisfaction to those who had been calling for a re-evaluation of Mao more drastic than that made at the Central Work Conference of November 1978; and he reaffirmed the central tenets of Deng's pragmatic philosophy, which had been questioned in the spring.

In mid-October, first Wei Jingsheng and then Fu Yuehua were put on trial. When Wei was sentenced to fifteen years' imprisonment and Mrs. Fu's trial began, it looked as though this might be the beginning of a series of trials of the most prominent activists, designed to deter others from writing and acting as they had done. There was puzzlement therefore when the trial of Mrs. Fu was suspended before it had run its course. This go–stop treatment of the imprisoned dissidents fueled speculation that there was uncertainty and disagreement in the leadership about how to handle the issue. The same ambivalence was apparent when an unofficial transcript of the Wei Jingsheng trial was put up on Democracy Wall and allowed to remain there for weeks, although copies of a mimeographed version were seized when they were put on sale.

There was no ambivalence in December when the Peking city authorities issued a notice prohibiting any further display of posters on Democracy Wall. The full force of the mass media was deployed to rally public support for the closing of the Wall.

Shortly before the ban on further posters went into effect on 8 December, one last poster went up. It was a lament written with a touch of hyperbole and with a little of that ambiguity the Chinese language encourages:

A POEM

The people have no rights,
Socialism is pure or impure,
Speakers are criminals,
Dictatorship is pure or impure.[14]

The sturdy ladies of the city's sanitation department scrubbed away the last scrap of poster-paper from the Wall, and the yellow-gray bricks returned to their original function of marking the boundary of a municipal bus depot a little more than twelve months after greatness had been pasted upon them. It looked as though they would spend the rest of their days in obscurity, but at least they would have a rich store of memories. No wall in China had won such a place in history, except of course that great one that lumbers its way across the land sixty miles to the north.

At Peking airport in 1979, Deng Xiaoping, the powerful Vice-Premier, stands a tactful two paces behind Hua Guofeng, the Party Chairman and Prime Minister. (*James Andanson/SYGMA*)

On Tiananmen Square: mourning the death of Zhou Enlai, January 1976 (*top*); noting inscriptions on wreaths dedicated to Zhou, April 1976 (*bottom*). (*G. Morley*)

After the Tiananmen demonstrations: these meetings with the Prime Ministers of New Zealand (*top*), Singapore (*center*), and Pakistan (*bottom*) in April and May 1976 were Mao's last with foreigners. (*New China Pictures Co.*)

The Gang of Four: after their arrest they were hung in effigy (*top*); and a streetcorner cartoon (*bottom*) showed Jiang Qing's courtiers dressing her for her role as "empress," in wig, false teeth, and crown. (*Author*)

Celebrating the Gang's arrest: with firecrackers
(*top left*), gong and cymbals (*top right*), and
dance music (*bottom*). (*Author*)

Hailing Deng's return to office: the boat dance was revived (*top*), and feminine charm was no longer taboo (*bottom*). (*Author*)

Democracy Wall: pasting up a poster (*top*); one night in December 1979, women streetcleaners scrubbed away the last trace of the last poster (*bottom*). (*G. Morley*)

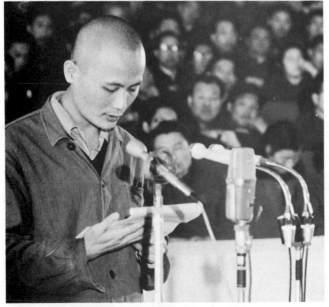

Wei Jingsheng, a leader of the democracy movement: as an officer in military service in 1970 (*top, at center*), and at his trial in 1979 (*bottom*). (*Anonymous* [*top*]; *New China News Agency* [*bottom*])

12

The Poster-Writer and the Poet

WEI JINGSHENG, the author of the poster *The Fifth Modernization* and the leading editor of the unofficial journal *Exploration*, was the most outspoken of the young activists of the democracy movement to emerge in the winter of 1978–1979. In his writing he displayed a spirit that was bold but not theatrical, skeptical yet not cynical. Under pressure, he was prone to act rashly, doing things he sorely regretted later. His boldness, his skepticism, and his impetuosity were evident in his assertion that the people had at last found their real leader, "the banner of democracy," in his claim that the Four Modernizations were just another promise to keep the Chinese people, "the old yellow ox," plodding along and in his warning that the people were in danger of falling prey to a new "political swindler."

He was twenty-eight years old when I met him in January 1979. Like many in his generation, he had already undergone experiences that had severely tested his character and shaken preconceived ideas. From sixteen to nineteen he had received an extraordinary political education in the Cultural Revolution. From twenty to twenty-three he had served in the army, becoming a squad commander and serving in the poor and backward Northwest China area. There he and his troops were called in aid of the civil power when local inhabitants, desperate from hunger, robbed public granaries and killed the guards. Upon demobilization he turned down a post as a junior official and took work as an electrician in the Peking zoo instead.

For years he had been developing thoughts that would cause him trouble, because no one can think as intensely as he thought and hope to keep his thoughts entirely to himself. To question Marxism–Leninism and the role of Mao as rigorously as he questioned them and to develop a desire for freedom as strong as his were bound to bring him into conflict with authority, and he knew it. He was one of the first to be arrested when the restrictions on free speech were reimposed in March 1979.

I had read Part 1 of *The Fifth Modernization* before I had the first of my few meetings with Wei, and I was intrigued to discover how closely his appearance matched his prose. His physique, like his writing, had the lean and sinewy qualities of a long-distance runner. The features of his face were cleanly chiseled. Close-cropped hair added to the ascetic look. His gaze was clear and level, and his manner dispassionate.

He dressed simply, in keeping with his job as an electrician: a gray Mao jacket and trousers, rough suede boots, and a brown corduroy cap when he went outdoors. He smoked a great deal but seldom accepted any drink stronger than tea.

His directness struck me when, at our first meeting, he gave me his home telephone number, saying "You can call me at home. My father does not approve of my opinions, but I do not hide from him what I am doing." Wei told me that he did most of his writing and editorial work at the home of a friend.

When I knew him a little better he told me that his friend was a woman he hoped to marry. Her name was Ping Ni, and her story was a remarkable one. Wei's relationship with her gave me an additional insight into his character. She was twenty-four years old and Tibetan. (For a member of the majority Han group to associate with someone of an ethnic minority, such as a Tibetan, was unusual.) Ping Ni's father had been one of the first Tibetans to enter the Communist Party, in the 1930s. He had taken part in the "peaceful liberation" of Tibet in the 1950s and afterward had held responsibility for military affairs at the highest level in that region. He had worked closely with the Dalai Lama at times. In 1961 he was arrested on grounds of being a foreign agent because he had been in contact with the Soviet and Indian Communist parties before 1949.

Ping Ni was seven years old when her father was arrested. Her mother was only twenty-six, having married very young, like many Tibetans; she was very attractive and had money. Many men wanted to marry her, if only she would do something which was quite common—divorce her imprisoned husband. Instead, she resolved to wait for his release. She was still waiting five years later when Mao launched the Cultural Revolution. As an official in her own right, she was a likely target of attack, so she warned her children "If ever I am dragged out to be struggled by the masses and imprisoned, I shall take my life."*

In 1968, she was dragged out and imprisoned. She took her life. Ping Ni was then fourteen years old, with an elder sister and two younger brothers. When day after day passed and their mother did not come home they felt terribly vulnerable. With their father still in jail, they were in effect orphans, in a society that not only regarded them as aliens but was itself in a state of anarchy. They lay on their beds and waited for death to take them. How hope and the will to live came back to them I do not know, but return it did, and through many vicissitudes Ping Ni grew up to become as attractive as her mother, as I learned from a source other than Wei Jingsheng. Through her father's imprisonment, which lasted until 1978, Wei learned about the conditions under which high-ranking political prisoners were held at Qin Cheng prison, some thirty miles north of Peking. He described these conditions in articles in *Exploration.*

In speaking Wei displayed the same boldness and clarity that marked his writing qualities. My interpretation of the way China's politics were developing differed from his in some important respects, but that was irrelevant to my purpose in meeting him—which was to gain a better understanding of such activists. I asked him whether he expected the democracy movement to

---

* To be "struggled" meant, during the Cultural Revolution, to be subjected to repeated, prolonged abuse (verbal and often physical) by a group or crowd of "outraged" citizens.

collide with the Party leadership at some stage. "Certainly," he replied, "because we want to go further than those Party leaders who have called for democracy and liberation of thinking."

"But those leaders have done much to show that they want more freedom in China. Why don't you accept that they want genuine democracy?"

"Because they have been Communists all their lives."

"You expect a confrontation to come sooner or later, and you know the punishment that may be awarded you. Why do you persist?"

"Because I know that democracy is the future of China and if I speak out now there is a possibility that I can hasten the day when the Chinese people will enjoy democracy. Two years ago it was pointless for us to speak or write as we do now, for we would have been arrested as soon as the words were out of our mouths. Now, through our posters and our journals we can make our voice heard." He had spoken in a matter-of-fact tone, but I sensed that living daily with the risk of imprisonment and being ready for it had developed in him an impatience for the crisis that would end the tension and realize the fate he had chosen.

Wei had spent his entire life under Communist Party rule, having been conceived in the year the People's Republic was born, and had been brought up by parents who were loyal to the Party. How was it that he had come to reject the political system created in China and to seek instead one that would provide an approximation of freedom and democracy as we understand them in the West? It was not by reading liberal philosophers or descriptions of liberal democracies, he said, but by reflecting on his own experience of growing up in China. In the early months of 1979 he set down an account of his growing up. In the following pages I will give a summary of the highlights, using his own language as far as possible.

*   *   *

When I entered my teens my father was a minor Communist Party bureaucrat. Of course he was devoted to Marxism–Leninism and Mao Zedong Thought, and made every effort to impart them to his children. He also encouraged us to read Liu

Shaoqi's book *How To Be a Good Communist*.* I could not fully understand the books my father gave me to read but I became convinced that I shared his faith. I remained a zealous Maoist until I was disillusioned by what I saw with my own eyes.

My mother bought novels and memoirs about the revolutionary struggles waged by the Communist Party in its early years and urged my sister and me to read them. I remember her telling my father once that we must have a clear-cut stand on what to love and what to hate, and that only by standing on the side of the people could we understand Marxism–Leninism and Mao Zedong Thought. She said that if a young man could not understand *how* the people suffer, he would not try to understand *why* they suffer, and would not know why we should make revolution. My mother instilled in me a conviction that we must make sacrifices for the common people who suffer hardship. Without that I would probably shrug my shoulders and say "That's just the seamy side of socialism" when I am confronted by the real situation of our workers and peasants. That's the way many children born into "good families" react when they see dirty, stinking beggars. They normally despise them as people who love to eat and hate to work.

I was sixteen when the Cultural Revolution erupted. With my friends, I joined the Red Guards in early 1966. Many of us who joined were dissatisfied with the state of society, disliking the inequalities that existed. We became a strong force but this force failed to destroy inequality. Why? Because our minds were still imbued with the ideas of autocracy. We attributed all inequality and unhappiness to the "class enemies" who, Mao Zedong told us, had wormed their way into the leadership. So, blind to the flaws in the system, we devoted our energy to dragging out these "bad" people.

* A guide to self-cultivation for Communists written by the man who was to become China's head of state and Mao's most prominent victim. The first edition had been published in 1949. Wei probably read the revised second edition, published in 1962. This edition retained passages that, in the context of 1962, when Liu was leading a major challenge to Mao's policies and style of rule (see p. 41 above), could only be interpreted as an attack on Mao. Between 1962 and 1966, fifteen million copies were sold, compared to a million and a half copies of the four-volume *Selected Works of Mao Zedong*.

At Mao Zedong's urging, we traveled across China to incite people to rebel against "bad" people in power in schools, factories, mines, and enterprises.* When our early zeal subsided, a question began to form in our minds: "If all power-holders are bad, doesn't that mean the state and Party are bad also?"

When we returned to Peking we were shocked to find that some veteran cadres whom we respected were under attack. They had been brought up among the suffering people and had joined the revolution when they were young; they weren't conspirators, they were loyal to the Party and socialism. Seeing this, Red Guard organizations began to splinter. Of the four hundred Red Guards in my school one hundred bowed out of the organization and the remainder split into five factions.

I was puzzled by what I saw and so, to get a better understanding of what was going on, I set out with several schoolmates to take a deeper look at society. We took a train heading northwest and after we passed Xian, the capital of Shaanxi province, I saw many people begging for food at railway stations along the way. I gave them food I had brought for myself.

When our train stopped at a station in the Gansu Corridor, a woman with a dirty face and long, loose hair came forward in a group of beggars. She stood begging below the window of my compartment, together with several teenagers. I leaned out of the window to hold out a few buns, but instantly fell back, because I saw something I could never have imagined: the woman with long, loose hair was a girl of eighteen and her body was naked. What I had thought were clothes were coal dust and mud that covered her body. As I shrank away, the girl and the youngsters with her raised their plaintive voices. I threw down a few buns and they scrabbled for them. A man sitting opposite me in the compartment said wryly: "This is the first time you've seen something like this, isn't it? But here we see it all around us . . ."

The naked girl stood on tiptoe and stretched her arms up

---

* Rail travel was free for Red Guards at that time, and they did not need permission to travel as in pre-Cultural Revolution days.

toward me, her eyes imploring me through her veil of dirty, tangled hair. I couldn't understand her dialect but I knew she still wanted food. Perhaps she had lost out in the scramble for what I had tossed down the first time. I gave my last buns to her and to the others who had missed out. The man opposite me gave me biscuits which I thrust into the outstretched hands. All down the train, other passengers were leaning out of their compartments feeding beggars. I was relieved when the train pulled out of the station. But the sight of the girl haunted me constantly for the next two days, making me search for the causes of her suffering.

I thought about the officials who were running that town. I seethed with anger against them. They deserved to be beaten to death for allowing such degradation to exist. And yet they were "comrades-in-arms" of my father. Was it because they were "bad" people that such suffering occurred, or was there something wrong with the socialist system?

The train carried us on to Xinjiang.* There I talked to all kinds of people in a production and construction corps which was farming newly opened land. There were many city-bred youths and demobilized soldiers who had been assigned there from the East. They had no sense of being heroic pioneers: they felt cheated. There were also people who had been labeled "rightists" and sent there as exiles. Despite their different backgrounds and purposes all these people had one thing in common: they were dissatisfied.

One woman rightist who was working as a journalist said that when she joined the Communist Party she could not have imagined that it would come under the control of such inhuman and brutal power-holders. This shocked me. Clearly she deserved to be labeled a rightist. But then she explained her views with many little stories from her own experience and the lives of

---

* Xinjiang is China's Far West. The name means New Dominion. Most of its original inhabitants were a Moslem Turkic people, the Uygurs, but since 1949 large numbers of ethnic Chinese have been settled there. This vast region of prairies, desert, and snow-capped mountains covers one sixth of the area of China but contains only 1 percent of its population. It has mineral resources, but the standard of living of its people has always been low.

those around her, and these carried a sense of irrefutable authority.

In her company I came to know many poor people in the region. One of them was the chairman of a poor and lower-middle peasants' association. As I sat in his home, he talked much of "revolution" and "revisionism." But I looked around as he talked: his home and its sparse contents were just like those of poor peasants before "Liberation," as I had read of them in the novels given me by my mother.

My journalist friend took me to a remote horse ranch. There we met some twenty young people who had grown up in Shanghai, two thousand miles away. They lived in shabby thatched huts by a fishpond. They were delighted to see us and when we let them ride our horses they yelled and whooped with joy. They asked us to photograph them so they could send pictures to their families. They insisted that we photograph them against the background of pine-covered mountains and not their shabby homes. In my naïveté I was puzzled by this and as I rode away with my companion at the end of the visit she explained to me: "They haven't sent photographs home for more than ten years. How would their families feel if they knew how their children were living? Didn't you see that they live just the same as the prisoners undergoing labor reform?" Had I missed seeing the prisoners? I thought a moment and then remembered a row of houses behind those of the young Shanghainese. I suddenly recalled people standing behind their windows looking at us in silence. "The young people are not allowed to ride horses on the ranch. They eat what the prisoners eat. They will spend the rest of their lives here."

I looked back across the mile or two of grassland which now separated us from the ranch. The young men and women were still standing outside their thatched huts watching us fade into the distance, unwilling to be parted from us.

Why did such things exist? Were they caused by people disobeying Mao Zedong's instruction? If so, why did he always trust people who disobeyed his instructions? I found no ready answer, but these young people from Shanghai and the peasant leader in his bare home joined company in my mind with the naked beggar girl in Gansu to make me keep on looking around and keep on seeking explanations for what I saw.

When I was getting ready to leave Xinjiang, my journalist friend told me that, after she was exiled there, her husband, a senior official in the news media in Peking, had divorced her and married another woman. "I don't blame him," she said. "I don't want him and the children to suffer by being involved with a rightist. And the children need someone to look after them, so I cannot ask him to live alone." She gave me some Korla pears and asked me to take them to "her" home and give them to her husband and children. On my return to Peking I found the house, but the husband would not see me. He even denied he had ever been married to the woman in Xinjiang. But he sent his daughter out onto the veranda to accept the pears I had brought.

As I walked away from the house, indignation and pain surged through me. Why should good people always be struck down and bad people rise higher and higher, turning bad luck into good fortune? Was it because party officials did not understand Marxism–Leninism and Mao Zedong Thought well enough? At first I thought so, but some of my Peking friends argued that there were flaws in Mao Zedong Thought itself. They said I should question Mao's thinking in the light of Marxism–Leninism. In their view, Mao had been a great man before 1957, but then began to make mistakes.

Many of the Red Guards who had answered Mao's call to rise up in rebellion at the earliest stage set out to study the realities of society as I had done. I heard that some even went dressed in rags to the Peking railway station to beg, believing that that was a way to "experience life." I did not need to experience life in this way. I learned more from listening to ordinary workers and peasants speak their mind than I could have learned from begging. Besides, it was not enough to study only one stratum of society; one should study them all.

My study of society was colored by a prejudice: I was convinced that all power-holders, unless they could furnish strong evidence to the contrary, were without a conscience, having risen to their position through the misfortune of others. My prejudice was widely shared by others of my age. We questioned everything and everyone that was official, theories as well as people.*

During that time, the people I associated with were occupied with all kinds of activities, and had little time for book-study. Our activities included staying in prison; holding meetings; smashing the Third Headquarters, which was a pro-Jiang Qing organization among university students; and attacking the Ministry of Public Security.†

The Red Guard organization which I had joined, the United Action Committee, was made up largely of the offspring of senior officials. We formed it late in 1966 but, because of anti-Jiang Qing activities, it was banned in 1967. We "Old Red Guards" felt an urgent need to have our own organization. So we associated ourselves with a choir that had formed in the western district of Peking. We expanded its range of musical activities and mobilized it for political purposes. I became involved in organizational work for this group. There was a choir of a hundred members and an orchestra of seventy instrumentalists. We gave concerts, ran a theatrical troupe, began making films, and put out a magazine called *Get Ready*. This kept me occupied and gave me experience in administration and leadership. But there were things I didn't like about the group, and they were typical of that time. Most of the funds for the group came from cash and goods, worth $120,000 U.S., stolen from a warehouse where they had been stored . . . after being seized by Red Guards. The main political activity of the group was voicing grievances on behalf of veteran cadres, to whom many of the members were related. I was dissatisfied that nothing was done for the common people.

---

* The statement that appeared on the lead page of the first issue of *Exploration* proclaimed this same spirit of skepticism. It gave this pledge to readers: "Our explorations shall be based on realities in Chinese and world history. In other words, we do not recognize the absolute correctness of any theory from any person. All theories, including current theories and those which may soon emerge, shall be the themes of our discussions as well as tools for analysis."

† In early 1967 Wei Jingsheng spent about three months in jail because of his participation in these activities but was released on 22 April 1967, together with other imprisoned activists of the United Action Committee.

Organizations supporting Jiang Qing began to take action against members of our group. There was one wave of arrests and we feared another. I was appointed to lead the choir in a move to Canton, where the political climate would be more favorable. When we arrived at the Peking railway station our party of several hundred was stopped by hundreds of soldiers. I gave orders that our party should return to their homes and myself entered the station to look for our advance party. I found my sister and a friend being detained by soldiers. With a dozen friends I surged forward and released them. We escaped on our bicycles. For three days the core group of the choir debated our predicament and then decided to dissolve the organization.

In the months that followed I kept busy but felt a growing sense of disillusion and emptiness. I could find no leader on whom I could rely, no one on whom I could pin my hopes. Workers and peasants foolishly trusted new bureaucrats who were oppressing them and exploiting them in place of the old bureaucrats. Soldiers followed any ruler. Some intellectuals had been won over by the group that was running the Cultural Revolution, while others were waiting timidly for their turn to be co-opted. I could find no force that could change the evil reality I saw around me.

As 1968 wore on I knew that I must be a target for arrest because of my work with the choir group. Pounded by the waves of massive arrests in Peking, I ran out of places to hide in the capital. In July I sought refuge in Tianjin, ninety miles away.* In August I escaped by only a hairbreadth from a police raid on a Tianjin office building. Friends gave me their last coins to buy a train ticket to go south. It was enough to get me to Changzhou [near Shanghai] where I sought refuge in the home of the girlfriend of a friend of mine. She helped me on my way to a village in Anhui province,† where my family had originated.

I had plenty of time to read in the countryside, so I studied the classic works of Marx, Engels, Lenin, and Stalin. Finding Marx and Engels more scientific than Lenin and Stalin, I re-

---

* The confusion that still reigned in China in mid-1968 would have facilitated Wei's unauthorized movements around the country.

† In central South China.

examined my political ideas in the light of their writings. Around me in the countryside class struggle was being waged in accordance with Mao's teaching. How did Mao's conduct of class struggle relate to Marx' and Engels' ideas? Marxist theory said that "classes are formed according to economic status." The landlords and rich peasants who were being struggled against had long since lost their economic status. The rich peasants had been stripped of their property fifteen years before and were now living at the level of the poor peasants. On the other hand, a whole new class of officials had grown up whose standard of living and political status set them apart from the ordinary peasants.

In Anhui I was surrounded by reminders of Mao's Great Leap Forward, which had taken place in 1958. I had been only eight years old then, so I had never fully understood its nature and its impact. Now I often heard peasants talk about it. The official explanation of the three years of hardship which followed the Great Leap Forward was that they were caused by nature. But the peasants told me that the hardship was the work of men who had pursued disastrous policies. They gave thanks that they had survived that terrible time when the "wind of communization" swept through the land. The rice crop itself had been left unharvested one year, because the peasants were so hungry that they could not move. They were starving because they had been forced to surrender to the state almost all their previous crop, to substantiate wildly inflated claims of increased output made by ambitious officials who were responsible for the region.* The peasants had been driven to physical effort beyond human endurance, to achieve impossible targets inspired by

---

* This practice did not end when the Great Leap Forward ended. It continued as a serious problem, at a less spectacular level, at least until 1976. On 25 March 1977, a Communist-controlled newspaper in Hong Kong, the *New Evening Post*, reported a "tense situation" with regard to the food supply in Chekiang, Kiangsi, Fukien, Szechwan, Yunnan, and Kweichow provinces. Factional strife had been reported in many of those areas in 1976. The newspaper said official exaggeration of "the actual statistics" might have been one factor leading to the food shortages. It said "Production was not all that abundant, yet they increased their figures. . . . Thus the state took its share of the grain according to the exaggerated figure. It looked like there was enough left for the people to eat, but in reality there was not."

Mao Zedong. At times they had joined night with day in an attempt to meet those targets. They had labored on grandiose water-control projects, some of which had inflicted damage instead of bringing benefits. They had been compelled to become makers of steel as well as tillers of the earth. The steel proved useless and the earth was neglected, but the army ensured that the will of Mao Zedong and the officials prevailed. When the time for harvest came, the starving, exhausted peasants could not summon the energy to work in the fields. The unharvested rice was buffeted by the winds until it fell where it had grown. The people died of hunger in the houses where they had been raised.

To keep death at bay, families exchanged children, to eat. These people were not executioners, but Mao Zedong's policies had forced them to batter children to death with hoes so that they themselves might live.* Now at last I understood how Marshal Peng Dehuai had mustered the strength to attack the Party Center headed by Mao Zedong for having launched the Great Leap Forward. Now I could see why the peasants had come to hate "communism," and why they could not understand Mao's attack on Liu Shaoqi's policies of private plots, free markets, small independent enterprises, and grain output quotas fixed by household: it was because they wanted to live, and to live without eating their neighbors' children, without handing over their own children to be eaten by their neighbors.

I was waking from a dream, but I was waking in a place of darkness.

One day I went with a relative to visit another village. On the way we passed an uninhabited village. The houses stood

---

* I have no way of verifying this statement by Wei Jingsheng. Its inclusion here does not imply that I endorse its veracity, any more than my quotation elsewhere of statements from official Chinese sources implies any endorsement of them. To judge whether it was possibly true, I told the story to someone who spent the first thirty years of his life in China, growing up as the son of a Christian missionary. He said that this was a practice which reappeared in the district of North China where he lived when bad harvests brought starvation. He had personal knowledge of several cases. On pages 148–149 of *In Search of History* (Harper, 1978) Theodore H. White cites cases he came across when he investigated the Honan famine in the winter of 1943.

open to the sky. Their roofs had rotted and grass had grown within their walls. The disorder of the wild grass within contrasted with the neat rows of the paddy fields outside. I asked my relative why the houses had not been pulled down to make way for ricefields. He replied: "Those houses belong to people. How can they be torn down without their approval?"

"But no one is living here!"

"Of course no one is living here. Most of the villagers died of starvation when the wind of communization blew, except for a few who went off to beg for food and never returned. But people said that surely some would return, so their houses were left standing while their land was given to others to till. Many years have passed and no one has come back. I am afraid that no one ever will."

As I walked on, I thought of what had once taken place in those roofless houses where the grass now grew. Men and women had sat down to eat those who had been born to be their companions and the companions of their neighbors. I saw children catching butterflies in the fields around; were they the reincarnation of the dead children? Who had made the villagers eat human flesh, which they had never dreamed of eating? I now know who were the executioners: They were Mao Zedong and his followers, with their criminal systems and policies.

I accepted this idea calmly. It neither frightened nor excited me. There was a question beyond it that I wanted to answer, which also had to do with Mao. Why did people continue to "warmly sing his praises" and "pledge to defend him with one's own life"? Weren't the army and police made up of peasants and workers and their children?

As I watched Mao Zedong whip up class struggle in the countryside, during my year in Anhui and later when I joined the army, I began to understand the answer: he put people into imaginary interest groups, and set them to struggle against each other so that they lost touch with reality and could no longer see where their true interests lay.

When I was posted as a platoon commander in Shaanxi province in the early 1970s I was involved in just such a conflict. The harvests in the region had been poor and the peasants had been forced to hand over too much grain to the state granaries. I was ordered to take my men to the rescue of another platoon which had been attacked while guarding a granary in an isolated stretch of country. As we advanced through the trees and the granary came in view, we saw that we were too late. The doors of the grain stores hung open and the only grain that remained was a scattering upon the ground. The remains of the platoon were more abundant. Their dead bodies lay all around.

We were ordered to remain in the area and assist the local authorities in bringing the culprits to justice. But no information on the attack was uncovered. It was not surprising: the local people were all poor and hungry, and the officials suffered too. So, to eat, peasants had killed soldiers who were the sons of peasants, and the officials turned a blind eye. But no one tried to change the system.

Mao Zedong's technique of controlling people by setting them against each other slowly lost some of its efficacy. We soldiers also turned a blind eye from time to time. Hungry peasants would break into military granaries and we let them . . . because everyone knew we could always get more.

We have come a long way since the Cultural Revolution started. In the beginning, people rose up in their anger to defend the man who was the author of their suffering. They opposed the slave system but worshiped its creator. They demanded democratic rights but despised democratic systems. They even tried to use a dictator's thought to win democratic rights. Eventually people recognized their mistakes. During the ten years of the Cultural Revolution great changes took place in their understanding. Many of those who in 1966 had stood in Tiananmen like idiots, with tears in their eyes, before that man who stripped them of their freedom, returned courageously in 1976 to oppose him in that same place.

I know very little of capitalist countries, but now when I see newspaper articles describing the "superiority of socialism over capitalism," I curse in my heart, saying "Go to Hell!" The books I have read say that capitalism is bad, but could anything be worse than what I have seen?

*   *   *

Wei was the only activist of the democracy movement, so far as I am aware, who made a sustained political challenge to the Communist Party of China. He was perhaps the only activist with an international reputation who could accurately be described as a dissident, a label that has been too readily applied to people who unlike Wei did not challenge the right claimed by the Communist Party to lead the nation. He saw himself as a democratic socialist and, like many in that tradition, perceived a great gulf separating democratic socialists from those who join and lead Communist Parties.

Arrested on 29 March 1979, Wei Jingsheng was brought to trial six months later, on 16 October. Because Wei's role in the democracy movement had become well known at home and abroad, and because this was the first political trial to be held in public view under the post-Mao leadership and since the extensive campaign to publicize the need for the rule of law, it was followed with close attention in China and overseas. The New China News Agency described the trial as a public one, and so it was—to the extent that it was publicly announced, selected citizens were issued passes to admit them to the trial, and there was some description of its proceedings in the Chinese news media. The friends of Wei were not admitted, nor was the foreign press. No official transcript was published although an unofficial one appeared on Democracy Wall and was permitted to remain on display for several weeks. (When a printed version of this unofficial transcript was put on sale at the Wall, the vendors and one customer were arrested.)

The trial lasted one day. Two and a half hours before it ended, the New China News Agency released a report describing Wei as a counter-revolutionary.

Wei was given the opportunity to engage a lawyer, but chose to conduct his own defense. Yang Guang and another co-editor of *Exploration* who had been arrested turned state's evidence and testified for the prosecution. The court sentenced Wei Jingsheng to fifteen years' imprisonment and deprived him of his political rights for an additional three years after the end of his sentence for "supplying a foreigner with military intelligence and openly agitating for the overthrow of the government of the dictatorship of the proletariat and the socialist system in China."

The official Chinese press devoted much space in the ensuing days to approving comments by people in many walks of life on the handling of the case. Very different views were expressed to foreign journalists by young activists who waited outside the courthouse as the trial proceeded. Lu Lin, a factory worker who had succeeded Wei as editor-in-chief of *Exploration*, called the verdict immoral and vowed "This will not be the end of it. We will not step back. We will not stop writing wall posters. . . . The longer the sentence they gave him, the more unseen trouble there will be in the future."[1]

A poster appeared immediately on Democracy Wall criticizing the trial and the official commentaries. It claimed that the tone of the *People's Daily* commentary on the trial was very reminiscent of one that had condemned the Tiananmen demonstrations in 1976. The author, who signed himself "An Upright Person," observed that Wei had published only half a dozen articles attacking China's political system and that this was a slim body of writing compared to that of Karl Marx, who had written thick volumes denouncing capitalism and had yet failed to bring it to its knees. "Are the new articles by Wei really more powerful than the works of Marx?" asked the Upright Person.

The U.S. State Department said it was "surprised and disappointed" by the severity of the sentence, and the spokesman revealed that the U.S. Ambassador in Peking had conveyed American concern over the Wei case to the Chinese authorities. In Moscow, Dr. Andrei Sakharov, the Soviet human rights leader, sent a telegram to Hua Guofeng, who was then visiting Paris. He appealed for a review of the sentence.

Within days copies of an unofficial transcript of the trial were circulating in Peking and were passed to foreign journalists. Then, on the weekend of 3–4 November, the editors of *April Fifth Tribune* pasted up a copy of their version on Democracy Wall. They had obtained a tape recording that people sympathetic to Wei Jingsheng had secretly made of the trial.

This unofficial transcript included the allegation that Ian Mackenzie, Reuters' chief correspondent in Peking, had promised to give Wei £200 or £300 (about $630) and was the recipient of the "military secrets" Wei had been found guilty of divulging. This was ironic; Mackenzie had not been among the most active reporters of the human rights movement. Wei made it clear that he had not actually received the money, as Mackenzie had never met Wei again after allegedly promising the money. From London, where Mackenzie was on holiday at the time of the trial, Reuters reported that Mackenzie had indeed been offered military information by Wei but that he had rejected the offer and had decided to have no further dealings with him.

The transcript gave extensive extracts from both the procurator's indictment and Wei's defense. The procurator charged that "Wei Jingsheng willingly became the running dog of Vietnam. Being a hidden enemy agent and a traitor, he supplied a foreigner with highly confidential and important military intelligence which directly concerned the interests of the state and affected the whole situation of the war." The intelligence was probably the information contained in articles by British, French, and Canadian correspondents in Peking which appeared on 20 and 21 February 1979. These said that the Chinese had killed or wounded 10,000 Vietnamese soldiers in their initial thrust across the border but had suffered only about 3000 casualties themselves, that the invasion had stopped ten miles inside the border, and that 200,000 additional troops had been committed at the last moment to reinforce frontier battalions numbering about 150,000. In addition, it was alleged that Wei had disclosed the names of the commander, deputy commander, and chief of staff of the Chinese troops. The procurator did not explain how this information had "affected the whole situation of the war."

In reply Wei said that as an ordinary man in the street the source of his information was hearsay and not any official government document. He claimed to have weighed and rejected the possibility that disclosure of the information could harm the Chinese forces: "For instance, I mentioned the name of the commander-in-chief on the front. Who has ever heard that one side lost a battle because the other side knew the name of its commander?" Nevertheless he recognized that under the prevailing circumstances he had erred in divulging military information to a foreign journalist.

Excerpts from the trial published by the New China News Agency confirmed that the "counter-revolutionary propaganda and agitation" with which Wei was charged referred to the articles he had written for *Exploration*. Wei did not deny that he had written these articles and admitted that he had "gone too far" when he wrote in the first issue: "It is a pity that in this People's Republic of ours, only those who are well fed and have nothing to do but read, write, and lead the lives of gods seize the power to dominate others. Should not the people have every reason to seize political power from these overlords?" But in general he claimed the protection of the Constitution for his writing:

> I published publications and wrote big-character posters on the basis of Article 45 of the Constitution: Citizens have freedom of speech, correspondence, assembly, publication, association, parade, demonstrations, and strike as well as the freedom to air their views freely, write big-character posters, and hold big debates. We published our publications for the purpose of exploring China and making China more prosperous and powerful. We believe that only by free, unrestrained, and practical exploration is it possible to achieve this purpose.

Wei's defense was in fact a counterattack. He challenged the notions of revolution and counter-revolution he claimed were current among those who condemned him:

> Some people have the following view: It is revolutionary if we act in accordance with the will of the leaders in power and counter-revolutionary to oppose it. I cannot agree with this debasing of the concept of revolution.
>
> Revolution refers to the tide which conforms to historical development and leads history forward. It also refers to waging struggles against things that hinder historical development. Revolution is the struggle between the new and the old.
>
> The debasing of the concept of revolution—to label the will of the people in power as forever revolutionary, to wipe out all divergent views and theories, and to think of power as truth—was precisely one of the most effective tools used by the Gang of Four in the past twenty years and more to suppress revolutionaries and the people. . . .

The current historical tide is a democratic tide, one which opposes feudal fascist dictatorship. The central theme in my articles such as "The Fifth Modernization—Democracy and Others" is that without democracy, there can be no Four Modernizations. Without the Fifth Modernization—democracy—all modernizations are doomed to failure. How can such a central theme be counter-revolutionary? People and things that oppose it should be justly included in the realm of counter-revolution.

To the charge that he had slandered Marxism–Leninism–Mao Zedong Thought, Wei replied:

A considerable portion of the theoretical core of the original Marxism consists of the description of a perfect society. This ideal realm is not peculiar to Marxism. This was the general wish of the working class and intellectuals in Europe at that time for freedom, equality, public ownership of property, and social justice. Marxism advocates a form of dictatorship with the combination of general democracy and the concentration of power to realize this ideal. This is the most obvious characteristic of Marxism.

After the past hundred years and more of practice, we find that governments organized under the form of dictatorship in which power is concentrated, such as the Soviet Union, Vietnam, and China before the Gang of Four was smashed, have without exception degenerated into a kind of fascist government with a minority of the leading class exercising dictatorship over the broad masses of the working people. . . .

What needs to be pointed out is that these conclusions, which I arrived at on the basis of the process of historical development of Marxism, may be correct and may be erroneous. This can be settled through further theoretical investigation. I welcome any criticism of them. But no matter whether the conclusions are correct or not, it is not a crime to carry out theoretical investigations and exchange opinions with other people in accordance with the principle of freedom of speech and publication.

In reply to the accusation that he had sought the overthrow of the socialist system, Wei reaffirmed the line he had taken in the chapter on "Socialism and Democracy" in *The Fifth Modernization*, saying:

I divide the socialist system into two big categories: the first is autocratic socialism on the model of the Soviet Union, charac-

terized by the concentration of power in a handful of people; the
second category is democratic socialism, which is characterized by
the concentration of power in all the people organized together in
a democratic way.

The wish of the majority of the people in our country is to
realize this democratic socialism. The aim of our exploration is also
to seek the road to reach this type of social system. I have taken
part in the democratic movement precisely to realize this kind of
democratic socialism in our country.

Wei concluded his defense with this reassertion of the right
and the duty of every citizen to criticize "unreasonable people
and things":

> It is the right of every citizen to criticize any unreasonable people or
> thing that he sees. This is also a responsibility which he cannot
> shift. Nobody and no organization has the right to interfere with
> this sovereign right. Criticism cannot possibly be nice and appeal-
> ing to the ear, or all correct. To require criticism to be entirely
> correct, and to inflict punishment if it is not, is the same as prohib-
> iting criticism and reforms and elevating the leaders to the position
> of deities.

That a poster should appear on Democracy Wall criticizing
Wei's trial was not surprising. More significant were two articles
that appeared in the *Guang Ming Daily*, the official paper for
China's intellectuals, on 24 October. The articles defended
freedom of speech, called for more democracy, and urged that
repression should not be used against those who do not believe
in communism. One of the articles, headlined "Methods of Dictatorship Must Not Be Used to Solve Problems of Ideology,"
asserted: "Violence can suppress a certain line of thought or
force people to surrender or even destroy them completely, but
it will never succeed in changing the way people think . . .
violence can never force people to believe what they cannot and
will not believe."

But what was most intriguing was the first substantive para-
graph of the other article, which contained this:

> We must not think that the set of Soviet "models" has solved all the
> fundamental questions concerning socialist politics; nor must we
> think that the works of revolutionary leaders have solved all the

questions in this respect, because practice in socialism has far surpassed what they could imagine at the time. We must conduct independent theoretical exploration [*tan-suo*], research and creation, in the light of the history and present conditions of our socialist political construction, and truly establish a Marxist political science.

The Chinese expression *tan-suo* was the one used for the name of the journal Wei Jingsheng had edited. It is a term I have seldom seen employed in Chinese political writing. To use it in such a context, only seven days after Wei's trial, at the start of a front-page article, could only have been a deliberate protest against the silencing of Wei.

The article was a report of an academic symposium on political science and sociology that had been held recently in Peking. It said that participants had insisted on the need to study the political structure of the state. The Gang of Four had made this a "forbidden zone" in the past to prevent discussion. "We must break down this 'forbidden zone,'" the participants were reported to have agreed. They also condemned the punishment of "ideological prisoners," and some of them "argued the need to give back to the law the authority it deserves and to clearly state that the power of law is higher than that of policy, higher than that of the instructions of any leader and higher than that of the decision reached by any party organization."[2]

The first issue of the left-wing Hong Kong monthly *Cheng Ming* to appear after Wei's trial focused on his case. Three articles commented on the judicial aspects of the case. They covered a range of viewpoints, but all were critical to some degree of the way it had been handled. One said the sentence was much too heavy; another said Wei should have been given some corrective education, then returned to his job; and a third atacked the whole basis of the charges laid against him. The editorial in the issue made play with the term *tan-suo* as *Guang Ming Daily* had done, placing it in the very center of the editorial page in the course of an appeal to the Communist Party to listen to the masses, even when they sing out of tune with the leadership. The editorial ended: "Separation from the masses can only lead to the death of the Party, or a party that exists in name only. The Chinese Communist Party has paid high tuition fees for many years past; surely it has learned the lesson of its experience?"

Is a poet any use in a revolution? In the 1960s, when it was fashionable on university campuses in the West to talk of revolution, poetry was less highly regarded than skill in breaking open safes and filing cabinets to extract administrators' files on investment policy or on individul students. But China's movement for democracy has been carried forward in thousands of poems and one poet has emerged supreme: Huang Xiang of the Enlightenment Society.

When Huang and his companions had come together some years before in their poor, remote home province of Guizhou "to study social problems, under the merciless oppression and cultural despotism of Lin Biao and the Gang of Four," they had asked themselves why China, with its long history of civilization, progressed so slowly, when Yugoslavia, also a "socialist" state, had developed quickly. Like many in their generation they concluded that the first thing to do was to establish respect for human rights and democracy. They differed from some of their contemporaries in that they read Western classics and respected Buddhism, Christianity, Islam, and Chinese mysticism. But what distinguished them more than anything else was the visionary poet in their midst. It is characteristic of the democracy movement that Huang Xiang was presented not as an individual but as a member of a group. Reading the poems and commentaries published by the society, it is clear he drew strength and enrichment from his companions. In turn he became their most eloquent voice.

Huang claimed that he was harassed by the authorities after reciting his poems before young people. The police searched for his manuscripts, but he had hidden them in candles by wrapping them in plastic bags, then rolling them around wicks, and finally molding wax around them. When the Gang of Four were arrested he melted the candles one by one to retrieve the manuscripts. Huang and his friends rejoiced at the smashing of the Gang of Four and at the political trend that emerged thereafter, but they were impatient at the pace of change. As one of them put it later, "The ice which locked China's great earth is now slowly and quietly melting. However, the melting is too slow."[3] To speed the thaw, in October 1978 Huang copied out his collection of political lyrics, the *God of Fire Symphonic Poems*, to make a big-character poster on about a dozen panels of poster paper. With seven friends he brought them from Guiyang to Peking "to meet the masses and undergo the test of social practice." On 11 October they pasted them up on the blank walls of an alleyway that runs beside the offices of the *People's Daily*, in the busy shopping center of the capital. Huang had taken trouble with the design of the posters to present as clearly and vividly as possible the poetry they bore. He chose white paper and brushed some of his large characters in red instead of black ink. He painted the emblem of the Enlightenment Society, a flaming torch of learning, at the beginning of the poster and between poems. After the last panel of poetry he pasted up three colored sheets, one green, one red, and one yellow, leaving them blank for readers' comments.

The poems immediately attracted so many readers that for days the alleyway was almost choked. Bicyclists who wanted to ride down the alley had to dismount to thread their way through the crowd. As they pushed their bicycles along they did not call out gruffly to those who blocked their path to stand aside, as people often did in Peking on other occasions; instead, they rang their bicycle bells. At first I was puzzled by the constant tinkling of bells and the fact that some people rang theirs even when no one was in their way. Then it dawned on me: the bells were being rung as much to express appreciation of the poems as to clear a path. With several bicycles in the alley at any one time there was a symphony of bell music to hail the poems on the walls.

Six weeks later, when free speech was blossoming on Democracy Wall, Huang wrote the poems out again as a new ninety-four-panel poster of even larger characters. This he displayed on seventy yards of fence high on an embankment in Tiananmen Square, facing Mao's mausoleum. The choice of this setting was not only a practical matter (the site enabled a thou-

sand people to read the poems at the same time); it was also an
act pregnant with political symbolism. The poems announce the
advent of a god who brings enlightenment to a people living in
the darkness of totalitarian dictatorship. According to the author, the poems had been condemned as subversive by the authorities because they violated "the imperial taboo"—they were
critical of the emperor. Now he displayed them face to face with
the Mao Memorial Hall.

Next to the poems, Huang Xiang and the seven friends who
had come with him to Peking displayed their notice announcing
the Enlightenment Society:

> To accord with the Constitution, we hereby formally announce the
> founding of the Enlightenment Society in Peking at 12 noon on 24
> November 1978.

Huang Xiang and his friends then signed the notice.

The society published a draft document setting out its aims.
This was a tactful document that began by expressing support
for the Communist Party of China and the socialist system and
acknowledged Marxism as "the fundamental guiding thought"
of Chinese society. There was no mention of Mao Zedong
Thought; instead there was a pledge to oppose the vulgarization
and dogmatization of Marxism. There was no mention of Lenin
or his "dictatorship of the proletariat"; instead, the main thrust
of the document was a commitment to the causes of constitutional government, democracy, human rights, intellectual freedom and creativity, and the rule of reason; and opposition to
"idols" and to the practice of establishing forbidden zones in the
realm of ideas.

Nine years before, Huang had written "I See a War" to
denounce the psychological war he believed was being waged
against the Chinese people by Lin Biao and the Gang of Four.
Now he included it among his *Symphonic Poems*:

I SEE A WAR

I see a war, an invisible war.
This war is waged in everyone's facial expression.
It is waged by numerous high-pitched loudspeakers.
It is waged in every pair of fearful and unstable eyes.

This war goes on within the nervous system in every brain.
It bombards every man, bombards every part and every aspect of
     man's physiological and psychological being.
The war is waged with invisible weapons,
Invisible bayonets, artillery and bombs.
This is the war of all the evils.

This is the invisible extension of physical war,
It is a war waged in the show windows of bookstores,
In every library,
In every song taught to schoolchildren,
In every elementary-school textbook,
In every household.
In numerous mass meetings.
In each stereotyped movement, line and image of the actors on
     stage.

I see the bayonets and spies, patrolling and spying between the
     lines of my poems,
Searching about in the conscience of every person.
A stubborn, ignorant, violent, feudal force
     Overruns everything, controls everything.

In the forefront of the attack by this unique, unprecedented and
     unrepeatable cultural dictatorship,
I see a group of wild animals trampling the spiritual world of man.
Oil paintings and canvases are lying to the people.
Poetry is panting in fear.
Music is crying.

Oh, invisible war, evil war,
You are the extension and continuation of 2500 years of war
     waged by feudal dictatorship.
You are the concentration and expansion of the war of spiritual
     enslavement that has been going on for 2500 years.

Come on, bomb, demolish, kill, hack down!
But people's democracy never dies,
The people's freedom of the spirit never dies.
Truth, Beauty and Goodness which live within the heart of man
     can never be uprooted, never be snatched away.[4]

The Enlightenment Society published Huang Xiang's *Symphonic Poems* in the first edition of its journal. In the second edition, Li Jiahua's commentary on them included these thoughts prompted by "I See a War":

> An irresistible mental war is going on in every autocratic country in the world. Its main task is to annihilate those who hope, endeavor, or dream; to destroy beautiful ideals and to prevent people's resistance to autocracy—a resistance that is possible, latent, brewing in people's minds, quietly going on and spreading inaudibly and invisibly. . . .
>
> Today, those who caused hatred, dissension, and disaster are dead, but the poems, drawings, and music they used as weapons . . . are still hidden in dark corners and an occasional glimpse of them disturbs our minds. . . .
>
> Now is the time to clean up the battlefields of mental war. The mines sown in our physical and spiritual worlds must be destroyed. The barbed wire must be removed and all the fighting trenches filled. We must smash the citadel from which they directed the war, we must discredit their theories and destroy the nerve center of this mental war. . . .
>
> We must rescue all the victims of this war and let them smile like normal people.[4]

Having denounced that psychological war which brings death to the spirit, Huang conceived and developed a vision of a revolution which would restore the spirit to life, indeed would establish the kingdom of heaven on earth. "Song of the Torch" describes the coming of the kingdom and the transformation of human society. It was written in 1969, the same year as "I See a War." (Li Jiahua commented: "In this revolution, the banner of the dignity of every individual will be planted again. They will no longer be enslaved and trampled upon, but with their personal traits and styles free from interference they will take their place independently in society.")

At the beginning of his "Song of the Torch" Huang Xiang shows us a great source of light:

> Moving above the horizon, far, far away,
> Swinging along on the great expanse of dark blue sky,
> Are the gleaming ranks of a marching column,
> A silently flowing river of fire,
> They light up the curtains that have always been closed.

As it comes closer, the poet's eye sees the source of light as a torch, and he calls on it to

> Awaken all the people of this generation.
>
> Those who have been forgotten by time, and those for whom time
>   has lost its value.
> Those whose thoughts are as dull as a machine.
>
> Those whose emotions are frozen stiff, and those whose blood is as
>   cold as ice.
>
> Those on whose faces are written anger and silence,
> Those who have numb despair carved at the corner of their mouth.
> . . .   . . .
> Ah torch, with a finger of light, you tap on the door
> Of the darkened room of every soul, calling for it to be opened.
>
> Bring strangers to understand each other,
> And help those who have strayed far apart come close to each
>   other again.
>
> Let those who are consumed with hatred be
>   filled with love,
>
> And let the suspicious doubt no more.
>
> Let those who are hated listen to the voice of goodness,
> And the eyes of the ugly be opened to beauty.
>
> In your irresistible and magic ring of fire,
> Mankind is allowed to experience the trembling of happiness.

In 1969 the Chinese people were being forced to worship Mao as a demigod, but Huang Xiang refused to accept that the idol is the ultimate reality. He put these rhetorical questions to those around him:

> Do you really mean to say the idol is more beautiful than poetry
>   and living,
> Do you really mean to say the idol can cover up the glow of truth
>   and science?
>
> Do you really mean to say the idol can suffocate the thirst for love
>   and the cry of the heart,
> Do you really mean to say the idol is the universe and the entirety
>   of living?
>
> Let people restore the dignity of man,
> Let living again become living.

Let man not guard against man,
Let every man be regarded as a man.

The darkness of night does not make men forget the morning
    light,
But only increases their longing for brightness.

Three years later, in 1972, Huang Xiang saw the Great Wall
of China as an ideological barrier between individuals and between peoples, and in "Confessions of the Great Wall" he let it
speak about itself. It begins by describing itself as the first
American astronauts told us they saw it,

The earth is small and blue,
I am a little crack in it

but it goes on to acknowledge:

Under the gray and low-flying clouds in the sky
I have been standing for a long time,
My legs are growing numb,
My support is giving way and I am losing my balance.
I will fall down and die of old age.

The marks left on me by the erosion of wind and rain
Are the dark blotches that old age brings to one's complexion.

The holes in my brickwork
Are gaps in my teeth . . .

I am old
My young sons and grandsons dislike me.
To them, I am a stubborn grandfather.

Why do the young so dislike the Wall? Because

I divide the great land into numerous small pieces,
Divide the land into many small, suffocating courtyards.

My body lies stretched out among the people
Dividing this group from that,
So that they are constantly guarding against each other,
Can never see the faces of their neighbors,
And cannot even hear their conversation.

They want to push me down and destroy me,
Because my huge body blocks their view,
Blocks them from the world outside their own little courtyards.

The wall was the web of controls that, at the time the poem was written, inhibited every Chinese, making him or her belong to a "unit"; confining him or her to one place, denying the freedom to travel to the next county, let alone to a neighboring country. It was the repression that cut Chinese off from each other's thoughts and feelings, the censorship that cut them off from what was happening in other lands, "the conversation of neighbors.* This poem foreshadowed the demands on Democracy Wall for freedom of movement and of expression and free access to foreign culture. The image of the wall

> Dividing this group from that
> So that they are constantly guarding against each other

reminds us of Wei Jingsheng's allegation that Mao whipped up artificial class struggle by dividing people into imaginary interest groups. But it was not only within the nation that young people believed artificial enmity was being maintained. In its declaration of 17 January 1979 the Human Rights Alliance would call for détente with the Soviet Union since, in their view, there was no longer any ideological basis for the Sino-Soviet dispute. So the young want to push down the barriers. The Wall knows that its days are numbered and that the future belongs to the young:

> They
> Are standing on the road of the new age,
> They
> Push aside my old black body, swaying, collapsing.
> They
> Strip me of my old traditions, of the ways of the mean in spirit, of the narrowness and conservatism that make up the shroud of tradition.
>
> The faraway places of the past
> Are now only a few feet away.
>
> My domain is disappearing on earth,
> Is collapsing in the minds of all mankind.

---

* The image had been used before. For instance, in 1957 Zhou Enlai had quoted a "rightist" as having said during the Hundred Flowers campaign, "Since 1952, campaign has succeeded campaign, each one leaving behind a Great Wall in its wake, a wall which estranges one man from another."

I am leaving,
I have died.

A generation of sons and grandsons are moving me into the
    museum. . . .

Mao's embalmed body lay just behind the crowd who read these
lines on Tiananmen Square. He had been born in 1893, and the
places that were faraway when he was young were nearby to his
sons and grandsons who had grown up reading about them in
Reference News and hearing about them in broadcasts beamed
to China by Russia, America, Japan, Australia, and Britain. In
the minds of the young, China was becoming part of the global
village and frontiers were indeed "collapsing in the minds of all
mankind."

Four years after he had written "Confessions of the Great
Wall," Huang Xiang's confidence in the future was tested by the
suppression of the Tiananmen demonstrations. That his confidence withstood the test is apparent in the poem he addressed
to the spirit of the square.

NO, YOU HAVE NOT DIED

Why do you hide your face, Tiananmen Square?
Why do your pale lips quiver, Tiananmen?
Why is your chest bleeding, why does your body shake so
    violently?
Answer me, Tiananmen!

I know what burning flames and molten lava are hidden in your
    chest.
I have heard you shake heaven and earth with your furious cries,
And I don't believe that you are just quietly dying,
I don't believe you are closing your eyes forever.
No, you will not die.
You have not died.

The whole world has seen the anger on your face.
Confronted by bayonets and rifle butts,
You did not shrink away.
Abused and trampled on by wild beasts, without a weapon in your
    hand,
You held fast, you would not give in.
In a pool of blood, you lay like a hero.

No, you are not dead, Tiananmen.
And you must not die.

You did not lower your banner in surrender.
Your silken ribbons bearing inscriptions were torn to shreds but
    their wings, red with fire, did not droop.
Your pamphlets and your poems have been gagged
But still they make their hoarse voices heard.
Your hammer-heavy fist still challenges and hits back, without a
    sound.
Your body, battered beyond recognition, still utters a silent
    accusation.

When Mao died and the Gang of Four was arrested, Huang
Xiang believed day was breaking at last. To celebrate the dawn,
he wrote the poem from which the whole set takes its title, "The
God of Fire." Like "The Song of the Torch" and "I See a War,"
the poem makes no specific reference to China or any Chinese
person, place, or event. The god transcends national boundaries:
"You belong to all time, you step over all planets, / All peoples
know your language." The image of a god of fire seems to have
replaced the torch as the force of salvation. The spirit has taken
on a more personal form:

You move about slowly, you sway gently back and forth,
You expose your naked body to me, without any inhibition.

Huang Xiang describes vividly his experience of the god of
fire coming into the hearts and lives of men, bringing a fire they
can use to purge themselves and the world around them of error
and unreason:

You are Prometheus, the bringer of fire, you are the liberator.
You liberated yourself and you broke the spiritual chains that
    bound the world.
God of Fire, I know you are approaching.
In the darkness of space I listen quietly to the sound of your
    footsteps.

Like the torch, the coming of the god of fire brings joy. The
curtains that have for so long shrouded the hearts of men are
opened.* Human relations are transformed. Strangers become

* A reference back to "The Song of the Torch."

friends, generosity replaces hostility, those who have been cheated regain a capacity for trust, those who have been pushed around are made part of society again, and those who have lost hope dare to hope again. The god of fire personifies universal law and will of justice; he sits as chief judge in the tribunal of practice, which replaces blind faith in a dogma. The god comes

Sprinkling a boundless rain of fire.

Allowing all living beings to cleanse themselves in that heavenly fire.

Burning to ashes the world of irrational and erroneous structures.

Ah, God of Fire, the unknown that is known to all, where you have descended, people rejoice.

Countless hearts are filled with your milky light.

You roll up the layer upon layer of curtain that covers men's hearts,

You walk nonchalantly toward the deep and far corners of men's souls.

You shake the inner halls of superstition and the deep inner palaces of unreason and error.

You sweep away the remnants of broken beliefs.

You are Prometheus, the bringer of fire, you are the liberator.

You liberated yourself and you broke the spiritual chains that bound the world.

You have found places in society for those who have been pushed around,

You have opened the door to knowledge to those who have been kept from the truth.

You have broken down the high, well-guarded walls of ignorance and prejudice that hold men prisoner.

You have removed the veil of disease that clouds the eyes of those who resist freedom more than tyranny.

Because of you, those who have been cheated and have lost their capacity to trust have regained it.

Because of you, those who have lost hope have courageously expressed hope.

Because of you, science is no longer sacrificed before the altar of tyranny,

Wisdom no longer has to breathe heavily and kneel before the feet
   of violence,
The will of one person can no longer represent the will of all.
Oh, God of Fire, Master of Time, Master of Space,
You are the incarnation of universal law,
You are the will of justice.

You are yourself the standard of truth and falsehood,
You are the measure of right and wrong.

Sitting at the seat of the chief judge in the tribunal of practice,
You conduct investigations and pass judgment on what is true.

The idol of the past is now tied to the pillar of torture by fire.
Among confusion and misconception inherited from ancient times,
   the voice of doubt has now been excited.

Your solemn judgment resounds throughout the universe.
"All that have been cast down are now established anew."

Ah, God of Fire, God of Fire,
You have come, come, come.

Huang Xiang wrote the first draft of this poem in 1976 and
revised it in February 1977 as the country waited for Deng
Xiaoping to return to office. He clearly believed that Deng and
indeed the whole movement for scientific socialism, for rational
government in place of dogmatism, and for national reconciliation, embodied much of the spirit of the god of fire.

Li Jiahua amplifies Huang Xiang's description of the god of
fire and at one point writes: "Yesterday, on the Huaihai
battlefield, your metallic voice traveled over thousands of miles
of gunsmoke.* Now, with your unflinching steadfastness and
your full warmth you are leading us on our march to the goal of
prosperity, democracy, and freedom. . . ." Neither Huang nor
Li is deifying Deng. To establish a new idol in place of Mao
would run contrary to the heart of all that the Enlightenment
Society was campaigning for. To them men are men and God is
God, and only when men make that distinction can the spirit of

* The Huaihai campaign was Deng's greatest military achievement. He
was secretary of the front committee that coordinated the 500,000-man Second Army and a supply system of two million civilians in this campaign that
broke the back of the Nationalist defense of Central and East China in 1948.

God enter their hearts and minds and work through them as it did, in their view, on the Huaihai battlefield.

Li Jiahua claims that Huang Xiang's description of the changes that the god of fire will bring to society is based on his faith in the future of communism, and the provisional draft program of the Enlightenment Society took Marxism as the fundamental guiding thought of the society. But their version of Marxism is very different from Lenin's version. Huang Xiang's predictions have nothing to do with the common ownership of property, and he believes in a god. His description of the god of fire echoes the Magnificat more than it does Marx.

The god of fire will

Pull down those who stand highest,
Raise up those who have been cast down,
Push down those who are deep-rooted, and
Steady those who have lost their support.

Li Jiahua compares Huang Xiang's visions of the future to those of pre-Marxian philosophers: to More's *Utopia*, Campanella's *City of the Sun*, and Owen's *A New View of Society*.* That Huang and Li managed to read such books in darkest Guizhou is proof of extraordinary determination—and a warning against imposing stereotypes on Chinese society.

The Enlightenment Society did not limit itself to publishing Huang Xiang's poetry and Li Jiahua's commentary on it. Its journal printed historical essays, including one on the European Enlightenment of the eighteenth century. Other poets' work was published, including a poem by Liang Qi expressing the wish that Voltaire, Diderot, and Goethe could be alive and in China to lend their strength to the Chinese Enlightenment. Seven pages were devoted to an open letter on human rights to President Carter by a writer using the pen-name Gong Min:

We are the younger generation of China, a generation which has painfully struggled amid disappointment, despair, and hope. For a

* Sir Thomas More (1478–1535) and Tommaso Campanella (1568–1639) conceived utopias ruled by reason. More's utopia was an atheist community based on the common ownership of property, as were the communities designed (and established in Britain, the U.S., and Ireland) by Robert Owen (1771–1858).

long time we have admired your country and the American people—our blue-eyed brothers. How we have wished to learn something about what is happening there in America, another continent under the same sky, under the Stars and Stripes, in the 1970s and 1980s! What are the American people thinking about, talking about, and doing?

However during this time, these widely held ideas of ours have existed under a sort of guilty conscience. We would have liked to sing this song to the American people: "I sing for you, Americans," but we dared not. An invisible iron curtain blocked us. . . .

Ever since our childhood, people have described you to us as "monsters and freaks" in the human world, as "tigers and wolves." . . . We have tried to peep through the gaps in the spiritual wall, to peep at the outside world through the breach caused by the wall's crumbling and collapse, asking ourselves: "What kind of monster is the United States?" But we could never see your true picture.

This writer, like others published by *Enlightenment*, displayed interest in and knowledge of the work of European philosophers, such as Montesquieu. The Enlightenment Society developed as an organization, founding branches in Peking and other cities. Its members numbered only a few hundred, a minuscule proportion of the nation, no larger than the Communist Party when it held its Fourth Congress in 1925, but it was an astonishing phenomenon, unprecedented in the People's Republic.

Sometime in the early spring of 1979 Huang Xiang and his friends returned home to Guizhou province, their presence in the capital having become something of an embarrassment to some of those in power, according to sources in the democracy movement. The Guizhou authorities took them into custody for a little ideological rectification and then returned them to their original work units. The voice of Huang Xiang and his friends was heard no more in public, at least so far as people in Peking could tell. No more was heard either of the branches of the Enlightenment Society in other cities.

13

Laws? Democracy?

AFTER THIRTEEN MONTHS' imprisonment, Zhang Zhixin was going home. But only for the time it would take her police escort to search through her belongings and confiscate whatever they decided to confiscate. This was but an hour's diversion in a day, 26 October 1970, devoted to her transfer from a rural detention center to jail in Shenyang city. Perhaps her children would be at home, her daughter of thirteen and her boy of three. She longed to see them but was frightened by the pain such a brief reunion could inflict on them and her.

The police escort pushed open the door of her home. There was no one there. They made their search and bundled Zhang Zhixin back into their jeep. As the jeep moved out from the sidewalk, Zhang Zhixin pressed her face to its small back window. Suddenly she saw her daughter running toward her calling out: "Mum! Mum! . . . Stop! Give me back my mother!" The driver accelerated down the street, leaving the young girl at the roadside.

Haunted by the glimpse of her daughter, Zhang Zhixin seized the first moment she could to write her a letter from Shenyang jail, and then waited for a reply. There was no quick response, and she had all too much time to herself to look ahead and look back. Ahead of her stretched a life term of indefinite duration.

The forty years that lay behind her had begun with joy.

As a child, there had been affection for her in her financially hard-up but cultured family, by the name of Hao.

In her teens, after the end of World War II, Zhixin attended Upper Middle School in Tianjin, the former treaty port where Zhou Enlai had received part of his schooling. She took pleasure in music and studied the violin. She had gentle but lively eyes set in an open handsome face. Besides the blessing of good looks she had a keen mind that won her a place at the Hebei Teachers Training College in Baoding. She entered the college in the autumn of 1950, a few months after the outbreak of the Korean war. In November, Chinese troops entered the war in massive numbers and Zhixin applied for a transfer to study at an officers training school. She hoped to be sent to the Korean front, but instead she was transferred in early 1951 to the Chinese People's University in Peking.

The Communist Party organization there found her suitable for party membership and encouraged her political development. In 1955 she was formally admitted to the Party. A year later she was sent to work in Shenyang, the capital of Liaoning province, an unlovely but businesslike city, one of the major centers of heavy industry in Northeast China. She worked in a section of the propaganda department of the Liaoning provincial government that dealt with literature and the arts.

This was a time of high hopes and considerable confidence for China, and life held promise for Zhixin. She and the "New China" were developing their potential, and there seemed to be a place in the new order of things for a woman with her education and character.

Marriage brought her a girl, LinLin, who shared her looks, and then, ten years later, a boy, to make a small family that matched the ideal of many young couples and did not strain the budget or the limited space at home.

In Shenyang the winters are grim. The temperature goes down to minus 30 degrees Centigrade and stays there for days on end. But Zhang Zhixin was no delicate lotus. She was rather tall for her generation, over five feet eight inches, and cut quite a figure as she strode through the northern cold, a bright red scarf thrown around her neck above a black overcoat.

But the New China did not fulfill its early promises to Zhang Zhixin. As the political balance swung between Mao and those who disputed his personal control of the nation, the Party demanded repeated changes of heart from its members. Among her colleagues and friends, including those with higher education, there were more than a few who followed the twists and turns of the party line without developing a viewpoint of their own. They preferred to close their minds to dangerous thoughts and concentrate on mastering the current orthodoxy. For Zhang Zhixin, upbringing and temperament precluded such a living death of the spirit.

The Cultural Revolution came, bringing a grotesque politicization to her daughter's education, strife in the Party of which she was a member, negation of the values she herself had acquired from her family, her schools and university, and violent disorder to the nation at large. It brought to a head doubts and dissatisfaction that had grown in her mind for several years, beginning with the dismissal of Marshal Peng Dehuai for his criticisms of the Great Leap Forward, continuing with the deification of Mao and growing with Mao's contravention of the letter and the spirit of the party Constitution. She confided these inner thoughts to a female colleague who was also a trusted friend. That friend was married to a man who worked in the same office, and she entrusted him with Zhang Zhixin's thoughts. He betrayed them to the leadership of the department. He was rewarded by promotion, and Zhixin was arrested in the autumn of 1969, one victim of a massive purge of the Party's ranks.

On 24 September 1969 citizens were assembled for a mass rally on a square in Shenyang. There, spread across the back of a stage, they saw a banner: "Struggle with the active counter-revolutionary Zhang Zhixin." Onto the front of the stage Zhixin was pushed and pulled by two hefty former colleagues from the provincial government and her military service. There she was held in the usual manner: one man twisted her arms up behind her back and the other forced her head down by pulling her hair

COMING ALIVE:

from in front, so that she could neither stand up straight nor squat down. A large board hanging from her neck proclaimed her "guilt."

In that position, she listened to accusations that she had opposed Mao's line and had slandered Jiang Qing and Marshal Lin Biao, Mao's most powerful collaborator in the Cultural Revolution. She did not deny that she had criticized these leaders but protested that she had a right to do so in a manner prescribed by party discipline. In the atmosphere of 1969 no one was going to heed that kind of protest. She was proclaimed guilty, formally arrested, and driven away in a jeep.

While in detention, it is alleged that her ankles were fettered and her arms were shackled behind her back in a manner widely used during the Cultural Revolution: one arm was stretched over its shoulder and down the back, to meet the other arm which was stretched behind the back and up from the waist. The two thumbs were held together by a small shackle. For a year and a half she was kept in a tiny cell where she could neither stand up straight nor stretch out full length on the ground. It is also reported that she was tortured and subjected to gang rape. Despite this treatment, she refused to admit that she had committed a political crime. It is claimed that she argued with her interrogators, insisting that she had a right to express doubts about leaders and policies. Jiang Qing and Lin Biao, she said, were not synonymous with socialism and the Party. She is quoted as having attacked Jiang Qing's impoverishment of Chinese culture through her personal cultural dictatorship. For her, Lin Biao was a "left deviationist." She had raised matters that touched on Mao himself: his condemnation of Marshal Peng Dehuai for daring to attack the Great Leap Forward and his purge of a group of veteran cadres known as the Clique of Sixty-One Traitors.

She kept her self-respect, mending her clothes with an improvised needle and threads taken from her prison uniform.

The prison authorities decided that she would not respond to the usual pressures, so one morning after breakfast two warders ordered her out of her cell and thrust her into the back of a prison van. Two ashen-faced fellow prisoners were already there. Guards stuffed a sponge into Zhixin's mouth to forestall any protest. She concluded that she was on her way to be executed. The prison van stopped at the execution ground, and she was ordered out with the other two prisoners. The other two knelt on the ground but Zhixin held herself upright. Shots rang out. The two men fell dead but Zhixin was not touched: she had been brought as a witness, to encourage her to admit to being a counter-revolutionary.

She recovered from the shock and maintained her defense under interrogation. The legal assessor responsible for "trying" her found her guilty of no crime and reported his conclusion to his superiors. The latter judged the assessor to have committed a grave error of right deviation and ordered a new assessor to try her. She again refused to repent. Back in her cell, she wrote a ten-thousand-word Manifesto of a Communist Party Member.[1] The assessor was faced with a dilemma; he could find no fault with the prisoner but he remembered how his predecessor had been criticized. He decided to award a stiff sentence: fifteen years. On 20 August 1970 his superiors revised it to life imprisonment, which meant an unlimited time.

It was with the prospect of endless years in jail stretching ahead of her that Zhixin had written to her thirteen-year-old daughter in October 1970. But she received no comforting reply. Instead there came a notice from a court informing her that her husband had divorced her. That meant that he and the children were suffering discrimination because of their connection with her. This had been common practice in China for years, as in the Soviet Union under Stalin, but it was still a terrible blow to know that it was now being applied to her family. They had been forced to move out of Shenyang to a remote mountain village. Her daughter had been refused membership in the Communist Youth League despite having denounced her mother repeatedly. Her son had been denied entry into the Shenyang music college's children's class even though he passed qualifying tests.

After serving five years of her life sentence, Zhang Zhixin still showed no sign of repentance. The story of her resistance began to become known in Shenyang and wall posters appeared demanding an investigation. Mao Zedong's nephew Mao Yuanxin was both the Chairman's secretary and the most powerful

figure in Northeast China. He began to fear that her example
might cause trouble, and one day in the spring of 1975, he said
"Zhang Zhixin would rather die than admit her crime. She fights
against us every day that she lives. Let us kill her and be rid of
her." The papers condemning her to death were duly drawn up
and signed.

There is a tradition in China that unrepentant rebels shout
defiant slogans as they face their executioner. The Shenyang
prison authorities practiced a discreet method of preventing
this: they muted the condemned prisoner by piercing a small
hole in his or her windpipe. The need to silence Zhang Zhixin
was obvious. So, on the morning of 4 April she was taken to
one of the prison offices and held down for the operation. The
pain made her scream and a woman guard fainted at the horror
of it, but the windpipe was soon pierced, putting an end to the
noise.

Zhixin was driven to the execution ground, and the Record of the Execution Ground shows that she was executed at
10:12 A.M. An eyewitness claims that as she walked from the
prison van to the execution spot she held herself well.

Although they had silenced Zhang Zhixin's own voice, Mao
Yuanxin and his colleagues had not heard the last of her. Wall
posters appeared in Shenyang protesting her fate. They were
ripped down but new ones kept appearing. Mao Yuanxin and
his colleagues had created a martyr who would be a more powerful opponent in death than she had been in life. Their
enemies kept bringing her case before the public eye in
Shenyang. That was embarrassing but by no means fatal while
Mao Zedong lived.

But then the Chairman died and Mao Yuanxin was arrested
trying to flee from Peking. For two years there were no major
developments in the story of Zhang Zhixin, but then in the
winter of 1978–1979 a new poster appeared in Shenyang giving
more details of her case and implicating in the decision to kill
her General Chen Xilian, who was still a member of the Politburo. That was but a prelude to the storm which burst in June
1979. The story of Zhang Zhixin had been chosen as a morality
tale, which was then told in a nationwide campaign on television

and radio and in the press. The moral to which the press pointed was the need for safeguards to protect the expression of nonconformist views on major issues of party and state. The choice of the case of a Communist Party cadre as an example is deliberate. If there is no democracy or freedom for party members there can be none for anyone else.

In July 1979 the editors of *Cheng Ming*, the left-wing monthly in Hong Kong, wrote: "The Zhang Zhixin case has provided us with profound lessons: First, the leftist line pursued by Lin [Biao] and Jiang [Qing] did great harm to the people; second, without democracy and the legal system, the people have nothing. . . . Those who emancipate their thinking and speak up without reservations are innocent. . . . Let us . . . strive for a society in which democracy and legality are combined to eliminate 'ideological offenders.'"[2] The campaign in the official Chinese press provoked articles and letters supporting the view that a person with ideological problems cannot be accused of having committed a crime and demanding that those responsible for Zhang Zhixin's death be brought to public trial.

Cheng Ming alleged that a high official with the surname of Chen and the most senior secretaries of the Liaoning provincial Party Committee concurred with Mao Yuanxin's decision to have Zhang Zhixin killed. A wall poster in Peking repeated the allegation already made in Shenyang that the Chen in question was Ferocious Tiger Chen Xilian, Commander of the Shenyang Military Region and First Secretary of Liaoning province at the time of Zhang's arrest. The poster-writer, who used the pen name "Someone in the Know," claimed that Chen Xilian had actually written the death warrant himself and was now protecting others involved.[3]

In October 1979, the democratic activist magazine *Autumn Fruit* put up on Democracy Wall the text of a letter written by Zhang Zhixin's mother to the President of the Supreme Court, Jiang Hua, on July 30. Mrs. Hao demanded the "opening of an inquiry" into the execution of her daughter and "the punishment of the guilty." Mrs. Hao accused General Chen of being one of the people who gave the execution order.[4]

The Zhang Zhixin morality play was wielded as a double-headed axe: to advance the cause of safeguards for dissent and to destroy opponents of Deng Xiaoping. Because factional politics are involved, one should be wary of accepting the story as the whole truth and nothing but the truth, but *Cheng Ming*—from which I have drawn this account—has earned a reputation for respecting the truth, and there is collateral evidence from Shenyang wall posters.

Zhang Zhixin's case was chosen by the Party from among tens of thousands of miscarriages of justice that occurred in the same period, one pebble on a stony beach. The administration of justice in China was in a state that could best be compared to that stable in ancient Greece in which King Augeas kept three thousand oxen for thirty years without once having it cleaned out. At a National Conference of Presidents of Higher People's Courts and Military Tribunals held in Peking in July 1979 it was announced that in the preceding eighteen months the courts in China had re-examined 708,000 criminal cases and had found more than 166,000 cases "from the period of the Cultural Revolution" involved false accusation or wrong verdicts. Earlier the President of the Supreme People's Court had told the National People's Congress that 40 percent of the charges against "counter-revolutionaries" in the same period had been found to be unjust. In some areas he said, the figure was as high as 70 percent.

In August 1979 a poster appeared on Democracy Wall that illustrated the mixture of maladministration of justice and lawlessness that had prevailed since the Cultural Revolution. Spread over nearly two hundred pages were the names of people allegedly killed in the Guangxi autonomous region in Southwest China during and after the Cultural Revolution: some in factional fighting, some as a result of illegal court actions, and many at the hands of people who were satisfying old grudges. In the introduction, the compilers of the list, a group of citizens from Guangxi, said that 67,500 people had met unnecessary and violent deaths in Guangxi in the period since mid-1968, which excludes the most violent period from 1966 until then. The full total would probably therefore be at least twice as high.

Execution and imprisonment of people for political crimes had occurred in waves since 1949. (It had happened before, of course, but on a smaller scale.) The Amnesty International report on China published in 1978 brought together some of the numbers that have emerged over the years. The categories of offender are necessarily vague in a society without a full code of law, but they do illustrate the dimension of the phenomenon.[5]

The Amnesty International report quotes documents collected and circulated by Red Guards during the Cultural Revolution which reveal that Chairman Mao said in April 1956, at an enlarged meeting of the Party Politburo, that "two or three million counter-revolutionaries had been executed, imprisoned, or placed under control in the past." From the texts of court notices published in China it is clear that some people convicted as counter-revolutionaries had done no more than express political dissent and had made no attempt to organize a "counter-revolution." In *Red China Today*, Edgar Snow quotes Zhou Enlai as saying that eight hundred thirty thousand "enemies of the people" had been "destroyed" up to 1954.

The judiciary, and the procuracy that was supposed to act as a watchdog over the administration of justice, were wide open to political interference. In December 1978, China's Chief Procurator, Huang Huoqing, voiced this complaint before the assembled Central Committee:

> It is nearly thirty years since Liberation and the procuracy has but hung up a sheep's head while selling dog's meat [that is, it is a fraud]. When will our judiciary and procuracy be independent as is stipulated in the Constitution? We have been criticizing the Nationalists for thirty years, but at least they can still say, with perfect assurance, that their judiciary and procuracy are independent. . . .
>
> As all men are equal before the law, should we prosecute the Secretaries [of the Provincial Party Committees] who are guilty of a crime? . . . The Public Security Bureau can take no action and the court can do nothing about them. Once the procuracy tries to intervene, it is rebutted with a question—should you obey the Party, or should the Party obey you? . . . Even some members of the Central Committee of the Party have flouted law and discipline.

The Chief Procurator bemoaned the ignorance prevailing in China about the role of law:

> I want to discuss how we can bring our comrades to have a better understanding of the law. Let us forget for the moment about people in distant and remote places. The participants here are all leading comrades of the party. Among the nine hundred million or so people of China, there are only a few hundred members or alternate members of the CCP Central Committee. However, how many of them can truly explain what law is? How many of them understand what role the law plays for us? Without the big-character posters which demanded the rule of law, we would not have put forward the issue of the rule of law to the central authorities. . . .
>
> There has not been a complete lack of law in the past thirty years, but, apart from the legislators and law enforcers, how many workers, peasants, students, and people of all trades actually understand on what law a verdict will be based if they violate the law? The procuracy has conducted a survey in seven counties and municipalities in four provinces. Most of the people only understand that our law contains the following sentences: "Leniency to those who confess their crimes and severity to those who refuse. Accomplices under duress shall go unpunished and those who render meritorious service shall receive awards." Or in another version: "The chief criminals will be punished without fail and those who are accomplices under duress will go unpunished. Those who have been led astray will be set free with a verdict of 'not guilty'; and people who turn against those with whom they have mistakenly sided will be regarded as rendering great service." If the law consists of these two points, then it is really the grief of socialism.[6]

The Augean mess in the field of justice was only one measure of the gap that had opened between the Chinese people and the Communist Party since 1949.

Deng Xiaoping showed concern about this gap in a more general sense. In his first published speech after his rehabilitation in 1977, he introduced a phrase which he repeated many times thereafter: he called on the Party "to revive and carry forward" its "fine tradition and fine style of work." The word *revive* was a key one. As Edgar Snow, John Service, and other highly professional observers had testified in the Yanan days, the support given to the Communist Party then by tens of millions of peasants and educated people was sincere and not the result of mass coercion. Because the liberal and patriotic policies pursued by the Party then were in step with the political development of the nation, the Party had been able to use methods that were comparatively democratic—and certainly more democratic than anything China had seen before. The rectification campaign of 1942 revealed the leadership's intention to impose strict ideological conformity, but its long-term effects were hardly discernible by the inhabitants of their base areas.

In August 1944, when Mao Zedong was bidding for American troops to be sent to China in large numbers to cooperate with his forces against the Japanese, he urged that the Americans should act as propagandists for democracy:

> Every American soldier in China should be a walking, talking advertisement for democracy. . . . After all, we Chinese consider you Americans the ideal of democracy. . . .
>
> Our experience proves that the Chinese people understand democracy and want it. It does not take long experience or education or "tutelage." The Chinese peasant is not stupid; he is shrewd and, like everyone else, concerned over his rights and interests.[7]

In the judgment of John S. Service, Mao's enthusiasm for American democracy was sincere but based on limited knowledge and an idealized image.[8]

The inadequacy of Mao's grasp of democracy was demonstrated on the eve of Communist victory on the mainland when he said the Communist-led government would practice "people's democratic dictatorship," which he defined as "democracy for the people and dictatorship over the reactionaries." The distinction between the people and the reactionaries was subjective and political, and no objective basis for making the distinction has yet been found.

The years that followed saw Mao and the Party move far away from the liberal reforms and democratic practices of the war years. But in those early years of their rule the Communist leaders were probably united in believing that their hold on power could not be consolidated or their land distribution accomplished without rigorous dictatorship and hundreds of thousands of executions. Immediately after these goals were achieved an influential body of opinion in the top leadership formed around the idea that rule by mass movement must give way to government by law in accordance with a written or unwritten constitution. Those who took this view also favored a gradual approach to economic reform. They were in no hurry to force collectivization of land or the nationalization of industry.

In 1954 the first Constitution of the People's Republic was made law by the First National People's Congress, which had been elected in accordance with an electoral law drawn up the preceding year. Deng Xiaoping had been secretary to the three committees that had drafted the Constitution and the electoral law and organized the election. The 1954 Constitution contained one hundred six articles and promised numerous rights to the citizen. It embodied the gradualist approach to economic reform and specifically promised protection of the rights of the peasants to own land, of handcraftsmen to own means of production, and of capitalists also to "own means of production and other capital." Peasants and handcraftsmen were to be encouraged, "on the voluntary principle," to form cooperatives. Capitalists were to be guided toward "various forms of state-capitalist economy."

Without a supporting body of law these provisions could have little practical effect, of course, and in the next few years a good deal of work was done on drafting laws and building up a legal profession. A system of "people's lawyers" was established, and by 1957 several hundred legal-counselor offices had been set up in various parts of China, staffed by trained lawyers. There were one hundred thirty-nine lawyers practicing in Peking alone.[9]

With the aid of lawyers, some defendants pleaded not guilty and successfully defended their innocence. Statistics collected in 1957 from fifty-nine legal-counselor offices showed that in 1204 criminal cases in which defense was put up by lawyers, the defendants were found not guilty in sixty-three cases and in another forty-nine punishment was waived.[10]

The body of codified law on which the legal system operated was very limited. The courts worked mainly by precedent, party policy, and "natural justice." The prospects for adoption of the laws then being drafted were reasonably good, but if the promulgation of laws was to make sense the Party must abandon rule by mass movement. In 1956, at the Eighth Party Congress, Liu Shaoqi, the Party's leading pragmatist who ranked immediately below Mao, gave his authority for just such a shift. In his speech to the congress he said that in the new period of the revolution "a complete legal system becomes an absolute necessity. Everyone in the country should understand and be convinced that as long as he does not violate the laws, his civil rights are guaranteed and will suffer no encroachment by any organization or any individual."

The congress also heard a speech on this theme from Dong Biwu, President of the Supreme People's Court, a Politburo member, a founder of the Party and later acting Chairman of the People's Republic. He said:

> We conducted mass movements in the past to emancipate the productive forces. What is the nature of the mass movement? It is a tempestuous revolution that relies in the main on direct action by the masses rather than on law, and reform, the movement against the three evils* and the movement against the five evils† were all conducted in the form of mass movements; in other words, none of them was a case of making laws first and then launching the movement. Our laws were born out of mass movements. . . . It was the Party's conviction at that time that the productive forces of the whole country could not be liberated in any other ways. . . .
>
> The situation is different now, in that the task of the state is to develop and protect the productive forces, while in the past it was to emancipate them. This calls for improving the people's democratic legal system. . . .
>
> We already have a constitution and some laws, but some other necessary laws are still lacking, such as a penal code, civil code, and the law of the criminal procedure and the law of the civil procedure. . . .
>
> As mankind entered civilization, the creation of legal systems became one of its hallmarks. A state without a legal system is not a state in the full sense of the term. Not all laws are necessarily

---

* Corruption, waste, and bureaucracy.
† Bribery of government workers, tax evasion, theft of state property, cheating on government contracts, and stealing economic information for private speculation.

written. Common law can serve just as well. Some have not had any written constitutions up till now, but that does not mean they have no legal system.[11]

Dong Biwu's personal commitment to these views was genuine, but he was not powerful enough to make such a speech on his own initiative. He was reflecting the views of those leaders whose influence in the Party was dominant at the Congress: Liu Shaoqi and Deng Xiaoping. But these pragmatists had already allowed themselves to be overruled and outflanked by Mao on the economy and they would soon let him have his way on the issue of mass movements versus law.

Paradoxically, it was Mao's initiative to encourage free speech, the Hundred Flowers Campaign,* which caused the damage. The anticommunist uprising in Hungary, which took place a month after the Chinese Eighth Congress closed, seemed to convince Mao that measures must be taken to forestall a similar uprising in China. His encouragement to the educated strata of society to speak their minds was intended, no doubt, to elicit "constructive criticism" that would lead the Party to correct those features of its style of rule which were harming relations with the noncommunist majority. He believed that the Party's leadership was basically accepted by the people and that the great majority of criticisms would be confined to minor complaints that would not strike at the fundamentals of the system. He had no thought of reforming the system by introducing laws to regulate freedom or institutionalize democracy. His approach owed much to Chinese tradition and nothing to Western-style democracy.

Mao had completely miscalculated. As one noncommunist put it, with gentle but deadly irony: "The consequences . . . were estimated by the venerable Mao . . . but the estimate was incomplete. It was not thought that the Party could have committed so many mistakes. The problems brought to light have far exceeded the estimate, and really 'the task has been over-fulfilled.' "[12]

* The policy was given the very traditional name the Hundred Flowers because, in expounding it, Mao had quoted the Confucian mandate "Let a hundred flowers bloom and a hundred schools of thought contend."

The demands and criticisms that poured out, once people had finally been convinced that the invitation was not a trap, mainly reflected a liberal democratic outlook. They were strikingly similar to those of the young activists of 1978. In 1957 as in 1978, there were calls for a system of law and the Party was accused of dogmatism, of mechanically copying Soviet society, of cultural dictatorship, of self-interested privilege-seeking, and of according exaggerated prestige to Mao Zedong. There were the same complaints that the lack of free expression was leading to unnecessary mistakes and a deadening of intellectual and cultural life.

In 1957 students in Wuhan called on Chiang Kai-shek to return to the mainland. In that year, when the collectivization of land had just been carried through, there were allegations that the policy had been effected by coercion and not voluntarily as was claimed. With the imposition of public ownership on commercial and industrial enterprises newly completed, there were complaints from workers and even from senior trade-union officials that the trade unions were acting as "worker control departments" and as the "tongues of the bureaucracy."

In 1978 the economic success of Taiwan was acknowledged, and posters and journals made it clear that the leaders on Taiwan had no devil image. Excesses of collectivization were again criticized. The transformation of state ownership into "social ownership" à la Yugoslavia was called for. In 1957 as in 1978 there was a common goal of putting an end to the monopoly of power of the Communist Party, although in 1957 this was expressed more bluntly than in 1978. In 1957 some went so far as to suggest that the Party should dissolve itself; in 1978, most young activists were concerned to speak within the framework of the Constitution. So, instead of challenging the Party's supremacy they called for institutional reforms that would curb its power.

In 1957 a student wrote: "The Party takes everything into its own hands and decides everything; the Party is the whole people; the Party is the State; the Party is the law."[13] In 1979, twenty-two years after this student was condemned as a rightist, the official press in Peking complained "A long-held viewpoint in our legal circles is that our party policy itself is law, because our party is the ruling party."[14] The students of 1957, like the poster-writers of 1978, condemned the Party's style of rule as fascist and bitterly criticized Mao, saying he had become a dictator remote from the people.

In 1957 as in 1978, some young people criticized the Party from a standpoint that was Marxist but not Leninist.

However, the relationship between the critics and the Party leadership was very different in 1957 from what it was in 1978. In 1957, Mao and the critics collided. In 1978, Deng and the critics were nearer to colluding than colliding. Mao's ideas on politics were directly opposed to those of the intelligentsia who bloomed at his invitation. He had no time for the "bourgeois" democracy and the rule of law that many of the critics wanted. The intensity and depth of their criticism caught him by surprise. In 1978, Deng was acting in a de facto alliance with the young activists. Together they were working for a greater reliance on law and a reform of institutions in a democratic sense, although the young probably wanted to go much further and faster than he. The wall posters of 1978 were a logical extension of themes of the official press, and Deng expected a whole range of views. "Not all of the opinions of the masses are well considered," he said, "and it is impossible for all their demands to be correct, but that is not something to be afraid of."[15]

The outcome of the two campaigns was also very different. In 1957, Zhou Enlai, as prime minister, gave a formal answer, on behalf of the leadership, to the demands that had been raised. On the crucial question of law, he said: "It was, and continues to be, difficult to draw up laws of a fundamental character suitable for the long term. . . . Under these circumstances, it is necessary and proper for the state to issue *provisional* regulations, decisions, and directives as terms of reference for general observance." (Emphasis added.)

After Zhou had given the formal reply, the Party proceeded to cut down the flowers that had bloomed. Three hundred thousand so-called rightists were purged. All lost their jobs and many were sent to labor camp or to exile in remote areas. Those among them who were at liberty when the Cultural Revolution was launched in 1966 were placed under house arrest and remained so restricted until release in 1978, two years after the Fall of the Four. The effect of the campaign was not confined to those labeled rightist. Even those intellectuals who had not been labeled were cowed and alienated. Few dared to exercise their creative talents to the full, and China lost a generation of trained minds and a generation of thought. Even in the short term the results were disastrous because Mao used the antirightist purge to open the way for an even greater lurch to the left, which brought the Great Leap Forward and a newly aggressive foreign policy. The nation—indeed, the Party itself—paid a terrible price for Mao's victory over those who had sought laws in place of mass movements. By contrast the conservative reaction of 1979, while it curbed the freedom of expression and slowed the pace of political change, did not stop the program of reform in social, economic, and foreign policy. All the essential features of that program were maintained, including adoption of the first criminal code of the People's Republic.

The antirightist drive of 1957–1958 virtually annihilated the legal profession described by Dong Biwu only a year before as "indispensable in judicial work." Many lawyers were condemned as rightists. The signboards of all lawyer's offices were smashed or removed, and those who escaped condemnation as rightists were forced to seek other work.

People became afraid to seek even a spare-time lawyer's aid. If they dared to plead not guilty at the formal court trial they were accused of showing a failure to repent for crimes that the earlier police investigation had proved they had committed. To appeal against a sentence often brought an increased sentence as punishment for failing to repent. (When I visited Puto district court in Shanghai in September 1978, the judge told me that in the twenty-five years of the court's existence nobody who had been brought before it had been found innocent.)

Abuse of the criminal process was not the only problem that was increased after the antirightist campaign. Statistically even more numerous, according to Professor Jerome Cohen, Director of East Asian Legal Studies at Harvard, were administrative sanctions that apparently resulted in loss of employment and reputation for hundreds of thousands of officials, scientists, and teachers. Professor Cohen adds that "Many of the hundreds of thousands or millions who have suffered 'rehabiliatation through labor,' which consists of long confinement in a labor camp in conditions not substantially very different from those suffered by convicted criminals, received no notice of any charges, no hearing, and no chance for appeal."

The application of these sanctions was particularly convenient against those whose offenses were political rather than criminal. Their number was legion: the Party *was* the law, so the law changed every time party policy changed, and it changed so much that during the period in 1977 between the Fall of the Four and the return of Deng this joke would circulate in Peking:

Three men are sitting on a bench in a cell in jail. The man in the middle asks the man on his right: "Why are you here?"

"I praised Deng Xiaoping. And you?"

"I opposed Deng Xiaoping."

They both turn to the third man and ask: "Why are you here?"

"I am Deng Xiaoping."

In November 1978, a correspondent of the *People's Daily* would look back over the disastrous effect on legal work of the mass movements of the late 1950s and say this of party officials who opposed and undermined the rule of law:

> For a long time they have avoided mentioning such things on the political and judicial front as "all are equal in the application of the law." . . . They avoided mentioning "the barrister system," "revolutionary humanitarianism," and even such things as "the regular legal system," "the legal system is not comprehensive," and "there is no law to follow." There not only exist forbidden areas on the political and judicial front, but they have been there for quite a long time. They were already well developed back in the fifties. . . .[16]

People came to fear using such provisions as the fledgling law made for the proper administration of justice:

For example, the law explicitly stipulated that "all citizens regardless of nationality, race, sex, profession, social background, religious belief, education, financial standing or period of residence are equal in the application of the law." . . . However, for a certain time, this became a forbidden zone and it was wrong and even sinful to talk about it. . . . In the past some of our comrades condemned the work of making warrant arrests [officially approved arrests] and filing indictments as looking for ways to "fetter the hands and feet of dictatorship." The Gang of Four and their remnant followers described the work of making warrant arrests and filing indictments as "interfering with the struggle against the enemy."[17]

In 1961–1963, when Liu Shaoqi and Deng Xiaoping were again able to shape domestic policy, they started a shift to greater reliance on law. Regulations setting out the rights and obligations of industrial enterprises and rural collectives were issued. The draft criminal code, on which work had begun almost ten years before, was supplemented, modified, and issued to some province-level administrations for comment. A code of criminal procedure was also drafted and views were widely solicited.[18] Measures were taken to restore some economic democracy: for instance families were permitted to farm land under contract to the production team and rural free markets were allowed to expand their operations. But when the Third National People's Congress was convened at the end of 1964, no codes were presented for its consideration. A year later, Mao fired the opening salvo of the Cultural Revolution, which was to reverse the trend to economic democracy and bring to China a reign of lawless violence that can only be compared with the early 1920s, when warlords preyed on society. Usually reliable unofficial Chinese sources estimate that four hundred thousand people died as a direct result of the Cultural Revolution.[19] (No official estimate for the whole nation is yet available, but the official press has said that "tens of thousands" died in the Inner Mongolian autonomous region in the early 1970s.[20])

Yet in the long run the Cultural Revolution was to make China more receptive to the ideas of the rule of law and institutionalized democracy. This was partly because of the sheer numbers of people who suffered from the lack of law and partly because, for the first time since 1949, high officials of the Communist Party found themselves on the receiving end of a mass campaign.

Hundreds of thousands of officials discovered what it was like to have no law to protect one's job, one's home, or one's body from the ravages of political campaign. Even the police could not defend themselves. In one province, Shaanxi, "over 80 percent" of the security officials and police were driven into a valley "where they were treated savagely and persecuted, under the pretext of running 'a study course.'" Two hundred eighty-one security organs and police stations in the province were attacked and one hundred thousand security files were stolen.[21] The system of law, such as it had been, broke down. Again in Shaanxi, sixty-one intermediate and middle-level courts and thirty-three courtrooms were sacked and looted.[22]

Obviously, under such circumstances the procuracy could do nothing to ensure proper administration of justice. After years of impotence and inactivity it was formally abolished in 1975.

During the Cultural Revolution, the institutes and faculties of politics, science, and law that had been training legal personnel were closed, and most of them remained closed until at least 1978.

Before the Cultural Revolution, an unwritten and unscientific rule had usually protected high officials who fell from grace: "The higher you are, the softer you fall." But from 1966 to 1968 they no longer suffered only a loss of office and honor. Physical and psychological torture, suicide under political pressure, death through medical neglect, and the betrayal of comrade by comrade afflicted the official class en masse. Liu Shaoqi, the Head of State, died in captivity of pneumonia while being moved by train from Peking to Hofei; one of Deng Xiaoping's children was crippled by an "accident" while under political interrogation; Ye Jianying's son-in-law, a concert pianist, had bones of one hand or arm broken by Red Guards to prevent him from playing "bourgeois" music; Tao Zhu, the "King of the South," died prematurely because he was denied medical treatment when he needed it; and Chief of Staff Lo Ruiqing broke a leg jumping from a window while under political interrogation, an "accident" that shortened his life. Experiences like this must have changed the pragmatists' attitude toward the rule of law from a political preference to a burning conviction.

Mao Zedong's opposition to reliance on law was not weakened by the Cultural Revolution. If it had been otherwise, China would not have had to wait three years after his death for a code of laws to come into effect.

The poster *Concerning Socialist Democracy and a Legal System*, which appeared in Canton in 1973–1974 signed Li Yizhe, and the interest displayed in it by the public had provided evidence that the Cultural Revolution had driven home to many people, far outside the leadership of the Party, the need for a legal system to safeguard democracy.

That poster had argued that the Cultural Revolution had not accomplished its aims, "because it has not enabled the people to hold firmly the weapon of an extensive democracy." It had claimed that in recent years there had been a "total rejection of the rule of law" and hundreds and thousands of cases had been framed against innocent people, and it attributed the lack of democracy to the fact that China "has been transformed into a socialist society directly from a semi-feudal, semi-colonial society. The feudal rule which continued for more than two thousand years has left its ideology deeply rooted."

The authors said that their earlier drafts had frightened some people because their themes of democracy and a legal system had once been raised by rightists in the Hundred Flowers Campaign. They made a pro-forma dissociation of themselves from those rightists, but it is tortured and lacks conviction.

They claimed that the dictatorship of recent years had "created a reaction to itself, a newly emerged social force"—the people whose eyes had been opened to the evil practiced in the name of Marxism–Leninism–Mao Zedong Thought. They said there had been an "upsurge of the democratic spirit." "The people demand Great Democracy; they demand revolutionary rights and human rights to protect the masses of the people. What answer do they get?" Those officials "who enjoy vested interests" reply: "What? You demand democracy? You are reactionaries! Because you are reactionaries, we shall give you no democracy!" If a legal system is to bring true democracy, said the Li Yizhe group, there must be tolerance for dissent, and for wrong-headed views: "It is not always easy to distinguish between fragrant flowers and poisonous weeds, there must be a process and the distinction must be tested by time. Therefore we should not be afraid of upright and honest opponents, as long as they refrain from intrigue and conspiracy."

The people's right to manage the state and society must be guaranteed, but the authors left it to the Fourth National People's Congress, which was about to open, to decide just how this should be done.

If the authors really hoped for any safeguards for democracy from the Fourth NPC they were doomed to be disappointed. A new state Constitution that reduced the 1954 Constitution to a collection of vague generalities was adopted. Rights were canceled out by obligations and most of the paper protections of the 1954 document were simply deleted, including the existence of the procuracy. If the Li Yizhe group drew any reassurance from the congress it was on more general political grounds: the pragmatists had left a strong stamp on the policies and appointments of the congress.

The continued denial of free expression even to those like their group, who acknowledged the leadership of the Communist Party and did not challenge Marxism, was made very evident when the central authorities in Peking condemned the poster as "reactionary through and through, vicious and malicious in the extreme."[23] The members of the group were arrested and forced to stand silent on the platform at more than a hundred criticism meetings in Canton. The "masses" attending the meetings were supposed to criticize the poster, but according to Cantonese travelers arriving in Hong Kong, they showed great reluctance to do so. The group refused to submit and the following spring wrote a wall poster refuting their critics. As a result they were again arrested and this time were sentenced to forced labor. They spent much of the next three and a half years in camps, but they must have derived satisfaction from seeing their assertion that "a new social force has emerged in reaction to the dictatorship of recent years" was so amply borne out by the resistance to the Gang of Four and the demands for democracy.

One can imagine their satisfaction also at seeing so much of what they had written about the surviving influence of feudal ideology, the damage done by the worship of Mao, the shortcomings of socialist democracy, and the molding of the Party into a "ruler-vassal and father-son party" being adopted by the official press in the course of 1978, even if they were never complimented on having been right four years ahead of time.

In March 1978 the Fifth National People's Congress adopted a new state Constitution that restored some of those protections promised by the 1954 version deleted in 1975. In particular, the procuracy was restored. In his speech to the congress, Chairman Hua said: "Our Constitution lays down in clear terms the rights of the people. The organs of the state at all levels must take effective measures to ensure that the people enjoy and exercise these rights. We should gradually make and perfect our socialist laws."

In July the President of the Academy of Social Sciences made his speech to the State Council, in which he called for reliance on legally binding contracts in economic life. The official press began to prepare public opinion on the issue of the rule of law well before the Central Work Conference of November–December 1978. Speeches that Dong Biwu had made in the 1950s advocating reliance on law were republished. Articles and editorials arguing the need for a proper legal system appeared in increasing numbers. The *People's Daily* and its Special Commentator lent their authority to a forceful exposition of the principle that all injustices must be redressed, no matter on whose authority they had been committed. Publicity was given to the start that was being made on redressing past injustices inflicted by the courts, and the scale and nature of past abuse of the law was gradually acknowledged.

When the National Trades Union Conference was convened in September, Deng Xiaoping announced the introduction of a limited form of industrial democracy. At the same time, a campaign was launched to institute elections for official positions at the grass roots of rural society.

General articles on the need for "socialist democracy" began to appear in the press in the fall of 1978. The Li Yizhe group was still in prison in November 1978 when, four years after they had spread their poster along the Peking Road in Canton, the official organ of the Communist Youth League, *China Youth* monthly, adopted the heart of their message. But before the year was out they had been freed. On 6 February 1979 they were fully rehabilitated.

The *China Youth* article was a milestone on the road of China's political development. No article in an official organ of the Communist Party of China or, so far as observers could recall, any other ruling Communist Party, had ever taken such a hard look at the deficiencies of the political system the Party had established. That the same points had been made by liberal democrats and by Marxist dissidents for decades did not detract from the importance of the development.

The two young women authors of the essay, Lin Chun and Li Yinhe, were writing at a time when it was still not acceptable to criticize Mao himself, so they spoke only of the evil done by Lin Biao and the Gang of Four;

> The disaster created by Lin Biao and the Gang of Four has made people think once again. With feelings of deep suffering, the people cannot help but reflect: How could the Gang of Four have run amok in such a way over the past several years? Why were the Chinese people tolerant of them? They were obviously the most evil criminals in Chinese history as they damaged inner-party democracy and people's democracy, trampled upon the legal system, persecuted revolutionary cadres and people, and led socialist China onto the path of a counter-revolutionary comeback. However, although the Gang of Four and their followers seized surprisingly great power, there were only a handful of them. Why couldn't the hundreds of millions of our people have exposed and overthrown them in time to prevent such a disaster and safeguard the revolutionary fruits of our decades of bloody sacrifice? Speaking of the counter-revolutionary coup d'etat of Louis Bonaparte, Marx said: "What the French people have said is not convincing: that their nation suffered a sneak attack. . . . Why was a nation of thirty-six million people put off guard and made prisoners, without resistance, by three well-dressed swindlers?" In other words: The viewpoint that advances and setbacks in history can all be attributed to or blamed on individuals cannot stand up. History cannot have occurred in vain. We have paid a high price but learned what we didn't know before. We have come to understand: The Gang of Four's emergence in the land of China had deep social and political

roots and was a product of history. The incompleteness of our laws, the imperfection of our legal system and the absence of reliable organizations and systems to safeguard socialist democracy gave Lin Biao and the Gang of Four opportunities to exploit. . . .

Only when the masses of people can truly make the final decisions on state affairs and really control their own destiny will our nation no longer be helpless before those "well-dressed swindlers"; only then will our people no longer need to worry—like children who cannot support themselves—that they might become orphans with no one to turn to because their fathers and elder brothers have left. When that time comes, the proletarian political power of our country will really be mature and consolidated.

The article reasserted the link between political democracy and the workers' ownership of the means of production, which had been submerged in China for so long.

Marx said: "Economic control of the workers by those who monopolize the means of labor—that is, the source of livelihood—is the foundation of all forms of slavery—that is, all social poverty, spiritual humiliation and political dependence." The economic liberation of the working class and other laboring people and their common possession of the means of production form the foundation of socialist democracy. The worker's real ownership in the economic field calls for corresponding democratic rights in the political field. . . . In places where there is no democracy, isn't it reasonable to look for the economic roots? *In places where people's democratic rights exist in name only, isn't it true that the worker's ownership in the economic field is in name only too?* [Emphasis added.]

Only by "concentrating the masses' experience and wisdom through democratic means" can the Party work out a line of principles and policies in the people's interests:

Since the victory of the revolution, we, in the position of the ruling party, need democracy and direct criticism from the masses more than at any time in the past. Practice has shown that, in any place, once democracy is abolished no one will dare to tell the truth and lies, boasting, and empty talk will bury and deceive us. With no one expressing any more opinions, we will be surrounded and corrupted by people who flatter and fawn upon us and sing our praises. . . .

In the spring of 1976, the Chinese people courageously rose up to the strains of the *"Internationale"* and wrote an extremely heroic, sad, and moving page in the history of the Chinese revolution, fully displaying the power of people's democracy. The incident provided an unprecedented education to the people. It taught us that using the methods of extensive democracy to expose and criticize careerists and conspirators like Lin Biao and the Gang of Four is the people's inalienable right and sacred duty.

Could it be that our people have followed the Communist Party in Revolution for decades only to have a bunch of new "overlords" sitting on their backs? . . .

Although the victory of the Chinese revolution has long since changed the Chinese people's historic destiny, traditional ideology still often entangles the people's minds like a lingering bad dream, and many people still cannot lift up their heads and stand up straight. When the Chinese nation was in its darkest period, Lü Xun bitterly pointed out: The Chinese people are so "lifeless" under the system of dictatorship. Only revolution and socialist democracy can fundamentally change the mental outlook of the people of our country and stimulate and mobilize the entire nation.

Marx cited a cautionary passage from *Paris Revolutionary Weekly* that was printed during the French Revolution: "Great men look so great because we ourselves are kneeling. Stand up!"[24]

We have already seen how, in the weeks that followed, young people rose from their knees one after another to make their criticisms of Mao on Democracy Wall and then went on to broader criticism and demands for freedom and justice. The language and ideas of the *China Youth* article could be found again in the posters of the strongest critics of the status quo, like Wei Jingsheng. It was as if two groups were calling to each other across an alpine valley. From one side came the voice of the reform group in the Party leadership, carried across the open space by the official press. On the other side, the voices of Democracy Wall took up the theme, developed it, and challenged the leadership to take it further. Sometimes the leadership accepted the challenge, sometimes it did not.

Behind the closed doors of the Central Work Conference, the issue was being dealt with both as a subject for argument and a focus for power play. The Chief Procurator gave his blunt assessment of the legacy of abuse and ignorance existing in his field. He complained of the lack of guidance he was being given. He had offered his resignation repeatedly, but each time it had been refused. The Politburo member who had been in charge of legal work, Ji Dengkui, was accused of having been "the root" of fighting and looting in his home Henan province during the Cultural Revolution and was reportedly stripped of responsibility for legal work. A beneficiary of the Cultural Revolution, Ji was not loved by the supporters of Deng Xiaoping, who had their own man in mind to take charge of this work. He was Peng Zhen, the former number five in the Party hierarchy and Mayor of Peking, who had encouraged and protected critics of Mao like Wu Han, the playwright, and Deng Tuo, the essayist, before being struck down in the Cultural Revolution.

The path along which he would lead legal work was officially signposted by the Central Committee which met after the Work Conference. It gave its official endorsement to the campaign for democracy and the rule of law. The communiqué it approved contained this passage:

> In order to safeguard people's democracy, it is imperative to strengthen the socialist legal system so that democracy is systematized and written into law in such a way as to ensure the stability, continuity, and full authority of this democratic system and these laws; there must be laws for people to follow, these laws must be observed, their enforcement must be strict, and law-breakers must be dealt with. From now on, legislative work should have an important place on the agenda of the National People's Congress and its Standing Committee.

In political circles Peng's name was associated with the cause of "socialist legality." It was he who twenty-two years before had laid a draft criminal code before the National People's Congress, only to see it swept aside by the antirightist drive. Before the Cultural Revolution, he had been in charge of legal and security work in the party secretariat. His advocacy of socialist legality had been used against him in the Cultural Revolution.

On 28 December 1978, Peng was flown back to Peking from his long exile in the Chining mountains of Shaanxi province. It was twelve years since he had been taken from Peking under arrest, having failed in his attempt to block the Cultural Revolution from the city. His return to the capital was unpublished because his rehabilitation had not yet been announced, but several hundred old colleagues, friends, and relatives went to the airport to greet him. Even for a tough seventy-six-year-old survivor of Nationalist jail and the Civil War, this must have been an emotional moment. Among those gathered to greet him were widows and orphans of friends who had died in the Cultural Revolution. There too were old colleagues who had survived persecution to be rehabilitated.

Peng grasped one of the survivors by the ears and tugged them, asking: "How are those ears, then?" The ears, which had not worked well for many years, belonged to Liu Yong, who had held responsibility for legal affairs in the capital when Peng was Mayor. Eight weeks later, an announcement was made that must have given great satisfaction to both men: Peng was appointed director of a newly created commission on legislative affairs of the National People's Congress. Within a few months he brought before the congress a criminal code that was a descendant of the one he had presented in 1957. As he pointed out to the Congress with unmistakable irony, the 1957 draft had been the twenty-second and the 1979 version was based on the thirty-third, which had been discussed by the Politburo standing committee in 1963, when he was still a member of that select body. The 1979 Congress adopted the criminal code and six other laws governing the courts, the procuracy, local government, elections for people's congresses, criminal procedure, and joint ventures with foreign business partners.

The new laws concerning the National People's Congress, and the status given it by the 1978 state Constitution, have not created a sovereign parliament. Article 2 of the 1978 state Constitution states that "The Communist Party of China is the core of leadership of the whole Chinese people. The working class exercises leadership over the state through its vanguard, the Communist Party of China." The Constitution also states that the guiding ideology of the People's Republic of China is Marxism–Leninism–Mao Zedong Thought. Even as a consultative and legislative body the NPC is rather unwieldy, for the new organic law states that the deputies "shall not exceed 3500 persons." For discussions between plenary sessions it divides into regional groups and a military group. Its potential as a voice of the people is further limited by the fact that the deputies are elected not directly but by the province-level congresses that are themselves elected by county-level congresses. Only at the county level and below are congresses elected directly by adult suffrage with secret ballot.

The provincial and local congresses have been somewhat strengthened in dealing with the central authorities under their new organic law as compared with that of 1954.

The new criminal code does not separate law from politics. One of its sections that has attracted most attention, because of its effect on political expression, is that which deals with counter-revolution. The Hong Kong left-wing journal *Cheng Ming* commented that neither the "Stalin" constitution of the USSR nor the criminal codes of capitalist countries defined a crime of counter-revolution, and to do so in the new Chinese law was a mistake. The journal pointed out that this had led to very vague wording. For instance, Article 90 defines counter-revolutionary offenses as "those for the purpose of overthrowing the political power of the dictatorship of the proletariat and the socialist system and jeopardizing the People's Republic of China." *Cheng Ming* commented that the concepts of the dictatorship of the proletariat and the socialist system are subjects of controversy among theoreticians and there is no universally accepted definition of them.[25]

At the NPC, a professor from Liaoning University argued for adding to the criminal law a clause that would make it illegal to define ideological and political problems as counter-revolutionary offenses. In an interview with the New China News Agency, the Vice-Minister of Public Security, Ling Yun, summed up the ambiguities of the law on this question: "We are firmly against resolving ideological questions and the problem of dissidence by judicial or administrative means. . . . However, those guilty of counter-revolutionary offenses must be convicted as such. It is wrong to describe them as 'dissidents.' "[26]

The Organic Law of People's Courts lays down that the courts "exercise their judicial authority independently and are only subordinated to the law." But their independence is limited by the fact that the judges are to be appointed and removed by local people's congresses which both constitutionally and in practice are under the leadership of the Communist Party.

The principle that everyone is equal before the law is asserted but is qualified to accord with the current practices of Chinese political life, as this explanation published by the *People's Daily* shows: "In our law we never say that everyone is entitled to equal rights. We take away the political rights of counter-revolutionaries, major criminals, and other exploiting elements who have not reformed themselves well."[27]

The article concerning the supply of "intelligence" to "the enemy" is as vague and sweeping as the section on counter-revolutionaries. In both cases, a very great deal will depend on precedents established by the courts and on the political climate. Commentaries published in Hong Kong and overseas on the conviction of Wei Jingsheng as a counter-revolutionary showed that the outcome of his trial had increased rather than diminished the concern expressed when the law was published.

The criminal code and the law on criminal procedure make very clear that the accused has the right to defend himself or to call on a lawyer to do so. Reasonable procedures are laid down for arrest and investigation, but it remains to be seen whether the pretrial investigation will be treated as just that or as the decisive test of guilt or innocence. The procedure is not based on a presumption of innocence.

So we see serious ambiguities in the new laws, and no grand strategy for a democratic revolution has been announced. Let us not be fooled, say the "realists," all this talk of law and democracy flows from the ignorant daydreams of young Chinese and the cynical manipulation of their Communist leaders, intent on duping their own people as well as gullible foreigners.

But if we look more closely we see that no extravagant claims have been made on behalf of the new laws. They are not presented as a fully developed system that will usher in a new era of democracy and the rule of law. Speaking to the NPC, Peng Zhen said:

> The laws to be examined and approved by the present session, and their subsequent enforcement, will make a big step in the

strengthening and perfection of our socialist legal system. Even greater tasks lie ahead. As our economic construction progresses, we shall enact a variety of economic and other laws on the basis of systematic investigation and study and thus gradually perfect our socialist legal system. The strengthening of the socialist legal system will inevitably involve sharp and complicated struggles to break down all kinds of resistance and obstruction put up by feudalism, capitalism, revisionism, and remnants of the factional setup of the Gang of Four.

Although no blueprint for a new age has been ballyhooed, if one puts the pieces of the jigsaw puzzle together a pattern emerges, and a strategy can be discerned.

After the congress a massive campaign to educate officials and the public on the need for law and the content of the new laws was launched. Colleges of politics and law and faculties of law in universities were reopened. An eight-year plan for the study of law was adopted, including many publications for both the general and specialist reader. Crash courses for officials were organized. A ministry of justice was established. The system of people's lawyers was revived and lawyers' associations re-established after almost a quarter of a century. Peng Zhen announced a decision to make a transfusion of fresh blood into the security forces. Those to be drafted would include experienced officials from other areas of work who had shown themselves to be "fair and honest" and new graduates from the revived system of legal education.* A law journal was published again. The Ministry of Public Security sponsored a conference on pretrial work at which attention was drawn to the need to bring pretrial

* The need for this was vividly illustrated by an article published in the unofficial journal *Exploration*, before the new laws were promulgated. The author of the article alleges that in a Peking reception station located in a former prison, now known as Virtue Forest No. 1, people were detained incommunicado indefinitely, without being brought to trial. The author quotes a prison official as telling prisoners: "Because you made trouble, you have been asked to come here to be suppressed. . . . We have arrested you according to the reports of various units, which are responsible for any erroneous arrests. We undertake no responsibility." One prisoner answered back: "I protest. Our newspapers have all publicized the constitution and the legal system. Haven't you heard about it?" The alleged response was: "We have five squadrons of a thousand policemen. We live by arresting people. Acting on orders from above, we must carry out our duties. Papers are propaganda media which live on propaganda. We are rail cars running on two different tracks."

arrest and investigation "into the orbit of socialist democracy and the socialist legal system." The courts continue their work of redressing past miscarriages of justice.

This Herculean labor fits into the work, now in hand, of drafting laws for industry, finance, and commerce. These in turn lock into economic reforms that give more freedom to individual enterprises and small groups of people running farms or businesses (see Chapter 15). A new reliance on market forces in economic decision-making is paralleled by a new readiness to trust the judgment of the public to sift the good from the bad in cultural life. In the sciences there is a new freedom of academic debate. Government is publishing statistics that have been classified for decades and the press shows a new interest in facts and a new aggression in exposing official incompetence, stupidity, and abuse of power. The philosophy of "seeking truth from facts," without which neither laws nor democracy can function, has begun to take hold. All these interlocking changes tend to diminish the area in which arbitrary political decisions can be imposed.

Even the centerpiece of the puzzle to which all the others must be joined, political democracy, is slowly—very slowly—taking shape. Of course this is the most difficult piece of all to fashion just because it relates to all the others. Much uncertainty remains: the counter-revolution sections of the new criminal code could be used to repress any criticism of the Party and its officials and there has been no hint of abandoning the "dictatorship of the proletariat" or of legitimizing factions within the Communist Party, let alone allowing the noncommunist parties to regain an identity of their own. Yet important developments are already visible.

The use being made of the martyrdom of Zhang Zhixin shows that the reformers are painfully aware of the disastrous effect on the Party itself, as well as the nation, of an absence of political democracy. They have exposed the "immaturity" and shortcomings of socialist democracy saying that in its own terms, bourgeois democracy is more effective. They have legitimized dissatisfaction with China's present political system and created an expectation of democratic reform that goes beyond the very limited steps taken so far. They have reminded the nation that democratic rights have to be won through struggle. If a ruler bestows them as a favor, wrote the editors of the *People's Daily*, he can withdraw them again. Everyone in China knows that is what happened to the Red Guards in the Cultural Revolution. So much has been said by the official press about the achievements of "bourgeois democracy" in overcoming "feudalism" that it is reasonable to expect that the reformers will continue to adopt features of bourgeois democracy to assist them in overcoming the feudal attitudes and practices they say still exist in China.

There is such an accumulation of past bitterness in China and so much evidence of a new readiness on the part of the people to shape events that only very foolish men would engage in a cynical manipulation of the slogan of democracy. To arouse the expectations that have been aroused if there were no intention of satisfying them would be the height of folly. And those leaders who are pushing the reform program in China today are not fools. But the history of earlier reform movements warns them that in a country the size of China, with strong feudal traditions and many conservatives in the ranks of officialdom, no leadership can conjure up a democratic revolution with a few pieces of masterly legislation. That kind of paper revolution has been tried before and has failed before in this century. In the last years of the Manchu emperors, and in the chaotic years of the Republic which followed, attempts were repeatedly made to graft foreign-inspired laws and democratic institutions onto Chinese society.* Some attempted too radical a break with contemporary reality, some were thwarted by the anarchy of the times, and others were swept aside by authoritarian rulers.

The brief, inglorious lives of parliamentary constitutions be-

---

* In the last years of the Qing dynasty a draft criminal code was put forward that was based on Japanese and German models, and would have distinguished law from morality. A less drastic reform was actually adopted and remained in force from 1910 to 1928. In the Republic that succeeded the Qing a great deal of compilation and codification of law was done. The overthrow of the Qing dynasty in 1911 was, of course, intended to open the way for democracy and the rule of law, and constitutions were promulgated in 1912, 1914, and 1928.

queathed by Britain to her African colonies for their independence shows how futile it is to attempt too much too quickly. The blocking of Khrushchev's reforms in the Soviet Union when they were only halfway down the road shows how important it is to have a carefully prepared, systematic approach. The fate of Dubček in Czechoslovakia was a reminder of the need for hard-nosed calculation of the strength of the opposition. The impetuosity of Khrushchev and the heroic naïveté of Dubček made exciting reading in our newspapers but were fatal to their reforms. For China to attempt to leap to democracy in one Peking spring would be suicidal.

There has been a complete reversal of the positions adopted sixty years ago by those Chinese intellectuals who favored an evolutionary approach to reform and those who wanted sweeping transformation. In 1919, Hu Shi, the spokesman for evolution, said: "Civilization was not created *in toto* but by inches and drops . . . there is no liberation *in toto* or reform *in toto*. Liberation means the liberation of this or that system, or this or that idea, or of this or that individual: it is reform by inches and drops. The first step in the recreation of civilization is the study of this or that problem."[28]

Li Dazhao, co-founder of the Communist Party, replied: "It is first necessary to have a fundamental solution, and then there will be hope of solving concrete problems one by one. Take Russia as an example. If the Romanovs had not been overthrown and the economic organization not reformed, no problems could have been solved. Now they are all being solved."[29]

After thirty years in power, China's Communist leaders acknowledge publicly that the problems are not all being solved—in China any more than in the Soviet Union, or anywhere else. So they have adopted a strategy that is evolutionary. There are six reasons why it stands a good chance of being sustained.

First, the goals of democracy and legality are being pursued by a powerful combination of the dominant group in the Party and a large segment of public opinion. Second, there exists a degree of order and stability in society which did not exist when attempts were made earlier in this century. Third, the gradual reform of institutions (governmental, judicial, and economic) is being combined with a campaign to inculcate values essential to democracy (respect for reason, for scientific enquiry, for principled dissent, for law and for the judgment of the marketplace; rejection of dogma and the deification of men). Fourth, the new movement is not drawn forward by romantic dreams or abstract notions but driven by bitter, recent experience and the sober realization that without some freedom, some democracy, and some law China will not escape from poverty and stagnation. Fifth, China is in touch with its own past again and so can draw on the strength of its own traditions, which, contrary to popular misconception, do include a tradition of law. Sixth, China is opening itself to a multitude of influences from liberal democracies which will tend to reinforce the strategy, not with a fanfare of trumpets but through the incremental influence of thousands of working relationships between people and institutions in every field.

To effect a transition from tyranny to a measure of democracy is surely the most perilous operation of statecraft. To do so in a nation of one billion people who have been governed by a Communist Party for thirty years is a test of statesmanship that has had few parallels in history.

The reform-minded Chinese leadership of the 1980s has to deal with a formidable array of conflicting forces and avoid all kinds of pitfalls. There is a metaphor current in China now to describe the political situation: "the two ends are hot and the middle is cold"—there is an ardent desire for change at the top of the Chinese hierarchy and among "the masses" but middle-level officials are, on the whole, cool to the idea. As Chinese readily admit, the situation is more complex than this handy summary indicates, because in China as anywhere else the top leadership includes people with a range of temperaments and different degrees of enthusiasm for reform.

Another set of difficulties is indicated by the fact that the opinions expressed during the two major periods of free speech since 1949, the Hundred Flowers campaign and the winter of 1978–1979, showed both the continuing hold of liberal-democratic values over the minds of many educated Chinese and the respect among the younger generation for the material achievements and the high level of personal freedom in capitalist countries. This is really rather awkward in a Marxist–Leninist state, and there is no reason to think that the party line that "bourgeois democracy" is a fraud and the workers of America are suffering terrible agonies because of the cost of running their cars or meeting mortgage payments on their privately owned homes is going to start convincing the young of China, now that windows onto the real world are being opened, when it has failed to convince them in the past. The statistics for legal and illegal emigration to Hong Kong, the United States, and other capitalist societies show that many Chinese workers are only too eager to start sharing the miseries of their exploited brothers and sisters overseas.

Moreover, it would be only reasonable to assume that the conflict between the impulses to liberate and control is, of course, not only an external one between competing opinion groups but also exists within the minds of the reform-minded leaders, who have spent their lives building up a highly authoritarian party and state.

If the leadership sets too fast a pace of change, it risks unleashing disorder from that ample reservoir of people who nurse grievances against the Party from the past, then revolt by the conservative middle ranks whose security in power is threatened by disorder. If the pace of change is too slow, the momentum for reform will be lost. The results of that would be catastrophic: rapidly worsening economic prospects for an enormous population and, at some stage, outright revolt by a people whose patience is finally exhausted.

With so many conflicting considerations to be balanced, it is not surprising that there have already been stops and starts in the progress of reform. There will be others.

If a lasting transition from tyranny is to be made, some degree of political pluralism must be allowed to develop, perhaps by tolerating the existence of factions within the Communist Party as is done in the Liberal Democratic Party of Japan. The slow-motion and nonvituperative manner in which the Whatever Faction, who dragged their feet over Deng's return to office in 1977 and opposed some of his reform, were removed from power in 1980 may have inaugurated an era of greater restraint in dealing with high-level political opponents.

If the demands for freedom are to be satisfied in any real measure, then the dictatorship of the proletariat will have to be relaxed as the body of law grows and its authority is more respected. As China moves along the political spectrum away from dictatorship and toward democracy, it will be useful to remember that the pragmatic side of the Chinese spirit has a special talent for changing the reality behind a hallowed phrase: the signboards of the "Dictatorship of the Proletariat" may, for political reasons, maintain their place in official doctrine while the policies applied in its name are changed. Whatever system the Chinese develop, it will certainly not be a carbon copy of anyone else's. But that has always been true in the migration of the idea of democracy. Moving from ancient Athens and Rome to the Europe of recent centuries and thence to America and the Anglo-Saxon dominions, to India, Japan, and Israel, it has always been shaped by the culture of its new hosts and taken on a somewhat different form.

The roots of China's present attempt to civilize her political system lie not only in the bitter memories of the Cultural Revolution and old men's nostalgia for the unity of the Party and people they knew in Yanan, but also in the long history of Chinese civilization. If the reformers succeed, they will have proved themselves to be worthy sons of the Yellow Emperor, the mythical founder of their race.

14

Opening to the World

Between the people of China and the people of the United States there are strong ties of sympathy, understanding, and mutual interest. Both are essentially democratic and individualistic. Both are by nature peace-loving, nonaggressive, and nonimperialistic.

America and China complement each other economically: they will not compete. China does not have the requirements of a heavy industry of major size. She cannot hope to meet the United States in its highly specialized manufactures. America needs an export market for her heavy industry and these specialized manufactures. She also needs an outlet for capital investment.

China needs to build up light industries to supply her own market and raise the living standards of her own people. Eventually she can supply these goods to other countries in the Far East. To help pay for this foreign trade and investment, she has raw materials and agricultural products.

America is not only the most suitable country to assist this economic development of China: she is also the only country fully able to participate.

For these reasons there must not and cannot be any conflict, estrangement, or misunderstanding between the Chinese people and America.

—MAO ZEDONG TO JOHN S. SERVICE
13 MARCH 1945[1]

I HAD LEFT PEKING in January 1970 convinced that nothing was more debilitating to China than her isolation from the international community. To end that isolation would be a revolution as important as that carried through when the Communist Party came to power in 1949. In my last year in Peking there had been signs that the Chinese leadership was preparing to break out of that isolation. The international situation, on balance, favored such an attempt. In the 1950s, diplomatic and economic isolation had in large measure been imposed on China by the many governments opposed to the Chinese Communist regime. By 1970 these governments had grown more flexible, and skillful diplomacy by China could probably induce them to establish friendly relations. Mao Zedong and Zhou Enlai were prepared to make the attempt.

In the six years that followed a great deal was indeed done to build bridges to foreign countries. Diplomatic relations were established with many nations, official visits were exchanged, the People's Republic occupied the China seat at the United Nations and in its agencies. New political relationships were launched with the U.S. and Japan.

All this was important for establishing the direction of Chinese foreign policy. A good deal of the activity was formal or purely political, but essential if substantive relationships were to be developed. Some substance was developed. Between the year I left, 1970, and the year of my return, 1976, foreign trade trebled from a low base. China made large purchases of foreign plant and equipment. The most remarkable contract was signed in Britain for the purchase of Spey engines and engine-manufacturing technology; this was the first time China had bought defense-related equipment and technology abroad since the break with the Soviet Union.

However, there was little immediate impact on the life of the ordinary citizen, and often the initial formalities were not followed up with any vigor or imagination. In some areas, such as culture and education, the development was not just limited, it was minuscule.

The trouble was that Zhou and the other pragmatists who wanted to develop foreign relations had run into political oppo-

sition at home. First, Mao's designated successor, Marshal Lin
Biao, had opposed the moves toward the United States. When
that obstacle was overcome, the pragmatists were foiled by
Maoist distrust of foreigners. In 1968, as the Soviet Union became more powerful and bolder in using its power and the
cutting edge of U.S. power was blunted by reverses in Vietnam,
Mao had recognized that China's security would best be served
by developing better relations with the U.S., Japan, and Western
Europe. But he allowed his leftist followers to block measures
to give content to those relations. The Maoists made a fetish of
self-reliance and described the policy of importing high-
technology plant, including that for producing desperately
needed chemical fertilizer, as "capitulation and national betrayal."

They were not simply trying to thwart an opposing faction.
For a hundred years before the Communists came to power,
Chinese had disputed among themselves the proper role of foreign ideas, trade, and technology in the strategy for modernization. In the 1890s conservatives had opposed opening China to
the world because they feared this would destroy the Confucian
essence of Chinese civilization. In the 1970s conservatives
warned that the revolution of Marxism–Leninism and Mao
Zedong Thought would be undermined if doors were opened.
Little has been disclosed about the relationship between the
Four and Mao on this issue, but we know enough of Mao's
distrust of Westernized Chinese intellectuals, his disinterest in
Western technology, and his general fears that the revolution
was about to be undermined to see that it would not have been
difficult for the Four to play on the conservative side of his mind
to elicit his opposition to proposals for closer economic and
social relations with capitalist countries. Mao was probably content if foreigners would follow his guidance and oppose the
Soviet Union.

As Zhou's strength ebbed from him in his last illness, he
could not muster the political support to overcome this Maoist
opposition.

On my return to China in 1976, I watched in dismay as the
Gang of Four, exploiting their ascendancy after Zhou's death,
set about the disruption of such relations as had been devel-

oped. The level of foreign trade declined for the first time since the Cultural Revolution. Negotiations with foreign suppliers of plant and equipment stalled. The shrewd and highly experienced Minister of Foreign Trade, Li Qiang, switched the emphasis of his policy to buying foreign food grain, which was less objectionable to the Four than purchases of advanced technology.

When the Four were arrested the way was opened to a resumption of normal relations. Chairman Hua Guofeng's loyalty to Maoist policies did not extend to an antipathy toward foreigners. But the first year after the Fall of the Four saw only one diplomatic spectacular, the visit of President Tito, and Mao himself had issued the invitation before his death; the reluctance had been on Tito's side.

If major new initiatives were to be taken to give substance to China's relations with capitalist countries, all kinds of Gordian knots would have to be cut, taboos broken, prejudices confronted, and advances made into previously "forbidden zones." Only a man of extraordinary self-confidence and strength could lead such an onslaught on tradition and the *status quo*. Lesser men would remember how, only four years before, a Minister of Foreign Trade had been removed from office for daring to suggest that Chinese industry could not be successfully modernized without joint ventures with foreign companies.

By the spring of 1978 Deng Xiaoping had achieved a position where he could set in train a series of foreign-policy initiatives that would make the next twelve months the most creative, sophisticated, and confident period of diplomacy China had ever known, and within those twelve months the Chinese people would see how the new activism could enliven and enrich their lives.

There was nothing mysterious or inscrutable about this diplomacy. Nor was it based on a thirst for recognition of China's importance or a desire to reshape the world in its image. Its goals of strengthening China's security and aiding her social and economic development were abundantly clear. It was the work of hard-headed men who knew where power and true strength lay in the world and were determined to make a reality of the old slogan "make foreign things serve China." But it was not just

based on a cold-blooded calculation of China's interests. It was
also based on trust: trust in the Chinese people and trust in
foreigners. The Chinese leaders believed that if their people
were exposed to the dynamic and materially successful societies
of Japan and the West they would be stirred into life, galvanized
into a great effort of nation-building. The agreements made with
these capitalist societies were based on trust because they would
open China's doors to foreign ideas, people, capital, and technology and would involve sending Chinese abroad in numbers
unprecedented in the thirty years of Communist rule. It was no
accident that the driving force behind this strategy for inter-
dependence with the outside world, Deng Xiaoping, had chosen
to go to France at the age of sixteen and had spent six years
there.

The Chinese leaders reached out in many directions, but first
across the East China Sea, in February 1978, to conclude an
eight-year trade agreement with Japan, their foremost trading
partner. This was designed to exploit the complementary
characteristics of the two neighboring economies: Japan is rich
in the skills, foreign exchange, and capital equipment needed to
exploit China's abundant natural resources. Combining the
strengths of the two economies would put to good use China's
embarrassing abundance of low-wage labor. This agreement established a model for others to come. It implemented the ideas
Deng had put into the Three Poisonous Weeds, such as using
deferred payments for importing capital equipment and paying
for equipment with product. It stretched the period for repay-
ment and extended the use of deferred payments into new
fields. These and other technical arrangements in the agreement
could not have been included if the Chinese side had not been
prepared to trust its foreign partner to a degree it had trusted
nobody since the break with the Soviet Union.

In August, Deng negotiated the historic Sino-Japanese
Treaty of Peace and Friendship in which Japan joined China in
undertaking to resist hegemony, a code word for the Soviet
Union. In the autumn Deng paid the most important visit to
Japan by any Chinese leader in the history of the two countries.
Ever since Japan had defeated China militarily in 1895, Chinese

reformers had looked with respect and envy upon the modernization of their neighbor. Deng paid tribute to the achievements of the Japanese and set the seal upon a new policy of explicitly learning from them. He was received by the Emperor with the honors due a head of state.

Next China reached out to Western Europe. For years, relations with the countries of the European Communities had been correct and courteous but very limited in substance. European heads of government had come to China and Deng had visited France in 1975, but there was little to relations apart from trade. In 1978–1980 that situation changed dramatically, with the negotiation of agreements on commercial, scientific, technological, educational, and cultural exchanges. More controversially, China made it plain that it wanted Western Europe to become, in addition, a major supplier of military hardware. This intention was dramatized in the autumn of 1977 when the first high-level Chinese military delegation toured France, the first such visit to an industrialized democracy since 1949. Thereafter talks were opened with France and other Western European nations for the supply of antitank aircraft and communications equipment. However, after the Politburo announced in 1979 a period of economic "readjustment" that entailed a substantial reduction of large-scale purchases abroad, it became clear that the talks would not lead to the signing of major contracts in the near future.

The seeds of a relationship with Western European nations were sown in other parts of the security field. Western European naval ships called at Chinese ports for the first time since the Communists came to power. Visits were exchanged between military staff colleges. The shortcomings of the Chinese armed forces in terms of equipment and training were deliberately disclosed to very senior European officers recently retired from their national armed forces.

These overtures to Western Europe, like the economic and political agreements with Japan, were proof of a new spirit of trust and openness to foreigners. Few relationships assume a greater readiness to work together over the long term than those in the fields of arms supply and military training.

The French and British response was to emphasize the need for a balanced relationship in which civilian trade would far outweigh military items. These and other West European governments proceeded with caution to avoid unnecessary damage to their relations with the Soviet Union, but it became evident that Britain at least would not grant the Soviets the right of veto they sought over this aspect of Sino–West European relations.

China grew increasingly bold in its relations with Yugoslavia and Romania. An agreement with Tito to re-establish relations between the Communist parties of Yugoslavia and China was no empty gesture. It was followed by visits to Yugoslavia by scores of Chinese groups studying almost every aspect of life there. Not since the 1950s had the Chinese leadership permitted its people to study another country in such depth. In return Yugoslav delegations toured China, explaining to ordinary Chinese how life runs in Yugoslavia, including the unique system of economic democracy. Incredulous Chinese workers in the bleak oilfields of Daqing heard Yugoslav trade unionists explain that their factory managers could be voted out of office by the work force if they did not give satisfaction. The same trade unionists forecast to workers in a Shanghai factory that they would soon live in a system where decisions on what goods the factory should produce would come from consumers, through their purchasing choices, instead of from bureaucrats in the Department of Light Industry. They were startled to hear their audience burst into applause at this prediction. A taste for the "Yugoslav Model" was not confined to young intellectuals. One of the best-received Central Documents of 1978 conveyed the Party Center's plainly stated view that there was much to be learned from Yugoslavia.

One aspect of Yugoslav economic policy that received particular attention was the system of joint ventures with foreign companies. When the National People's Congress passed "The Law of the PRC on Joint Ventures Using Chinese and Foreign Investment" Chinese commentators quoted the Yugoslav experience in support of the measure. (One hundred sixty-four cooperation agreements between Yugoslav and foreign enterprises were signed in the years 1967 to 1977, with an aggregate investment of $1.45 billion, 22 percent of which was foreign exchange.)[2] Romania's foreign economic policy was also of interest to China, for it had established joint companies with capitalist nations.

Of course there was a strategic dimension to China's growing friendship with these two Balkan socialist states. China supported their assertion of independence from Moscow in foreign policy and Yugoslavia's role in the nonaligned movement. President Ceausescu had followed Tito to Peking at a few month's interval and Hua Guofeng returned the visits in August 1978. Soviet commentators waxed indignant when Hua's Romanian and Yugoslav hosts permitted him to make thinly veiled attacks on Soviet foreign policy from their soil.

As China built a new relationship with relatively liberal Yugoslavia, relations with Yugoslavia's illiberal little neighbor, Albania, went into decline. The new Chinese strategy in domestic and world affairs was anathema to the Albanian leadership, which denounced China's reconciliation with "revisionist" Yugoslavia and the U.S.

As Tito walked on Tiananmen Square in 1977, Albanian diplomats had scurried around Peking delivering to diplomats and journalists copies of a pamphlet entitled "Khrushchev Kneels before Tito" that reprinted an article, first published twenty years before, to attack Khrushchev's own reconciliation with Tito. It was a colorful piece of propaganda work and accurately anticipated China's interest in Yugoslav worker self-management but only served to hasten Albania's march to isolation. In July 1978, after enduring a year of attacks by Albania without making public reply, China printed its side of the story and cut off aid to the little Balkan state. So long as the Albanians did not invite the Soviet Union to revive a once-intimate relationship, the Chinese leadership was glad to be rid of "friends" whose repressive rule was an embarrassment.

The swings and roundabouts in China's relations with Yugoslavia and Albania were mirrored in Southeast Asia. Nations that had once had reason to fear a China bent on subversion—Thailand, Singapore, the Philippines, and Malaysia—were now offered the hand of friendship, while Vietnam became the chief enemy in the region. In relations with these free-enterprise countries of Southeast Asia, considerations of strategic security were not the only operative factors: in addition, the Chinese leaders intended that the many skilled and wealthy Overseas Chinese entrepreneurs in these countries should contribute to China's economic development through commercial joint ventures and trade and hoped overseas Chinese intellectuals would lend their skills in such fields as education and medicine.

The greatest achievement of Chinese diplomacy in 1978, and one that will do much to make China a secure and relatively open country in the long term, was the agreement to normalize relations with the United States. No decision required more self-confidence on the part of the Chinese leaders who favored this step. The issue at the heart of the negotiations was the future of Taiwan. To reach agreement, concessions had to be made by China as much as by the U.S., although this was largely overlooked by foreign commentators. There were two crucial concessions by the Chinese: first, they made it abundantly clear that they would seek a *peaceful* "return of Taiwan to the Motherland" and would not force socialism on the island. It seemed that their refusal to give a specific assurance not to use force was based on a need to guard against any possible Soviet interference. The second Chinese concession was to go ahead with normalization even though the U.S. had made it plain that it would continue to ensure that Taiwan received arms after revocation of the formal defense treaty with the Republic of China.

Either of these two concessions would have been used by the Four to accuse Deng of betraying the nation and the revolution, if they had been around to do so. It is not beyond the bounds of possibility that the Whatever Faction would have liked to do so if they could. But Deng, the tough old campaigner, timed his negotiations with Ambassador Leonard Woodcock of the U.S. Liaison Office in Peking in such a way as to minimize this possibility. The crucial concessions by China were made immediately after the pragmatists' resounding victory over the Whatever Faction at the Central Work Conference in November–December 1978. He brought the negotiations into their most delicate phase when the denunciations of Wang Dongxing, Wu De, Chen Xilian, and Ji Dengkui were still ringing in the delegates' ears and poster attacks on Deng's opponents were in their crescendo. The intimate relationship between Chinese foreign policy and domestic politics has never been more clearly demonstrated.

The path to normalization had been prepared with energy and skill by the Chinese and United States governments. The two-way flow of invited visitors had been increased geometrically and the visitors selected and wooed in such a way as to give a wide range of interest groups in both countries a glimpse of what they stood to gain by better relations. The underlying theme was "Look what we can do to our mutual advantage now! Think what more we could do after normalization!" Key leaders of the U.S. Congress were involved in the process and became one channel for communicating with the American public, particularly on the key question of Taiwan.

In 1978 the Chinese leaders decided to make a massive increase in the number of students who would go abroad to study. A target figure of ten thousand a year was established. Here was another example of the leadership going open-eyed into a situation fraught with risks and requiring the reversal of established practices. The great majority of these students were to go to capitalist countries, where they would see for themselves the combination of affluence and personal freedom. The cream of China's young intellectuals could no longer be expected to believe the old propaganda that capitalist countries are overwhelmed by appalling economic and social problems.

A foreign diplomat was shown a copy of the document that had been submitted to Deng Xiaoping. There, in his handwriting, was a comment, in effect: never mind if one thousand defect, the other nine thousand will come back to work for the nation. Explicit instructions were given that the students might live like any other foreign students in the host countries: in campus dormitories, halls of residence, or off-campus rented accommodations, as appropriate. Previously Chinese had, wherever possible, been housed in separate groups where they could control each other.

Since some students of social science, law, and the humanities were to be sent alongside scientists, engineers, and medical students, there was no doubt that the Chinese leaders wanted their people to absorb ideas as well as technology. Of course there was no suggestion of abandoning socialist principles but, in a speech to the State Council, the President of the Academy of Social Sciences had quoted with approval Lenin's opinion that socialism could only be built on the basis of the whole inheritance of capitalist culture, using the word *culture* in a sense that included economic as well as social life.

In the autumn of 1978 a conference was held in a city of Northeast China at which senior officials at about vice-ministerial level were invited to discuss in a free-ranging way what kind of system China should have. A senior diplomat recently returned from Western Europe spoke along these lines: We should have a socialist system, but socialism as practiced in the world so far has been disappointing. There is no socialist country anywhere which has an economy as efficient as the most efficient capitalist economies. Therefore we must reform our system to take account of the strong points of the capitalist countries.

On the eve of his visit to the United States, Deng Xiaoping said: "Any country, if it wants to develop itself, must mainly rely on itself and its own potentialities. But it is also necessary to obtain capital from the developed countries [and] to learn from the experience of the developed countries."[3]

I remember that two young members of our embassy's Chinese staff, who were employed as cleaners but whose main occupation under the Gang of Four had been sleeping, suddenly came to life, like Sleeping Beauty after she had been kissed, when Peking Radio started broadcasting English lessons. I would find them bent over a transistor radio imitating the radio teacher's pronunciation of such sentences as "Down with the

Gang of Four!" Over in the French Embassy the drivers were learning to say, "A bas la bande de quatre!"

Television as well as radio was mobilized to teach English, Japanese, and French. To speak a foreign language became a source of pride instead of a cause for suspicion. In Shanghai alone some four hundred fifty thousand English textbooks were distributed for use with radio classes in 1978. The standards attained by some students of English I met were remarkable considering they had never left China or had a friend who was a native speaker. The days of Chinglish were fast ending. Flying to Peking from Canton in June 1978 I sat next to a young woman reading Advise and Consent by Allen Drury. I showed interest in her book and she told me she had just taken an exam to select those who would be sent abroad to study English. She feared that she had failed because she had prepared for the exam by reading the Chinglish of some English-language magazines published in China. "But there was none of that in the exam," she said; "the English texts were mostly from English novels by Jane Austen, Charles Dickens, and others. So I'm making up for my mistake now." The examiners had rewarded those subversive types who had studied their Jane Austen in secret defiance of Jiang Qing.

Foreign literature, banned in its entirety from bookshops by the Maoists for a decade, was published in translation again. A Chinese version of Hamlet was sold out in Peking in three hours, so great was the thirst for good foreign (as well as Chinese) writing. The cultural commissars began, very prudently, by publishing familiar classics like Shakespeare, Balzac, Dickens, and Mark Twain but then ventured into the contemporary world. A party of American publishers visiting China in 1979 learned that translations were being made of books by Herman Wouk (The Winds of War, War and Remembrance), Alex Haley (Roots), and Saul Bellow (Humboldt's Gift). In 1980, it was the turn of Dr. Kissinger: NCNA announced that the extracts from his memoirs published by Time magazine were to be translated and distributed all over China. The NCNA announcement did not reveal whether Kissinger's characterization of Mao as demonic would be expurgated or not.

One day I was walking in the traditional Yü Gardens in Shanghai with a visiting colleague from the Foreign Office in London. Music that struck my ears as familiar floated across the ornamental pond from a loudspeaker hidden in the eaves of an ornate pavilion. "That," said my colleague, "is a Bach toccata and fugue." So it was, in an arrangement played by the Canadian Brass Quintet, a witty and original group of musicians then touring China. Their tour in March 1977 was one of the first moves in the final lifting of the ban the Maoists had first imposed on Western classical music in 1966.

On billboards in the streets of Peking there appeared the ample bosom of Gina Lollobrigida, advertising a film version of *The Hunchback of Notre Dame*, and tickets were so much in demand that the black market sprawled into the roadway outside the theaters. A Japanese film about a woman sold into prostitution in Southeast Asia during World War II opened while Deng was in Japan, and the Minister of Culture took it off in response to parental outrage. But when Deng returned he put it back on, insisting that the young should know what went on in the wide world. Charlie Chaplin's *Modern Times* packed cinema houses, and military men watched the film *Patton*, once a favorite of President Nixon. The first British film to appear was *The Million Pound Note*, which tells of the adventures of that million-pound note when it blows out of the hand of its owner as he is walking to the bank.

Into Chinese theaters came foreign orchestras, drama groups, and ballet companies. Beryl Grey, the British dancer who had been born in Shanghai, brought the London Festival Ballet to dance not only a safe and jolly *Coppelia* but some erotic modern pieces that would have thrown Jiang Qing into a fit of public Puritanical horror. Onto television screens came documentaries about foreign countries made by foreigners, foreign plays in translation, and foreign films. There were other eyeopeners. For instance, on New Year's Eve 1978–1979, as I was dressing to go out I switched on television to watch a special

program that showed various provinces of China. Suddenly
scenes of Taiwan province appeared on the screen and, for the
first time since television came to China, viewers could see
downtown Taipei and, more surprisingly, a priest officiating in a
well-maintained temple. I learned later that the film had been
bought from the Taiwan tourism promotion office in Hong
Kong. When the Chinese New Year arrived a month later there
waltzed onto our television screen a beautiful young Chinese
woman in an off-the-shoulder black dress, with her long hair in a
ponytail. She and her partner were taking part, it transpired, in a
televised dance party and she was dressed to perform a Spanish
flamenco. Someone in the Broadcasting Bureau had answered
Chairman Hua's call to liberate his mind a bit. The Chairman's
reaction is not available. Such a sight, commonplace in Manila or
Bangkok, was exciting in Peking.

When Hua and Deng made their first major visits abroad
Chinese television stations broadcast daily transmissions received by satellite. This was unprecedented in China and added
enormously to the impact of their tours. For the first time
Chinese people saw their leaders being cheered by hundreds of
thousands of well-dressed Europeans living in modern blocks of
flats, being received in discreet luxury by the Emperor of Japan,
or delighting a rodeo crowd in Texas by donning a ten-gallon
hat. The public could see that, under the new leadership, China
had joined the world and had acquired successful and powerful
friends on three continents and with a variety of skin colors.
This increased the self-confidence of the ordinary Chinese as
well as respect for their leaders.

During Deng's visit to the U.S. television gave many
Chinese their first glimpse of life in an industrialised democracy,
taking viewers inside the home of an IBM executive and showing the informal ease with which a young singer like John Den-
ver would address a man of state like Deng Xiaoping. Peking
Radio's sendoff for Deng on his visit to the U.S. included a
half-hour program of American folk music that included songs
by Bob Dylan and Joan Baez.

Nineteen seventy-eight saw the start of a long-term strategy of tapping China's vast potential for earning foreign exchange from tourism. In the first year of the new policy China received slightly over a hundred thousand foreigners and six hundred thousand overseas Chinese and Chinese from Hong Kong and Macao.[4] In 1977 there had been only about twelve thousand foreign and three hundred thousand Chinese visitors. Plans for building new hotels and other facilities and training new staff were hurriedly drawn up. Overseas Chinese and foreign investment was sought. The Chinese leaders must have been as aware as anyone of the "cultural pollution" that is one of the negative aspects of tourism, but they seemed to have concluded that the Chinese people would gladly put up with some of that if it would raise their standard of living above the subsistence level.

The opening of China to mass tourism was only one corner of the field of economic relations with foreign countries into which the government led the Chinese people. Other parts of the field were strewn with mines, many of them laid in the course of China's dealings with the West and Japan in the years from 1840 to 1949.

No people in the world have a more vivid sense of the past than the Chinese. Their verbs have no tenses, and often when they speak of some thousand-year-old incident from history it is as if it happened yesterday. Mao, the revolutionary, illustrates this. Long-dead emperors lived in his mind, were the unseen companions of his days as if they were recent presidents of China. The ten-year-old daughter of a Chinese friend of mine in Hong Kong would regale my friend and me after supper with the strategems and statecraft of generals and emperors from fifteen hundred years ago as if they were our contemporaries. The record of the West and Japan in China from 1840 to 1949 is not an episode in a dusty history book.

I am proud of much of Britain's imperial record, but I can think of no more shameful episode in that record than our use of armed force to promote opium sales to China in the mid-nineteenth century. I admire much that the British and others did in Shanghai, and I used to resent the way China Travel Service guides, for years, presented only the bad side of Shanghai's history. But the dark side had been all too real. There was rapacious greed and heartless exploitation by foreigners who prided themselves on their civilization; and if some Chinese capitalists and gangsters surpassed the foreigners in evil, that does not alter the fact that the evil flourished precisely in Shanghai, a city engendered, born, and raised on a mud flat where foreigners and Chinese came together in economic union.

Capitalists have no monopoly on acts of selfishness in China, and the Chinese do not have to reach back to the 1940s for examples of abuse of economic power by foreigners. After the Soviet Union withdrew its engineers, technicians, and advisers in 1960, a campaign was launched to denounce the way the Soviet "elder brothers" allegedly had taken advantage of their Chinese "younger brothers." And earlier, while the "fraternal" Chinese Communist Party was still fighting for power, the Soviets took advantage of their entry into Manchuria to fight the Japanese (for the last ten days of the Pacific war) to strip that region of its industrial plant, which it then transported to the Soviet Union.

The boom in the narcotics trade in the West in the past twenty years and the use of million-dollar bribes to secure lucrative contracts for the high-technology goods of the industrialized world are evidence that we, who live in the very countries with which China is now developing a new economic partnership, have not become angels. It is simply no use pretending that careful management can shield China from the sins of the outside world. In any case, the *People's Daily* has carried enough stories of embezzlement, corruption, and exploitation of the Chinese people by their officials for us to know that China is not a land populated by saints.

The Chinese reformers need no reminding of the dangers attendant on their new economic partnership with the industrialized countries, but in this area as in many others they have chosen to face the dangers and the rough-and-tumble of the marketplace rather than the often illusory virtue and safety of monastic seclusion because they see a prize to be gained: new vitality for China.

The present leadership has accepted that foreign trade and investment can play a dynamic role in China, even if it does only amount to a small percentage of the gross national product.

China now shares with most other Third World countries the recognition that, properly handled, foreign investment, foreign long-term credit, compensation trade, deferred payments, and other conventional arrangements of international business will bring China the benefits of additional capital, new technology, the skills of foreign managers and designers and marketing networks, all adding up to accelerated growth and a transfer of skills and knowledge. This view was consolidated as official policy when the June 1979 session of the National People's Congress adopted "The Law of the PRC on Joint Ventures Using Chinese and Foreign Investments."

Foreign companies are unlikely to make investments on the scale hoped for by China unless they have some control over the workforce. This is a minefield that evokes many unhappy memories from the past, but one Chinese old enough to have known Shanghai in the "bad old days" assured me that Chinese would welcome the chance to work in foreign-run enterprises. "They reckon," he said "that at the very least foreigners would not treat them worse than some officials have treated them in the last twenty years." Of course we shall have to do better than that to make the partnership flourish and avoid handing a club to the opponents of those who have risked their careers for this policy.

The new policies brought some particular advantages to China in dealing with two issues in her relationship with Japan that carried the seeds of a long-term conflict of interests. The first was exploitation of the continental shelf that stretches from China to Korea and Japan. This is believed to be rich in oil deposits, but there is no agreement between the two countries as to the geographic limits of their exploitation rights. So the Japanese proposed joint development of the seabed around the Senkaku Islands, which are claimed by both Japan and China, and the Chinese gave their full approval.[5] Secondly, the new policy enabled the Chinese leadership to give assurances that foreign businesses will be allowed to continue to operate on Taiwan if and when the island is reunited with the mainland.

To alleviate the job shortage in China, the government announced that it was prepared to export laborers. Reliable sources indicated that a target of sending a million people to work abroad within three years had been set up. China was willing to negotiate contracts for joint ventures and partnerships under which it would supply labor for factories, farms, ships, construction companies, and service industries.[6] The workers would be allowed to send one third of their earnings to their families. The potential lies in labor-deficient developing countries, like Saudi Arabia, rather than highly industrialized and highly unionized countries where there is at present a surplus of labor. The success of South Korean and Indian construction companies in overseas markets proves there is something to the idea.

Of course this new policy, like others, raises unhappy ghosts from the past. The conditions under which contract labor went to the United States to build railroads in the nineteenth century or to British colonies to work on plantations were often harsh. Only a self-confident leadership could have taken the view that "The past is past. We have the strength now to protect our laborers' interests. Let us make China's new strength work to their advantage, and earn foreign exchange for the nation."

There is of course a great potential strategic dividend to China in giving foreigners a stake in her development, especially in such crucial fields as energy resources: the foreigners then have a vested interest in seeing China made secure against foreign attack. It was not surprising therefore that in 1980 Chinese officials began to invite foreign oil companies to search for oil inland, not just in the heartland of China but in the Far Western region of Xinjiang, which many foreign military experts have identified as a prime target for foreign military and political intervention.

Self-confidence and openness are no guarantee of success, and China faces the common difficulty of Third World countries of judging correctly the pace at which it can absorb foreign technology and the level to which it should increase its foreign debt. (Just how many new plants can be run in any one year with China's present and future stock of engineers, technicians, and skilled workers? What will the size of the foreign markets be for Chinese commodities and goods five or ten years from now?)

The inexperience of the Chinese government in the new fields and the lack of experienced operating personnel has already promoted a major readjustment of economic plans and the cancellation of contracts with Japan worth two billion dollars. Mutual confidence has suffered and might suffer again. The use of Overseas Chinese intermediaries can only mitigate, not prevent, such difficulties.

Those conservative cadres who do not have what it takes to exploit the new opportunities and who see their control being undermined by the opening to the world will latch onto the bad side effects of the new relationships. In the future they will get much more ammunition and they will be able to make veiled accusations that Deng and his fellow pragmatists have promised some things that they cannot deliver.

How far can the opening of China and the learning from other countries, including capitalist countries, go before China ceases to be a "socialist" state? Will China go as far as Yugoslavia in relying on market forces and the price mechanism? The man who assumed charge of China's economy in 1979, Chen Yun, had advocated study of the Yugoslav model twenty years ago. After his appointment, a book was published that brought together essays written in the 1950s and 1960s by the economist Sun Yefang, calling for reforms that would carry China's economy at least as far as Yugoslavia has gone in setting prices according to production costs, using profits to determine the success or failure of enterprise management, expanding the powers of decision of enterprises, and basing relationships between enterprises on contracts.

Some Chinese regard even Yugoslavia as only a politically acceptable way station on the road to more radical reform. One Chinese official told a West European resident in Peking for many years: "Because it is a socialist country, pointing to Yugoslavia is a gentle way of introducing ideas for reform that would be shocking if you lifted them straight from a capitalist economy."

In their opening to the world, as in their internal reforms, there will be times the reformers will have to slow down or make tactical retreats under pressure. But they believe it will be disastrous in the long run not to press ahead. In July 1979 the *People's Daily* commentator wrote: "Some comrades become panic-stricken whenever the word 'reform' is mentioned. . . . In a certain sense, changes mean readjusting power and interests. . . . Therefore behind hesitations and reservations to change there probably lie considerations of power and interests. . . . We should have an unswerving will to fight and a strong determination to carry out reforms. We must on no account give up halfway because of obstructions and pressure. Take the reform movement of 1898 during the last days of the Qing dynasty for example. . . . 'Obstructed by high officials' and 'attacked by old colleagues,' the movement was compromised."

The chances of success today are greater than they were in 1898. The reformers of today are not a minority faction in a conservative court. Since December 1978 they have been in a dominant position. Today's struggle to open China is backed by a mass of ordinary citizens who, starting in 1976, have shown where their allegiance lies. They are pleased that their rulers are less and less treating them as children who must be screened from anything foreign that might divert their attention from work and political study. By their decisions as purchasers of foreign books and tickets for international sports matches, foreign films and drama, by their posters, by their applications to emigrate, by their enthusiasm for studying foreign languages and for travel and study abroad, and in a dozen other ways they have shown that they are delighted that China is joining the world.

When Deng Xiaoping donned a Stetson at the Texas rodeo in February 1979 he was not just playing for the American crowd. He was doing something for his people back home as well.

Speculation on how far the Chinese will go is tempting but should not obscure an important fact: to close the door that has been opened to the world would be as difficult in today's China as to restore the doctrine of the infallibility of Mao. During the 1960s, the nation had such a profound and prolonged demonstration of the sterility of autarky that if one leader or group of leaders tried to close the door he or they would find that their opponents could easily mobilize overwhelming forces against them.

The young men at Democracy Wall who defined their goals for China as *fu-guo qiang-bing* (a prosperous and secure nation) placed as much importance on security as on prosperity. Their leaders have done the same. One of the two fundamental aims of the explosion of their diplomatic activity in 1978–1980 was to achieve a strategic alignment between China, the U.S., Japan, and Western Europe against the Soviet Union and its allies. Deng Xiaoping said on the eve of his departure for the U.S.: "It is not only of interest to China but also of great significance to world peace, world security, and world stability that there be friendly relations between China and the U.S., Europe, and Japan."[7] He went on to repeat what Chinese leaders had been saying for years with increasing clarity and force: "Since the early 1970s the U.S. has been on the strategic retreat . . . the true hotbed of war is the Soviet Union, not the U.S."

The facts that had led the Chinese to this conclusion included a fast-growing Soviet military capability on China's perimeter. This Soviet buildup began in 1965–1966. Two years later the Soviet Union signed a mutual defense treaty with Mongolia and introduced its troops into that country. In 1968 it conducted its first large-scale military maneuvers in Mongolia, timing them to coincide closely with those maneuvers in Central Europe that were suddenly transformed into the invasion of Czechoslovakia. The alarm that these actions aroused in China was reinforced by the armed clashes between Chinese and Soviet forces on China's northeastern and Xinjiang borders in 1969. It was at this time that the Chinese press began to indicate to their own people and the world at large that the USSR was now the nation most to be feared: "The ghost of Foster Dulles walks the streets of Moscow" was one colorful sentence used to put this message over.

Between 1966 and 1971 the Soviets increased the number of their divisions deployed along the Sino-Soviet border and in Mongolia from about thirteen to forty-four. According to Chinese and Western military strategists, the number of Soviet divisions remained at this level thereafter and only a third of them were kept at full strength.[8] In terms of numbers, the Russians had created a local balance of deterrence. But in terms of military hardware they enjoyed great superiority. The state of readiness of their forces can be rapidly increased, and their equipment is being modernized still further.

The Chinese, like the Japanese, also noted with concern the increase in Soviet naval strength in the western Pacific, to the point where it far exceeded that of the U.S.

As a result of their buildup, the Soviet forces deployed around China accounted for about one third of all Soviet army, air, and naval forces in 1979. The decision of the Vietnamese government to align itself with the Soviet Union, and to sign a treaty of peace and friendship with it in 1978, means that Chinese defense planning must now also take account of the Vietnamese forces of 650,000 men armed with a great quantity of modern equipment left behind by the American army and air force at the end of the Vietnam war.

China's armed forces are large but twenty to twenty-five years behind those of the U.S. and USSR in terms of equipment. Strengthening them will take much time and money. For instance, the backbone of China's air force is its fifteen hundred MIG-19s, introduced by the Soviet Union in 1955. Just to replace these planes alone would cost billions of dollars. The U.S. Department of Defense has calculated that procurement of sufficient goods and services from the U.S. to give China the capability to defend itself against any Soviet attack by conventional forces and weapons would cost from forty-one billion to sixty-one billion dollars. Given the inferiority of China's economic, scientific, and technological base, it cannot hope to buy or make the equipment to tip the military balance with the Soviet Union *in its favor* in the foreseeable future, and many Western analysts believe the gap between Chinese military capabilities and those of the Soviet Union may actually widen over the next decade.

Chinese strategists assert that since the advent to power of Secretary Leonid Brezhnev in the mid-1960s, and especially since the early 1970s, the pursuit of an offensive strategy of global expansion has been a dominant feature of Soviet foreign policy. They point to the huge growth of Soviet military expenditure and armaments production, the buildup of the global reach of the Soviet armed forces, and the increasing readiness of the Soviet Union to use force itself or encourage and equip others to do so as evidence to support their assertion that the Soviet Union is on the strategic offensive. They also assert that the Soviet leaders are seeking to gain overall military superiority over the U.S. in the long run.[9]

The Chinese have devoted an immense amount of energy to educating the world on what they regard as the harsh realities of Soviet expansionism—global hegemonism, as they call it. For years their warnings on the illusions of détente and the ambitions of the Soviets fell on deaf ears, but they persisted.

They believed in teaching by deeds as well as words. The invasion into Vietnam in February 1979 was designed to teach the Vietnamese a lesson and to set an example to others who have to deal with allies of the Soviet Union and with the Soviet Union itself. The Chinese judged that, with careful management, they could inflict punishment on Vietnam for ignoring China's interests and feelings and yet not provoke the Soviet Union into retaliation. The action was unpopular in a world that had grown unaccustomed to the use of military force against allies of the Soviet Union, but the Chinese judgment of the risk of Soviet military response was proved correct. From then on, people began to attach rather more weight to Chinese statements on foreign policy. China could no longer be accused of being content with merely lecturing the world on how to deal with the expansion of Soviet power.

The Soviet invasion of Afghanistan made many people listen to the Chinese views with a new respect. It is clear therefore that when the Chinese recommend alignment of foreign policy with the U.S., Japan, and Western Europe they do not think in terms of simply reshaping their strategy along anyone else's lines but of a joint search for viable ways of checking the Soviet Union. For their part they have considerably adjusted their own position on a number of major international issues over the years. They have become supporters of NATO, European unity, Atlantic unity, close strategic relations between the U.S. and Japan, and Japanese rearmament. They have reduced their support for Communist parties engaged in armed struggle and they have been quietly sympathetic to U.S. efforts to achieve a peace settlement in the Middle East. They have also ended their boycott of arms control talks in Geneva, although their skepticism on this matter has not evaporated.

While the Chinese leaders always have a highly developed overall view of the world to present to their own people and to foreigners, they do not overrate their present capacity as a global actor. On the eve of his visit to the U.S., Deng told his American audience "China is quite poor, and you have made a poor friend." Within East Asia China has acted boldly, for example in its relations with Vietnam, but it recognizes that it does not have the capability to build or sustain an air or sea bridge to another continent, such as Africa, to support a major intervention there. But China is taking measures that will extend its reach. It has acquired both the aircraft and the landing rights for a major extension of its international civil air network, and in the years 1977 to 1979 spent $1.2 billion buying merchant vessels, mainly in the secondhand market.

It is of course the long-run potential value of China's friendship that attracts the West. If China achieves a new economic, social, and military strength and maintains a close alignment with the West and Japan, this could bring a new stability to relations with Soviet Union.

Few decades can have begun with so much anger and uncertainty in the air as the 1980s. In that bitter beginning, China's opening to the world provided a much-needed ground for hope that the decade would end on a happier note.

Since the 1969 peak of danger in Sino-Soviet relations,

China and the Soviet Union have devoted some effort to lessening the tension between them at various times, but the first major exploration by the post-Mao leadership was talks at vice-foreign ministerial level in Moscow in October 1979. They made little progress, so far as could be detected from the meager disclosures to the press, although reports from well-informed sources in Peking while the talks were under way indicated that the Chinese leaders had prepared their own people for removal of the "revisionist" tag they had attached to the Soviet Communist Party in the 1960s. The Chinese have now adopted much of the pragmatic and materialist approach to economic policy they once denounced in the Soviet Union, which represents a limited victory for common sense. But China's disputes with the Soviet Union today are less ideological than geopolitical, and in that field the Moscow talks showed no progress. Still, the question continues to be asked, will China and the Soviet Union ever come together again in an anti-Western alliance like that of the 1950s? This has an obvious bearing on Western willingness to sell arms to China.

There are strong grounds for believing that there will not be a new Sino-Soviet alliance. In its search for prosperity, China does not wish to be tied to the Soviet model for development that has been tried and rejected as a failure in China. Since it is hardly possible for the socialist camp to have a dual Chinese-Soviet leadership, the Chinese would be subordinate to the Russians and would then be constrained in their experimentation with different social and economic forms. Secondly, the pragmatism of the present Chinese leadership leads it to seek partnership with those nations who are most successful economically, market-economy countries like the U.S., Japan, and West Germany. For China, only the best will do. With a billion people now, and perhaps 1.3 billion by the end of the century, she cannot afford to do otherwise.

This does not mean that the trend of recent years to increase trade between the Soviet Union and China could not be accelerated. There is room for that, particularly when China's new investment in light industry increases her export capacity in that sector. As for exchanges in other fields, much will depend on the general state of relations between the Soviet Union and the West, Japan, and China. As the 1980s began, the prospects were for a refreeze rather than a new thaw.

In 1944 and 1945, the small band of U.S. Foreign Service and military officers and journalists who went to the primitive little town of Yanan reported the readiness of the Communists to trust and work with America. This chapter began with a quotation from one such report, in which John Service summarized the hopes of Mao for Sino-American cooperation. In quantitative terms, the strength of the Communists was derisory compared to that of the Chiang Kai-Shek Nationalist government. If anyone could have fed all the numbers into a computer at the Department of Defense in Washington and projected the future course of the contest between Mao and the mighty Chiang—a household word in American homes, *Time* magazine's Man of the Year for 1938, savior of China to Henry Luce and all whose minds he swayed, and author of the book *China's Destiny*—the answer would surely have come back: Chiang will win.

Yet John Service, John Paton Davies, and others in that small band of observers, faced with what they had learned in that dusty town about the "derisory" Communist forces, judged that "China's destiny is not Chiang's but theirs." For insisting that this was a reality which the American government should take into account, Service and his colleagues were driven out of China by Ambassador Patrick Hurley, Roosevelt's hand-picked emissary to Chiang, and were later hounded from the U.S. Foreign Service or shunted into posts where their Far Eastern expertise was irrevelant. America was not able to heed the prophets on its payroll or hear the message of Mao in the spirit in which it was sent. It allowed Chiang to retain his monopoly in speaking for China. So the Chinese Communists concluded that they had no alternative but to lean to one side—the Soviet side.

Today, John S. Service's collected dispatches have been published in a volume called *Lost Chance in China* and, as the 1980s began, America and her allies have another chance to work with China. We can hardly believe our luck because it is so rare that life gives a second chance. The years between have brought a little wisdom along with the bitterness, but there are as many awkward realities in China today as there were in John Service's time. Earlier chapters have touched on some of them. Will we be better at dealing with them than our predecessors thirty-five years ago? The recent history of Iran stands as a warning against complacency.

"Seek truth from facts" is a slogan of the Communist Party of China that we might put on our walls, along with one from Isaiah:

> Behold, the former things are come to pass,
> And new things do I declare:
> Before they spring forth I tell you of them.

If, this time around, we can adjust to the awkward new things before they become the clichés of history, then someday someone may write a book, *Second Chance in China*, in celebration.

15

But What Is Socialism?

China at present is not even capitalistic. Its economy is still that of semifeudalism. We cannot advance at one jump to socialism. In fact, because we are at least two hundred years behind most of the world, we probably cannot hope to reach socialism until after most of the rest of the world has reached that state.

First we must rid ourselves of this semifeudalism. Then we must raise our economic level by a long stage of democracy and free enterprise.

It is impossible to predict how long this process will take. But we can be sure that it will be more than thirty or forty years, and probably more than a hundred years.

—BO GU, CPC POLITBURO
MEMBER, TO JOHN S. SERVICE,
3 SEPTEMBER 1944[1]

The relation between Marxism–Leninism and the Chinese revolution is the same as between an arrow and a target.

—MAO ZEDONG, 1 FEBRUARY
1942[2]

Of course we must keep to the socialist road. But what is socialism?

—ZHAO ZIYANG, CPC POLITBURO
MEMBER, NOVEMBER 1979

IN THE EARLY AND MID-1950s, day-to-day leadership of the Chinese economy was exercised by the senior Deputy Prime Minister, Chen Yun. He and a group of other political leaders and highly placed economists favored studying the Yugoslav road to socialism and insisted on the importance of profits, prices that reflected costs, contracts, adequate powers of decision for enterprises, and the role of the market as a guide to investment and pricing. Chen also advocated a steady pace of economic development and structural change as opposed to headlong rushes. When Mao launched his Great Leap Forward in 1958 in direct contradiction of the views of Chen and his other senior advisers, Chen stepped back out of the limelight. Day-to-day control of the economy had been taken from him.

In 1962, following the failure of the Leap, Liu Shaoqi and Deng Xiaoping put forward their rightist program of economic reforms which included closing uneconomic plants, ceasing work on uneconomic investment projects, the free marketing of some agricultural produce, and the organization of grain production by households instead of by collectives (see page 37). Naturally, Chen was in accord with the Liu–Deng reform program and stepped out of the shadows to call for emergency measures to deal with the economic crisis, which had produced a budget deficit that was enormous by the conservative fiscal standards of the Chinese Communists. Liu proposed that Chen be appointed head of the Financial Commission of the Central Committee of the Chinese Communist Party. When Mao blocked the Liu–Deng reforms he also blocked Chen's appointment to the Financial Commission.

Seventeen years later, in 1979, after Deng Xiaoping's ascendancy in the Politburo had been established, Chen Yun at last was formally given charge of the nation's finances, as head of a newly created Economic and Finance Commission. And in 1979, as in 1962, there was a budget deficit that needed to be trimmed. The great difference between 1962 and 1979 was that now there was no Mao to stand in Chen's way. Deng would listen to him with great respect and he was supreme in the economic field. This frail figure of a man who fifty years ago had been a typesetter in the *Commercial Press* in Shanghai was one of many septuagenarians who had come into their own after years of frustration. A certain youthful exuberance must have lifted his spirit when in December 1978 he was reappointed to the Standing Committee of the Politburo after two decades of eclipse. At last he had the power to give a mighty push forward to those ideas for the sake of which he had for so long sacrificed his place in the front rank of the leadership. He could set in motion a whole series of measures to adapt Yugoslav methods to China on a trial basis and to establish the role of price, profits, markets, incentives, and enterprise autonomy as he had been itching to do for twenty-five years or more. But his style of leadership would be very different from that of the adventurous Deng Xiaoping. The only public pronouncement he made in the first months after his return to high office ostensibly had nothing to do with politics or economics, but was a few remarks on the Southern Chinese art of singing stories to the accompaniment of a three-stringed Chinese guitar. He said that the traditional nature of this art must be preserved, and he quoted an old Confucianist saying, "Things pushed to an extreme make a comeback."

The tasks Chen and his subordinates faced on the economic front, as they took up the reins of power in early 1979, were daunting. Mao's economic legacy has been described with increasing candor by the Chinese leaders; Deng was not exaggerating when he warned the Americans, before his visit to the U.S., that they had made "a poor friend."* The following account of the problems inherited by the post-Mao leadership is based entirely on Chinese sources.

In 1979, one quarter of China's state-owned enterprises were making a loss. To realize the dimension of catastrophe this represents one has to remember that it is to enterprises owned by the state rather than to neighborhood collectives that the government has directed almost all funds for industrial investment from the national budget and given first claim on human and material resources—the precious capital funds, scarce raw materials, equally scarce power supply, and transportation and

---

* He made it clear to his *Time* interviewer, Hedley Donovan, that by "poor" he did not mean "bad."

the inadequate flow of trained manpower. It has been the spearhead of China's modernization effort since the 1950s. Its employees not only enjoy cradle-to-the grave welfare but also the highest wages paid in any sector and political privileges denied to some others.

Unemployment stood in 1979 at ten million—or twenty million, if one accepts the accuracy of a report published by the reliable noncommunist Hong Kong daily *Ming Pao*, quoting an unpublished speech by Vice-Premier Li Xiannian.[3] That is not ten or twenty million out of the national workforce; in the countryside the work is shared among all able-bodied adults. It is ten or twenty million out of an urban-workforce of 70 to 100 million.[4] The true figure of nonproductive adults is far higher because—as stated in Deng's 1975 Poisonous Weed on industry—in some units 30 to 40 percent of the work force are (or were then) employed on nonproductive work.

A Central Committee document on agriculture adopted on 22 December 1978 stated that in 1977 the national average amount of food grain per person was *slightly less than in 1957*, and somewhat more than a hundred million peasants had inadequate food grain supplies.[5] In 1977 the national average annual income for the agricultural population was sixty yuan ($39).*[6] In an unpublished speech in May 1979, Li Xiannian said that the grain ration for urban workers—thirty-one pounds per month— was not enough to sustain hard work. This was despite massive grain imports. In 1977, *not* a year of unusually high grain imports, China's net grain imports accounted for about 15 percent of her expenditure of hard-won foreign exchange. That is, China had to spend about a billion U.S. dollars on importing food for consumption rather than machinery for production.

According to estimates by China's State Statistic Bureau, the real earnings of staff and workers in China's commercial and industrial sectors were lower in 1979 than in 1965.[7] In the course of 1979, the Chinese press, in keeping with the new spirit of seeking truth from facts, surveyed conditions in rural China and gave examples of low growth in rural incomes: it

---

* This is presumably the average *cash* income and excludes income in kind—share of collective grain production.

reported that in one Shandong county "conditions have improved very little since Liberation in 1949." So far as I know, no journalist or official had been permitted to acknowledge such a thing before. Another report showed that in the relatively well-endowed Jiangsu province per capita income for peasants increased by less than sixty-five U.S. cents per year between 1966 and 1976.[8] This was in line with the national average for peasant income.

I was startled to read in an NCNA despatch one day in January 1979 that an official of a forestry farm in Gansu province, where Wei Jingsheng had met the mud-coated, naked beggar girl, had said to one of the agency's reporters:

> The peasants here are poverty-stricken. How can you expect them to work hard to restore the sabotage that has been committed in agriculture if they have to live from hand to mouth? Beginning in 1959, one political movement was launched after another in our villages. With each one, the peasants' life became a little more intolerable.
>
> The peasants had their private plots confiscated, allegedly to help them get rid of their traditional "money seeking mentality." . . . Formerly the peasants were allowed to plant fruit trees around their houses, raise a few sheep, and grow vegetables on their private plots. Then, when they were about to benefit from these domestic sidelines, their trees were felled and the sheep and plots confiscated. The peasants hope that the party and the government will never again go back on their word.
>
> Having suffered so much, the peasants are asking for a little breathing space to get back on their feet.[9]

As China entered the 1980s her economic infrastructure suffered from gross imbalances. According to *Cheng Ming*, "China's fuel, power, raw materials and processing industries are out of balance. In the power sector many electric generators were out of action in 1978 because there is a shortage of coal and gasoline. . . . In some of the country's provinces, 30 to 40 or even 50 percent of the production capacity of industrial and mining enterprises is not being used because of the power shortage."[10]

Major modernization projects involving billions of dollars

each have been launched on the basis of utterly inadequate feasibility studies. For instance, the Baoshan steel works in Shanghai, designed to produce six million tons of steel a year with plant imported from Japan, was built on a site that had not been properly surveyed. After construction started it was discovered that there was too much quicksand in the ground there and the problem was not even solved by pouring several hundred thousand tons of reinforced concrete into the ground. In Wuhan, the famous iron-and-steel works acquired rolling equipment from West Germany that could produce four million tons a year. Only after construction was started were the power requirements of the mill calculated. It was then discovered that if the rolling plant were to come into full operation, the entire electricity supply of Hubei province would not be enough to supply its needs. Even before the new plant came on stream, other factories in Wuhan had to close down to permit the iron-and-steel works to operate.[11]

Labor productivity has stagnated and, in some cases, seriously declined. According to Xue Muqiao, an economist who is adviser to the State Planning Commission and Director of the Institute of Economics under the Commission, the labor productivity of China's large factories is five to ten times lower than that of developed capitalist countries.[12] Other indicators are equally somber: coal mines with an annual production capacity of 600,000 to 900,000 tons used to take two to four years to be completed but by 1979 were taking four to seven years; a five-story dormitory with a floor space of 3000 square meters, which used to be finished in four to five months, required eight or nine months in 1979. For these and other reasons construction costs had increased by a factor of two or three.[13]

It has been widely believed outside China that Chinese workers do not exercise their constitutional right to strike or use their industrial power for political purposes. This kind of illusion survives because neither the workers nor the authorities in China use the word *strike* to describe industrial stoppages, and the strikers do not parade through the streets carrying banners in support of their demands. But on numerous occasions before the death of Mao workers absented themselves en masse from work to express their grievances.

The epidemic of strikes across the nation in 1976 was a clear response to the swerve to the left in political direction after Zhou Enlai's death (see page 138). The effect showed dramatically in the overall indices of production for that year: for example crude steel production dropped from twenty-four million tons in 1975 to twenty-one million in 1976, a low it had not touched since five years before. In early 1977, some people expected a rapid recovery because the Gang of Four had been smashed, but the recovery was slow. In the early spring bus drivers in Peking were not just going slow but sometimes stopping altogether. For a week or so it became a common sight on the Avenue of Eternal Peace to see a bus or trolley stopped, empty by the roadside, while the driver squatted on the sidewalk or casually dusted his windshield—something drivers seldom did in any manner, casual or otherwise. I mentioned my puzzlement over this to a Chinese friend, who remarked not very cryptically, "Many people are impatient for the return of Deng Xiaoping." (The decision on Deng's return was just then being debated by the leadership in secret conclave.)

These are only a few illustrations of a phenomenon the post-Mao leadership knows it has to deal with. The workforce has lost its old enthusiasm and has developed a readiness to reduce its level of attendance, cooperation, and effort if it takes exception to party policies or leaders. They have identified industrial action as a substitute for that ballot box to which they have little access.

Another part of the legacy with which China's leaders are now saddled is a highly developed practice on the part of middle-level and not-so-middle-level officials to use statistics unscrupulously to advance their careers. The *People's Daily* has explained how this is done. A county, or at least a county's leaders, may want to win an honorable title such as that of a "Dazhai-style county." To exaggerate the per-acre yields it is obtaining, it cuts down the figure of land sown, thus increasing the per-acre yield. Elsewhere, as we have seen in Chapter 4, output figures are not reported from below by the producers but are simply assigned from above. In industry, said the *People's Daily*, there are many ways of falsifying gross-output value figures. Low-quality products are passed off as high-quality ones, and "there are many regions, departments, and units which send in false reports about the number of workers, wages, and labor efficiency." The situation has become so bad in some places that people scoff at statistical tables, saying "30 percent statistics and 70 percent guesswork."[14]

Statistics were reasonably accurate until the Great Leap Forward, but the insane targets then set left junior officials with little alternative but to make false claims. So wildly did people exaggerate that the government sensibly cut back severely on the number of statistics published. This at least reduced the incentive to lie but clearly did not succeed in eliminating it.

The regulations issued in the early 1960s setting the administrative framework for rural life in theory gave a certain autonomy of management for the lowest level of organization, the production team. The team members were supposed to feel that they were the collective owners of their land and other property. But, over the years, officials at the higher levels interfered frequently, issuing arbitrary orders on how the teams should manage their business and ordering them to produce groups of men and women for collective labor on schemes which might or might not be designed to benefit that team and for which the laborers might or might not be paid. As a result, the members of many teams had ceased to have much sense of ownership; the results in terms of stifling initiative and effort can be imagined.

The people of Nanzhuang in Zhengding county, Hebei province, have a story to tell which illustrates this. In the spring of 1979, they studied the major policy document on agriculture that had been issued as a result of Deng's success at the November–December meetings in Peking. This laid down twenty-five policies; first among them was that of allowing peasants to plant whichever crops were best suited to local conditions, provided they took into account the state plan. Policy No. 16 encouraged the peasants to grow cash crops (such things as cotton, tobacco) provided they did not neglect grain.

The members of Nanzhuang production brigade had culti-vated only grain for years and their income from this had been low. On the basis of the "new" policy document they "summed up their experience of getting poorer and poorer because of the practice of a single-product economy" and considered planting just six acres of watermelon, sweet potatoes, and snake melon—crops they could sell for cash. They reckoned this would bring a return of almost fifty dollars per brigade member and a total return of sixty-five hundred dollars to the brigade. This modest sum was very attractive to them, so they decided to go ahead.

When the melons had grown to the size of rice bowls the officials who were in charge of the commune (the administrative unit to which the brigade is subordinate) heard about Nan-zhuang's little venture into the cash economy and were furious. They condemned the brigade members for "growing things freely in a capitalist way" and forced them to destroy the entire crop.[15] The national press publicized this abuse of power as an example of the kind of thing the peasants were up against in making a reality of their status as collective owners of their land.

If the workers and the peasants had suffered a loss of morale, economists and others whose job it was to think about the econ-omy as a whole were, if anything, in a worse state. One example was Sun Yefang, who in the 1950s had written studies on the issues of profit, price, and autonomy to which Deputy Premier Chen Yun attached importance. Sun was one of the nation's foremost political economists, but he could not get many of his essays published. His was not a case of "publish or perish" or even "publish and be damned"; he was damned even without having had much published, and he nearly perished. He was sent to jail for seven years and was released only because the leftist tide receded in time. His writings of the 1950s and 1960s were published in 1979. The persecution of Professor Ma

Yinchu, President of Peking University, for having warned of
the dire consequences of Mao's policy of unrestrained population growth in the 1950s, is one other example. He was rehabilitated in 1979, at the age of ninety-seven.

Of course these are only two cases out of thousands of economists who were silenced. Those who remember the paralyzing
effect on U.S. policy toward China caused by persecution in the
McCarthy era of four American Foreign Service officers and a
handful of academic sinologists will be able to grasp the paralysis
of thought that descended on the economic field in China as a
result of the infinitely wider Chinese witch hunts of the 1950s
and 1960s. As the reformers of today search for ways to revive
China's economy, they are hampered by the lingering fear that,
according to the Chinese press, still inhibits the minds of many
economists.

This catalogue of troubles contrasts strangely with the evidence that greets the eye of the visitor arriving in China from
Hong Kong. Chinese farmland looks in apple-pie order as one
journeys from the Hong Kong border to Canton in an air-conditioned railway coach.

For years Chinese economists suffered in silence while
Panglossian propagandists asserted that in China all was for
the best of all possible worlds. Now they have their chance to
take grim reality as their starting point, as exhorted now by
Deng and twenty years ago by Liu Shaoqi.

The diagnosis the Chinese are making of their ailing economy is many-sided, but two key weaknesses have been particularly stressed since Deng's return to power. The first is the inadequacy of decision-making power granted to enterprises in all
sectors. This is as true for agriculture (remember the melons of
Nanzhuang) as for industrial and commercial enterprises. The
second is the past neglect of the interests of the individual. Both
are recognized as having contributed to the low state of morale,
but official writing devotes more attention to the former, while
the young democracy and human-rights activists stress the need
for more rights for the individual.

The combination of welfare-state responsibilities and managerial impotence that characterizes Chinese enterprises is truly astounding. The cradle-to-grave welfare responsibilities with which many are saddled were briefly described earlier. Their managerial impotence can be grasped if we remember that a state-owned enterprise is not empowered

- to decide upon new investment
- to decide its product line
- to purchase capital goods
- to purchase raw materials
- to recruit or dismiss personnel
- to market its own product
- to price its products
- to fix its wage levels and reward systems
- to retain its profits.

Control over all these matters has rested and still in most cases rests with departments of local or central government who allocate labor, capital, capital goods, and raw materials; distribute the products; and take away the profits. Of course there is some degree of consultation with the enterprise, but the impediments to developing any sense of identity or corporate pride are daunting, to say the least.[16]

With so little autonomy, enterprises can hardly be held responsible for their profits and losses. Moreover, in the past *profit* was a dirty word and the state would subsidize all lame ducks (however unprofitable), so there was no reward for efficiency and no punishment for incompetence and idleness among either management or workers. In such a situation it is hardly surprising that cost accounting was regarded an academic exercise.

This disinterest in profits has been reinforced by the state enterprise's role as a mini-welfare state and by the job assignment system. The workers have not chosen their enterprise and the enterprise has not chosen them. The association is an arranged marriage that is not likely to draw forth the best efforts from the workforce. "We're here, because we're here, because we're here," the old British solder's song, might have been the marching song of many Chinese workers.

Those who are assigned to large state enterprises providing all the welfare benefits consider themselves fortunate. Since they cannot normally be dismissed, they feel they have acquired an "iron rice bowl," to use a phrase coined long before the Communist Party came to power and much heard these days. In a world of mass movements and zigzag politics, an iron rice bowl is not something to be jeopardized by efforts or thoughts that mark you out from the crowd or by firm leadership that will make you some enemies who can seek their revenge the next time a campaign needs a scapegoat.

Successive campaigns have left their legacy of enmities not only at the eternally talked-of level of Deng versus the Gang of Four but in almost every workplace across the land, because those who joined opposing factions in, say, the Cultural Revolution are still living and working together years later. When instability rose again in 1976, factories in parts of the country showed signs of splitting into old factions, and buried hatchets (and guns) were dug up again, literally.

Industrial enterprises learned that they could not rely on the quality of production goods and spare parts they did not make themselves. They also learned that the system of allotting such supplies did not work too well, and so there arose a tendency to take the slogan "We Must Rely on Our Own Efforts" to extremes. There appeared a phenomenon described by Chinese leaders as "big-and-complete and small-and-complete," meaning that big factories and small ones alike tried to achieve self-sufficiency to a degree unknown in industrially developed nations. As a result, China's leaders and economists now are struggling to develop specialized division of labor at a comparatively late stage in China's industrial progress.

With the supply of raw materials subject to uncertainty, enterprises have developed a tendency to carry uneconomically large inventories of raw materials, fuel, and labor.

To overcome supply bottlenecks, a breed of Mr. Fix-Its has grown up in China, as in the Soviet Union. These men operate outside the national plan, setting up unauthorized cash and barter deals between companies. Their existence depends on their ability to bring willing buyers and willing sellers together to circumvent the rigidities of the planning system. It is not just they who profit by their role of middlemen. Often managements make sure that their enterprise employees benefit from the increased production that results, distributing illegal bonuses or laying on fine meals. These middlemen are part of what is in effect a free market in parallel with the planned one. For instance, the managers of a farm-machinery corporation in Qinghai province used their positions to arrange deals involving the bartering of eight thousand dollars' worth of farm machinery spare parts for twenty-four hundred kilos of rice, which they distributed to their workers and used for throwing parties and as gifts to oil the wheels of other deals. They bartered seven tractors, four hand tractors, and four diesel engines for large quantities of cement, timber, rolled steel, and other building materials.[17] They were small-time operators compared to men like Wang Weichun, the deputy secretary for economic affairs in Hebei province (see pages 73–74).

The first broad-ranging critique of the state of the economy, and outline of measures to reform it, made after Deng's return to power was the speech made to the State Council in July 1978 by Hu Qiaomu, President of the Academy of Social Sciences.[18] The Academy serves as the pragmatists' principal "think tank." This speech will surely stand as a landmark in the history of Chinese socialism. (In its English version, published in the widely distributed *Peking Review*, it covered thirteen pages). Hu began by affirming that economic laws are objective in their nature. He quoted Lenin, who said that these laws are "not only independent of human will, consciousness and intentions, but, rather, on the contrary, determine the will, consciousness and intentions of men." By opening his speech with this theme, Hu was seeking to counteract the deep influence which Mao had wrought in precisely the opposite direction.

Hu went on to point out to his audience that the socialist system does not of itself guarantee that an economy will develop in a planned way and at a higher speed than in a capitalist society. Indeed, in practice the opposite has sometimes been the case, and "socialism has not yet given rise to a labor productivity higher than that under capitalism." Why? Because, compared with capitalism, socialism is in its infancy and is little developed as yet. Also, capitalism has a built-in safety device for limiting the impact of mistakes that socialism lacks. Hu quoted something Stalin said at the Fourteenth Congress of the CPSU in 1925:

> No mistake of any magnitude, no overproduction of any magnitude, or serious discrepancy between production and total demand takes place in capitalist countries without the blunders, mistakes, and discrepancies being corrected by some crisis or other. . . . There we see economic, commercial, and financial crises, which affect individual groups of capitalists. Here, in our country, things are different. Every serious hitch in trade, in production, every serious miscalculation in our economy, results not in some individual crisis or other, but hits the whole of our national economy. In our country, every crisis, whether commercial, financial, or industrial, may develop into a general crisis that will hit the whole state.

"What was described by Stalin," Hu commented, "took place in the Soviet Union both before and after this statement of his, and occurred in China as well."

What is to be done to avoid a repetition of such general crises in China? Hu answers in very general terms, but the answer is not without interest because it links socialism with political democracy: "To reduce the twists and turns in the process of development, it is necessary to integrate the socialist economic system closely with the socialist political system, i.e., the people's democratic system, as well as with the economic, managerial and natural sciences. In short, socialist economy means highly socialized mass production based on public ownership."

Hu left open the question of what is meant by public ownership. His omission was surely deliberate because he called for a period of experimentation and exploration with different "systems of management," a term that could develop a very wide meaning in China now and could be used as safe umbrella for discussing different forms of ownership.

Another major part of Hu's answer to the question of what is to be done was "Study foreign countries." Foreign socialist countries? By no means—they are not mentioned anywhere in the speech. The countries to be studied are the advanced capitalist countries. Hu acknowledges "the highly efficient planning and other managerial functions carried out in today's big corporations" and adds that there is a degree of planning within branches of capitalist countries' economies, such as agriculture in the United States. It is done rather well, he says, continuing:

> It is precisely in respect to this first function of the management of capitalist enterprises . . . that the proletariat can and must learn from the capitalist class. Lenin said: "When people . . . say that socialism can be won without learning from the bourgeoisie, I know this is the psychology of an inhabitant of Central Africa. The only socialism we can imagine is one based on all the lessons learned through large-scale capitalist culture." The proletariat "could not retain power by dictatorship, by force, by coercion alone; power can be maintained only by adopting the whole experience of cultured, technically equipped, progressive capitalism and by enlisting the services of all these people."

Hu then catalogued the shortcomings of China's economic system, covering almost all those listed above. He was especially blunt in acknowledging the failure to motivate management and workers to strive for the success of their enterprises. Hu attached importance, of course, to the role planning has to play in setting the economy right. The form of planning he envisaged is a fairly flexible combination of direct planning for state-owned enterprises and indirect planning for enterprises under collective ownership. In the latter case the plan passed down to these units by the state is merely a kind of demand, and the state helps its realization by adopting certain economic policies and signing contracts with these units. In this indirect way, the state controls their main economic activities and is able to bring them into the orbit of state planning. The combination of the two kinds of planning will constitute the unified plan of the state: "The targets set by the state must be geared to the orders and contracts received by the various enterprises with a view to effectively resolving existing contradictions due to a certain degree of

dislocation between production and need and imbalance between supply and demand."

Hu advocated increased decision-making power for the enterprises, and this will facilitate a closer linking of the performance of the enterprise and the rewards and punishments for
the individual. Here he produced yet another striking quote
from Lenin: "We say that every important branch of the economy must be built up on the principle of personal incentive.
There must be collective discussion, but individual responsibility. At every step we suffer from our inability to apply this
principle." "How true!" commented Hu. "Haven't we too suffered at every step? And how true are Comrade Mao Zedong's
words: 'Empty talk is useless; it is imperative to bring the
people visible material well-being.'"

The first major decision taken after Chen Yun assumed supreme responsibility for the economy in 1979 was to designate
the next three years as a period of readjustment. The highly
ambitious targets Hua Guofeng had set out at in his speech to
the Fifth National People's Congress in March 1978 were to be
drastically scaled down, and the three years from 1979 to 1981
used to bring the different sectors of the economy into somewhat better balance. These three years were also to be used as a
time for devising, testing, and popularizing better systems for
managing the economy.

The main imbalance in the economy identified by Chen Yun
and his colleagues was the backward state of agriculture compared with industry. For years agriculture had been treated
mainly as a source of investment funds for industry. Within the
industrial sector, it was judged that heavy industry had been
given too great a share of investment funds. China's planners
decreed an improvement in the terms of trade for agriculture,
announcing substantially higher prices for grain as well as other
agricultural products, and increased the share of state funds to
be invested in the sector from 10.78 percent of the national
budget in 1978 to 14 percent in 1979. Heavy industry's share of
state investment was cut from 54.7 percent to 46.8 percent.
Investment by the state in light industry was increased by only a
small amount, .4 percent, but it was to be helped in other ways

that may be more important in the short run. It was to be given priority in obtaining fuel, power, and raw and semifinished materials.

The reform aspect of the leadership's economic strategy was summed up and put in perspective by Xue Muqiao, adviser to the state planning commission, in an article published by the Party's main theoretical journal in October 1979:

> The present economic management system of our country is seriously hampering the development of the national economy, dislocating supply and demand and causing serious waste. China today is still basically following the economic management system we learned fifty years ago from the Soviet Union. We have placed too much emphasis on administrative management and are not good at utilizing the law of value and the regulatory role of the market. The CPC Central Committee has decided that, after the proportions of the national economy have been properly readjusted and economic management work reorganized to basically overcome the chaotic conditions, a thorough reform of the economic management system must be instituted, and the right of the localities and, in particular, the enterprises to make their own decisions must be increased, so that the economic activity of the enterprises need not be restricted by departmental and local administrative organs and supply and marketing can be directly linked. Naturally, reforming the management system of the national economy is a very complicated matter, and we still lack experience in this direction. That is why many important reforms must still go through investigation and study and be tested at special points, and experience must be obtained before they can be gradually popularized.

The most important reform instituted so far in agriculture is the new Output Responsibility System, authorized by the Central Committee on a trial basis in December 1978. Under this system the production team—which groups about thirty families together—remains the basic unit for accounting, but its leaders have authority to divide the team into smaller work groups. These work groups, which may consist of ten to fifteen adults, are allotted a share of the collective property of the production team—land, tools, and draft animals—and in return they contract for a share of the production planned for the year by the team. If they produce more than they contract for, they are entitled to special rewards. Ownership of the land, tools, and draft animals remains with the team. Except where the fields and houses are scattered over a wide area, the groups are not to be formed along family lines. Nor is free association of labor allowed; and when the work groups are organized, attention is to be paid to balancing strong and weak members in the different teams. This is a less radical reform than that Liu and Deng proposed in 1962, but it is a genuine attempt to bring about a better balance between socialist ideals and incentives for the individual.[19]

Other new policies for rural areas were put into effect in 1979, such as a liberalization of regulations governing rural markets. For years these markets had literally been regarded as manifestations of capitalism which could at most be tolerated under strict supervision as a necessary accommodation to the unreformed instincts of the peasantry. Now the aura of sin has officially been lifted from them and peasants are strongly encouraged to take their sideline production and surplus production from collective and household labor to market for sale. Markets on the outskirt of cities where peasants can sell their vegetables, fruit, eggs, chickens, peanuts, and tobacco have been revived. These are in competition with the state marketing system. The regulations governing their markets include provisions against profiteering, so evidently there is a degree of price control.[20]

Country people are now allowed, as they were twenty years ago, to sell handicrafts on city streets again. I remember the first one I saw on the streets of Peking, driving along the Avenue of Eternal Peace on a windy and sunny day in early December 1978. News of the decisions made by the Central Work Conference had begun to filter out and hearts in the city were lifting. Emerging from one of those elaborate inhuman knots of concrete complete with underpasses, crossovers, and exit roads that highway engineers the world over create in the service of the motorcar, I saw a solitary peasant walking along the sidewalk bedecked with a whole array of toy windmills he had made of

wood and pink plastic. The stiff winter wind spun their sails at a
dizzy speed. There was not a potential customer anywhere in
sight, but the peasant hawker was not in the least dismayed. He
was enjoying his freedom to sell the work of his hands and stroll
in the city to marvel at the concrete monstrosity of the modern
world. He reminded me of the street vendor created by Jacques
Tati in his film *Mon Oncle*, whose mild anarchy and humanity
are at odds with the highly regimented and automated world
around him.

At the end of the first year of operation of the new policies
governing rural life, the New China News Agency reported that
China had achieved its highest-ever level of food production
and attributed the increase in production largely to the new
policies.

Further reforms in agriculture are the subject of experiments now underway. One of these can be observed in Deng
Xiaoping's home province, Sichuan, which has been chosen as
one of the testing grounds for new economic policies. It was a
good province to choose because it has problems and potential
shared by other provinces. It used to be one of the great
granaries of China, but social and economic deterioration in the
1960s put an end to that, at least for a while. Its population
swelled to almost a hundred million and a decline of social order
after the Cultural Revolution played havoc with the economy.
Sichuan's top Party man in 1979 was Zhao Ziyang, an unequivocal supporter of Deng and a vigorous implementer of his
pragmatic line. Chinese pay tribute to Zhao's ability by using a
phrase that is just about the highest compliment that can be paid
in these pragmatic times, *ta hen neng gan* (he knows how to get
things done).

After a tour of Western Europe in 1979, Zhao launched a
drive to encourage farmers to join forces across the demarcation
lines between communes that had previously been sacrosanct.
He encouraged production teams to form cooperatives for specialized common purposes, such as food processing and animal
husbandry, irrespective of which commune they belonged to.[21]
This was not just another chapter in the checkered history of the
cooperative idea; it was an indirect assault on the semifuedal

system perpetuated and even reinforced in China under the "progressive" title *commune*. The commune organization has in fact been one of the main constraints on the free movement of people and ideas in China, the rural equivalent of the all-embracing urban unit, dividing Chinese from their neighbors, as Huang Xiang wrote in "The Confessions of the Great Wall":

> I divide the great land into numerous small pieces,
> Divide the land into many small, suffocating courtyards.
>
> My body lies stretched out among the people
> Dividing this group from that,
> So that they are constantly guarding against each other,
> Can never see the faces of their neighbors,
> And cannot even hear their conversation.

In industry the experiments of 1979 concerned pay and powers—the way wage-packets are calculated and the powers that are granted to individual enterprises. The testing of new (or revived) wage systems was begun in all parts of China, although two thousand enterprises in Sichuan and elsewhere seemed to be given a license to experiment more than others. The principles behind the work on wages are simple: "More pay for more work" and "If production rises wages will rise, step by step." The ways in which these principles are being applied are many and various. Does this sound like a capitalist philosophy? The Chinese nation is being taught that this is a fundamental principle of socialism, and texts from the founding fathers are being produced to prove it. So far there have been no protests by workers against the application of a principle that was resisted in their name for so many years by self-appointed "proletarian revolutionaries." By the standards of Chinese wage levels the amount workers can now earn in bonuses for more and better work are substantial and put him or her well ahead of inflation.

A hundred industrial and transportation enterprises in Sichuan are participating in a national experiment with granting more powers to individual enterprises. The power of their "mothers-in-law" to order them around is being curbed. The companies in the experiment have been given greater freedom to develop strategies that take account of local conditions. This includes greater financial autonomy (retaining some of their profits and more of their depreciation funds and taking more credit from banks), the power to hire and fire workers and dismiss unsatisfactory managers, and authority to enter into direct relationship with foreign firms and to adjust production to consumer needs based on market research. The actual extent of the increase in autonomy appears to be very modest and the use made of it very restrained, according to an investigation made by a group from *The Economist* of London.[22] But there is nothing modest about the claims made for its impact on performance: an average increase in output of 56.7 percent in the first six months of the experiment, together with a "large" increase in profits.[23]

In the long run the establishment of joint ventures with foreign companies in China will affect wholly Chinese enterprises. Modern management methods, incentive schemes, and the whole culture of modern business are bound to be contagious. More than that, it may well lead to revival of the 1950s policy of encouraging joint enterprises between the Chinese state and Chinese private entrepreneurs. At present Overseas Chinese are setting up joint ventures with the Chinese state. Some of these people have relatives still living in China, some of whom have substantial bank accounts preserved from earlier days.

Consider the case of two brothers, whom I will call Wang Jiafu and Wang Jiaqing. In 1949, when the Communists took over China, Wang Jiafu moved to Hong Kong, taking with him a part of the savings his family had accumulated from their textile business. In Hong Kong he set up his own small garment factory and it flourished. Today, seeking to take advantage of the lower wage rates in China, he is setting up a joint venture with a Chinese state corporation in Canton, the city in which he and his brother grew up. His brother, Wang Jiaqing, stayed on in Canton when the Communists came and the Communist government has made a certain amount of use of his knowledge of the textile industry down the years. He had a rough time during the Cultural Revolution, and his bank account—in which he kept his share of what was left to the family by the government in the 1950s—was confiscated. Now it has been returned to him, with interest, and he would like to join his brother in his joint venture in Canton, but he is not free to do so. It is illogical that the brother who "deserted" the country in 1949 can be a capitalist in China, but the brother who stayed behind "to help build socialism" cannot.

Viewed from another angle, if the offshore oil all along the China coast is to be developed jointly between the Chinese state oil company and capitalist foreign companies, what logical reason could there be for excluding a Chinese capitalist from joint ventures with his own state's enterprises? Even politics are not impervious to logic, and it seems unlikely that this barrier will be maintained indefinitely.

In 1979, I spotted one straw that showed the wind was blowing in that direction. When the government announced its decision to restore to China's surviving capitalists or their families the funds and private property that had been confiscated from them during the Cultural Revolution, many leading "former capitalists" attended a meeting in Peking to hear the announcement and give their reaction to it. One of the main speakers at the meeting, a former capitalist named Hu Juewen, called on his fellows to apply themselves to developing tourism, service trades, foreign trade, and joint ventures. Another speaker, Rong Yiren, soon to be appointed to head the China International Trust and Investment Corporation (CITIC), encouraged his wealthy friends to place their "extra funds" with credit and investment companies that would finance high-priority capital projects.[24] Putting two and two together, it began to look as though one day there might once again be room in China for joint state-private ventures where the "private" partner could as well be Chinese as foreign.

A reform that is being pushed ahead nationwide now and does not require a period of experiment is revitalizing and expanding collective enterprises. These differ from state-owned enterprises in several ways. First, they are controlled exclusively by municipalities or neighborhoods instead of by ministries of the central government. Second, in theory, they have always been responsible for their own profits and losses. Third, they have in the past been regarded as a less "socialist" form of organization than state enterprises and have been discriminated against in many ways. They are the nearest thing in China to Yugoslav-style self-managing companies, and that helped account for their second-class status while Tito and his Yugoslav League of Communists were the pariahs of the socialist camp.

Collective factories and workshops produce 79 percent of total annual output value of household goods manufactured in China and 40 percent of all light industrial goods. They employ twenty million people. Housewives and grandmothers beaver away in makeshift workshops of the kind found all over Asia producing prodigious quantities of plastic sandals, shoehorns, zippers, shirts, blouses, combs, net baskets, and thousands of other low-cost articles with the aid of rudimentary machines or pedal-operated sewing machines. Some work as economical subcontractors for larger enterprises.

Today the Party leadership is taking steps to make more of a reality of the autonomy of collective enterprises. This is not easy, because for years many city officials have disregarded their supposed autonomy, and hard-pressed city revenue collectors have been taking advantage of their stepchild status to cream off their profits. At the same time the collectives have been expected to pull themselves up by their own bootstraps with a minimum of capital handouts from the city or the banks and a low priority on the waiting lists for machinery, raw materials, and skilled manpower. Despite all these handicaps the collectives have thrived, providing work for millions of city-dwellers who would be otherwise unemployed or forced to move to the countryside. Their strength has probably stemmed from the sense of identity that comes from being neighborhood businesses on a personal scale. It is now official Party policy to capitalize on the inherent strengths of this kind of enterprise, and as the Chinese economy becomes more of a free market this policy should bear fruit.

There are hundreds of gaps in the economy waiting to be filled. According to Xue Muqiao, adviser to the State Planning Commission, many of these gaps have been created by the Party's own policies of public ownership and bureaucratic control. In a radio interview in July 1979 he said:

> Before Liberation the Johnson Taxi Company and house-moving and other companies in Shanghai were all run very well, to the great convenience of the residents. In Peking in the 1950s, one

could find a cart for house-moving, but now such carts cannot be found. In the past there were people who helped carry bags at railway stations and airports, but now there are none.

Before Liberation, in many large and medium-size cities, there were laundry services in each residential area. Now washing clothes is a burden second only to cooking.

What I have mentioned are trades and professions that should be set up in the cities. In the past, some people regarded them as "capitalist loopholes" that were too numerous to be plugged. Now we need to change these "loopholes" into front gates to develop enterprises under collective ownership.[25]

It is vital that the collectives should flourish because the Party is placing great reliance on them in dealing with the urgent and massive problem of how to ensure that city youths are employed. With three million young people graduating from city schools each year, state-owned enterprises cannot possibly absorb them all, and few if any of these people want to work in the countryside. So the city administrators are being directed to help these young (and other not-so-young) people in need of jobs to set up collectives, particularly in light industry, the service industries, and trade.

In many towns and cities 70 to 80 percent of new entrants to the labor force are absorbed by the collectives. But in the view of economists like Xue Muqiao this system is still too rigid. In his July 1979 radio interview he said:

At present, job assignments for young people are handled exclusively by the labor departments. This system can no longer be maintained. Even though the state wants to issue an "iron rice bowl" to everyone, there are not enough bowls for all the people. The labor departments must find another method. And there is only one method: Do not handle everything by yourselves if you are unable to do so, but permit the young people awaiting job assignments to organize production in a certain way by themselves.

Instead of prohibiting them, we should assist and lead them in organizing their production. At present there are innumerable employment opportunities in the cities, but the question is whether or not we will permit ourselves to find these opportunities.

If people awaiting jobs are allowed to find these opportunities themselves, organize their own cooperatives or cooperative groups, and be responsible for their own profits and losses, the state will not be required to pay them wages. Besides, the laborers' enthusiasm will be greater, and their attitude toward providing services will be better. Also, one person will do the work that normally is done by several persons, and the income from his work will not be lower than that of third- or fourth-grade workers. Why, then, do we prohibit such things? If we allow them, we can not only solve the employment problem of a large number of people but also provide tremendous convenience to the people living in the cities, thus, in essence, hitting two birds with one stone.

The idea of grouping young people together in collective (or "cooperative") enterprises is also being applied in the countryside. With three million young people coming into the urban labor pool every year and the rate of creation of new urban jobs still inadequate, the policy of sending school-leavers to the countryside is going to continue, but since 1979 they are not supposed to be inserted into the labor force of existing production teams but helped to set up their own collective farms. This should alleviate some of the tensions and problems caused by the old system.

Peasants often resented the arrival of the city youths, whom they regarded as a burden on their economy. The city youths found the culture gap between themselves and the peasants intolerably wide. Now there is some chance that the groups of literate and reasonably like-minded young people will create viable farms that will use whatever new methods are available and such new equipment and inputs as they can afford and can lay hands on.

The strategy outlined by Hu Qiaomu in his July 1978 speech and the ideas so long advocated by Chen Yun are being elaborated and institutionalized in numerous other ways also. To provide a framework for the expanded use of contracts and the modest increase in the autonomy of enterprises, laws regulating economic activity have been promised and specialized courts are being set up. The role of the banks is being expanded; one effect of this will be to apply economic criteria to investment decisions to a greater extent than in the past. Barriers to competition and to the exchange of goods between provinces are being broken down. Bureaucratic control over prices was sharply reduced in November 1979, when it was announced that price control was being removed from ten thousand products, making up about one fifth of all commodities on sale.[26] (Capital goods and raw materials are still allocated, not sold.) Specialized corporations are being set up to group together enterprises that are engaged in the same line of business; the corporations are supposed to strengthen the managerial expertise of the enterprises, leading them to operate on more commercial, market-oriented lines and giving them more clout in the competition for scarce resources. They would perform some of the functions that are now performed by the semilegal Mr. Fix-It. They are also empowered to authorize such a seemingly simple matter as overtime working, which has been bound up in red tape in the past.[27]

Chen Yun's preference for a gradual pace of development was evident in the decision to lower the target rate of "capital accumulation"—savings by enterprises and individuals. So it was in the announcement that unprofitable enterprises were to be closed down if they could not make themselves profitable within a reasonable period and if there were no mitigating circumstances. (Hua Guofeng, speaking at the July 1979 session of the National People's Congress, set a one-year time limit, but given all the factors beyond the control of enterprises that make it difficult to achieve profits, it seemed likely that this deadline would not be rigidly adhered to.)

These changes apply not only to the two thousand enterprises participating in the controlled experiment but to all the scores of thousands of enterprises across China. The changes have been cumulative. They have not been thrown at the enterprise managers in one package. This is wise, because although the operating principles may be as familiar to a Westerner as ABC, to many Chinese officials they are as strange as hairy crabs. Exhorting Chinese managers to overcome their timidity, which was inhibiting them from applying the new policies, the *People's Daily* quoted Lu Xun, China's great social satirist of the 1930s: "Dare to eat hairy crabs for the first time!"[28] The cautious pace of change is partly due to the nation's bitter memories of experiments launched by Mao at breakneck speed. Too many necks were broken. It also stems from the opposition of conservative-minded officials to any reform that increases anyone else's freedom of action. These officials have for decades lived with a minimum of legal restraint on their own actions while exercising a maximum of administrative restraint upon those of other people. They are afraid of what will happen to them and to society if they let go.

The Chinese Communists would be the last people in the world to neglect the intangibles that affect economic behavior. It is not surprising therefore to see that the power of the press that formerly was deployed to exhort the peasants and workers to set their hearts against filthy lucre is now engaged in encouraging a very different set of values. The most basic message now is "It's okay to be rich."

In the past, production successes were celebrated for the benefits they bring to society as a whole, but in 1979 the press began to play a new theme, publicizing the achievements of families who were making a better living for themselves through hard work and enterprise, provided they shared their efforts between "public" and "private" work.

One example cited was a family in a farming commune in South China's Guangdong province. In 1978, the family of eight, including three able-bodied workers, earned a net income of more than $3800, more than ten times the national average for a peasant's cash income. Of this, 60 to 70 percent came from raising pigs and poultry and growing vegetables and mushrooms in their spare time. This and other examples were publicized, wrote NCNA, to stress "the need to carry out the newly adopted policy of encouraging those peasants who are more efficient or who have better conditions to go first in achieving prosperity. The policy represents a further move to eliminate egalitarianism. . . . Facts have proved that it amounts to sheer illusion to suppose that socialism can be built by deliberately preventing people from getting rich. It is equally absurd to maintain a low level of income for people in relatively prosperous areas or units to prevent a possible polarization of society."

A drive was under way to rid people of the notion, instilled into them over many years, that to seek prosperity was sinful and for one man or one family to get ahead of others was a failure of socialism. This was part of a wider campaign against the "antisocialist" error of egalitarianism.

Some of the articles written on the subject reminded me just a little of the "Do you sincerely want to be rich?" evangelism popular in the West in the 1960s. I could hear again the cheers ringing in the ears of Bernard Cornfeld at a meeting of those who put money into his Investors Overseas Services. The crucial difference was that in China this was part of an effort to relieve rock-bottom poverty. Here are excerpts from one article that advocated "Getting rich through labor."

When the leftist line of Lin Biao and the "gang of four" ran wild, "getting rich through labor" was vilified as a "revisionist" slogan, and anyone who thought of "getting rich through labor" was considered guilty of the heinous crime of believing in the "superiority" of "capitalism" and given a head-on blow. In their reactionary theory, there was no room for prosperity in socialism because "prosperity will lead to capitalism and revisionism." Socialism means being poor, for only the poor can make revolution, and people make revolution because of poverty. Therefore, the poorer, the more revolutionary; and the more revolutionary, the poorer. Is this socialism? No! This kind of "socialism" cannot be found in Marxism.

Is "getting rich through labor" advocating the development of capitalism? This notion is totally incorrect. First, "getting rich through labor" means opening the door of prosperity to the masses of laborers and not to a handful of exploiters. Second, the key to "getting rich through labor" lies in getting rich by means of "labor" and not by means of "exploitation." Third, "getting rich through labor" means opening the door of prosperity to the masses of laborers and not to a handful of exploiters. Second, the key can advance only along with the contributions he has made in raising the level of the collective and the whole country.

Even now, the pernicious influence of Lin Biao and the "gang of four" is still very deep. Some people still look upon egalitarianism as something of a "socialist" or "communist" nature to worship and adore. Small production complacency and envy are liable to be encouraged. They do not want to be superior to others and are afraid that others will be superior to them. When they notice other people "getting rich through labor," they see red.

To build socialism in China we must practice to each according to his work and advocate "getting rich through labor." Not only must we do so in the countryside, but we must also do this in the factories and other departments. Getting rich through labor should be encouraged and protected.[29]

The return of private property to former Chinese capitalists in January 1979 was given strong publicity and there was a mixed reaction among the Chinese public when they learned that in Shanghai seven thousand families each had more than six thousand dollars returned to them and some received far larger sums.

The readers of the *People's Daily* are being taught by many a news story many of the lessons in enterprise management that capitalist businessmen had to learn for themselves the hard way before Harvard founded a business school: "Stop being obsessed with your product and find out what the market wants!" "Learn to entice your customer!" and the oldest adage of them all: "Maximize your profits!"

In more ways than one can count, let alone describe in the space of single chapter, the leadership of the Communist Party of China is moving the Chinese economy away from the Soviet model they chose to copy in the 1950s, and they are rejoining the international market economy upon which they turned their backs in 1949, as the Soviet Union had done in the 1930s. That this is happening in the world's most populous developing country is of political as well as economic interest.

There is no mystery about the direction in which the Chinese leadership is headed, but there is a question as to how far they go in that direction—how literally they will apply Lenin's teaching, quoted by Hu Qiaomu, that the proletariat must adopt the whole experience of capitalism.

There is theoretical justification for Marxist–Leninists to turn the clock back and retrace steps taken prematurely toward socialism and then communism, and, in his November 1979 speech to officials of Sichuan province, Zhao Ziyang said that because of ultraleftism in the past, China had put the cart before the horse in changing the structure of her economy. Marxist–Leninists are supposed to adapt "the relations of production" (the system of ownership) to the growth of the "productive forces" (the increasing scale and sophistication of economic operations in the economy), but, said Zhao, China had laid emphasis "solely on changing the relations of production with the result that these relations have gone far ahead of the level of productive forces." This justifies reforms, such as devolving production responsibility from the team to the work group in the countryside, which are a step back from conventional socialism. It could be used in the future to justify more drastic reforms.

Cold-shouldered by the United States in the late 1940s, the Chinese Communists felt obliged to abandon their strategy, outlined to John Service by Bo Gu in 1944, of a gradual transition to socialism through "democracy and free enterprise" over a period of thirty to a hundred years. Instead, they tried to leap into Soviet-style socialism in less than five years. They skipped over the capitalist stage in the Marxist scheme for the march to socialism. They all know now, as some of them warned then, that this was unwise.

In 1942 Mao said that Marxism–Leninism was an arrow he and his comrades would shoot at their target, the Chinese revolution. Prosperity for the Chinese people was part of that target, and the arrow has not yet hit the target. Are Chinese leaders discarding the arrow of Marxism–Leninism to pick up one made by Adam Smith or Milton Friedman? Or are they refashioning the arrow in a way Marx and Lenin and the whole panoply of socialist saints would approve if they were alive today and faced China's problems and opportunities?

To judge again by what Zhao Ziyang said to his provincial subordinates, Party leaders will do nothing they cannot call socialist. The *Peking Review* gave this account of Zhao's speech:

> Of course, we must keep to the socialist road. But what is socialism? [In the past] there was confusion in the people's minds, and many things which are not socialist were regarded as sacred and inviolable principles. Marx and Engels were the founders of

scientific socialism, but they did not and could not work out concrete measures for its realization. And Lenin did not impose a fixed pattern to restrict the people's initiative and creativity.

The hallmark of socialism is the public ownership of the means of production, and the principle of socialism is "to each according to his work." So long as these two principles are upheld, a demarcation line is clearly drawn between socialism on the one hand and capitalism and all other social systems based on the private ownership of the means of production and exploitation of man by man on the other. With these two principles as the prerequisites, we should adopt whatever system, structure, policy, and method are most effective in promoting the development of the productive forces and in bringing the superiority of the socialist system into play. We must never cocoon ourselves like silkworms.

Is the demarcation line as easy to draw as Zhao suggests? On which side of the line should one place the decisions to let individual handcraftsmen and hawkers ply their trade again on the streets of the cities: the peasant with his pink windmills whirling, and all the cobblers, photographers and watchmenders and peddlers of homemade editions of *Hai Rui Dismissed from Office* who followed him? How about the handing back of small shops and restaurants that were municipalized in the late 1950s? How about the joint ventures with foreign capitalists? What is socialism and what does "public ownership" mean? If the Tianjin stock exchange was reopened and the state allowed the public to buy shares in previously state-owned enterprises, would that increase the public character of their ownership or diminish it? In the early 1950s Liu Shaoqi invited the capitalists of Tianjin to send him a proposal for reopening the city's stock exchange. He did not promise to see it was done, but he did say he would consider it very seriously and that his view counted for about 50 percent on such decisions.

16

Unfreezing the Mind

At present there is too much studying going on and this is exceedingly harmful.

—MAO ZEDONG, 13 FEBRUARY 1964

The main task of students is studying.

—DENG XIAOPING, 22 APRIL 1978

ONE SUNLIT MORNING in May 1976, my wife and I climbed a terraced hillside just outside the small town of Yanan. First we visited the sturdy stone building resembling an Episcopal church where the Communist Party of China had held its Seventh Congress in 1945. Climbing again, we saw ahead of us a flat, open grassy space where a couple of hundred people could sit on the ground for a meeting. On another May morning, thirty-four years earlier, the political and cultural leaders of the Communist Party had gathered here to listen to Mao Zedong talk about party policy for literature and the arts. The line he laid down that day, and in a second speech later in the month, remained the orthodox line on culture for the rest of his life.

The grassy space, the cool of the morning, and the blue sky above reminded me of happy moments spent on similar hillsides in Hong Kong when I would gather my Gurkha soldiers together for a short rest after a company exercise.

As we walked onto that Yanan meeting place, I noticed a photograph, framed and mounted on a stake. Our guide explained it was a photograph taken after Mao had finished his talk on 2 May 1942. A number of the best-known writers, poets, and party officials had been gathered with Mao for a formal group photograph. I asked our guide to identify them for me. Among them was a young woman called Ding Ling.

I knew something of Ding Ling's history. She had come to Yanan as a talented young writer, a vivacious young woman whose early writings had reflected the struggle of Western-educated women of her generation to free themselves from the controls of the traditional Chinese family. She was one of those intellectuals who looked on the Communist Party as a liberating force against the corruption and repression of Chiang Kai-shek's government. After joining the Party in the early 1930s she had soon found herself in a Nationalist jail. On her release she had made her way to Yanan, where she was given quite a welcome.

This emancipated young woman from a well-to-do home, who had been nurtured on Flaubert and Maupassant, Gorki and Tolstoy[1] and intrigued by the views on free love held by early Russian Communists,[2] contrasted oddly with the tough little band of women who had made the Long March and the simple fighters of peasant origin like Peng Dehuai whose ideas on liberating China owed nothing to Flaubert. But she threw herself into organizational work with women and wrote some articles and short stories about life in Yanan. These were to spell the beginning of trouble for her, because the reality of life there did not live up to the ideals which had drawn her to the Party. She protested against examples of incompetence, elitism, and male chauvinism that she saw around her, laying the blame on senior party leaders who, she alleged, did not practice what they preached. Her courage inspired a few other writers to expose the darker side of life in the guerrilla base.

As she sat listening to Mao on 2 May 1942, Ding Ling must have been cast into gloom. The line he was laying down was irreconcilable with her own beliefs on what a creative artist's role should be and at odds with her love of Western literature, as a source both of values and of forms suitable for expressing a modern consciousness.

Mao's speech was presented as his original doctrine but, according to Merle Goldman, a leading scholar in this field, much of it could have been translated from the speeches of the Soviet literary czar, Andrei Zhdanov. He served notice that henceforth literature and all phases of intellectual activity were to be dictated by party policy. Art would serve politics and political criteria would have priority over artistic criteria. The forms used should be readily understood by "the masses"; Western ones were ruled out. No longer might left-wing intellectuals claim the right to independence of conscience. Mao had put China's intellectuals into a Soviet-style straitjacket.

Ding Ling and others who sat with Mao that morning were pressured in the weeks that followed to disown their views and criticize fellow writers whom they respected. It was their first taste of "thought reform." Ding Ling did what she was told, and as a result she found it impossible to write with her old vitality. After the Communists won national power in 1949, she wrote a novel about land reform which took the party line sufficiently to win the Stalin Prize, but thought reform had not changed her innermost thoughts about the freedom an artist or writer needs. So, like many other intellectuals, she spoke out in the Hundred Flowers campaign, appealing to the Party to remove the straitjacket that was stifling her. She was duly purged when the whistle blew. She disappeared without trace, and as I looked at her photograph in Yanan I believe she was still undergoing "re-education through labor" or a similar regimen.

The enforcement of Mao's doctrine on the arts had led to the persecution and even death of hundreds of thousands of creative writers, artists, and thinkers by the time I came to Yanan. Why did the Party still display the photograph that showed Mao sitting with people whose voices he had smothered in the succeeding thirty-four years? Those who had been silenced were still silent; those who had died had been buried without any announcement and therefore unmourned by those who had valued their work.

Mao himself was dying now in Peking, politically and physically, and his end had been hastened by the demonstrations of April 1976, which showed that people would no longer tolerate his kind of dictatorship. On Tiananmen Square he had reaped the harvest sown on this hillside.

On 1 November 1979, Ding Ling, gray-haired and lined of face at the age of seventy-five, stood in the Great Hall of the People to pay silent tribute to writers and artists who had died under the persecution by Lin Biao and the Gang of Four. She was one of 3200 delegates to a National Congress of Writers and Artists.[3] She had survived a dozen years of hard labor and five years of prison and was now editing some of her new and old writings for publication.

Among the one hundred writers and artists named in the speech of mourning at the congress was Wu Han, whose play *Hai Rui Dismissed from Office* had been brought onto the streets of Peking in a hand-printed edition by hawkers at the hour of Deng's triumph at the Work Conference in November 1978. Now the play was back onstage in Peking.

Almost all the writers and artists attending the congress had spent years in official disgrace, some since the Cultural Revolution, others since the Great Leap Forward. They had survived to be brought back from the "memory hole."

After Mao's death, when the press had begun to speak of the start of a new era of vigor in the arts and literature, I had set up some milestones in my mind that, if passed, would mean substantial progress. One of them had been the restoration to honor Deng Tuo, the satirist who, with Peng Zhen's protection, had turned his talents against Mao in 1961 and 1962. Another had been the restoration of Hu Feng, the critic who in 1955 had championed the right of the Marxist writer to an independent conscience. By November 1979, Deng Tuo had been restored to honor, posthumously, and his work was being republished. Hu was not at the writer's congress. He was out of jail but he had not reappeared in public. One milestone had been passed, another still lay ahead.

These two writers had been treated differently because Deng Tuo had attacked Mao, not only to defend certain values but also to advance the political goals of a faction in the Party that in 1979 was riding high; by contrast, Hu Feng had challenged a prerogative of the Party itself—its right to final arbitration in creative work—and had launched his challenge without the backing of any faction in the leadership. Hu Feng was a symbol of the intellectuals' demand for a degree of freedom the Party was still not prepared to grant.

But the speeches made to the congress showed that the reformers led by Deng did want to loosen the reins considerably. Deng himself and Zhou Yang, Vice-Chairman of the China Federation of Literary and Art Circles and the Party's chief literary commissar since the 1930s, both spoke to the congress, and their speeches showed how far Party policy had evolved since the death of Mao. A speech by Bai Hua, a writer with a military background who had been purged as a rightist in 1957, showed what hopes were still unfulfilled.

Deng's speech was a political balancing act. He gave encouragement to diversity and individual exploration without giving away the Party's role of final arbiter. Nowhere did he mention the Yanan Talks by name, and his reference to Mao's ideas was vague in the extreme.

His audience must have been encouraged to hear him say:

> Any artistic creation that provides education, enlightenment, entertainment, and aesthetic enjoyment on a grand scale or small, written in a serious or humorous vein, lyrical or philosophical, all should be given a place in our literary and art field. Feats of heroism or daily labor, the struggle of ordinary people, their joys and sorrows, the life of today's people as well as that of the ancients should all be portrayed.

He advocated freedom of choice of style for the artist or writer and free discussion about artistic creation. From the very father of modern totalitarian dictatorship, Lenin, Deng's resourceful researchers had found a quotation about giving "plenty of room for individual creation and plenty of room for different ideas, imagination, forms, and content."

Deng forbade party committees to issue orders to creative writers. The bureaucratic way of doing things must be discarded and "administrative orders in the sphere of literature and art creation and criticism must be abolished." Writers and artists must make full use of the *individual* creative spirit because their work was so complex. "The subject matter and method of presentation can only be explored and decided step-by-step by the writers and artists themselves in their artistic work. *No outside interference should be permitted."* (Emphasis added.)

Zhou Yang's speech was as much of a landmark in Party policy as Hu Qiaomu's 1978 speech on economics. It is 25,000 words long and covers thirty pages in English, and in it Zhou Yang reviewed the whole history of Chinese left-wing cultural creation and Party policy in this field before giving guidelines for the future. In the historical review Zhou Yang acknowledged that the Party had made numerous errors and specified them, without attributing blame, except in the case of "Lin Biao and the Gang of Four." He did not reconcile Hu Feng to the Party, but restored to honor almost every other writer and critic of note who suffered from the Party's leftist dogmatism.

In setting guidelines for the future he reinforced the points made by Deng and elaborated on them. The guidelines he set will certainly encourage greater diversity and more experimentation. He said: "With the prerequisite that literature and art should observe the objective laws of reflecting real life, every artist and writer must be free to adopt any method in his or her creative work." He strongly defended the need for works which exposed the dark side of life under Communist Party rule, provided that authors did not simply spread "passive, listless, and nihilist ideas and feelings," but sought to help the people avoid the recurrence of past tragedies.

Zhou Yang defined the relationship between politics and literature and art as being, in essence, that between "the people" and literature and art. "So long as literature and art give true expression to the needs and interests of the people, it is inevitable that they will exert a great influence on politics." The relationship was not a one-way street, with literature and art playing a supporting role in implementing a certain concrete policy or a limited task for a certain place at a certain time. The arts were not mere "tools of class struggle," and stereotyped, "formula" works at the superficial level of slogans or posters were useless.

Zhou Yang did not sign away the Party's right to decide what was the "true expression" of the needs and interests of the people, but he did say "We must never try to provide guidance in a peremptory, patriarchal manner or by indulging in personal whims. Writers and artists must enjoy the freedom to decide what and how to write. . . . Free competition among different schools of art should also be encouraged . . . but conformity must not be imposed."

Some people in the Party had charged that "emancipation of the mind" had gone too far, leaving the masses ideologically confused. Zhou Yang retorted that, on the contrary, emancipation had not gone far enough. He warned against "anarchism, extreme individualism, and the tendency toward capitalist 'liberalization' " and the dangers of people being corrupted by "capitalist cultural thinking and lifestyles." He saw a danger too of people accepting Western cultural thinking with such devotion as to forfeit their own national self-confidence and self-respect. But he did not use these dangers as a pretext for curbing access to foreign culture. Indeed, he emphasized the need for increased cultural exchanges and spoke of the "common spiritual wealth of mankind." Echoing precisely the line by Hu Qiaomu on the economy, Zhou Yang said that the Marxist classics, including Mao Zedong Thought, did not offer ready-made solutions to all problems existing in literature and art. Marxist theory on literature and art must be integrated with China's "time-honored cultural traditions" and the nation's "two-thousand-year history of literary and artistic theoretical criticism."

Organizationally, Zhou Yang indicated that great reliance would be placed on the China Federation of Literary and Art Circles and various literary and art associations in all parts of the country. The editors of literature and art magazines were to shoulder "great responsibilities" for encouraging young talent and for opposing those who sought to suppress it.

Zhou Yang called for thousands upon thousands of "pathbreakers" to lead a revival of art and literature. To show what he meant, he quoted Lu Xun, China's greatest writer of the century (and an opponent of Zhou Yang's sectarian ways in the

1930s): "In the old China, Lu Xun deeply regretted the 'silent China' and prayed for a 'valorous pathbreaker' who would dare to 'break away from traditional ideas and methods' and break the silence that reigned in the cultural arena."

Zhou Yang agreed that the leftists had almost turned new China into the old "silent China," but "the voice of the liberated and highly conscious people" had burst out in April 1976, using poems as weapons of political struggle.

He ended, of course, by striking a note of confidence in the future and the note did not ring false. But Bai Hua, the army writer who had been pushed down China's memory hole in 1957 and had been rescued only after Deng Xiaoping's return to power, struck a more somber and more skeptical note.

He began with a bitter-sweet comment on the congress itself: "I highly value my chance of being able to speak at the Fourth National Congress of Writers and Artists. Many of our comrades and comrades-in-arms have not seen each other for more than twenty years. It is as if they had been living in different worlds. . . . Some comrades and comrades-in-arms have left us forever. We can still remember how they hoped and fought as we did. They left behind for us their hopes and struggle."

In a brief review of the People's Republic, Bai said: "Our motherland had a bright and beautiful morning. In the morning, we were sober and made great sacrifices to achieve our goals. At that time, our Party was fully confident and had inexhaustible power. All the people responded to its calls, because it had taken root among the people. . . . However, we later fell back. . . . Even today, when we oppose modern fetishes and advocate science, we can still see scenes which resemble those before the revolution of 1911, where anyone who smashed an idol was surrounded and beaten to death."

Writers who want to reflect the realities of China are faced with hard questions, and Bai posed some of them: "Should we cover up the social contradictions which no one can cover up? Should we eulogize the state of ignorance for which we have made great material sacrifice? Should we keep silent before the bureaucracy which has tied us hand and foot? Should we preserve the prestige of the one who practiced the 'rule by the voice of one man alone,' the practice of which has nothing to do with a Communist Party? The people will not allow us to do so."

At one point Bai seemed to challenge very directly Deng's words about the need for party leadership. He said: "The tasks of writers and artists are assigned by history. Anyone who violates the law of development of history, applies pressure on literature and art workers, and subordinates literature and art work to his political interests will fail in the end. We must not neglect this phenomenon, which has rare precedence in the history of mankind. We must study its emergence and development, its terrifying success, and its ignominious failure."

Bai pointed out that while the Central Committee and "the people" had given writers and artists the right to express their views, some officials were still trying to protect the ultraleftist line, the "cancer" that brought such harm to the country. "They do not allow the people to touch the cancer. They accuse those who touch it of opposing the Party and lacking socialist virtues."

Bai spoke of the legacy of fear that inhibits many Chinese from even thinking, let alone speaking:

> Many kind-hearted comrades and readers have written to me saying: "You are far from safe." I am very grateful to them for their kindness. It was very sensible of them to think so. The Chinese nation has many fine qualities. Honesty is one, but for a time, many honest people lost their personal freedom, their minimal standard of living, and even their lives. At the same time, many hypocrites gained fame, profit, and high official positions without having to do any work—just by scaring other people. Some of them came to a bad end, like Yao Wenyuan, but only a very few. Over the past years, stories of how people made rapid advances in their careers were taught to the old people, youngsters, and children of China every year and every month. A social mentality took shape: hypocrites are safe and the honest are in danger. I often heard comrades who had children say: "My son will surely be put in jail in the future, because he does not know how to tell a lie." Others said contentedly: "My son has a promising future, because he is now a young double-dealer." After the smashing of the Gang of Four and especially after the Third Plenum of the Eleventh Central Committee, much has been done to eliminate confusion and restore order. Fewer and fewer people have been punished for

their speeches. However this does not mean that the "all clear" signal has been sounded. The majority of intellectuals have personally learned this lesson: when you are allowed to express opinions, there is a danger of tightening up controls; when you express opinions, you are preparing conditions for blows, labels, and imprisonment. Did the cold wind which blew after the Third Plenum last spring not clearly show this? . . .

Deng had claimed that writers now experienced "ease of mind," but Bai cautioned "It is not yet time to say that writers and artists are relatively safe. Are there not people who write and speak about arresting some people and putting labels on them again?"

One sign that even China's most highly regarded writers still feel restrained is the failure of any of those who have been restored to honor to produce a major work since their rehabilitation. That may soon change, but it had not changed before they held their congress. Ba Jin, Ding Ling, and others had all told interviewers that they were busy writing but none of them had actually published anything new that could be compared with their great pre-1949 work.

Bai called for encouragement for young writers, claiming that the unofficial journals, which had all but disappeared by the time he made his speech, had published writers of talent who had been cold-shouldered by established writers. He showed more sympathy for them than Deng, who had called for "setting strict demands" on them. The thinking of the young writers shocked their elders, who called it "terrible," but it was the history of their lives which had made it so. They could produce excellent work in the future because they lived at the grass roots of society, they had courage, and they knew how to think for themselves. "We must not neglect them but must try to understand and guide them. It is absolutely wrong to train young writers who can neither think independently nor find a voice of their own. If there is more freedom for literary creation, these young writers will mature sooner."

Bai applauded the principle, enunciated by Deng Xiaoping, of doing away with outside interference in creative work but warned that junior officials ignored the Central Committee's instructions. "The reason is that flagrant interference is the one thing they know how to do. Not only that, they will lose their jobs if they don't interfere. . . . They will appear to be unintelligent and lacking in wisdom if they allow the writers and artists to show their intelligence and wisdom. . . . The Party Central Committee only put forward some correct principles. We have never heard of anyone being dismissed or demoted or having his salary cut for having inflicted ultraleftist persecution over intellectuals, not to mention being punished according to the law. Therefore the basic conditions needed for creating art and literature will have to be won through long-term unremitting struggle."

While Bai spoke of the risks that writers still ran, he did believe that conditions were improving and forecast: "If this situation continues to develop, excellent works will appear in a few years. Today, different opinions may be brought up to contend. . . . Nothing like this has existed in the past three decades."

Bai ended his speech with this appeal: "We must be courageous. Without courage, we cannot make a breakthrough. Without a breakthrough there can be no literature."[4]

The *People's Daily* published excerpts of the speech totaling over five thousand words in the English translation. A speech that went further than Deng had gone in calling for freedom for the artist and in criticizing the atmosphere of fear maintained by junior cultural commissars would not have been published at such length by the *People's Daily* without the blessing of some group in the top leadership. The handling of this speech and the whole management of the congress demonstrate how the reformers in the Party are cutting back party control in this field as in others.

The tactics used are a mixture of direct and indirect pressure. On the first day, Deng makes a speech that embodies a reformist line, without going so far as to leave his political flank unguarded. The next day the leading cultural commissar underlines Deng's reformist ideas and elaborates on them. Then along comes Bai Hua, who speaks in the language of a wall-poster writer rather than a party official, and he pushes the reformist line further than Deng or Zhou Yang could do at this stage. His speech is given nationwide publicity by the *People's Daily*. It does not follow that Deng endorses every word that Bai has spoken, but he approves of the general thrust of his remarks and of the effect their publication will have in preparing the ground for future developments. Deng and his allies are not infallible political tacticians—they suffered a major reverse on the issue of wall posters in 1979—but in the long run they do manage to roll the circus ball in the direction they want. And the direction is away from totalitarianism toward something more tolerant of diversity.

To judge by their words and deeds of the years 1977 to 1980, the reformers in the Chinese leadership today are not totalitarian either in their ambitions or their methods. It is my view that they know full well that "thought reform" never really reformed the thoughts of China's intellectuals, it only taught them what orthodox thoughts they must mouth to stay out of trouble. The reformers have accurately assessed the damage done to the nation's vitality by the Yanan straitjacket; they recognize that it split at the seams in the Qing Ming demonstrations in April 1976 and on Democracy Wall in 1978–1979, and they have no intention of trying to stitch it back together again. This is not only because they are political realists who know an impossibility when they see one, but also because they themselves no longer believe, if ever they did believe, that Marxism–Leninism provides them with a blueprint for the society of the future. Only people who believe they have such a blueprint have the will and the "moral" force to impose totalitarian rule.

As Hu Qiaomu's speech to the State Council in July 1978 made very clear, the reformers look on Marxism–Leninism not as a set of pat solutions to all problems that may arise but as a scientific method of studying the world and solving problems as they arise. One may dispute the value of this "scientific method," but the point is that the reformers are looking for solutions, not imposing them ready-made. This is not a totalitarian frame of mind.

A Chinese friend of mine with a good feel for the political

pulse of the reformist leaders told me in 1979: "A major goal for the Party's work for years to come will be the eradication of dogmatism," and I accept this as a fair claim. But as sworn enemies of dogma who have as their only instrument of politics and government a bureaucracy that has grown highly dogmatic over the past decades, Deng and his allies must often proceed in a manner which is far from direct. They have shown that they judge there are times for frontal assaults on dogmatism and bureaucracy and times for oblique attack. The policy for art and literature is no exception. They proclaim the continuing need for effective leadership by party committees, but they encourage people to read novelists like Saul Bellow or essayists like Deng To, who urged China's leaders to "seek advice from all sides." They keep Stalin's portrait on display in Tiananmen Square but give a hero's welcome back to an unrepentant Ding Ling, who tells an interview that in China "When there are two people together they tell the truth; when there are three, they tell jokes; and when there are four, they tell lies."[5]

Nobody who has been in Chinese politics as long as Deng or Zhou Yang is going to leave his flank unguarded by making wholly unambiguous statements on any major issue, least of all on one as controversial as party leadership over culture, but the fact is that, since their return to power, the Chinese public has been given vastly increased access to foreign and Chinese culture. In literature, republications and new publications have ranged from the complete works of Shakespeare to Herman Wouk on the foreign side, and from *The Twenty-four Histories* to Ba Jin on the Chinese side. In philosophy, after an unvaried diet of Marxism–Leninism for many years, Chinese can now turn to Adam Smith and other classical authors. A spokesman for the publishing industry claimed that in 1977 and 1978 a total of 6.3 billion copies of 25,000 titles was published.

Many of the finest musicians, dancers, and actors of the Western world and Japan followed each other to China in rapid succession in 1979. Pop culture had a place in the opening: perhaps the most electric moment in this encounter between the long-frozen Chinese culture and the West was when two black American dancers, Peaches and Herb, disco-danced their way down the marble steps of the Hall of Prayer for Good Harvests (which stands near the Temple of Heaven and is often mistaken for it) to a crowd of Chinese schoolchildren, who joined them in the dance, picking up the rhythm with consummate ease. This was part of an officially sponsored breakthrough, a television spectacular built around Bob Hope and nostalgically entitled *Road to Peking*.

A domestic breakthrough, whose origins were far from official, was an art show that took place in Peking in late November 1979. At first the artists had applied for permission to exhibit their work at the National Gallery of Fine Arts, but were turned down. Their next move was to display their work on the sidewalk outside the gallery; when the police appeared and started to dismantle the show, established artists belonging to the Peking Artists Association took the exhibits inside the gallery to prevent the police from confiscating them. The young artists then staged a protest march to the city hall.

The twenty-three artists and some eighty supporters marched on the thirtieth anniversary of the founding of the People's Republic. They assembled at Democracy Wall, and before setting off some of them made speeches. One asked "Why are some people allowed to exhibit and others are not? Aren't we all equal? There is no more protection for the ordinary people now than under the Gang of Four."

Several leaders of the march were representatives of unofficial literary and political journals, including *Exploration*, *Today*, and *Fertile Ground*. *Exploration* had brought out a special issue to mark the anniversary which claimed that China's youth was losing its faith in the Communist Party, which was itself undergoing a crisis of faith.

As they marched to the city hall they shouted slogans against dictatorship and carried a banner that read "In politics we want democracy and in art we want freedom." Several leaders of the march were allowed to enter the city council offices to present their case to officials.[6] They were given permission to show their work for ten days in the Bei Hai Park in Peking. Nothing quite like it had been seen in Peking before: abstract renditions of an imperial palace, impressionistic street scenes, a dozen nudes, and some powerful, abstract sculptures that mocked arrogant bureaucrats and other less-attractive facets of Chinese society.[7]

It is not just young democracy activists and artists who link democracy and art. A week after the artists' march, a sober group of academics met in another part of town under official auspices to discuss the relationship between art and politics. Some among them argued that, first, art and literature cannot be separated from politics and, second, there can be no artistic democracy without political democracy. The official press reported their message clearly.[8]

The first twentieth-century novel to be republished under the policy of enabling Chinese to get in touch with their cultural roots again was Ba Jin's *Family*. One of the great works of the golden age of modern Chinese fiction, first published in 1931, it is the very opposite of the formula novel of stereotyped proletarian revolutionary heroes that had been churned out in the 1970s. Ba Jin' himself was more of an anarchist than a Marxist when he wrote it. The novel tells of the tensions of the 1920s between feudal family controls and the desire of modern-minded young people to realize personal and social goals that conflict with feudal values and discipline. There is an analogy between those conflicts and the conflicts of today caused by young people rebelling against the controls imposed by their work units or by the whole Soviet-style bureaucratic apparatus of the state. Those who chose *Family* to head the republican list cannot have been blind to the analogy.

The first foreign play to be republished in Chinese was *Hamlet*, and the hesitating prince in that play hardly conformed to the archetype of the proletarian revolutionary hero. It sold out within three hours of being put on sale in Peking. In September 1979 the Shanghai People's Publishing House republished work by Chinese writers that had first been published around 1957 and had been denounced in the antirightist movement as antiparty and antisocialist. The title given to the collection was *Fresh Flowers That Have Bloomed Once Again*.

There is such a thirst for these and other publications of any merit that lines form around the block when they go on sale. People stand in line for hours to buy them, and then a discreet secondhand market develops. Before the republishing of classics of the past and the best of new foreign work there was a system of hand-copying in force: among a class of students of a foreign language a book would circulate—say, Steinbeck's *Cannery Row*; as each student read it he or she was honor-bound to copy one chapter. In this way a new copy of the book was built up for circulation.

The same happened with Chinese writers' work. In 1965 a young man from Changsha, capital of Hunan province, was sent down to live in the countryside, under the policy of sending urban youths to live in the villages if there was no job for them in the city. His name was Zhang Yang, and two years earlier he had started writing a novel that described the lives and loves of Chinese scientists of his parents' generation. Living in Zhongyue commune, he completed the first draft in 1970. After rewriting it six times in his leisure hours, he circulated handwritten copies. So many people recopied it that news of it reached Yao Wenyuan, the Politburo member in charge of culture. He ordered that the author of the book be tracked down and arrested. As a result, Zhang was sent to jail in 1975 and remained there until his case, like those of many others, was reviewed in 1979. He was released from jail and a few months later the novel was published officially under the title *Second Handshake*, which it had acquired in the course of being recopied. From the time Zhang had first put it into circulation until it was formally published, tens of thousands of copies were made by hand, and some of those who made them were persecuted for doing so.[9]

Starting in late 1978, a revival of the Chinese theater began, and in the next two years hundreds of new plays were produced in Peking alone. Foreign plays were also staged by Chinese companies. The new Chinese plays did not stray outside the ideological frame set by the more liberal theoretical writers in the official press, but none of them could conceivably have been performed during Mao's last decade. One play that helped break down invisible barriers to thought and speech was *The Call of the Future*, performed in a workers' club in Peking in October 1979 by a neighborhood amateur drama group. It described contention between two Communist officials and made the main protagonists credible characters. A love theme was woven into the plot, which also dealt with such sensitive topics as security clearances for someone with a questionable class background and the degeneration of an official who had once been innovative but later thought only of politics, revolution, and class struggle. The audience snickered when this official walked over to a gilded bust of Mao and gazed at it reverently in an attempt to put his opponent in an argument at a disadvantage.[10]

The relaxation of dictatorship after Mao's death also permitted a slow revival of religious worship. Chinese religious leaders and their followers of the Buddhist, Christian, and Moslem faiths were allowed to resume their activity and selected places of worship all over China were renovated and reopened after years of neglect following the vandalism of the Cultural Revolution. In 1979 it was announced that both the Koran and the Bible were to be reprinted, but there was a more cautious attitude on the republication of the Buddhist scriptures. The number of Christians who resumed activity was tiny compared even to the 1950s, let alone the years before 1949, when the Roman Catholics numbered about three million and the protestant sects totaled about seven hundred thousand. The number of active Muslims has always been much higher than that of Christians, and should probably be counted in the tens of millions. Buddhism is of course more widespread and more sinicized than either Christianity or Islam, and Zhao Puchu, the urbane Acting President of the Buddhist Association of China, told foreign journalists in 1979 that lay believers could number a hundred million or more.[11] Daoism, the religion most interwoven with peasant superstition and a traditional source of inspiration for peasant revolts, seemed destined to remain under official disapproval. There were no reports of Daoist temples being reopened, but in the countryside I noticed that burial mounds were receiving more attention after 1977, indicating that traditional practices were being quietly resumed.

After his return to public office in July 1977, Deng Xiaoping first devoted his attention to formal education and science and technology. Surveying these areas at that time was rather as it must have been to survey West European industry in 1945. The landscape was strewn with the wreckage of past endeavors, the people were tired by a long war, many of the most talented and experienced people had been scattered by the war, but there was a great yearning for reconstruction and rejuvenation.

Officials described education as a disaster area. Their judgment was supported by the results of a test given in the fall of 1977 to university graduates working in scientific and technical jobs in Shanghai, China's most modern city. The tests were based only on high school course requirements, and the Shanghai authorities gave those to be tested adequate time to prepare for the exam; 68 percent failed in mathematics, 70 percent failed in physics and 76 percent in chemistry. The NCNA report on the test said that the most shocking thing was that "some people could not answer one question in their own specialty's most basic knowledge. They just handed in blank papers."[12]

Fang Yi, a member of the Politburo and President of the Chinese Academy of Sciences, said that before the Cultural Revolution China had been close to catching up with international levels in some fields of science but by the late 1970s had fallen so far behind that it was fifteen or twenty years behind in some fields and more in others.[13]

A quick international comparison shows how desperately China lags behind in training top-flight minds. If one uses the measure of the number of students engaged in tertiary (higher) education per thousand people in the population, the United States has 50, Canada 36, Argentina 24, Japan 21, France 19, the USSR 16, Brazil 11, South Korea 9, India 5, and China 0.1—one fiftieth of the Indian ratio.

China's problems of scientific manpower are not limited to lack of educational facilities. There has also been misuse of trained minds. The system of compulsory assignment to posts selected by the state was supposed to have the advantage over a free labor market of ensuring the rational deployment of manpower. In practice, the reverse seems to have occurred. As early as 1956, Premier Zhou Enlai was moved to say that "some are assigned one task today and another tomorrow, but are never given a job for which they are qualified." After this, the State

Planning Commission studied the problem and reported that of the 98,000 engineers and technicians who graduated from higher education between 1949 and 1957, only 22 percent were involved in engineering. The anti-intellectualism that was propagated during the Great Leap Forward and the Cultural Revolution aggravated the problem. As part of an attempt to correct it the government organized a survey in 1979 to find out how the nation was using or wasting its trained linguists.[14]

One of Deng's first moves in tackling the task of intellectual reconstruction was to assure intellectuals in general that the Party now regarded them as bona fide workers as much as those who work with their hands. This helped remove some of the stigma that had attached to them for years past. His promotion of more general policies of redressing injustices perpetrated in the Cultural Revolution was of especial benefit to intellectuals, who had suffered more than any other sector of the population. So was his drive to get the Central Committee to remove pejorative class labels from former landlords, capitalists, and others. The ruling that the children of such people were to be judged mainly on their own merit and not by the sins of their fathers and mothers opened the doors of higher education to a number of young people from educated homes.

The press ran articles refuting the line taken by "Lin Biao and the Gang of Four" that truth has a class character. This had been used to stifle academic debate. Truth, wrote a *People's Daily* contributor, "is objective and independent of any individual or class, [although] the recognition of that truth or the attitude taken toward it may be strongly influenced by individual or class considerations."[15]

Speaking at a national conference on education in April 1978, Deng insisted that China could not meet its modernization goals unless schools imposed strict standards and enforced rigid discipline. "The main task of students is to study," he said. China should follow a "practical, down-to-earth revolutionary style of work that will help us turn lofty ideals into reality step by step." Quoting from Mao in a vein we had not seen in the Chairman's pronouncements in his later years, Deng added that after ten thousand years there would "still be a gap between the advanced and the backward" and that different people have different abilities.[16]

The selection system for entry to higher education was reformed by bringing back the pre-Cultural Revolution nationwide examination, and some innovations were made to reduce political bias in selection. Deng ruled that any citizen who met the age requirements could apply to take the exam, whether or not his work unit agreed, and he downgraded the importance to be placed on family background in the final selection—the main criterion from now on was to be academic ability, not proletarian or peasant origin. The universities and technical colleges, which had been recruiting far below their student capacity, quickly increased their intake. But it is a sad comment on the neglect of the intellect that had marked Mao's last years that it was forecast that by 1980 Chinese universities and colleges would only have returned to the 1963 level of two hundred thousand graduates per year.[17]

Another reform introduced by Deng was the establishment (or perhaps the re-establishment) of key schools. These were schools, universities, and colleges that were to be allocated a higher-than-average share of resources to enable them to provide the best education China could devise for students of outstanding promise, who would be selected by examination. (At the secondary level they would be China's equivalent of the grammar schools that Britain had abolished a few years earlier out of respect for the very principle of egalitarianism that the Chinese Communist Party was now denouncing as a deviation from true socialism.) China had concluded that it could not afford *not* to develop its talents to the full.

The launching of a mass campaign to teach foreign languages by radio and television was only a foretaste of bigger things to come.

I watched more ambitious plans for educational television unfold with a special personal interest. Driving along the road from Peking to Tianjin in the dark days of 1968, when China was still in the grip of obscurantism, the sight of underemployed country people (one man tending one sheep, another spending his morning collecting animal manure from the highway) set me to thinking how, in an ideal world, one would accelerate the development of China. Would it be a massive injection of capital funds, a Marshall Plan for China? That would be only part of the solution, and the funds would be useless if there were not enough trained Chinese minds to put them to work in new industries and trades. Surely a major part of the strategy would be to turn the underemployment of so many Chinese into a virtue by using mass media to train and educate them in the hours they were not fully occupied with production. I started looking into the history of the application of mass media to education in China. I discovered that China had been one of the first countries to use television for education. Its pioneering efforts were first spoiled by the Great Leap Forward, and when they were relaunched in more favorable circumstances in 1960 the television side never reached mass dimensions because of the lack of sets in China. By 1968 satellite-broadcast television was being adopted on a major scale for education and development by India and Indonesia, and so I dreamed of the day when the international climate would allow China to use this promising technology. In 1978, after the visit to Peking of the science adviser to the U.S. president, it was announced that China was negotiating for the purchase of a communications satellite and Chinese broadcasting officials told me the plan was to use it for educational television, in addition to telephone communication. However, the Education Ministry and the broadcasting authorities were not waiting for the satellite to relaunch educational television. In early 1979 they announced the opening of a television university using existing equipment. They expected millions of students across the nation, and I was told that study sessions would be organized by factories and other work units. A communications satellite will carry broadcasts to those vast areas of China which have no microwave distribution system. Then China will advance toward a goal that was dear to Mao, reducing the gap between the city and countryside, by means of that kind of Western science that seemed to interest him so little.

In March 1978, Deng Xiaoping opened a National Science Conference, an event without parallel in China's history. His speech to that conference gave China's scientists reason to believe that at last there was proper understanding in high places of the contribution they could make to the nation's development. Fang Yi strengthened the scientists' grounds for optimism when, later in the conference, he unveiled a national plan for science. The goals he listed to be attained before 1985 included:

• Approaching or reaching advanced world levels of the 1970s in a number of important branches of science and technology, by means of 108 key projects.
• An increase in the number of professional research workers to 800,000.
• Establishment of up-to-date centers for scientific experimentation.
• Establishment of a nationwide system for scientific and technological research. (Lack of communication between Chinese scientists has struck recent foreign visitors very forcibly.)

The 108 key projects lay within eight "comprehensive spheres" of science and technology:

• Agriculture.
• Energy.
• Materials (e.g., metals and building materials).
• Electronic computers.
• Lasers.
• Space.
• High-energy physics (an experimental base was to be built within ten years, incorporating a proton accelerator of 30,000 to 50,000 million electron volts in the first stage and a "giant one" with a still larger capacity in the second five years).
• Genetic engineering.[18]

I have seen no expert analysis of this plan and am quite unqualified to judge it. But one thing is clear even to the layman: it is highly ambitious and will require huge investments. If it proves overambitious it will no doubt be scaled down in time, like the overambitious economic plan. But in political terms it showed that science had arrived in a big way. It demonstrated that Deng was not just flattering the conference when he said that "the crux of the four modernizations is the mastery of modern science and technology." That most of the students being sent abroad are to study science, and many of the foreign teachers being recruited to work in China or visit for limited teaching or research engagements are also scientists, are further indications of the importance the new leadership gives to this aspect of modernization.

The achievements of Chinese scientists in the distant past are legendary, a source of inspiration for the present that should not be underrated. Even under the adverse conditions of recent years they have made notable advances in molecular biology and advanced work has been done on the applications of lasers. In the more favorable climate of the United States, postwar achievements by Chinese-Americans have been striking and it is no accident that three winners of the Nobel Prize in physics since 1957 have been of Chinese descent. It is likely that if the political environment in China continues to improve, China's scientists will have much to be proud of ten or fifteen years from now.

In May 1976, on the same excursion that took us to Yanan, my wife and I visited the model agricultural brigade at Dazhai. The brigade kindly sent a car and one of its members to meet us at the nearest railway station, forty miles away. That member of the brigade, a man in his late fifties, acted as our guide and host during the next two days. During that time he never initiated any conversation, and killed all our attempts by monosyllabic answers. Two of my attempts to start a discussion I recall with special clarity. On the first occasion, I complimented him on the great increases in production that had been achieved in the brigade and the technical innovations that had been introduced and asked: "How do new ideas emerge in the brigade?"

"What do you mean?" he said.

"Well, do your new ideas all come from the minds of your brigade members or do you sometimes get them from books or from visits to other places where people are doing work similar to yours?"

He looked at me as though I was a simpleton, and said "They come from here."

"Do you mean to say you have learned nothing from outside in the past twenty years?" I asked.

"Nothing," he said dully.

The next day, I asked him who were the last visitors he had escorted, and he told me they were a party of Japanese farmers.

Surely he would have found it worthwhile talking to them; I could understand that he would consider it a waste of time talking to a nonfarmer like me, but the Japanese knew as much as anyone in the world about intensive farming to get high yields from terraced, irrigated farmland like Dazhai's. Had he asked them about the yields they were obtaining? No. Had he talked at all about farming techniques with them? No.

Dazhai was held up to the nation in those days as a model of self-reliance, but this was self-reliance carried to the point of obscurantism.

Six months later I visited a vegetable-growing brigade in a suburb of the northeastern industrial city of Shenyang. There I found what seemed to me a truly dynamic example of collective enterprise. The brigade had built miles of underground storage tunnels to serve as a giant deep-freeze when the temperature fell below zero. They were experimenting with new breeds of plants, using native and foreign varieties. They had started raising chickens in cages of a foreign design and had established a factory to prepare frozen chickens for sale at home and abroad. They were proud of the rising incomes of the brigade members and impatient at the shortages of consumer goods, which meant that their members were unable to spend their savings when they wanted to. That Shenyang brigade might have been in another country from Dazhai. It seemed to have got away with disregarding the Dazhai model and to be vigorously implementing the "right-wing revisionist line," which was still being castigated at that time. Today Dazhai has lost its status of a model for emulation nationwide. Instead encouragement is given to the spirit of outward-looking collective entrepreneurship that I saw in Shenyang. I suspect that if I returned to Dazhai today I would find little trace of the old closed environment—that there too obscurantism would had gone out of style. Someone might even ask me a question about British farming. And I would not know how to answer.

In November 1978, I organized a small exhibition in Peking of paintings by the Hong-Kong–based artist Rosamond Brown. Through the Ministry of Culture I invited some Chinese painters, art teachers, and students to come and to my delight a group came, even though the exhibition was purely private. In the group was a painter whose name I recognized, Zhang Anzhi. He told me he had studied at the Courtauld Institute of Art in London in the late 1940s. He looked tired and worn and said he had not painted for more than ten years because of bad health. It was no time to ask whether the politics of the Cultural Revolution had contributed to his health problems, although any former student of a "bourgois capitalist" institution like the Courtauld would have been an obvious target for the Red Guards. Instead, I showed him an illustration, in a book on twentieth-century Chinese art,* of a drawing that he had made in wartime Guilin, in Southwest China. It was a portrait of the young headmaster of a school for war orphans. The face was a handsome one, and Zhang had captured on paper a character that combined integrity, open intelligence, and unpretentious nobility. I told him that during the Cultural Revolution, when there had been much hostility between Britain and China and the faces I saw in the streets of Peking were sullen or tense, I had often looked at his drawing of the headmaster and had taken comfort from it, because there in black and white was proof of qualities that anyone would admire. But it had also made me wonder why I did not find those qualities in the faces of 1968. Zhang Anzhi looked at me intently for a moment, and then asked: "Have you seen that man recently?" I had to admit that I had not.

A few days before I left China in the spring of 1979, I attended a cocktail party given for some young teachers of English who were about to depart for Britain for advanced study. I found myself talking for longer than I should to a young woman from Southwest China. I was moved by that same combination of good looks, intelligence, and openness that I had seen in the features of the young headmaster drawn by Zhang Anzhi forty years before. Here was a face of someone who was ready to walk through China's opening door to the outside world, someone who might move Zhang Anzhi to take up his drawing pencil again.

* Michael Sullivan, *Chinese Art in the Twentieth Century* (London: Faber & Faber, 1959), plate 39.

17

For Tomorrow:
The Men and the Issues

AS THE 1980s began, China's leaders addressed themselves to a cluster of issues in which past, present, and future mingled in a volatile mixture.

The Cultural Revolution had left some charges of dynamite in the basement of the Chinese house of politics. What was to be done about its most prominent victim, the former Head of State, Liu Shaoqi? What was to be done about the man who had "personally launched and personally led" it, Mao Zedong? Any change in the official evaluation of the two dead giants of the revolution would affect the fate of tens of thousands of office-holders still alive. Should the Politburo bring the Gang of Four to trial? To do so would raise the thorny issue of their relationship with Mao and might evoke unfortunate (and unfair) comparisons with the Stalinist show trials in Moscow in the 1930s. On the other hand, if they were *not* brought to trial the matter would hang in space, unresolved.

In dealing with these packs of dynamite, the leadership based its actions on the judgment that the fuses were long and the explosives could be removed with due deliberation.

Other issues that faced them were:

- how to rejuvenate the aging leadership
- how to overcome the fear of a leftist backlash in the future
- how to reconcile the need for order with the popular desire for more freedom
- how to reward those who carried responsibility, and yet not tolerate excessive privilege
- how to legitimize a regime that had become heavily reliant upon the police and the army for the maintenance of its authority
- how to overcome a crisis of faith in Marxism–Leninism.

Some of these are the perennial stuff of politics in any society, but the recent history of China had given all of them a special urgency and a particular character.

When the Central Committee was convened in February 1980 it took decisions that affected to some degree all the issues on this list and those bequeathed by the Cultural Revolution. This Plenum of the Central Committee gave Liu Shaoqi an unqualified rehabilitation. It further eroded Mao's prestige by declaring that the appraisal of the situation in the Party and the country on which the Cultural Revolution had been based was entirely wrong; the author of this appraisal was not named, but everyone knew it was Mao. The Central Committee approved the "requests to resign" made by Wang Dongxing, Ji Dengkui, Wu De, and General Chen Xilian. In other words, the Whatever Faction had finally made its exit from the Politburo, and without the bitter denunciations that had accompanied leadership changes for fifteen years past.

The Central Committee promoted to the highest rank two men in their sixties who would form part of the group to whom the Party elders—Marshal Ye Jianying, Deng Xiaoping, and Li Xiannian—would progressively transfer power. These two younger men, Hu Yaobang and Zhao Ziyang, were both close followers of Deng Xiaoping. Hu, after being Secretary-General of the Party for the past fourteen months, was given the title of General Secretary and made a member of the Standing Committee of the Politburo, changes that substantially enhanced his power. Zhao, the boss of Sichnan province who had been made a vice-premier shortly before, was now also promoted to the Standing Committee of the Politburo.

The Central Committee also moved to strengthen the central machinery of the Party by re-establishing a secretariat such as had existed before the Cultural Revolution. This secretariat is a group of ten who devote themselves full-time to the day-to-day management of the Party, and since the Party lays down the line for the state they are likely to be an extremely influential group of administrators. (Their nearest counterparts in the British system would be the permanent secretaries of the various government departments.) The men appointed to the secretariat were a mixture of technocrats and more political types. The latter all shared the distinction of having been purged by Mao—or, in one case, simply attacked heavily during the Cultural Revolution.

As a result of these and earlier appointments there is now in place a group of experienced and relatively pragmatic leaders who are likely to ensure the continuation of Dengist policies after Deng has left the scene. These appointments, coupled with the resignation of Wang Dongxing and company, the powerful symbolism of Liu Shaoqi's posthumous rehabilitation, and the increasingly fundamental condemnation of the Cultural Revolution all served to diminish the fear of a leftist backlash that had been inhibiting lower-level officials from vigorously implementing the policies of pragmatic reform.

The Fifth Plenum emphasized order and discipline rather than liberalization and took its keynote from a speech made by Deng Xiaoping at the start of the year. On that occasion Deng had warned of what he called a "new phenomenon" of attacks from the right. He called on the leaders of the Party and state to criticize "the trends of bourgeois liberalization," and the phenomena of "ultraindividualism" and "blind faith in capitalism" that he said had emerged.[1] Some Western observers immediately declared that this signaled an end to liberalization in China.[2] On the internal evidence of the speech alone this interpretation was suspect: Deng had condemned *bourgeois* liberalization (which he had always condemned), *ultra*individualism (who would ever defend it?) and *blind faith* in capitalism (not that scientific study of capitalist management methods for which the president of the Academy of Social Sciences had called).

The interpretation was nonsense when viewed in the perspective of the whole panoply of reform policies and a thousand and one minor decisions that never make newspaper headlines. In early 1980, the first joint ventures with multinational corporations were being concluded, delegations were visiting the U.S. at the record rate of a hundred a month; and the *People's Daily* was writing that a more flexible attitude must be taken to the collective ownership of land because—remarkable admission—one hundred million people (one-eighth of China's rural population) had "drawn no real benefits" from it.

The decisions announced to the session of the National People's Congress held in September 1980 provided further proof that Deng and his allies were well able to hold Chinese politics to the course of reform that they had charted. In the economic field, the liberal reforms that had been tested in Sichuan province were now extended over much of the rest of the country, giving a greater role to market forces and to profits as a measure of performance, increasing competition, allowing managers a greater say in the running of their enterprises, and making those enterprises take more account of financial realities by requiring them to pay interest on their operating and investment capital. The economic plan for 1981–90 was rewritten on the basis of these new operating principles.

In the structure of government, the Congress endorsed the principle of separating party and state, and gave it dramatic expression by accepting the resignation of Hua Guofeng as Premier, while he retained the post of Party Chairman.

The Congress strengthened the role of law in society by enacting a number of new laws. Further revision of the state constitution was promised, and word circulated in Peking that the revised version would restore many of the safeguards included in the original 1954 Constitution whose implementation had been stymied by the mass movements of the late 1950's and the 1960's.

With that delicious irony that so often characterized Chinese politics in this period, Hua Guofeng, in his swan song as Premier, endorsed Dengist reforms with a warmth he had not displayed before, and announced the nomination of that full-

blooded Dengist reformer, Zhao Ziyang of Sichuan, as his successor. A little more than four years after Mao had said to Hua
"With you in charge, I am at ease," Deng was moving his most
un-Maoist game plan for the succession into its final phase. And
he was executing it with a cool deliberation seldom seen when
power changes hands in a communist-run state.

The program of reforms—political, legal, and economic—
endorsed by the Congress of September 1980 would in time
create the socioeconomic base for a larger measure of individual
and group freedom. Looking back from that vantage point to
the order-oriented pronouncements of Deng and the Central
Committee in January and February, it was clearer than ever
that one purpose of those pronouncements had been to strike a
balance between democracy and discipline. For many reasons, it
is going to be hard to strike the right balance for years to come.
The impatience of the urban youth for Western-style freedom of
the individual has to be balanced against the opposition of
middle-level officials who resent the loss of control that reforms
will bring. Power of decision must be shifted to farms and factories and away from bureaucracies without provoking a fatal
backlash from dispossessed party *apparatchiks*. The reservoirs
of discontent created by the errors of the past and by a poverty
that long predates Communist rule mean that China cannot be
run like a school debating society. Add to this a crisis of faith in
Marxism–Leninism–Mao Zedong Thought so widespread that it
has been frankly discussed in the official press, and it is clear why
the gradual evolution toward a measure of democracy and some
degree of freedom of expression in China is bound to be
marked by periods of stop as well as go.

One reason Mao was able to launch his Cultural Revolution,
mobilizing millions to rise up against the Party hierarchy, was
the resentment ordinary people felt at the privileges officials
bestow upon themselves. That resentment still exists long after
Mao's campaign against privilege has been discredited. No society is entirely free of this sentiment, but the absence of free
elections for public office in China can only intensify it and
multiply its causes.

In his January speech to the leaders of party and state, Deng addressed this problem, warning those who were indulging in abuses of power and privilege that they must change their ways or face dismissal. The problem was particularly serious among senior military officers, he said, but the malpractices of civilians and military alike were threatening the viability of the Party and the state. Over the next three years the ranks of the Party would be purged, and those who failed to reform would find themselves targets of the purge. (New regulations have been issued to define the extent of the legitimate privileges of office. Such regulations have been issued and ignored in the past, but today's leaders probably have both the will and the authority to enforce the new ones with some vigor. Popular resentment is such that Deng's warning of the dire consequences of failure to do so is no empty threat.)

When the Communist Party swept to power in China in 1949 it had a kind of legitimacy. The vast armies of the Nationalists had melted away, whole units deserting or surrendering, and scores of millions of civilians had withdrawn their support from the Nationalist government in ways that were less dramatic but no less fatal. On the other side, the Communist armies had swelled with volunteers. But in the last ten years of Mao's life the gap between rulers and ruled had grown to a yawning chasm. After Mao's death, the new leadership had moved to narrow the gap by purging the special targets of popular hostility and adopting policies more likely to win public support. They went some way to restoring a rough and ready legitimacy. As we have seen, provision was made for a somewhat more democratic system of electing the hierarchy of the People's Congress. The February 1980 Plenum, in announcing that the Twelfth Congress of the Communist Party was to be held ahead of time, stipulated that the delegates should be elected by secret ballot—another small but not unimportant innovation. But none of this amounted to a final solution to the problem.

The challenge presented by what Shanghai's largest newspaper called the "crisis of faith" was equallly formidable.[3] In his January speech, Deng did not use the term *crisis of faith*, but concern over the phenomenon was at the heart of what he had to say. He told his audience that for more than ten years Lin Biao and the Gang of Four had spread confusion in China's political life and deeply damaged the general mood of society. "As a result," he said, "anarchist and extreme individualist ways of thinking are still widespread among our people. We have a problem of re-educating this generation, particularly some of the young. All levels of officials, including officials of the older generation, also need re-education."

The education Deng had in mind was something other than a mechanical regurgitation of the Communist classics. He insisted that careful consideration must be given to the methods to be used in this effort, and as to content, he did not speak of Marxism–Leninism–Mao Zedong Thought. Instead, he said, "The supremely important lessons which they must learn are to value centralism, respect discipline, be concerned for the overall situation, give preference to public interests over private ones, and moreover restore and develop, step-by-step among all our people, the good moral standards which we used to have." The accent Deng put in his speech on public interest rather than private ones has to be set in the perspective of the policies developed under his leadership which have led to a rebirth of the individual in China. But because the long neglect of the individual by the ultraleft diminished devotion to the public good instead of strengthening it, so now, as the rights of the individual are slowly restored, an effort must be made to guard against ruthless self-seeking. Deng's generation has a vivid memory of the exploitation of man by man to which extreme individualism gave rise before 1949. Many in the audience to whom he delivered his speech joined the Communist Party in the 1930s and 1940s to fight against such exploitation. In the privacy of their minds they may regard Marxism–Leninism as an arrow that failed to reach its target, but they remain attached to the values that once led them to see it as a guide to making a better China. If Deng is to engage the older generation of officials wholeheartedly in the reform of China he must calm its fear that the values for which it fought are being abandoned.

Besides, the sheer size of China intensifies the need for "public spirit." Watching Zhou Enlai at receptions in the latter days of

the Cultural Revolution, when Mao's strategy lay in shreds and
Zhou was exerting every fiber in his body to pull China back
together again, I was always awed by the number of people
whose fate depended on his success or failure. Although his
brisk step and ready wit showed that he did not feel it a burden,
the invisible carrying pole across his shoulders bore the number
800 million. One evening in 1980, Nigel Wade of the London
Daily Telegraph was being walked to his car by some students
of a foreign-language institute in Peking to whom he had been
lecturing about the press in Britain. As they walked, one of
them said to him, "Always remember two things about our
country, Mr Wade: One billion people and three thousand years
of feudalism."

That is a terse warning against the kind of oversimplification
that has so damaged the West's relations with China in the past.
The oversimplified portrayal of Chiang Kai-shek as the savior of
China during World War II distorted U.S. policy in those years,
and an oversimplified view of monolithic world communism
prevented proper exploration of the possibilities of Sino-
American rapprochement in 1955 and 1956. The mass media
are as prone to oversimplify today as they were in 1945 or 1955.
The advent of television has made the problem worse, not better.
    China fits none of our ready-made categories for classifying
the world. As a nation it is sui generis: a Third World country
whose leaders deal with their First World counterparts without a
trace of psychological inferiority. China's present poverty and
industrial weakness are an accident of history: culturally, intel-
lectually, China is a permanent member of that group of great
nations whose stature is recognized by a seat in the Security
Council of the United Nations.
    China is not following a path that any nation has beaten
before her. Yugoslavia's rejection of Stalinism after 1948, bold
and resolute though it was, was an accomplishment on a smaller
scale quite simply because Yugoslavia is a country on a smaller
scale. The limited rapprochement between the Soviet Union
and the West of the 1960s and 1970s never saw the Soviet

Union sending its brightest and best young people to the West for their higher education, and the Soviet Union never looked to the West for the technology with which to strengthen its armed forces against an expansionist power that threatened both of them.

A foreign policy made of such elements will of course have a deep impact on domestic policies in the long term. It is part of the movement from totalitarian tyranny to a system more humane, part of a struggle by this nation to free itself from a straitjacket woven of feudalism, Marxism-Leninism, and twentieth-century technology. There is no true precedent for this, and there is no country that will be unaffected by its outcome.

Appendix
Notes
Bibliography
Index

Appendix

Excerpts from the Nineteen-point China
Human Rights Declaration,
by the China Human Rights Association
(or League),
January 1979

AFTER THE ASSOCIATION was founded in Peking on 1
January 1979, branches were quickly established in other cities and the
Association began to publish its own journal. Like all the other nonofficial groups and their publications, the Association and its journal were
not officially sanctioned, but neither was their existence contrary to any
law. Their life was determined by the political climate: when tolerance
of free expression was the norm, they flourished; when expression was
curbed they disappeared from view one by one.

Leaders of a number of groups of democracy activists came together in the Association and participated in drafting the Declaration.
It was therefore a representative document in organizational terms as
well as in the character of its propositions.

The China Human Rights League was officially established in Peking on 1 January
1979. The league discussed and approved the human rights declaration. In the final
analysis, the 1976 Tiananmen Square incident was a human rights movement. The
significance of human rights is more far-reaching, profound and lasting than anything
else. This is a new mark of the political consciousness of the Chinese people and is a
natural trend in contemporary history. With a new content and a unique spirit, our

human rights movement this year has again won the support and approval of the whole world. This has hastened and promoted the establishment of relations between the Chinese and U.S. governments. To stimulate the development of our social productive forces and promote world peace and the progressive cause, we put forward the following nineteen points:

1. The citizens demand freedom of thought and freedom of speech and the release of everyone in the country found guilty of offenses connected with these two freedoms. It is likewise absurd to incorporate individual thinking in the constitution and have a successor listed in party regulations and the constitution. This is against the principle of freedom of speech and against the law of human thought. It is also against the materialistic principle of the "diversified nature of matter," is a manifestation of feudalism, and is regarded with great disgust by the people throughout the country. Nothing is sacred, unchanging, or inviolable. The citizens demand the thorough elimination of superstition, deification, and personality cult, the removal of the crystal coffin in favor of a memorial hall and the building of a memorial hall dedicated to Premier Zhou, the commemoration of the "4 May" movement every year, and the emancipation of faith from the confines of superstition.

2. Citizens demand that the constitution safeguard in a practical manner the right to criticize and assess party and state leaders. To save the present generation and all future generations from suffering, to protect truth and justice and develop productive forces, citizens demand that the feudal imperial criterion of equating opposition to "individuals" with "opposition to revolution," a criterion which is still being applied, be given up forever. They demand that our society really be built on the basis of the principles of people's democracy.

3. Give the minority nationalities sufficient autonomy. Our country is not only multinational but also has many political parties and factions. In our socialist development, we should take the existence of various political parties and factions into due consideration. Various parties and groups should be allowed to join the National People's Congress. It is most ridiculous that various parties and factions cannot join the NPC, which claims to be an organ with supreme power in the country. This is a manifestation of replacing the government with the party and not separating the party from the government. This is incompatible with democratic centralism. It will inevitably result in the continuous development of bureaucratism. Our country's citizens do not want a "showcase" constitution.

4. Citizens demand that a national referendum be held to elect state leaders and the leaders at all levels in various areas. Deputies to the fourth and fifth National People's Congresses were not elected in a general election involving all the people. This was a scathing lampoon of our socialist democracy. It made a mockery of the human rights of 970 million citizens. The citizens demand the establishment of a "citizens' committee" or "citizens' court" through a direct vote of all the citizens. It would be a standing organ of the NPC able to participate in discussing and voting on policy matters and to exercise supervision over the government. The citizens demand that the state punish those party and state leaders who have violated the law, and uphold the law under their supervision.

5. Every PRC citizen has the right to demand that the state make the national budget, final financial statements, and the gross national product public.

6. The NPC cannot convene in camera. The citizens demand the right to attend as observers and witness the proceedings of the NPC, its Standing Committee conferences, and its preparatory meetings.

7. State ownership of the means of production should be gradually abolished in a transition to social ownership.

8. China and the party have altered their understanding of the theory and practice of Comrade Tito and his Yugoslav version of socialism. Major changes in our domestic and foreign policies and guidelines in recent years have borne full testimony to the bankruptcy of "revisionism" in theory and practice. There is no objective basis for ideological differences and disputes to exist between China and the Soviet Union. The citizens demand détente. The Soviet people are a great people. The people of China and the United States, China and Japan, and China and the Soviet Union must be friends for all generations to come.

9. The citizens demand realization of the Marxist doctrine that the socialist society is one in which everyone can develop freely. Any socialist country's form of government is a continuation of the traditional form of capitalism. Without the material civilization of capitalism, socialist democracy and freedom cannot survive. The basic thinking of this classic doctrine is also an important lesson that the Chinese people have obtained after more than twenty years of groping in the dark. We must not only draw on Western science and technology but also on Western traditions, democracy, and culture. The citizens demand that the state continue to keep closed doors open. Let ideas smash through the confines of prisons. Let freedom spread far and near. Let the wise people of China share the treasure of the whole of mankind. Let the suffering generation enjoy freedom. Let the younger generation be spared suffering. Eliminate class prejudices and ban deceptive propaganda.

10. Citizens must have the freedom to go in and out of foreign embassies to obtain propaganda, the freedom to talk to foreign correspondents, and the freedom to publish works abroad. Make available all "inside reading matter" and "inside movies" and let everyone be equal in enjoying culture. The citizens must have the freedom to subscribe to foreign magazines and newspapers and listen to foreign television and radio stations. Citizens demand that the state grant publishing and printing rights that are true to the constitution.

11. The system in which a citizen devotes his whole life to a unit where he works must be resolutely abolished. Citizens demand the freedom to choose their own vocations, the freedom to express support [for a leader], and freedom of movement. Abolish all regulations and systems that stand in the way of solving problems of husbands and wives being separated in different places.

12. Citizens demand that the state ensure basic food rations for peasants and get rid of beggars.

13. Educated young people on state farms should enjoy reassignment rights. Educated young people in agriculture demand that the state abolish inhuman treatment. They demand political equality, an improved standard of living, and a wage increase.

14. Citizens demand that the state ban the use of deceptive means to recruit various technical workers. Those cadres and units that practice deception should be punished by law. Those who give bribes, especially those who receive bribes, should be punished.

15. While undivided attention is being paid to promoting modernization, no less attention should be given to the firm implementation of policy. The citizens demand that the state put into action the policy once applied to those Kuomintang officers and soldiers along with their families who came over to our side in the early postliberation period.

16. Secret police and the party committee of a unit have no right to arrest citizens or investigate them. The secret police system is incompatible with socialist democracy. Citizens demand its abolition.

17. Get rid of slum quarters and crowded living quarters where people of three generations or grown sons and daughters are packed close together in the same room.

18. We are "citizens of the world." Citizens demand that the borders be thrown open, trade be promoted, culture exchanged, and labor exported. They demand the freedom to work and study abroad and the freedom to make a living or travel abroad.

19. This league appeals to the governments of all countries in the world, to human rights organizations, and to the public for support.

[Signed] China Human Rights League

Prepared 17 January 1979 in Peking.*

* *Zhongguo Renquan* (China Human Rights), Peking, February 1979, pp. 1–5; JPRS 073421, 10 May 1979, pp. 67–70.

Notes

PROLOGUE

1. *Ming Pao*, Hong Kong, 4 June 1977.

CHAPTER 1

1. Based on accounts by Chinese residents of Peking.

2. Agence France Presse, 2 February 1976.

3. *Far Eastern Economic Review*, 19 March 1976, p. 9.

4. *People's Daily* editorial, 28 March 1976; *Peking Review*, No. 14 (2 April 1976), pp. 4–5.

CHAPTER 2

1. Edgar Snow, *Red Star Over China* (New York: Random House, 1938), p. 71.

2. Joseph W. Esherick (ed.), *Lost Chance in China: The World War II Dispatches of John S. Service* (New York: Vintage Books, 1975), pp. 195–196.

3. Article by Wu Han in *China Youth*, vol. 8, no. 18 (1949), p. 19.

4. Article by Wu Han, quoted in Ting Wang (ed.), *Zhonggong wenhua dageming ziliao huiben*, vol. 4 (Hong Kong: Ming Pao Publishing Company, 1969), p. 267.

5. *Cheng Ming*, Hong Kong, No. 24 (October 1979).

6. Maurice Meisner, *Mao's China: A History of the People's Republic of China* (New York: Free Press, 1977), p. 133.

7. Source for this is "From Bourgeois Democrats to Capitalist-Roaders" by Chih Heng in *Peking Review*, No. 13 (26 March 1976). It is the only item in the list of struggles for which I know of no independent evidence, but it is not the kind of charge a Maoist propagandist would have fabricated.

8. In an interview with the American journalist Anna Louise Strong.

9. Chinese government statement 1 September 1963; *Peking Review*, No. 36 (6 September 1963), p. 10. Quoted by Stuart Schram in *Mao Tse-tung* (Harmondsworth, Middlesex, England: Penguin, 1966), p. 291.

10. Strobe Talbott (ed. & trans.), *Khrushchev Remembers* (Boston: Little, Brown, 1970), pp. 467–468.

11. Schram, *Mao Tse-tung*, p. 304.

12. Ibid., p. 298.

13. *The Case of P'eng Teh-huai, 1959–1968* (Hong Kong: Union Research Institute, 1968).

14. *People's Daily*, 16 June 1959, p. 4: "Hai Rui Scolds the Emperor," published under the pen name Liu Menzhi (possible meaning "Please be guided by this Mr. Liu"). English version from D. W. Y. Kwok's introductory essay to C. C. Huang's translation of Wu Han, *Hai Jui Dismissed from Office* (Honolulu: University of Hawaii Press, 1972), pp. 14–15.

15. Joseph W. Esherick (ed.), *Lost Chance in China: The World War II Dispatches of John S. Service* (New York: Vintage Books, 1975), p. 195.

16. Peking New Literature and Art, No. 3 (8 June 1967). Quoted in Peter R. Moody, *Opposition and Dissent in Contemporary China* (Palo Alto, Calif.: Hoover Institute Press, 1977), p. 169.

17. *People's Daily*, 27 July 1966.

18. *People's Daily*, 16 August 1966.

19. *Qian Xian (Front Line)*, Peking, 2 October 1961; quoted in translation in Jurgen Domes, *The Internal Politics of China 1949–1972* (New York: Praeger, 1973), p. 125.

20. Edward E. Rice, *Mao's Way* (Berkeley: University of California Press, 1972), pp. 182–183.

21. Agnes Smedley, *Battle Hymn of China* (London: Gollancz, 1944), p. 169.

22. Schram, *Mao Tse-tung*, p. 139.

23. Smedley, *Battle Hymn of China*, p. 169.

24. Mao Zedong speech to Enlarged Central Work Conference, January 1962; *People's Daily*, 1 July 1978.

CHAPTER 3

1. Edgar Snow, *The Long Revolution* (New York: Vintage Books, 1973), pp. 18–19, 66–71, 169–170.

2. *Peking Review*, No. 1 (2 January 1976), pp. 5–6.

3. NCNA in English, Peking, 18 August 1966.

4. Speech by Lin Biao to Red Guard rally in Peking, 18 August 1966.

5. Robert Elegant, *Mao's Great Revolution* (New York: World, 1971), p. 200.

6. *People's Daily* editorial, 4 June 1966.

7. Pamphlet produced by Red Guards of middle school attached to Qing Hua University, 20 July 1966.

8. Quoted from Yao Wenyan's article "On 'Three Family Village'—The Reactionary Nature of Evening Chats at Yenshan and Notes from Three Family Village," *Chinese Literature*, No. 7 (1966).

9. *Survey of China Mainland Press*, No. 4070 (30 November 1967), p. 6.

10. AFP, Peking, 3 February 1979; FBIS-CHI-79-25, 5 February 1979, p. E2.

11. Chi Hsin, *Teng Hsiao-ping* (Hong Kong: Cosmos Books, 1978), p. 263.

CHAPTER 4

1. The account that follows is based on the text of the documents published in Chi Hsin, *The Case of the Gang of Four* (Hong Kong: Cosmos Books, 1977), pp. 203–295.

2. NCNA, Peking, domestic service in Chinese, 18 November 1978; FBIS-CHI-78-220, 14 November 1978.

3. *People's Daily*, 23 April 1979; FBIS-CHI-79-082, 26 April 1979, pp. L5–L8.

4. *People's Daily*, 26 July 1978, p. 2; FBIS-CHI-78-152, 7 August 1978.

CHAPTER 5

1. All figures quoted are from *China: Economic Indicators*, published by CIA's National Foreign Assessment Center in December 1978. The CIA calculated that the

industrial production index for China had risen from 48 in 1952 to 100 in 1957 and 502 in 1976. Coal output had grown from 66 million metric tons in 1952 to 488 in 1976, and crude steel from 1.3 million to 21 million metric tons in the same period.

2. I learned of such cases through foreign students in Peking. Other evidence is cited in Claudie and Jacques Broyelle and Evelyne Tschirhart, *Deuxième Retour de Chine* (Paris: Editions du Seuil, 1977), pp. 41–47, and in Edgar Snow, *The Long Revolution* (New York: Vintage Books, 1973), p. 46.

3. *New York Times* report from Hong Kong, 12 October 1969.

4. *Wo kanjian yichang zhanzheng*, published in *Qimeng*, No. 1 (11 October 1978), pp. 19–20. Photocopy in East Asian Collection of the Hoover Institution, Stanford University.

5. Melinda Liu, "Replacing a Lost Generation," *Far Eastern Economic Review*, 15 September 1978.

6. NCNA, 6 July 1978; FBIS-CHI-78-133, 11 July 1978, pp. H2–H4.

7. This and other quotations from the poster are based on the English version of the text published in *Issues and Studies*, Taiwan, January 1976, pp. 111–148.

CHAPTER 6

1. The account that follows is based on a report published by the *People's Daily* on 10 March 1979 (p. 4.); *JPRS* 73360 of 1 May 1979, *Translations on PRC* No. 515. Main features have been confirmed by foreign diplomatic and other visitors to the city.

2. For details see FBIS Daily Reports for PRC for the period 17 November to 1 December 1978 and reports published in mid-April 1976 by Agence France Presse, *The New York Times*, and the *Washington Post*.

3. Taiyuan Shaanxi provincial radio service, 17 November 1978. Report on an undated article by Wang Lishan (phonetic), worker at a machinery plant in Shaanxi, FBIS-CHI-78-225, 21 November 1978, pp. K3–K4.

4. Quoted in a 1978 speech by Zhang Pinghua, director of the propaganda department of the Central Committee of the Chinese Communist Party, published in *Issues and Studies*, Taiwan, December 1978.

CHAPTER 7

1. Dennis Bloodworth and Ching Ping Bloodworth, *Heirs Apparent: What Happens When Mao Dies* (New York: Farrar, Straus, 1973), pp. 85–95.

2. *Ming Pao*, 3 November 1976, p. 11.

3. This account of Hua's career is based largely on Ting Wang's excellent "A Concise Biography of Hua Guofeng" in *Chinese Law and Government*, XI, No. 1 (Spring 1978). Additional material comes from the NCNA report of an interview given by Hua to Felix Greene in September 1979; NCNA report 17 October 1979, FBIS-CHI-79, 18 October 1979.

4. This account is based partly on an article by Tso Yu-chin, "The Operation to Round up the Gang of Four," published in *Cheng Ming*, No. 12 (1 October 1978), pp. 32–37 [FBIS-CHI-78-196, 10 October 1978, pp. N1–N3], and partly on reports published by *Ming Pao*, 26 October – 1 November 1976.

5. This account is based largely on reports published in *Cheng Ming*, numbers 11-16 and 18-19 (September 1978 to May 1979), themselves based on official documents published for internal circulation in China. The main features of the *Cheng Ming* accounts are corroborated by wall posters that appeared in Shanghai in October and November 1976.

CHAPTER 8

1. *Ming Pao*, 27 May 1977 (overseas edition). A reader sent the newspaper a paraphrase of the letter, the text of which he had seen in CPCCC Document 15, 3 May

1977. The fact of circulation was confirmed by the communiqué of the Third Plenum of the Tenth Central Committee (*Peking Review*, No. 31 [29 July 1977], p. 5).

2. *Cheng Ming*, No. 20 (1 June 1979), p. 30; FBIS-CHI-79-114, 12 June 1979.

3. *Ming Pao*, 24 March 1979, and Central News Agency, Taiwan, same day.

4. Two detailed accounts of the meeting are the report by Alain Jacob in *Le Monde*, 31 March 1977, pp. 1, 6, and *Ming Pao*, 26 May 1977 (international edition).

5. Stuart Schram, *Mao Tse-tung Unrehearsed: Talks and Letters 1956–1971* (Harmondsworth, Middlesex, England: Penguin, 1974), p. 61.

6. *Ming Pao*, 27 May 1977 (international edition).

7. *Peking Review*, No. 36 (2 September 1977).

8. *Peking Review*, No. 35 (26 August 1977).

9. See for example the article by Lo Ping in *Cheng Ming*, No. 20 (1 June 1979), pp. 29–33; FBIS-CHI-79-114, 12 June 1979, pp. U1–U10.

10. *People's Daily*, 3 November 1977; FBIS-CHI-77-214, 7 November 1977, pp. E9–E13.

11. *People's Daily*, 5 November 1977, p. 2; FBIS-CHI-77-219, 14 November 1977, p. E14.

12. NCNA, 5 June 1978; FBIS-CHI-78-109, 6 June 1978, p. E1.

13. NCNA, 16 October 1978. Text of speech published in *Peking Review*, Nos. 45 and 46 (10 and 17 November 1978).

14. *People's Daily*, 18 October 1978; newsletter by Wang Yung-an; FBIS-CHI-78-206, 24 October 1978, pp. E10–E13.

15. NCNA in English, 26 September 1978; FBIS-CHI-78-188, 28 September 1978, p. E20.

16. *People's Daily*, Peking, 16 September 1978, p. 4; FBIS-CHI-78-186, 25 September 1978, p. E15.

17. *Kyodo*, Peking, 15 September 1978; FBIS-CHI-78-180, 15 September 1978, p. K1.

18. *Dong Xiang*, Hong Kong, No. 4 (16 January 1979), pp. 14–17; FBIS-CHI-79-16, 23 January 1979, pp. N1–N6.

19. *People's Daily*, 19 September 1977, article by Xu Xiangqian; FBIS-CHI-77-182, 20 September 1977, pp. E1–E10.

20. Ibid.

21. *Ch'ishi Nientai*, Hong Kong, November 1978, pp. 6–13; FBIS-CHI-78-218, 9 November 1978, pp. N2–N5.

22. *Kyodo*, Peking, 15 November 1978; FBIS-CHI-78-221, 15 November 1978, p. E1.

CHAPTER 9

1. *People's Daily*, 28 September 1978; FBIS-CHI-78-192, 3 October 1978, pp. E4–E19.

2. *People's Daily*, 2 October 1978; FBIS-CHI-78-199, 13 October 1978, pp. E14–E16.

3. *People's Daily*, 9 October 1978; FBIS-CHI-78-201, 17 October 1978, pp. 6–7, and 204, 20 October 1978, pp. E14–E17.

4. *People's Daily*, 19 October 1978; FBIS-CHI-78-204, 20 October 1978, p. E6.

5. *Guang Ming Daily*, 19 September 1978; FBIS-CHI-78-192, 3 October 1978, pp. E31–E32.

6. *Guang Ming Daily*, 15 November 1978, p. 3; FBIS-CHI-78-225, 21 November 1978, pp. E5–E12.

7. Peking Domestic Radio, 18 November 1978; FBIS-CHI-78-224, 20 November 1978, p. E7.

8. *Ch'ishi Nientai*, February 1979, pp. 7–17; FBIS-CHI-79-32, 14 February 1979, pp. N1–N4.

9. *Ming Pao*, 15 January 1979, p. 1; FBIS-CHI-79-13, 18 January 1979, pp. E1–E3.

10. Ibid.

11. NCNA, Peking, 1 February 1979, Item 020126.

12. *Dong Xiang*, No. 4 (16 January 1979), pp. 14–17; FBIS-CHI-79-16, 23 January 1979, pp. N1–N6.

13. *Ming Pao*, 15 January 1979, p. 1; FBIS-CHI-79-13, 18 January 1979, pp. E1–E3.

14. *Ta Kung Pao*, Hong Kong, 27 November 1978, p. 2; FBIS-CHI-78-231, 30 November 1978, pp. N1–N2.

15. *Kyodo*, Tokyo, 29 November 1978; FBIS-CHI-78-230, 29 November 1978, pp. A3–A4.

16. These quotations were published in a Cultural Revolution tabloid edited by a group of Red Guards that called itself the Liaison Station of Peking Red Guards Congress for Crushing the Liu–Deng Counter-revolutionary Line in Youth Work.

17. *Qimeng*, No. 2 (24 November 1978), Peking. Photocopy in East Asian Collection of Hoover Library, Stanford University. Translation as in JPRS 73215 *Translations on the People's Republic of China* No. 509, amended by the author.

CHAPTER 10

1. Quotations from the text of posters given in this chapter are from the author's collection of notes taken at the time by him and others and from dispatches of journalists, particularly the Agence France Presse Bureau, Nigel Wade of the London *Daily Telegraph*, and John Fraser of the Toronto *Globe and Mail*.

2. *Qimeng*, Peking, No. 2 (24 November 1978). Copy in the East Asian Collection of the Hoover Library, Stanford University.

3. Agence France Presse, Peking, 26 November 1978; published in *The Times* of London, 27 November 1978, p. 1.

4. Agence France Presse, Peking, 27 November 1978; FBIS-CHI-78-229, 28 November 1978.

5. Agence France Presse, Peking, 29 November 1978; FBIS-CHI-78-230, 29 November 1978.

6. Agence France Presse, Peking, 7 December 1978; FBIS-CHI-78-237, 8 December 1978, p. E1.

7. Ibid.

8. *Cheng Ming*, Hong Kong, No. 22 (August 1979), p. 44, and Fraser report in Toronto *Globe and Mail*, 10 August 1979.

9. *Dong Xiang*, No. 4, Hong Kong, 16 January 1979, pp. 27–31.

CHAPTER 11

1. S. Bonavia and P. Griffiths, *Peking* (New York: Time-Life Books, 1979), p. 000.

2. For personal testimony on conditions for city youths in the countryside see Jean-Jacques Michel and Huang He, *Avoir Vingt Ans en Chine: À la Campagne* (Paris: Editions de Seuil, 1978).

3. NCNA, Peking, 27 November 1978; FBIS-CHI-78-229, 28 November 1978, p. E7.

4. *People's Daily*, 22 January 1979, article by Zhang Xianyang and Wang Guixin; reported by NCNA's English-language service on the same day; FBIS-CHI-79-17, 24 January 1979, p. E2.

5. Based on reports quoted in China News Analysis No. 1153, Hong Kong, 27 April 1979, p. 5.

6. Agence France Presse, Peking, 4 January 1979; FBIS-CHI-79-4, 5 January 1979, pp. M1–M2.

7. *Liberation Daily*, Shanghai, 28 February 1979.

8. Ibid., 11 February 1979.

9. Melinda Liu, "China's Justice on Trial," *Far Eastern Economic Review*, 19 October 1979, p. 38.

10. Report by Nigel Wade in Peking, London *Daily Telegraph*, 2 April 1979, p. 4.
11. Agence France Presse, 28 May 1979; FBIS-CHI-79-104, 29 May 1979.
12. Agence France Presse, Peking, 1 August 1979; FBIS-CHI-79-150, 2 August 1979, pp. L29–L30.
13. *The New York Times*, 16 September 1979, report from Fox Butterfield in Peking.
14. San Francisco *Chronicle*, 8 December 1979.

CHAPTER 12

1. Based on reports published on 17 October 1979 by reports from the Peking correspondents of the London *Daily Telegraph*, *The New York Times*, and the Los Angeles *Times*.
2. *Guang Ming Daily*, 24 October 1979, pp. 1–3; FBIS-CHI-79-210, 29 October 1979, pp. 6–8.
3. Li Jiahua, "The Call of the Square," *Qimeng*, Peking, No. 2 (24 November 1978), p. 214; PRS 73215, 12 April 1979, p. 28.
4. The poems are in *Qimeng* (*Enlightenment*) No. 1, published in Peking on 11 October 1978 and in Guizhou on 21 October. The commentary and an epilogue are in *Qimeng*, No. 2, published in Peking on 24 November 1978 and in Guizhou on 29 November. Photocopies are in the East Asian Collection of the Hoover Library at Stanford University. Translations were published in JPRS 73215, 12 April 1979, *Translations on the People's Republic of China*, No. 509. That translation is the starting point for the version here.

CHAPTER 13

1. A summary was published in *Guang Ming Daily* on 12 June 1979.
2. *Cheng Ming*, Hong Kong, No. 21 (July 1979).
3. London *Daily Telegraph*, 1 July 1979.
4. Agence France Presse, Peking, 2 October 1979; FBIS-CHI-79-192, 2 October 1979, pp. L33–L34.
5. *Political Imprisonment in the People's Republic of China* (London: Amnesty International Publications, 1978), pp. 28–29.
6. This account of the speech, which had not been published officially in China, appeared in the reliable noncommunist *Ming Pao* daily, Hong Kong, 12 July 1979, p. 15; FBIS-CHI-79-146, 27 July 1979, p. U1.
7. John S. Service, *The Amerasia Papers: Some Problems in the History of U.S.-China Relations* (Berkeley: University of California Center for Chinese Studies, 1971), pp. 167–173.
8. View expressed in a discussion with the author in September 1979.
9. NCNA, Peking, 22 July 1979, newsletter by Xinhua reporters An Zhongnan and Huang Zhimin.
10. NCNA, Peking, 19 June 1979.
11. NCNA, Peking, 13 September 1978; FBIS-CHI-78-178.
12. Report in *People's Daily* (4 July 1957) on speech made by Zhang Pojun, first deputy chairman of the China Democratic League, on 6 June 1956; quoted in Roderick MacFarquhar, *The Hundred Flowers* (London: Stevens and Sons, 1960), p. 170.
13. Dennis J. Doolin, *Communist China: The Politics of Student Opposition* (Palo Alto, Calif.: The Hoover Institution, Stanford University, 1964), p. 49.
14. *Guang Ming Daily*, 24 February 1979, p. 3; FBIS-CHI-79-045, 6 March 1979, p. E5.
15. NCNA Domestic Service in Chinese, Peking, 27 November 1978.
16. *People's Daily*, 7 November 1978, p. 3; FBIS-CHI-78-222, 16 November 1978, p. E10.

17. Ibid.

18. *Guang Ming Daily*, 2 November 1978, p. 2, article by Law Institute of the Academy of Social Sciences; FBIS-CHI-78-172, 5 September 1978, p. E9.

19. Agence France Presse, Peking, 3 February 1979; FBIS-CHI-79-25, 5 February 1979, p. E2.

20. *People's Daily*, 4 September 1979, p. 1.

21. Shaanxi Provincial Radio Station, 3 September 1978; FBIS-CHI-78-172, 5 September 1978, pp. M2–M3.

22. Ibid., p. M1.

23. *Issues and Studies*, Taiwan, January 1976.

24. Lin Chun and Li Yinhe, "It Is Necessary to Bring Democracy into Full Play and Consolidate the Legal System," *China Youth*, No. 3 (1978), republished in *People's Daily*, 13 November 1978; FBIS-CHI-78-221, 15 November 1978, pp. E2–E11.

25. *Cheng Ming*, Hong Kong, No. 22 (August 1979), p. 13.

26. NCNA in English, Peking, 30 June 1979; FBIS-CHI-79-131, 6 July 1979, p. L12.

27. *People's Daily*, Peking, 24 July 1979, p. 3; FBIS-CHI-79–150, 2 August 1979, p. 14.

28. Maurice Meisner, *Li Ta-chao and the Origins of Chinese Marxism* (Cambridge, Mass.: Harvard University Press, 1967), p. 107.

29. Ibid., p. 28.

CHAPTER 14

1. Joseph W. Esherick (ed.), *Lost Chance in China: The World War II Dispatches of John S. Service* (New York: Vintage Books, 1975), p. 372.

2. *Liberation Army Daily*, 21 July 1979, "Talk on Current Events" column by Li Yongji; FBIS-CHI-79-142, 23 July 1979, pp. L17–L21.

3. Interview published in *Time* magazine, 5 February 1979, p. 16.

4. NCNA, Peking, 17 February 1979, item 021726.

5. *Mainichi Shimbun*, Tokyo, 16 July 1979; FBIS-CHI-79-141, 20 July 1979, Annex p. 2.

6. *Cheng Ming*, Hong Kong, 1 July 1979, pp. 11–12; FBIS-CHI-79-141, 20 July 1979.

7. *Time* magazine interview, 5 February 1979, p. 16.

8. "Some Problems Concerning the Soviet Military Strategy," paper presented by Cheng Minggun and Yao Wenbin, research fellows, Institute of World Politics, Chinese Academy of Social Sciences, to the Sino-American Conference on International Relations and the Soviet Union, organized by Columbia University, meeting in Washington, D.C., in November 1979.

9. Drew Middleton, "Pentagon Studies Prospects of Military Links With China," *The New York Times*, 4 January 1980, p. 2.

CHAPTER 15

1. Joseph W. Esherick (ed.), *Lost Chance in China: The World War II Dispatches of John S. Service* (New York: Vintage Books, 1975), pp. 311–312.

2. Stuart R. Schram, *The Political Thought of Mao Tse-tung* (Harmondsworth, Middlesex, England: Penguin, 1969), p. 174.

3. *Ming Pao*, Hong Kong, 14 June 1979.

4. "Appraise and Treat Urban Collective Ownership Correctly," article by Contributing Commentator, *People's Daily*, 4 August 1979, pp. 1–4; FBIS-CHI-79-165, 23 August 1979, p. L14.

5. According to *Cheng Ming*, Hong Kong, No. 19 (1 May 1979), pp. 9–13 [FBIS-CHI-79-092, 10 May 1979, pp. V1–V6], two hundred million Chinese are in a state of semistarvation.

6. "CPC Decisions on Accelerating Agricultural Development," published in *Zhanwang*, Hong Kong, No. 417 (16 June 1979), pp. 21–24, and No. 418 (1 July 1979), pp. 23–25; FBIS-CHI-79-171, 31 August 1979, pp. L22–L37.

7. *Cheng Ming*, Hong Kong, No. 19 (1 May 1979), pp. 9–13; FBIS-CHI-79-092, 10 May 1979, pp. V1–V6.

8. NCNA, 28 January 1979.

9. NCNA, 11 January 1979.

10. *Cheng Ming*, Hong Kong, No. 19 (1 May 1979), pp. 9–13; FBIS-CHI-79-092, 10 May 1979, pp. V1–V6.

11. Ibid.

12. *People's Daily*, 18 July 1979, pp. 1, 4.

13. *Cheng Ming*, Hong Kong, No. 19 (1 May 1979), pp. 9–13; FBIS-CHI-79-092, 10 May 1979, pp. V1–V6.

14. *People's Daily*, 20 April 1979.

15. NCNA, Peking, 26 July 1979; FBIS-CHI-79-147, 30 July 1979, pp. 12–34.

16. For a comprehensive study of the defects of this system and recommendations for reform, see Ma Hong, "Transform the Economic Management System and Expand the Decision-making Power of Enterprises," *Red Flag*, No. 10 (2 October 1979), pp. 50–59; JPRS 74680, 30 November 1979, pp. 83–89.

17. *People's Daily*, 26 July 1978, p. 2; FBIS-CHI-78-148, 7 August 1978, pp. E19–E20.

18. "Observe Economic Laws, Speed up the Four Modernizations," *Peking Review*, Nos. 45 and 46 (10 and 17 November 1978).

19. *Red Flag*, Peking, No. 4 (3 April 1979), pp. 40–43; JPRS 073650.

20. NCNA in English, 21 September 1979.

21. *The Economist*, London, 29 December 1979, pp. 23–24.

22. Ibid., pp. 27–29.

23. *People's Daily*, 14 July 1979, p. 1; FBIS-CHI-79-148, 31 July 1979.

24. NCNA in English, 25 January 1979.

25. NCNA Domestic Service in Chinese, 18 July 1979; FBIS-CHI-79, 23 July 1979, pp. L12–L13.

26. London *Daily Telegraph*, 2 November 1979.

27. David Bonavia, "Of 'Mothers-in-law' and 'Hairy Crabs,'" *Far Eastern Economic Review*, 23 March 1979, pp. 21–23.

28. Ibid.

29. *Guang Ming Daily*, 15 April 1979, p. 3, article by Jin Wen; FBIS-CHI-79-084, 30 April 1979, pp. L1–L4.

CHAPTER 16

1. Merle Goldman, *Literary Dissent in Communist China* (New York: Atheneum, 1971), pp. xiii–xiv.

2. Agnes Smedley, *Battle Hymn of China* (London: Gollancz, 1944), p. 163.

3. The fourth National Congress of Writers and Artists, held in Peking in October and November 1979. See FBIS-CHI-79-212 to 219, 31 October to 9 November 1979, and FBIS-CHI-80-008, 11 January 1980, Supp. 009.

4. *People's Daily*, 13 November 1979, p. 3.

5. Asian *Wall Street Journal*, 1 June 1979.

6. London *Daily Telegraph*, 2 October 1979.

7. Linda Mathews, "China's Artists Exhibit Daring Nudes, Abstracts," Los Angeles *Times*, 30 November 1979, pp. 11–12.

8. *Guang Ming Daily*, 4 November 1979, pp. 1–2; FBIS-CHI-79-218, 8 November 1979, pp. L17–L19.

9. NCNA, Peking, 23 July 1979; FBIS-CHI-79-147, 30 July 1979, pp. L20–L21.

10. Fox Butterfield, "Peking Theater Reflects a Shift from Mao Era," *The New York Times*, 15 October 1979.

11. Report by Graham Earnshaw of Reuters, Peking, published in the Los Angeles *Times*, 14 December 1979.

12. *The New York Times*, 24 October 1977; report from Hong Kong, datelined the same day and based on an NCNA dispatch.

13. Fang Yi, report to the National Conference on Science and Technology, Peking, April 1978.

14. *Guang Ming Daily*, 5 May 1979, p. 1; FBIS-CHI-79-098, 18 May 1979, p. 11.

15. NCNA, Peking, 1 December 1978; FBIS-CHI-78-234, 5 December 1978.

16. Fox Butterfield, "Teng, Challenging Mao Ideology, Says Students' Role Is To Study," *The New York Times*, 1 May 1978.

17. Study by J. P. Emerson, quoted in Melinda Liu, "Replacing a Lost Generation," *Far Eastern Economic Review*, Hong Kong, 15 September 1978, pp. 10–11.

18. NCNA, 28 March 1978.

CHAPTER 17

1. *Cheng Ming*, Hong Kong, No. 28 (February 1980), p. 28. In fact, as *Cheng Ming* made clear, Deng made two very similar speeches at this time and the magazine's report combines the main points of the two.

2. See for example Agence France Presse dispatch from Peking, 14 January 1980; FBIS-PRC-80-014, 21 January 1980, p. L14.

3. Guo Loji, "Crisis of Faith," *Wen Hui Bao*, Shanghai, 13 January 1980.

Bibliography

I have drawn heavily on material published by the following periodicals, news agencies, newspapers, and translation agencies:

Agence France Presse (AFP) dispatches from Peking
ANSA (Italian News Agency) dispatches from Peking
Cheng Ming (Contention), Hong Kong
China News Analysis, Hong Kong
China Quarterly, London
Chinese Law and Government, edited by International Arts and Sciences Press, White Plains, New York
Ch'ishi Nientai, Hong Kong
Daily Telegraph, London
Dong Xiang (Trend), Hong Kong
Far Eastern Economic Review (FEER), Hong Kong
Foreign Broadcast Information Service (FBIS) Daily Reports—People's Republic of China, published by National Technical Information Service, Springfield, Virginia
Guang Ming Ribao (Guang Ming Daily), Peking
Hongqi (Red Flag), Peking
Issues and Studies, Taiwan
Jiefang Ribao (Liberation Daily), Shanghai
Jiefangjun Bao (Liberation Army Daily), Peking
Kuang Chiao Ching, Hong Kong
Kyodo News Agency dispatches from Peking and Hong Kong
Le Monde, Paris
Ming Pao Daily, Hong Kong
New China News Agency (NCNA), known as Xinhua since January 1979
Newsweek
The New York Times
Peking Review, Peking; from January 1979, known as *Beijing Review*
Problems of Communism, Washington, D.C.
Qimeng (Enlightenment), Peking and Guiyang

Renmin Ribao (People's Daily), Peking
Reuters News agency dispatches from Peking and Hong Kong
Ta Kung Pao, Hong Kong
Tansuo (Exploration), Peking
Time
The Times, London
Toronto *Globe and Mail*, Toronto
U.S. Joint Publications Research Service (JPRS) *Translations on People's Republic of China*, known as *China Report* since mid-1979. The *China Report* is published in several series: (a) Economic, (b) Agriculture, and (c) Political, Sociological, and Military Affairs.
Wenhui Bao, Shanghai
Zhongguo Qingnian (China Youth), Peking

I have found the following books helpful to an understanding of China. This does not pretend to be a definitive list of the best books on modern China, and with the exception of a few books in French is confined to English-language works.

Amnesty International. *Political Imprisonment in the People's Republic of China*. London: Amnesty International Publications, 1978.
Asia Research Center. *The Great Cultural Revolution in China*. Hong Kong: Asia Research Center, 1967.
Aubert, Claudie, Lucien Bianco, Claude Cadart, and Jean-Luc Domenach. *Regards froids sur la Chine*. Paris: Seuil, 1976.
Barnett, A. Doak. *China and the Major Powers in East Asia*. Washington, D.C.: The Brookings Insitute, 1977.
Bonavia, David, and Peter Griffiths. *Peking*. New York: Time-Life Books, 1978.
Broyelle, Claude and Jacques, and Evelyne Tschirhart. *Deuxieme Retour de Chine*. Paris: Seuil, 1977.
Bowie, Robert R., and John K. Fairbank (eds.). *Communist China 1955-1959: Policy Documents with Analysis*. Cambridge, Mass.: Harvard University Press, 1962.
Chai, Winberg (ed.). *Essential Works of Chinese Communism*. New York: Bantam, 1969.
Cheng Ying-Hsiang, and Claude Cadart. *Les Deux Morts de Mao Tse-tung*. Paris: Seuil, 1977.
Chi Hsin. *Teng Hsiao-ping: A Political Biography*. Hong Kong: Cosmos Books, Ltd, 1978.
Chow Tse-Tung. *The May Fourth Movement: Intellectual Revolution in Modern China*. Cambridge, Mass.: Harvard University Press, 1960.
Ciantar, Maurice. *Mille Jours à Pekin*. Gallimard, 1969.
Clark, Anne B., and Donald W. Klein. *Biographic Dictionary of Chinese Communism, 1921-1965*, Cambridge, Mass.: Harvard University Press, 1971.
Cohen, Jerome Alan. *The Criminal Process in the People's Republic of China, 1949-1963*. Cambridge, Mass.: Harvard University Press, 1968.
Crankshaw, Edward. *The New Cold War: Moscow v. Peking*. Harmondsworth, Middlesex, England: Penguin, 1963.
Dittmer, Lowell. *Liu Shao-ch'i and the Chinese Cultural Revolution: The Politics of Mass Criticism*. Berkeley: University of California Press, 1974.
Domes, Jurgen. *The Internal Politics of China, 1949-1972*. London: C. Hurst, 1973.
Donnithorne, Audrey. *China's Economic System*. London: George Allen & Unwin, 1967.
Eckstein, Alexander. *China's Economic Revolution*. Cambridge, England: Cambridge University Press, 1977.

Eckstein, Alexander, Walter Galenson, and Ta-chung Liu (eds.). *Economic Trends in Communist China*. Edinburgh: Edinburgh University Press, 1968.

Eighth National Congress of the CPC. Peking: Foreign Languages Press, 1956.

Eliot, T. S. *Collected Poems 1909–1962*. New York: Harcourt Brace Jovanovich, 1963.

Esherick, Joseph W. (ed.). *Lost Chance in China: The World War II Dispatches of John S. Service*. New York: Vintage Books, 1975.

East Asia: The Modern Transformation. London: George Allen & Unwin, 1965.

Fairbank, John K., Edwin O. Reischauer, and Albert M. Craig. *East Asia: Tradition and Transformation*. Boston: Houghton Mifflin, 1978.

Fairbank, John K. *China: The People's Middle Kingdom and the U.S.A.* Cambridge, Mass.: Harvard University Press, 1967.

Fitzgerald, C. P. *The Birth of Communist China*. Harmondsworth, Middlesex, England: Penguin Books, 1964.

Goldman, Merle. *Literary Dissent in Communist China*. Cambridge, Mass.: Harvard University Press, 1967.

Guillermaz, Jacques. *A History of the Chinese Communist Party, 1921–1949*. New York: Random House, 1972.

Hinton, William. *Fanshen: A Documentary of Revolution in a Chinese Village*. New York: Vintage Books, 1966.

Howe, Christopher: *China's Economy: A Basic Guide*. New York: Basic Books, 1978.

Hsu Kai-yu. *Chou En-lai: China's Gray Eminence*. Garden City, N.Y.: Doubleday, 1968.

Huang, C. C. (trans.). *Hai Jui Dismissed from Office*. Honolulu: University Press of Hawaii, 1972.

Isaacs, Harold. *The Tragedy of the Chinese Revolution*. Stanford, Calif.: Stanford University Press, 1951.

Kissinger, Henry. *White House Years*. Boston: Little, Brown, 1979.

Lau Yee-fui, Ho Wan-Yee, and Yeung Sai-cheung. *Glossary of Chinese Political Phrases*. Hong Kong, Union Research Institute, 1977.

Leys, Simon. *Chinese Shadows*. New York: Viking, 1977.

Leys, Simon. *Images Briseés*. Paris: Editions Robert Laffont, 1976.

Lieberthal, Kenneth. *A Research Guide to Central Party and Government Meetings in China 1949–77*. White Plains, New York: International Arts and Sciences Press, 1976.

Lifton, Robert Jay. *Revolutionary Immortality*. New York: Random House, 1968.

MacFarquhar, Roderick (ed.). *The Hundred Flowers Campaign and the Chinese Intellectuals*. New York: Praeger, 1960.

Meisner, Maurice. *Mao's China: A History of the People's Republic of China*. New York: Free Press, 1977.

Michel, Jean-Jacques, and Huang He. *Avoir 20 Ans en Chine*. Paris: Seuil, 1978.

Middleton, Drew. *The Duel of the Giants: China and Russia in Asia*. New York: Scribner, 1978.

Milton, David, and Nancy Dall Milton. *The Wind Will Not Subside: Years in Revolutionary China—1964–1969*. New York: Pantheon, 1976.

Moody, Peter R. *Opposition and Dissent in Contemporary China*. Palo Alto, Calif.: Hoover Institute Press, 1977.

Oksenberg, Michel, and Robert B. Oxnam (eds.). *Dragon and Eagle: United States–China Relations: Past and Future*. New York: Basic Books, 1978.

Pye, Lucien. *Mao Tse-tung: The Man in the Leader*. New York: Basic Books, 1976.

Reischauer, Edwin O., and John D. Fairbank. *East Asia: The Great Tradition*. Boston: Houghton Mifflin, 1960.

Rice, Edward. *Mao's Way*. Berkeley: University of California Press, 1972.

Richman, Barry M. *Industrial Society in Communist China*. New York: Random House, 1969.

Schram, Stuart. *Mao Tse-tung*. Harmondsworth, Middlesex, England: Penguin Books, 1966.

Schram, Stuart (ed.). *Mao Tse-tung Unrehearsed: Talks and Letters 1956–1971*. Harmondsworth, Middlesex, England: Penguin Books, 1974.

Schram, Stuart. *The Political Thought of Mao Tse-tung*. New York: Praeger, 1969.

Selected Works of Mao Tse-tung (4 vols.). Peking: Foreign Language Press, 1961.

Smedley, Agnes. *Battle Hymn of China*. London: Gollancz, 1944.

Snow, Edgar. *Red Star Over China*. New York: Random House, 1938.

Snow, Edgar. *The Long Revolution*. New York: Vintage Books, 1972.

Sutter, Robert G. *China Foreign Policy after the Cultural Revolution, 1966–1977*. Westview Press, 1978.

Talbot, Strobe (ed. and trans.). *Khrushchev Remembers*. Boston: Little, Brown, 1970.

Tregear, T. R. *A Geography of China*. London: University of London Press, 1965.

Union Research Institute. *The Case of P'eng Teh-huai, 1959–68*. Hong Kong: Union Research Institute, 1968.

White, Theodore. *In Search of History*. New York: Harper & Row, 1978.

Whiting, Allen. *The Chinese Calculus of Deterrence: India and Indochina*. Ann Arbor: The University of Michigan Press, 1975.

Zagoria, Donald S. *The Sino-Soviet Conflict, 1956–61*. Princeton, N.J.: Princeton University Press, 1962.

Index